Charles Bennett Lewis

The Life of John Thomas

Surgeon of the Earl of Oxford East Indiaman, and first Baptist Missionary to Bengal

Charles Bennett Lewis

The Life of John Thomas
Surgeon of the Earl of Oxford East Indiaman, and first Baptist Missionary to Bengal

ISBN/EAN: 9783743335202

Manufactured in Europe, USA, Canada, Australia, Japa

Cover: Foto ©ninafisch / pixelio.de

Manufactured and distributed by brebook publishing software (www.brebook.com)

Charles Bennett Lewis

The Life of John Thomas

THE LIFE

OF

JOHN THOMAS,

SURGEON OF THE EARL OF OXFORD EAST INDIAMAN, AND FIRST BAPTIST MISSIONARY TO BENGAL.

BY

C. B. LEWIS,

BAPTIST MISSIONARY.

London:

MACMILLAN AND CO.

1873.

[The Right of Translation and Reproduction is reserved.]

TABLE OF CONTENTS.

		Page
Chapter	I.—*Mr. Thomas's Early Life,* 1757-83,	1
,,	II.—*Calcutta in the latter half of the eighteenth century,*	13
,,	III.—*Voyages to Calcutta and engagement as a Missionary.*—1783-87,	37
,,	IV.—*The first year at Malda.*—1787-8,	77
,,	V.—*Controversy and Disaster.*—1788-9,	107
,,	VI.—*Harla Gáchí.*—1789-90,	153
,,	VII.—*Reconciliation and Return to England.*—1790-92,	173
,,	VIII.—*Missionary Projects for Bengal,*	199
,,	IX.—*The Baptist Missionary Society and its First Enterprise,*	211
,,	X.—*How the Lord made room for His Servants, that they might dwell in the Land.*—1793-4,	247
,,	XI.—*Moypaldiggy.*—1794-7,	269
,,	XII.—*Having no certain dwelling place.*—1797-9,	321
,,	XIII.—*Serampore.*—1799-1800,	339
,,	XIV.—*Cast down, but not destroyed.*—1799-1800,	349
,,	XV.—*Dinajpur and Sadamahal.*—1801,	375
,,	XVI.—*Concluding Observations,*	401
Appendix.		415

PREFACE.

FOR many years I have felt deep interest in the character and history of Mr. Thomas. The earliest records of the Baptist Mission contain so much, and yet so little, about him,—there is so much to awaken, and then to disappoint, curiosity, in the particulars there given,—that a strong desire arose in my mind to search out and to arrange in a consecutive narrative all that could be ascertained regarding him. This desire induced me to put together the substance of all the notices of Mr. Thomas which I could discover in the first volumes of the *Periodical Accounts* and in several old magazines. The result was a series of papers published in Calcutta, in 1853, and reprinted in England in the *Baptist Magazine* for 1853-4.

Since that time many interesting documents, hitherto unpublished, have come into my hands. Chief amongst these are (1) MS. letters and several volumes of Mr. Thomas's journal, with a Common-Place book and other miscellaneous papers, very kindly sent out to Calcutta, from his native place, Fairford, by his grand-daughter, (2) a copy of his letters preserved at the Baptist Mission House, London, and (3) a number of his letters to Dr. Carey, for the use of which I am indebted to J. C. Marshman, Esq. I was hopeful of obtaining through the same friend some correspondence preserved amongst the papers of Mr. Charles Grant; but the death of the late Lord

Glenelg, before his consent could be gained, unhappily defeated that expectation.

Many facts in Mr. Thomas's history were withheld from publication by the early friends of the Baptist Mission, there can be no doubt, because they were felt to be discreditable. His debts and his misunderstandings with his friends involved so much that was unpleasant, that it was thought well to keep them out of sight, and himself with them.

We can hardly wonder at this decision, or at its consequences. Our first missionary has gone out of the remembrance of the denomination to which he belonged; and the little notice he has obtained from those who have written of Indian missions seems to be due to the desire to use him as a foil, setting off the excellencies of others, rather than to any wish to relate his services to the cause of Christ.

The following narrative is not encumbered with controversies. Using all the documents I could obtain, in the light of all available contemporary information, I have endeavoured to weave my story with the strictest regard to truth. I have not attempted to disguise Mr. Thomas's foibles or faults. Let him appear just what he really was. Any how, he was the first man who made it the business of his life to convey the gospel to the Bengali-speaking people of India. Perhaps still more may be said as to his precedence in the great missionary work. Not a few missionaries before him had devoted themselves to the evangelization of India; but not one of them was an Englishman. Englishmen too were missionaries before him; but not in India. He was, it is believed, the first English missionary who laboured in the East. He was also the instrument employed to lead the Baptist Missionary enterprise in the direction of Bengal. To him it was largely owing that

that enterprise was carried into effect amidst all the difficulties which obstructed its early progress. That he was also an eccentric, erratic man, in disgrace amongst his contemporaries, because of his debts and failures, does not alter all this. And if, in the wisdom of God, such a man was employed to accomplish that which great influence, ample wealth, and unimpeachable respectability tried in vain to do, I cannot see why we should not now look the facts in the face, and gratefully accept the result in the knowledge of them all.

The *Baptist Magazine* for the years 1813, 1814, and 1835, contains some letters by Mr. Thomas, and use has been made of them here. Of a few of these the originals were sent me from Gloucestershire; and, in my extracts, these have been followed, the alterations made by the editor of the magazine having been for the most part rejected. I have, however, taken the liberty to modify some expressions and to amend the grammar of the originals, just as far as I thought fairness to the writer required. Mr. Thomas wrote rapidly and negligently, never supposing that his words were to be printed. I have treated him in this respect as I myself would wish to be dealt with, if my own private letters were put to press.

The materials in my hands are very unequal in different periods of the story; so much so that I have often been tempted to lay them aside, as insufficient for the production of a symmetrical biography. I have felt it, however, to be a duty to secure and arrange the facts, such as they are, that they may not be lost; which would probably be the case, if the tattered faded papers before me were suffered again to be dispersed.

C. B. LEWIS.

CALCUTTA,
February 1st, 1873.

CHAPTER I.

Mr. Thomas's Early Life.—1757-83.

NO intelligent reader will overlook the first pages of a biography.

The child is father of the man ;

and a knowledge of the dispositions evinced by any one in childhood, and of the influences under which they were formed, is of the greatest value in enabling us to understand his subsequent career. The early life of John Thomas might therefore be here described with much advantage; but very few materials for the purpose are in existence. His boyhood was full of incident, often, it is to be feared, of a kind most vexatious to his friends: for he describes himself as "a hopeless child ;" but, with the exception of a few memoranda, too brief to be well understood, his childish exploits and transgressions are all buried in the oblivion which covers the particulars of other home-life a hundred years ago.

He was born at the town of Fairford, in Gloucestershire, on the 16th of May, 1757. He had a brother James, two years older than himself, and two sisters, Elizabeth and Sarah. The fond mother of this family was taken from them when John was in his eleventh year. Their father, Mr. John Thomas, was a deacon of the Baptist Church, which has existed at Fairford from the year 1700. He was a man highly esteemed for his excellent Christian character, and his household was governed in the fear of God. Ready to take part in every good work, he was well known to the neighbouring ministers of the gospel, and his home was often honored by their presence. It must not be thought that such a house was gloomy and uncongenial to the young people belonging to it. The reverse of this was the case. It was a high day for the children when good Mr. Beddome of Bourton on the Water,—whose hymns are well known to us all,—or any other pillar of nonconforming piety was their father's guest; and it was a gala time to them when, on the occasion of an Association or a Ministers' Meeting at Fairford, they were allowed to attend the services, long protracted and numerous as they sometimes were. As to him whose history the following pages are to unfold, it is most evident that unwelcome as he may sometimes have found the restraints of his home, his recollections of it in after-life were full of tender affection. His father and his father's chosen friends were the examples from which his ideal of practical excellence was derived. In them he saw the realization of that Christian morality and piety, which he himself strove to attain.

Like so many other lads similarly brought up, John cherished a very early ambition to become a preacher. "From a child," he wrote, many years afterwards, "I always had extraordinary stirrings of mind to the work of the ministry." "I preached before I was five years old, and from that time till I was fourteen or fifteen, I never dropped the bent; but, whenever I was alone, in lanes, and hedges, and high roads, I used to preach aloud; and oftentimes from 1 Corinthians xv. 58, which I never had heard preached from."

But although he deeply felt the reality and priceless value of that godliness which he saw within the circle in which his father moved, and, even as a child, "coveted the best gifts" there exercised, he did not soon yield himself to the restraints and direction of divine influence. He says of himself:—

I had many serious convictions from my childhood, which were stifled by various cares, pleasures, scenes of dissipation and wickedness, too horrible to remember without deep abasement of soul and detestation of myself. I was quite sensible all the while of the truth and reality of the word of God, the certainty of future judgment, and the danger of my utterly perishing, which I was sure of in case of death; still I went on in paths of sin and forgetfulness of God. Sometimes, after a sharp sermon, I would set up stated prayer, and continue it for a little while, with reading the Scriptures and other good books, determining never to leave it off; but the first temptation proved that the change was founded only on brittle resolutions, and not the work of the blessed Spirit, who only can renew the heart. We may start out of our common course, when shook, like the needle of a compass; but, the disturbance over, we turn to our own track again. When, however, we are thoroughly convinced of the evil propensity of our own hearts, and of our utter inability to change them, or to escape wrath, and are brought by the Spirit of God to see an able Saviour calling us to look to Him and be saved, and are grounded and settled in love of Him and His ways, then we are still like the compass, effectually and chiefly inclined, not now, however, to that which is evil, but to that which is good. Yet notwithstanding this good bias of the mind and will, we are moved to evil by the shock of temptation; but return, bent in the main to that which is 'holy, and just, and good.'

Meanwhile, his constitutional "flightiness" gave his friends no small anxiety. His brother James was a lad of far quieter disposition, and afforded satisfactory evidence of early piety; but it may be feared that Jack, as he was called by the Fairford community, did much to earn for himself the reputation of a "ne'er-do-well," who was likely to cause his father endless trouble. With excellent natural abilities, he gave little satisfaction to his friends by his progress at school; but bird-nesting, shooting, fishing, and any other sport in which he could engage, was followed with the utmost alacrity. How difficult it was to find the boy a calling in which he would abide, and how troublesome he must have been to all concerned in his bringing up, appears from a list of "some of the most remarkable things" which happened to him, which, with much sadness, he drew out about six weeks before his death. This memorandum speaks of his having run away from home, and of his going to London, and of eight or nine fruitless attempts to settle him as an apprentice, as well as of several narrow escapes from death. At last, he was placed at Westminster

Hospital, and in his medical studies there he found an employment in which he took very deep interest, and wherein his proficiency was acknowledged by most competent judges. Having attained the requisite qualifications, Mr. Thomas first secured an appointment as Assistant Surgeon on board H. M.'s ship *Nymph*, and then was removed to the *Southampton* frigate. Here he narrowly escaped shipwreck, under circumstances thus described by himself in a paper written in March, 1784.—

We had been out to sea in the *Southampton* frigate, together with three other frigates and two line of battle ships, in search after Paul Jones, and, it being winter, every one of the ships returned to port before her appointed time, with considerable damage from a severe gale of wind in the Bay of Biscay. Our ship had, some months before this cruize, run foul of H. M.'s ship *Phœnix*, and, being a very old vessel, she suffered very much in her timbers, and the repairs she received in dock were insufficient to fit her for such a terrible tempest as this proved to be in the Bay. She soon sprung a large leak, and this leak continually increased, till the ship was thought to be in very great danger. Every method that could be devised was made use of, with very inconsiderable success, and all the hand pumps, working both night and day, hardly sufficed to preserve us from sinking. To make our fearful situation more terrible, we were utterly separated by the storm from all the ships of the squadron; and after several days' fear and alarm, which we thought hardly capable of increase, we discovered ourselves in danger of driving on a rocky coast; to avoid which we were obliged to carry a press of sail, and so increased the leak. Our hopes were almost driven to distraction; vast seas threatening every moment to swallow us up; no ship to be seen; no port, but what was either foreign and too far, or else the foul wind was increasing our distance from it. And when Providence favored us with a change of the boisterous wind, we sprung our main-mast, and so were disabled from using the last chance for our lives in that measure which our driven thoughts panted for. But that immeasurable goodness, that unsearchable Providence, which so often banishes our terrors and fears, though ever so violent, adapted our relief to the measure of our distress so nicely, that we did not let go our hope till it was swallowed up in the enjoyment of a safe arrival in harbour. This affecting preservation from death changed my opinions on religious matters, which otherwise had about this time been strongly biased by principles of rank infidelity and deism.

In a letter to a friend, Mr. Thomas says of this same time of trouble :—

I shall never forget what happened to me. All was given over for lost. I heard the boatswain say we were like men under sentence of death. My terror was exceedingly great within, though outwardly I calmly begged the captain's clerk to lend me his cabin. There I went ; and, kneeling down, vowed to the Lord to live a new life, if He would spare me this once ; and, if the ship was to be lost, to save my soul. I cried out, and feared exceedingly ; being well enough acquainted with the truth we know assuredly that, if I died, I should die in my sins, and so perish for ever and ever. I knew I should die unconverted and accursed. I believe it was the same day, the wind changed, the storm abated, and we set sail for England. We got safe into port, and there I was too base at heart to think much of the tender mercy of God to my poor perishing soul. Psalm cvii. 31. I hardened in harbour into my old sins, and forgot the God of my mercies. I soon felt the truth of the observation : 'If they hear not Moses and the prophets, neither will they be persuaded, though one rose from the dead.'

Shortly after this, he was seized with a violent fever, and was carried into the Haslar Naval Hospital, insensible. Let him again narrate his own story.—

Being often delirious, my physician had blistered me and ordered the other necessary applications and medicines, and then delivered me to the care and attention of the appointed nurses. In the night time, after having reflected, with uneasy fears, on the danger of my disorder, I renewed my thoughts for and against the immortality of the soul and other matters of revelation, till the force of the fever involved me in a mixed multitude of puzzling thoughts, which jumble I sensibly remember, and which was the effect of approaching delirium ; and at last I was lost in pain and confusion. I very plainly recollect my becoming unconscious of surrounding objects, either by sight or touch ; that the pain of my head was almost insupportable ; and that I settled within my thoughts that it must immediately occasion my death ; and, though I was certainly delirious, the arrangement of these circumstances of thought was very plain, together with all those very extraordinary feelings that did accompany the more wonderful parts of the following vision.

I thought the violent pains of my head continued till I expired ; and I thought I did expire, and felt an utter freedom and separation of the soul from my body ; and this moment of departure was sensibly distinguished by a total exemption in one moment from all pain of the body. As soon as I felt myself clearly satisfied that my death was fully over, I heard a sound of words, as though a voice has uttered them, to this very purport: 'There; *now* you *see* the immortality of the soul!' My feelings were at this time exercised in such a manner, that though I could ever recollect it clearly, yet it was unutterable. I thought myself unspeakably filled with joy and freedom. I thought myself in the midst of immensity, and capable of sweeping through immeasurable distances in a moment, with extasy and vast power. I saw myself surrounded with appearances of substance, which, whether they were angels or souls, I do not remember to have determined; but with my happy situation and their appearance, (which was not beheld in so much splendour as with heartfelt enjoyment,) I was filled with inexpressible awe and admiration. This most delightful of all sensible enjoyments endured but for a short time, when I began to think whether that was heaven, and what *I* was in heaven for; when, on a sudden, the Almighty spoke, and in a moment I beheld the world beneath me consuming in flames of fire, and I myself insensibly forced thither; and, feeling the scorch of that fire, I became lost in dreadful astonishment and fear.

And so ended the vision, which I have never yet had occasion to think had any remarkable utility or design in its accomplishment. But thus it happened to me exactly; immediately after my fever, I was clearly convinced in my judgment of the reality of my immortal soul, and that it was, without the body, capable of both enjoyment and suffering.' The importance and the strangeness of it had some temporary influence on my affections, but, these, after a little while, together with the remembrance of the vision, declined and fell away very fastly. My prayers, which had been offered up by the force of these occasional feelings, soon became short and lifeless, and at last were totally neglected.

As little regard as ever was now paid to the things of religion; and the time that elapsed between this period and my marriage was of no consequence to my present design, for it was spent in sinful courses of life, neglect of worship, worldliness, hardness of heart, and forgetfulness of God.

From Haslar he was transferred to Winchester Hospital, and then was appointed "Hospital Mate for Barbadoes." But he very soon after left the navy, and began business as a Surgeon and Apothecary, in Great Newport Street, London. The paper already quoted goes on to say:—

In my more youthful days, when the thoughts of my future life, blended with the ripeness of my years, often led me to the subject of matrimony, I very customarily formed a maxim in my mind that I would never marry any person but one of my own religious tenets, and more inwardly religious than I myself was. But being entwined with the world, and with almost all sorts of vice and habitual sin, this became a matter of no particular importance to me, so that I wonder, from circumstances which I cannot forget, why I was not permitted to marry one of those who were lost to all sense of comeliness in virtue and religion, except certain forms and customs, which the generality of people can by no means openly dispense with.

At the solemnization of my marriage, which happened in March, 1781, being then twenty-four years of age, I was sadly lost to a proper sense of those solemn requisites that must alone, at the bar of conscience and in the sight of God, constitute a right to that communion. But I feel at this moment emotions of praise and thankfulness in my heart, that notwithstanding my wrong motives, by which I naturally exposed myself to the common misery and unhappiness of a married state, yet God was pleased to give the person I had taken for a wife a true love and affection for me, which was so evident to me on many occasions that it could not but win my regard. Her religious principles were different from mine, she being a strong advocate for the Church of England, and I still harbouring sense enough of religion to make choice and preference, which I bestowed on the Baptist persuasion; but by what I have already said, you will perceive that nothing of this kind was then matter of trouble to me.

After marriage, I now and then attended places of worship on a Sabbath day, and once I accidentally dropped in where Mr. Robert Robinson of Cambridge was preaching on the instability of the natural man, and his words very much affected me, being very applicable to my case. After this sermon, I felt my inclination lean more naturally to some place of worship; and resolutions, prayers, and reformations were again set up and carried forward for a short time with self-approbation, till either the pleasures or cares of the world had recovered their usual dominion; and then all was laid aside, except public worship, or rather the attendance at public worship, once or twice on a Sabbath day. The next remarkable impression was under the ministry of Dr. Stennett, whose manner of delivery and language had ever some weight with me. He was now preaching from those words, in John xvii. 20, 'Neither pray I for these alone, but for them also which shall believe on me through their word.' I have nearly lost the memory of the discourse, but recollect that that part of it which was delivered from the last clause had a peculiar effect upon my heart. It was about this time that I had many troubled thoughts of the eternal danger I was in, and felt much of the burden of guilt; so that I was afraid to be alone. Very often, I was almost distracted, starting up in my bed, and crying out with fear. One afternoon, I had retired for prayer, and I was so apprehensive, that I thought I felt Satan come and touch my heel, which gave me great fear and mental distress. Notwithstanding these great emotions of mind, I was so allured with a sporting pleasure that was seasonable about this time of the year, that, after many endeavors to stifle the thoughts of it, I one day deliberately determined that, though it should be to save me from hell itself, and give me a possession in heaven, I would not deny myself the pleasure of the approaching sporting day. That determination convinced me that all was wrong, and inclined me to believe that all I had felt was nothing more than a working up of my imagination, whereas I was sensible that the work of conversion, for which I seemed to have great desires, was the operation of God on the heart and principles, and not barely on the mere affections.

It was before the month of August, 1781, had expired, when I heard Dr. Stennett preach from these words, 'Labour not for the meat which perisheth, but for that meat which endureth unto everlasting life, which the Son of man shall give unto you: for him hath God the Father sealed.' John vi. 27. Now if ever I was effectually called by the grace of God out of natural darkness into spiritual light, it was on this occasion. My heart was strongly moved by what was said on the promise, particularly the enforcement of the word 'shall.' On the same day, I heard with uncommon pleasure a sermon preached by a stranger in Eagle Street, from these words, 'All things are yours,' (1 Corinthians iii. 21,) wherein there shone such inestimable privileges of the people of God, and so much of the bounty and goodness of God through Christ to all those who are his true worshippers, that I was very much amazed and affected. The scriptures now became more particularly the object of my thoughts, both night and day, sleeping or awake. On the following Tuesday, Dr. Gill's Exposition of the Gospel of Matthew had for some time engaged my meditations; but I remember no particular word or passage by which I was encouraged; but towards evening I had such an apprehension of the method of salvation by Jesus Christ, of his sufferings, and suretiship, that I could hardly behave myself moderately before those whom I considered as destitute of any right knowledge of such things. Many days and nights were spent in the enjoyment of believing that Christ had suffered for *me* in particular. ME, ME, so insignificant, so worthless! that such an one as *I* should be a partaker of his benefits!—this thought attended me for many days; and wherever I was, I had many tears of joy and gladness. Once, the effect it had on my affections was so powerful that I became apprehensive of losing my senses suddenly; on which occasion I earnestly besought the Lord for more moderation. Not many days after this, I detected myself in sinning with my tongue so deliberately that it gave me trouble, and I was humbled on the occasion; and I described what I had said before some Christian friends, thinking nothing at all of their thoughts of me, in comparison of that apprehension of myself before God. The word of God became very precious to me, and was read with a new ability of understanding and clearness. My zeal was often very strong, and I inwardly thought that the Lord was going to make an eminent Christian of me. Dr. Stennett, in or about September, had preached from these words, ' Let not him that girdeth on his harness boast himself as he that putteth it off.' 1 Kings xx. 11. This was mentioned to me by a Christian friend, and he made remarks on what the Doctor had said, that were so suitable to my case that I bitterly lamented I had not been there. Now I began to think that, after all, I might, according to the Doctor, only have been warmly moved in my passions, and that the amount of all was an ignorant zeal or a fit of enthusiasm. But this thought did not give me much concern, because I thought my inclinations and desires were so different from what they formerly were, that I must have undergone the great change of regeneration. My assurance of pardon and everlasting happiness ran high and strong, without any intermission for a long time.

If I were now to describe what passed in my soul after the end of four months, I must write with such words as would deeply affect me. I must relate sad instances of declension; awfully sad indeed. It is true, I constantly attended the preaching of the word; but, oh, how grievously did my life and conversation differ from that of a disciple and follower of Christ! No words are strong enough, no language is severe enough, to express my thoughts of my conduct which yet fall infinitely short of the baseness and disingenuousness with which I now walked before God. What lamentable occasions did I furnish to the enemies of the Lord for blasphemy. Their words to my face were piercing; and what must their thoughts have been ? They saw me intemperate, resentful, impatient, and furious, with such other irregularities as raise my wonder why I was suffered to live, why eternal vengeance did not utterly consume me ; only His compassions fail not. Dear me! who can utter anything adequate concerning the patience of God ? My affairs in worldly respects were very distressing, and my sufferings were not small, and though I heard the word with now and then some comfort, yet I do not remember much else left that was Christianlike. I grew so poor that, after being teased by many people, very often in a pressing manner, for debts I could not pay, after being arrested and for two days imprisoned, I left off business, and had much difficulty and distress in raising a shilling to defray the expenses of a day. Almost every valuable I had was in pledge for money, and the money all gone ; so that I did not know where to look. Well! an unexpected messenger came to my mournful house one day. A friend, unsought, offered to procure for me the surgeoncy of a ship bound to the East Indies; and this offer led me to discover by enquiry two such ships. The one my friend meant was under imperial colors ; but that I chose was the *Earl of Oxford*, one of the Hon'ble East India Company's ships, to which I was very readily appointed, by a number of helps from entire strangers, who introduced me to the captain, who received me with partial favor.

My poor wife was sadly distressed at this prospect, and for several days it was an affliction of great weight to her. But I am amazed as I look back on the multitude of providential circumstances that brought me through every difficulty that stood in my way, and so quickly and so effectually placed me in this new office; for I had on lesser occasions humbly solicited a host of friends, by whom I was sadly mortified. Oh how greatly does the insincerity and selfishness of friends embitter what are called the misfortunes of this life!

Here the guidance of Mr. Thomas's autobiographical sketch is suddenly lost. Although thoroughly a Baptist in his religious sentiments, he for the present made no public profession of his consecration to God. Like his temporal affairs, his religious connexions seem to have been unsettled. He was frequently a hearer of the Rev. Dr. Samuel Stennett, at Little Wild Street; but he also sought to recommend himself, with a view to being baptized by him, to the Rev. Abraham Booth, who knew some of his relatives. Mr. Booth, however, regarded him as too wild and enthusiastic to deserve much encouragement, especially as he was very desirous of becoming a preacher. He received from Mr. Booth therefore only some good advice, and a copy of Chauncy's *Doctrine according to Godliness*, from the study of which he derived much benefit. Meanwhile his appointment to the *Earl of Oxford*, 758 tons burden, John White, commander, was confirmed. He appears to have gone on board early in January, 1783, and, on the 11th of March, sailed with the Indian fleet, leaving his poor "tender and delicate wife," who was very shortly to become a mother, in painfully straitened circumstances, and to a large extent dependent upon the generosity of her friends.

The foregoing narrative, imperfect as it is, lays bare the guilt and misery of a life misspent notwithstanding much knowledge of God's will. From the time of his marriage to his leaving England, the unhappy man must have suffered inexpressible distresses and mortifications, and, alas, he only too well deserved the most of them. But these painful details are given because they may help to an understanding of the following story. Who that reads this account of Mr. Thomas's vision, of his secret terrors, his floods of happy tears, his extasies of rapturous confidence and his fits of despondent gloom, his eager entire consecration and his so speedy obliviousness of the restraints of dutiful obedience, with the other contrasts and extravagancies here exhibited, can fail to perceive that his mental constitution was not evenly balanced, but was peculiarly liable to disturbance? His brain was easily excited to a morbid activity, he was impulsive and imprudent, his imagination was vivid, his affections fervid, his purposes precipitate,—and then there came the reaction. For such a man, the even path of tranquil steady trust and obedience was very hard, nay, was impossible, to tread. If indeed his restless, easily perturbed spirit had been regulated by wise early discipline and soothed by all that propitious circumstances could yield of quiet happy influence, his character might have developed itself far differently; but cast, as he was, into fierce temptations in his youth, and subsequently becoming the victim of so many failures, disappointments, hardships, reproaches, conflicts, throughout his whole life, mostly passed amidst the aggravations of an Indian climate, what marvel was it that he was always erratic, and that on some occasions the poor overwrought brain yielded to assaults of positive mania? What wonder if there be found in this narrative occasions for the exercise of patient forbearance? And, if notwithstanding all such instances of defect and infirmity, there be traced in it the indubitable results and the final triumph of divine grace, what abundant reason will it afford to ascribe glory to Him whose goodness conducts His feeblest and most erring children, and makes them "more than conquerors" over the difficulties and temptations which beset them throughout their earthly way?

But a yet higher interest belongs to the history this book will relate. Whatever were the infirmities or faults of the subject of it, "out of weakness" he was "made strong" to labour for Christ in circumstances of most peculiar difficulty. He was the first to preach the gospel to the idolators of Bengal, and, through him, other labourers were brought in to a vast field for Christian effort, which had before been close shut against the messengers of the cross. He whose life issued in such grand results lived not in vain. No apology need be offered for recording the facts of his career. They form part of the history of the progress of the gospel, and may claim affectionate remembrance by those who desire the glory of Jesus Christ in the salvation of men.

CHAPTER II.

Calcutta in the latter half of the Eighteenth Century.

IN order to the better understanding of the subsequent narrative, a few pages must be devoted to an account of the city whither the *Earl of Oxford* was bound, and, more particularly, to an attempt to describe the state of religion there and in the great province of Bengal, in the latter half of the eighteenth century.

In 1756, a woeful calamity befell the English factory at Calcutta. Siráj-ud-Daulah, having recently succeeded his grandfather as Nawáb of Bengal, in displeasure at some proceedings of the British, resolved upon the destruction of their settlement, and suddenly attacked it with a force said to number seventy thousand men. Our countrymen were ill-prepared to meet his attack. They had originally come to Bengal only as merchants, and their fort was designed for the protection of their commerce, not for resisting the power of the princes of the country, to whose haughty sufferance they were indebted for their highly-prized right to dwell and traffic in the land.

But, for whatever purpose designed, their fort was now in disrepair. Arrangements to restore and strengthen it had been for years under consideration; but had been frustrated by the sickness or death of the engineers charged with the important duty. New guns had been sent out by the East India Company for its protection; but, until the ramparts could be made strong enough to bear them, these were lying unmounted under the walls. All the regular troops in the garrison fell short of two hundred men. Their supply of ammunition also was very scanty.

Such was the condition of the settlement when this overwhelming danger threatened it. A considerable number of civilians of all ranks hastily volunteered to bear arms; and the 18th of June witnessed a spirited resistance to the host of invaders. By the next morning, however, the president had lost all heart, and, together with some of the chief military and civil officers, the ladies, and most of the other residents, he took refuge in the shipping and dropped down the river beyond the reach of the enemy. Only one hundred and seventy men were left behind. These bravely held the fort till the forenoon of the 20th, when, utterly exhausted, they could sustain the conflict no longer. Twenty-five were killed, and seventy wounded. In sheer helplessness, they surrendered themselves; and that evening were all mercilessly thrust into a single ill-ventilated room, eighteen feet square, for confinement through the sultry night. When the morning came, the door was opened; but, out of one hundred and forty-six prisoners,* twenty-four only were living. The rest had expired in the agonies of suffocation.

For half a year after this horrible catastrophe, there was little left besides the blackened ruins of the fort and factory buildings, to show how a company of adventurous Englishmen had made an abortive attempt to settle on the fertile plains of Bengal, and to establish commercial relations between their own distant island and the nations of Northern India. A large native town remained, which had rapidly grown up around the factory; but it was Siráj-ud-Daulah's resolve to wipe out all traces of British occupancy from the country over which he ruled.

Those who escaped from the besieged factory lay " on board a few defenceless ships at Fultah, the most unwholesome spot in the country, about twenty miles below Calcutta, and destitute of the common necessaries of life:" but by the assistance of the French and Dutch, and partly

---

* This number was made up by the presence of a woman, Mrs. Carey, who would not be separated from her husband. He perished; but she was taken out alive, and lived to be the last survivor of the Black Hole prisoners. She died in the year 1801.

by the help of the natives, who privately sold them all kinds of provisions, they supported the horror of their situation till August. Then two hundred and forty men came from Madras. But evil was still before them. Disease, arising from "bad air, bad weather, and confinement to the ships," with the want of proper supplies, now broke out, and swept off " almost all the military, and many of the inhabitants."

How little were the strange issues of these dismal events foreseen! Intrepid Britons soon came with Admiral Watson and Colonel Clive from Madras, to the succour of those of their countrymen who had escaped destruction. Victory attended the little army whithersoever it advanced, and before the anniversary of the unhappy siege came round, Calcutta had been triumphantly retaken, the battle of Plassey had been won, and the throne of the Nawáb was occupied by a partisan of the English. By those who had been his own creatures, the fugitive tyrant was put to death, while the British obtained that firm footing and that arm of power in Bengal which speedily led to their acknowledged supremacy there. In short, the foundations had been laid of that great Indian empire whose growth has been as marvellous as its beginning. The history of British India must be strangely read by any one who fails to discover in it the providence of Him who ruleth among the nations. Valiant as our countrymen are, and daring as their exploits in India have been, "they got not the land in possession by their own sword, neither did their own arm save them; but His right hand, and His arm, and the light of His countenance, because He had a favour unto them."

The tragedy of the Black Hole has been related here because the present city of Calcutta may be regarded as dating from it. The English factory was first founded there before the year 1690, and a considerable town had sprung up around it. But very few features of old Calcutta can be traced in the modern city. The sites of some of the principal buildings are known; but only to the antiquarian. The present city, like the empire of which it is the metropolis, has come into existence since the year 1756.

Calcutta did not immediately acquire that elegance which has gained for it the designation of the CITY OF PALACES. In 1769, when Mr. John Shore, afterwards Lord Teignmouth, came to it, it consisted of "houses, not two or three of which were furnished with venetian blinds or glass windows; solid shutters being generally used; and rattans, like those used for the bottoms of chairs, in lieu of panes; whilst little provision was made against the heat of the climate." Another writer of about the same period says that Calcutta was "one of the filthiest places in the world." Down to a much later date, the extreme nastiness of the streets, and the absence of all sanitary regulations, afforded occasion for frequent animadversion in the newspapers.* The dead bodies of indigent natives were dragged naked through the crowded thoroughfares to the river, into which they were thrown; and sometimes a corpse in a state of putrefaction was left lying in close proximity to some crowded bazar, until the distressed neighbours would liberally fee the *Háris* or scavengers charged with the duty of removing it. The country around the city was very insalubrious, and epidemic diseases often devastated the settlement. Early in the eighteenth centu-

* One illustration may suffice. *Hicky's Bengal Gazette* for March, 1780, says, "Would you believe it, that in the very centre of this opulent city, and almost under our noses, there is a spot of ground measuring not more than 600 square yards, used as a public burying ground by the Portuguese inhabitants, where there are annually interred, upon a medium, not less than 400 dead bodies, that these bodies are generally buried without coffins, and in graves dug so exceeding shallow as not to admit of their being covered with much more than a foot and a half of earth, insomuch that, after a very heavy fall of rain, some parts of them have been known to appear above ground, that when the pressure of the atmosphere happens to be at any time diminished and the effluvium arising from the accumulating mass of corruption has room to expand, the stench becomes intolerable and sufficient to give the air a pestilential taint? Moreover the quantity of matter necessarily flowing from it assimilating with the springs of the earth can scarcely fail to impart to the water in the adjacent wells and tanks a morbid and noxious quality, laying by this means the foundation of various diseases among the poorer sort of people, who are obliged to drink it; nor can those in more affluent circumstances, from the natural indolence and deception of servants, promise themselves absolute exemption from it."

This burial ground was, it is believed, in the vicinity of the Armenian church.

ry, out of twelve hundred Europeans, four hundred and sixty burials took place in six months; and for some years after the reoccupation of Calcutta, it was a most unhealthy place. This was probably owing to the salt water lake to the east, and to swampy fields and tracts of uncleared jungle, the lurking place of the tiger and the leopard, within a very short distance from the town. So great was the annual mortality, that it is said that the European residents met on the 15th of October in each year, to congratulate one another on their escape from the pestiferous influences of the rainy season. Towards the end of the eighteenth century, however, the healthiness of Calcutta was well established in the opinion of its inhabitants; and it has continued ever since to be a very salubrious place, notwithstanding its great natural disadvantages. European residences were at first collected around the Old Fort; but, as confidence grew stronger, " garden houses" sprung up in the suburbs, and the area of the town was enlarged. The thatched huts of the natives composed most of the streets, and accidental and incendiary fires annually produced wide-spread devastation amongst them. In March, 1780, no fewer than fifteen thousand " straw houses" were thus destroyed; and a hundred and nineteen persons perished in the conflagration. Famines were also frequent and frightfully destructive. One which extended over 1770 and 1771 was the most terrible in its consequences; but others of shorter duration occasioned unspeakable suffering. In 1788 it was necessary to give daily allowances to upwards of twenty thousand starving people in Calcutta; whilst "the crowds of those who surrounded the city and lined the roads to it exhibited a scene of misery and wretchedness which words could not paint or tongue express."* The European resi-

* " So numerous," says the *Calcutta Chronicle* of October 9th, 1788, " are the wretches who daily expire on the roads leading to Calcutta, that there is scarcely a sufficient number of men of the *Hári* caste to carry the bodies away before they turn putrid and infectious." The *Chronicle* proceeds,—

" Some more decent, and less shocking manner should be practised in carrying the dead bodies to the river, instead of that now in use. Sometimes they are loosely flung across a bamboo, and frequently tumble off on the way. At other

dents were always generous in aiding such sufferers; but it was often declared that the opulent natives seemed to be utterly regardless of the woes of their miserable countrymen,* and gave only when superstition extorted what philanthropy would not yield. The most revolting practices of Hinduism were unblushingly exposed to public view. The editor of one of the newspapers complains, in October, 1792, that he had just seen about fifty *Sanyásis* parading the streets of the city, all utterly naked. ·Widows were burned with the bodies of their husbands, or, in some inferior castes, were buried alive with them, close to the city; and there was reason to believe that, now and then, the bloody goddess Káli was propitiated by a human sacrifice at the celebrated shrine in the south-eastern suburb, from which, most probably, the city takes its name. The police regulations in these early days were very inefficient. Dacoits, those red-handed robbers, who ruthlessly combined most cruel atrocities with destructive pillage, abounded in many districts of Bengal, both on land and upon the rivers; and the consternation their daring exploits produced was felt in Calcutta itself.† Murders and robberies

times, the feet and hands are tied together, and in this shocking and indecent manner the bodies are carried naked through the streets."

* So the *Calcutta Chronicle* of November 19th, 1789, says,—"It is really shocking to humanity to behold in the streets of Calcutta so many poor wretches, dying of hunger, chiefly women and children. Not an instance occurs of the least assistance being afforded to any of them by their callous and inhuman countrymen."

† The *Calcutta Chronicle* of February 19th, 1789, relates, with strong expressions of disapprobation, an instance of the punishment of a gang of dacoits found guilty of burglary at a place near Kishnagur, and sent by Francis Redfearn, Esq., to be tried at the Criminal Court at Salkea, on the western bank of the river, opposite to Calcutta.

At 1 o'clock, on Sunday, February 15th, the fourteen criminals were brought out, to undergo the sentence passed upon them, to the Sair Bazar, a little to the southward of the Orphan House. The horrible scene is thus described.—

"One of the dacoits was extended upon his back, with a fillet or band covering his mouth, and tied at the back of his head, to prevent his cries being heard by the others, who were witnesses of the fate they were themselves to experience. He was then pinioned to the ground with only his right hand and left leg at liberty. This done, the operator began to amputate the hand. It was performed with an instrument like a carving knife, not at a stroke, but by cutting and hacking round about the wrist, to find out the joint; and in about three minutes the

were of very frequent occurrence in the heart of the city; and, in the suburbs, armed gangs of these marauders sometimes boldly paraded the highways by torch light.* Slavery also existed in Calcutta. The old newspapers publish many advertisements of slaves—chiefly " Coffries," or negroes,—for sale, or of rewards for the recovery of those who had run away from their owners. The most numerous class of slaves, however, were Bengalis who had been sold in childhood by their parents in times of scarcity.† When the

hand was off. The same mode was observed in amputating the foot, at the ancle joint. Both operations took up together from six to eight minutes in performing. After the hand and foot were off, the extremities of the wounded parts were dipped in boiling ghee; and then he was left to his fate. The other thirteen were served in the same manner; yet, what will appear very strange, not one of them expired under the severity of the operation.

" The hands and feet of the criminals were thrown into the river. Four of the men have since died; but more from the influence of the sun on the wounded parts, and through want of care, than from the more than savage cruelty of the operation."

In April, 1780, the same punishment was inflicted upon an incendiary at Murshidábád. It was a Muhammadan penalty, and was resorted to in the case of the dacoits in the hope of striking terror into the hearts of the numerous robbers who were devastating the country in so many districts, and producing everywhere so much alarm. It is hoped and believed that the above was the only instance in which so ferocious a punishment was administered under British authority. In 1793, a Regulation of Government made it illegal to inflict mutilation, and prescribed imprisonment in lieu of it.

* Within the city, where offences against life or property were perpetrated more cautiously, craft took the place of effrontery. The single thief committed his nightly depredations, having his naked body smeared over with oil, so that it was next to impossible to hold him. *Hicky's Gazette* recommended that a long bamboo with a triple iron hook at the end of it, should be kept in readiness for detaining such visitors. In November, 1788, two Bengali policemen were apprehended in an attempt to rob the house of a wealthy native, in a very different style.—" They had disguised themselves in the dress of Portuguese, with their hair curled, frizzed, and powdered, cocked hats, and very smart coats, shoes, stockings, &c."

† Sir William Jones, in a charge to the grand jury at Calcutta, in 1785, described the miseries of slavery existing at that period, even in the metropolis of British India. " I am assured, from evidence which, though not all judicially taken, has the strongest hold on my belief, that the condition of slaves within our jurisdiction is, beyond imagination, deplorable; and that cruelties are daily practised on them, chiefly on those of the tenderest age and the weaker sex, which, if it would not give me pain to repeat, and you to hear, yet, for the honour of human nature, I should forbear to particularize. If I except the English from this censure, it is not through partial affection to my own countrymen, but because my information relates chiefly to people of other nations, who likewise call themselves

indignation of the British Parliament was directed against slavery in the West Indies, the Calcutta newspapers declared that " the barbarous and wanton acts of more than savage cruelty daily exercised upon slaves of both sexes in and about Calcutta by the native Portuguese" made it most desirable that the system of bondage in the East also should be brought under the restraints of the legislature. If drunkenness was introduced amongst the natives of Bengal through the influence of European example, that effect was produced very early. The oldest prints complain loudly of the number of arrack shops everywhere set up, and of the difficulty of obtaining domestic servants whose sobriety could be relied upon.

These general remarks upon old Calcutta might easily be expanded by the introduction of many similar facts. Let these suffice, as introductory to the particulars regarding the religious state and history of the city and the circumjacent province, which are now to follow.

It is surely more than probable that amongst the earliest adventurers in the East India Companies, there were some God-fearing men, who looked with indignant grief upon the cruel idolatries of the land in which they had come to sojourn, and who heartily wished that Christianity might supplant and destroy them. But such engagements and circumstances as theirs were very unfavorable to the life of religion in their own souls, as may easily be supposed; and there is reason to fear that the representatives of our native country in the far East did but little to show that they came from a land blessed with the pure light and the excellent morality of the gospel of Jesus Christ.

The Charter conferred upon the East India Company by William III. in 1698, made careful provision for the spiritual interests of the servants of the Company employed in

Christians. Hardly a man or a woman exists in a corner of this populous town, who hath not at least one slave child, either purchased at a trifling price, or saved, perhaps, from a death that might have been fortunate, for a life that seldom fails of being miserable. Many of you, I presume, have seen *large boats filled with such children, coming down the river for open sale at Calcutta ;* nor can you be ignorant that most of them were stolen from their parents, or bought, perhaps, for a measure of rice in a time of scarcity."

the East. It expressly stipulated that "in every garrison and superior factory," there should be " set apart a decent and convenient place for divine service only ;" that one minister should be constantly maintained in every such place ; and that every ship of 500 tons and upwards sent by the Company to the East Indies should carry a chaplain approved by the Archbishop of Canterbury or the Bishop of London. It was further provided that all such ministers as should be sent to reside in India should be obliged to learn, within one year after their arrival, the Portuguese language, and should also apply themselves to acquire the language of the country where they should reside, the better to instruct the Gentoos who should be the servants or slaves of the Company or their agents, in the Protestant religion.

We know not that there is any evidence to show that either the letter or spirit of this enactment was observed in the Bengal factories and in other parts of India. In Calcutta, a handsome church was erected by subscription about the year 1715, and it is said that the chief persons in the factory were regular in their observance of the public worship of God.* The portion of the settlement occupied by Europeans was small, and the Governor walked to church, attended by the civilians, and by the military not actually on duty.

The fate of this old church was remarkable. In 1737, its much-admired spire was thrown down in a most furious cyclone, accompanied, as it was said, by an earthquake. The re-erection of the steeple was repeatedly talked of,

---

* "About fifty yards from Fort William, stands the church, built by the pious charity of merchants residing there, and the Christian benevolence of sea-faring men, whose affairs called them to trade there, but ministers of the gospel being subject to mortality, very often young merchants are obliged to officiate, and have a salary of £50 per annum, added to what the Company allow them, for their pains in reading prayers and a sermon on Sundays.

"In Calcutta all religions are tolerated but the Presbyterians' and that they brow-beat. The pagans carry their idols in procession through the town. The Roman Catholics have their church to lodge their images in, and the Mahomedans are not discountenanced ; but there are no polemics except what are between our High Churchmen and our Low, or between the governor's party and other private merchants in points of trade."—Captain Alexander Hamilton's *Travels*, published in 1727.

but as often postponed; and when the fort was besieged, the church immediately fell into the hands of the enemy, who, under the shelter of it, directed a galling fire upon the unfortunate garrison. After the siege, the remains of the building were wholly demolished by Siráj-ud-Daulah, who employed his brief period of dominion in Calcutta, in erecting a mosque there, as if to give his triumph a religious aspect. The two chaplains were also victims of the siege. One of them, the Rev. Jervas Bellamy, perished in the Black Hole, and was found lying amongst the dead there, his hands fast locked in those of his son, a young Lieutenant. The Rev. R. Mapletoft escaped with the fugitives to Faltah; but soon died there of the malarious fever which swept off so many more, as they in impatient misery awaited the arrival of the relief looked for from Madras.

Specific and sufficiently ample compensation for the church which had been destroyed was exacted by Colonel Clive; but he and his companions were too intent upon the dazzling prospects of dominion and wealth which had suddenly opened before them to be able to bestow much care upon the ordinances of public worship. The compensation money was therefore not devoted to the erection of a new church; but was thrown with other sums into a charitable fund, subsequently applied to the foundation of the Calcutta Free School. Not until thirty years after the English had returned in triumph to Calcutta, was a church built there to take the place of the one destroyed by the Nawáb's troops. In the meanwhile, however, a succession of chaplains performed public service for those who cared to attend it, at first in the Portuguese or Roman Catholic church, and then in a thatched bungalow in the Old Fort. The fact was, without doubt, a significant one, and was so noted at the time: Calcutta had "a noble play house, but no church." The history of religion is not indeed a history of buildings for public acts of worship; and if any better and surer indications of the existence of spiritual life amongst our countrymen at that time in Bengal were obtainable, we would gladly record them. None such have been discovered. "In those days," wrote one who remembered them, "the Lord's-day was nearly as little regarded by the British as by the natives : the most noted distinction being hardly more than the waving of the flag at headquarters ; except as it was the well known signal for fresh accessions of dissipation ;" and when at last the Presidency church of St. John was built, it could scarcely be regarded as an expression of the religious sentiment of the community for whom it was to be the house of prayer. Sir John Shore wrote of the undertaking at the time ; "A pagan gave the ground ;* all characters subscribed ; lotteries, confiscations, donations received contrary to law, were employed in completing it. The Company contributed but little : no great proof that they think the morals of their servants connected with their religion."

But if religious observances were long neglected by the so-called Christians in Calcutta, there were yet fewer traces of them in the other European stations in Bengal. Four or five military chaplains were usually distributed amongst the places occupied by British troops; but little indeed was done by them to enforce the claims of the holy religion of which they were the acknowledged ministers. What were called "surplice duties" made up their ordinary work.† A sermon was very rarely delivered in those days, out of the metropolis. Nor was this always the fault of the clergyman. The commanding officer at a military

* The ground upon which St. John's church stands, was the old British cemetry of Calcutta, and, together with an adjacent piece of land, was given by the proprietor, Maharaja Nabakissen, for the purpose. It was remarked that the natives, especially Musulmans, who regard all human remains with superstitious feelings, were horrified at seeing coffins disturbed and the bones of the fathers of the English settlement shovelled away that the foundations of the new sanctuary might be laid.

† In a pasquinade upon the Calcutta doctors, published in *Hicky's Bengal Gazette*, for February, 1781, the negligence of the clergy even as to some of these duties seems to be hinted at in the last verse.

"Thus to Pluto's domain, by the vulgar called hell,
    Those excellent doctors dispatch us pell mell.
    In a very few days you're released from all cares.
    If the *Padrie's* asleep, Mr. Oldham reads prayers,
    To the grave you're let down with a sweet pleasant thump,
    And there you may lie, till you hear the last trump."
Mr. Samuel Oldham was the undertaker of the settlement.

station sometimes obstinately refused to permit public worship to be held. This was the case at Barrackpore, only fifteen miles from Calcutta. Claudius Buchanan was chaplain there for about three years, and was allowed to address no congregation but such as he could collect within his own dwelling. In view of such facts, we can well believe that Mr. Tennant, one of the king's chaplains, affirmed nothing beyond probability, when he wrote of British soldiers at the period,—"It must happen that many persons have left England at an early age, and resided in India for twenty or thirty years, without once having heard divine service till their return."

In May, 1798, the Court of Directors addressed a letter to the Governor-General of India, in which attention was called to the flagrant profanation of the Lord's day by the officers of Government, and the general neglect of public worship was severely censured. "We have now before us," wrote the Hon'ble Court, "a printed horse-racing account, by which it appears that not less than eight matches were run at Chinsura in one day, and that on a Sunday. We are astonished and shocked at this wide deviation from one of the most distinguished and universal institutions of Christianity. We must suppose it to have been so gradual that transitions from one step to another have been little observed ; but the stage at which it is now arrived, if our information be true, must appear to every reasonable person highly discreditable to our Government and totally incompatible with the religion we profess. We enjoin that all such profanations of the Sabbath as have been mentioned be forbidden and prevented ; and that divine service be regularly performed, as in England, every Sunday, at all the military stations ; and all European officers and soldiers, unless hindered by sickness or actual duty, are required punctually to attend, for which such an hour shall be fixed as shall be most suitable to the climate. The chaplains are to be positively ordered to be regular and correct in the performance of their duty ; and if any one of them neglect it, or by his conduct bring discredit on his profession, we direct that he be dismissed from our service."

It appears from the wording of this extract that the Court of Directors had no very strong confidence in the piety and zeal of their clerical servants. A very low estimate would indeed seem to be fully justified by the testimony of Sir John Shore, the Governor-General, in 1795. " Our clergy in Bengal," he wrote, " with some exceptions, are not respectable characters. Their situation is arduous, considering the general relaxation of morals, from which a black coat is no security." Perhaps it may shed some light on the general character and social influence of the Calcutta chaplains of this period if it be here stated, that of three of them retiring from the service towards the close of the last century, one, after twenty-three years' incumbency, was reported to carry away with him, £50,000; another, after thirteen years, £35,000; and the third, after ten years, £25,000.* The gentleman last referred to, the Rev. John Owen, was a correspondent of the excellent Cecil, and, as may be judged from an address he delivered in 1796, was himself a man of thoroughly evangelical opinions and of very superior abilities. That his influence for good in Calcutta, in the dark period to which he belonged, is not more manifest, may well be regarded as matter for surprise.

But, leaving the Calcutta chaplains, let us see what missionary effort was directed to the enlightenment of Bengal in the eighteenth century.

To Frederick IV., king of Denmark, belongs the honor of first sending a Protestant mission to the East Indies.

* The "salary" allowed by the Court of Directors to a chaplain was only £50 per annum; but gratuities and various allowances which "crept in by custom and connivance" very considerably augmented this insignificant stipend. In January, 1759, the Court ordered that each chaplain should have a consolidated annual allowance of £230. In 1764, an additional Rs. 100 monthly was conceded in consideration of "the great increase of expenses in Calcutta."

The Presidency chaplains, however, had another source of far greater emolument in their share in certain monopolies, particularly salt, beetle-nut, and tobacco,—and, as appears from the instances above given, they found means to realize large fortunes. That this was true not only of the Calcutta chaplains, or of those of a particular period, may appear from a letter written in September, 1691, by the Rev. Jethro Brideoake, when about to sail as chaplain to Madras. He says: "I am told of those chaplains who have got very great estates there, whither I am going, and particularly of one Evans, who, having been there but a short time, is now coming home worth above £30,000."

In the year 1705, Bartholomew Zeigenbalg and Henry Plutscho were sent under his auspices to establish themselves at the Danish settlement of Tranquebar; and, subsequently, missions were also conducted at Madras, Cuddalore, and Trichinopoly. The work commenced by Zeigenbalg and his companions soon attracted the attention and sympathies of British Christians, and from the year 1710 the reports of the venerable Society for Promoting Christian Knowledge contain notices of the progress of the Danish missions in the East; and the Society generously aided them by contributions of money, paper, and printing materials. Amongst these notices, mention is made of the Rev. Mr. Aguiar, who, after living for ten years "as a Protestant missionary at Calicatta, in Bengal, was appointed Portuguese preacher at Colombo and other places at Ceylon," about the year 1742. At the same time, it it stated that "Mr. Sichterman, the Dutch Director at Houghly in Bengal, greatly wishing a Protestant mission might be established at Calicatta, had promised to give any missionaries all the liberty and encouragement in the Dutch territories, in his power."

No other references to missionary work in Bengal are discoverable until the period when Calcutta was emerging from the ruins of the old factory. In 1758, the mission at Cuddalore was broken up by the French troops under Count Lally, and the missionaries had to retire to Tranquebar. One of them, the Rev. John Zachariah Kiernander, a native of Sweden, was then invited by Colonel Clive to transfer his labours to Bengal, and to establish a mission in Calcutta. He gladly accepted the invitation, and, in September, 1758, began operations with all the encouragement Colonel Clive could give him, and with the approval of the chaplains. The Governor put at his disposal a house rent free; and the children sustained by the charity fund were placed under his instructions.

These facts must be felt to be very remarkable. They stand quite alone, and are in strong contrast with the policy of the Government in regard to the propagation of Christianity, and indeed with its customary indifference to all Christian interests. Was it so, that, at the outset of British conquest in the East, there was a disposition to acknowledge the claims of religious duty, and to honor the Lord in the sight of the heathen, which disposition was afterwards destroyed by the selfishness engendered by unprecedented prosperity? We see no reason to think this was the case. Far more probably, Colonel Clive's patronage of the distressed Swedish missionary arose out of the personal kindliness he cherished towards him as the brother-in-law of his fellow-soldier, Colonel Fischer of the Madras army.

Nor was that the only consideration. There was political importance in such a mission as Mr. Kiernander was to conduct. It was apprehended that, in case of a conflict with the French, the Roman Catholics would refuse to bear arms against their co-religionists. "The public exercise of the Roman Catholic religion" was therefore forbidden upon the return of the English to Calcutta, and priests were not allowed to reside within British bounds. Even before the siege, the Rev. R. Mapletoft had obtained help for the charity school boys, on the plea that "the original design of the school was to educate children in the Protestant religion, and keep them so when they had got from under the master's care." In perfect consistency with this design was the mission conducted by Mr. Kiernander, as appears from his appeal to Governor Vansittart, November 23d, 1763. "I need not mention," he wrote, "what advantage it will be to any Protestant Government to have the number of such subjects as are by their very religious principles bound to be haters and enemies, lessened not only, but reduced to the same principles; which cannot well be expected, so long as they have not an opportunity to be better instructed." Therefore he urged that "a convenient place for a Protestant Portuguese church should be granted, "which, as it would be a public benefit for the town, it may not be improper that the public should provide the same." Nor did he plead in vain. A house which was formerly the Collector's Office was granted to the missionary for the Charity School, and the permission of the Council was given, that it might be used " also as a church for his converts."

The mission thus inaugurated was conducted by Mr. Kiernander down to the year 1787, and the reports of the venerable Society with which he corresponded contain records of his proceedings, and exhibit an amount of success as resulting from them, which the friends of any modern mission might well rejoice over. Within twenty-eight years, not fewer than two hundred and nine heathens, including natives of Siam, China, and Macassar, and about three hundred Roman Catholics, of whom at least three were priests, were spoken of as the fruits of the mission. The Rev. Dr. Claudius Buchanan in his *Apology for Promoting Christianity in India*, says :—

The Honorable Company's ships brought out the annual supplies for this mission, and, before the year 1770, religious tracts were translated into the Bengali language; and Hindu Christians preached to their countrymen, in the time of Hastings, in the town of Calcutta.*

It must be added that much mystery rests upon these alleged facts. They altogether escaped the notice of some most observant men who dwelt in Calcutta at the time they are said to have occurred. And if this be accounted

* Dr. Buchanan's reference to the time of Warren Hastings seems to invite a reference to the observations of that gentleman on this mission, given in his evidence before the House of Commons, on the 30th of March, 1813. In reply to questions as to whether he recollected if any persons employed themselves as missionaries in India during the time of his residence there, &c., he said,—

" I do. I remember a very worthy gentleman, in that character, Mr. Schwartz, in the Carnatic; another in Bengal, named Kiernander: I do not know whether I can call him a missionary; he was sent out from London, and supported, I believe, by the Society for Propagating the Gospel. I remember his conversion of one Indian, because it was announced with great pomp and parade. ..... Mr. Kiernander, whom I too inconsiderately named as appertaining to this character, was a constant resident in Calcutta."

On the same occasion, William Cowper, Esq., mentioned Mr. Kiernander, but stated that he had never heard of a single instance of conversion to the Christian religion amongst the natives of India.

To these testimonies, may be added that of the Rev. D. Brown, who was personally intimate with Kiernander, and who took charge of the mission church on his retirement from Calcutta. In a letter, written in 1787, he says, " Out of ten million natives, we know of no Christian."—Yet in the previous year alone, Mr. Kiernander had baptized *" twenty heathens."*

for by the common indifference of worldly men to Christian effort and success, we have still to ask, What became of all the numerous Hindu and Musulman converts Mr. Kiernander is said to have baptised? and how could a work of such a nature have been carried on so successfully and so long, without leaving, at the close of the eighteenth century, at least some perceptible traces of its reality and power? How passing strange, that men deeply interested in all that related to the spread of the gospel in Bengal, and who were familiar with all the different classes of society in Calcutta, should with unfaltering and sustained confidence have regarded Krishna Pál as the very first Hindu native of Bengal who abandoned his caste by submitting to the rite of Christian baptism!

It is, we believe, an unquestionable fact, that Mr. Kiernander never learned either Bengali or Hindustani. The language he used was Portuguese, and Mr. Charles Grant no doubt correctly stated that his labours were " confined to the descendants of Europeans," and " hardly ever embraced a single heathen." His work was always spoken of in the correspondence with England as "the Portuguese mission."

Mr. Kiernander, however, left behind him in Calcutta a very valuable and interesting monument of his earnest desire to promote the Christian religion there. By a second marriage he became a wealthy man, and he resolved to erect a mission church; which appears to have been completed with a very inconsiderable amount of help from others. His personal outlay upon the building was said to be between five and six thousand pounds. It may be noted, as an indication of the state of European morality at that time, that Mr. Kiernander's friends claimed remarkable credit to him because he did not suffer the bricklayers to work upon his church on Sundays. It was opened for worship in 1770, and services were from that time held in it both in English and Portuguese. It would accommodate two hundred persons, but its internal arrangements were clumsy and uninviting. It was therefore pronounced by the European community to be altogether beneath their notice, and to be " fit only for stable boys and low Portuguese." Perhaps if it had been much more elegant, they would have been little better disposed to frequent it. As it was, it accomplished very little, at the time it was built, in the direction of influencing the European population of the city to yield a more decorous attention to the forms of religion. Mr. Kiernander built a school house, close to his church, in which between two and three hundred children might be accommodated. He also erected at his own cost a dwelling house, for the residence of two missionaries. The reader who knows Calcutta as it is, and remembers Mission Row, may smile at the statement, made in 1777, that this mission house stood "near the church, the school, and the industrial school, in a delightful situation, whence all the ships could be seen, as they passed up and down the Ganges."*

The munificence exhibited in these and other acts is worthy of perpetual remembrance; but we would gladly discover facts, showing that this worthy man himself clearly apprehended, and fully and effectually made known to those who came under his teaching, the divine way of salvation. Such facts we have not found. Memoranda of his own, still in existence, show that he was a man of remarkable simplicity and benevolence, but they do not bear the testimony we desire that he gloried in the cross of Jesus Christ.†

* The mission was also provided with a press, but little was effected by it, and Mr. Kiernander incurred some obloquy because, to oblige a friend, he lent his "Gospel types" for secular uses, and thus disturbed the balance of power amongst the few members of the fourth estate then in Calcutta!

† The following statement has the great disadvantage of being reported after the death of the narrator. The circumstantial character of the anecdote and the intelligence and integrity of the Rev. Joseph Ivimey, who wrote it, entitle it, however, to full confidence.—It is extracted from the *Baptist Magazine* for 1828, page 254.

"Having called upon Mr. Charles Grant, on business connected with the Baptist Missionary Society, on the 26th November, 1814, I mentioned to him a letter just received from the Rev. Dr. Carey, which shewed the increase of Christians in Calcutta, and I observed how different this was from the period, 1783, when Mr. John Thomas advertised in the *India Gazette* for a Christian. Mr. Grant said,—' I was in India at that time, and resided at Malda. About seven years before the arrival of Mr. Thomas, I lived at Calcutta, and was brought under

Thus then, seventeen years before the Presidency church was opened, the generosity of a Swedish missionary provided a house of prayer in addition to the bungalow near the Old Fort, used by the chaplains. Even after the new St. John's church was consecrated in June, 1787, its superior accommodations attracted few of the citizens. If the Governor-General was in Calcutta and was expected to attend church, it was fashionable to be there.* Otherwise, few persons chose to devote their leisure to such an engagement. Lord Cornwallis was remarkable for his decorous observance of public worship; but Sir John Shore, though himself a religious man, rarely went to church;† and the indifference of men inferior in character and position was therefore in no way remarkable. Ungodliness was the

deep concern about the state of my soul. There was no person then living in Calcutta from whom I could obtain any information as to the way of a sinner's salvation. I at length went to the Dutch Missionary, (the same who had built what is called the Old Church,) but he had outlived his zeal, and, I suppose, was a man destitute of religion. I found him lying on his couch. My anxious enquiries as to what I should do to be saved appeared to embarrass and confuse him exceedingly; and when I left him, the perspiration was running from his face, in consequence, as it appeared to me, of his mental distress. He could not answer my questions, but he gave me some good instructive books."

* So a letter from a young man at Malda, dated November 30th, 1787, says,— "There are some churches in Calcutta, but, till lately, our good and worthy countrymen hardly ever frequented them. However, when Lord Cornwallis came to Bengal, he attended every Sunday, regularly, which at once made going to church fashionable, and every Englishman mostly in the settlement went to hear sermon, because the Governor did so. So it continued for a considerable time; but it happened, at the end of a month or two, that his Lordship went into the country on Saturday for four weeks, and did not return to town again till the Monday morning following. The people in Calcutta thus seeing their Governor staid in the country four Sundays, thought he had left off going to church; so they by degrees gave it up too. Now, what the Governor meant by this, I cannot say, but, on the fifth Sunday morning, he returned from the country and went to church, and found it almost deserted. In the course of the week, the people heard that the Governor had been at the church, and so, next Sunday, it was as throng as ever again. From the circumstances of this story, it is but too apparent that vital religion is little known in this country. The morals of both sexes are in general but depraved. It is a wonder to see how indelicate some of them are. They glory in things that they ought to be ashamed of."

† Some excuse for infrequent attendance at public worship might have been pleaded, because of the great heat of the climate, to which there was then no mitigation, except by the use of a lady's fan. *Punkahs* and *tatties* were first introduced into the churches at the suggestion of Lord Wellesley, in 1801.

prevailing rule amongst all classes of society, and any manifestations of piety were rare indeed.

Many painful details as to the general depravity of morals at this period might easily be collected. Christianity appeared to great disadvantage in the conduct of those who represented it before the heathen and Muhammadan population of the city. The Portuguese, or "black Christians," were almost wholly Roman Catholics; and, with a few exceptions, they formed "the most debased and despised class in Calcutta," whilst the English and their descendants, who were mostly called Protestants, were still less religious, and perhaps not more moral. "Europeans had their work carried on, their assemblies and routs, on the Lord's-day the same as any other day; and a man when he arrived in India showed what he would have been in England, if there had been no restraint there." Duelling was very frequent, and was encouraged by the example of some of the chief persons in the settlement. Deism was the fashionable profession; yet, for the sake of gain, or from other motives as ignoble, the idolatrous ceremonies of the natives were encouraged by the contributions, and honored by the presence, of the representatives of Protestant England. Drunkenness, gambling and profane swearing were almost universally practised. The public journals testify to the absence of "decency and propriety of behaviour" in social life. In December, 1780, one of them complains that "Europeans of all ranks" ordinarily made Christmas festivities "a plea for absolute drunkenness and obscenity of conversation, &c.,— that is, while they were able to articulate at all," and urges that respectable men ought not to subject their wives to such impure and injurious associations. Another, in 1788, complains of "a very general depravity of conversation and manners, both in mixed and male societies," such as he "hoped, for the honor of human nature, was not the case in other countries." Nearly all the unmarried Europeans,—and few were married in those days,—lived in acknowledged concubinage with native women.*

* Perhaps the following illustration of this statement may be admitted. In

Such was Calcutta in the eighteenth century. Mr. William Chambers, Master in Chancery in the Supreme Court, often used to say that Calcutta and Batavia were the two vilest cities upon earth, and he called them Sodom and Gomorrah.*

Notwithstanding this general irreligiousness, there were unquestionably some excellencies which sustained the credit of the European settlers with the natives of Bengal, and which, if not the immediate fruits of our holy religion, were traceable to its influence upon the character of every community in which it is acknowledged. Mention has already been made of the generosity displayed by English residents in Calcutta towards those who suffered in times of scarcity. To the needy amongst themselves also, they were ever ready to afford most liberal aid. Dr. Edward Ives bore his testimony to this, shortly after the reoccupation of Calcutta, in the following strong language : " It is not possible to point out a part of the world where the spirit of charity is more nobly exerted than in our East India Company's settlements. Numerous instances may be mentioned, where princely subscriptions have in a few hours been

---

1810, a work, called the *East India Vade Mecum*, was published by Captain Thomas Williamson. It was intended to contain a compendium of information valuable to persons about to settle in India, and was dedicated to the Honorable Court of Directors of the East India Company, as designed particularly to be a guide to young gentlemen in their service. In this work, concubinage is regarded as a matter of ordinary necessity, and advice is given as to the female establishment a young man should set up, its proper cost, &c. The impossibility of marriage with Englishwomen is shown, by the declaration that an English lady could not be landed in India, "under respectable circumstances throughout, for less than £500," and the connexions recommended are justified by the statement that "the number of European women to be found in Bengal and its dependencies, cannot amount to two hundred and fifty; while the European male inhabitants of respectability, including military officers, may be taken at about four thousand."

* The public prints at this period bear unmistakable testimony to the universal depravity of social life. A writer in *Hicky's Bengal Gazette*, in June, 1780, speaks of himself as having been "led by the hand of fate from Christendom to the land of Pagans," adding, "The Oriental morality differs from the Hyperborean, as much as heat from cold, and darkness from light. It is not for me to determine which is better or worse. While I remain in this Paradisial region, it is sufficient that I conform to its customs; never affecting singularity, and keeping in mind the maxim of the Apostle, ' *Cum Romano Romanus eris*' " !

raised, and applied to the effectual relief of many unfortunate families." So also in reference to truthfulness and commercial integrity, the reputation of the English in India stood very high. The Rev. John Owen states,—" There are exceptions, in the character of worthless adventurers, which the natives know how to make ; and when they have made them, you will daily see them reposing their fortunes with Englishmen, in such ways as they will tell you they dare not with persons of their own complexion."

But in the midst of the general ungodliness of European life in Bengal, there were, even at this early period, a few Christian men whose exemplary lives shone brightly in contrast with the darkness around them. Conspicuous amongst these, was Mr. Charles Grant, a civilian of high position and very great influence. Mr. Grant's first introduction to India was in the military service, in 1767, but he soon went home, and returned as a writer on the Bengal establishment, in 1772. Shortly afterwards, a number of painful domestic afflictions led him to seek earnestly the consolations of the gospel; and throughout his subsequent career in India, and then for a long series of years in England, where he became Chairman of the Board of Directors of the Hon'ble East India Company, his hearty endeavors were directed to the promotion of Christianity in India and elsewhere. Mr. Grant brought out from England, with his wife, her mother and sister.* The last mentioned lady afterwards became the wife of Mr. William Chambers, a man of unquestionable piety, who had formerly resided near the excellent missionary Schwartz, and was deeply indebted to his influence and instructions. When he came round to Calcutta, he brought with him another pupil and friend of the same missionary. This was Mr. J. C. O'Beck, who became Mr. Grant's steward, and appears to have been a very good man. In

* It is a curious fact that at this period several elderly persons ventured upon life in India for the sake of the society of their children. Thus, in the circle spoken of above, besides Mrs. Frazer, Mr. Grant's mother-in-law, there had been Mrs. Chambers, the mother of Sir Robert and Mr. William Chambers ; and, a little later, there was added to it Mrs. Udny, the mother of the brothers of that name.

1781, Mr. Grant's appointment as Commercial Resident at Malda gave him an influential position amongst a number of young Europeans ; and he strove earnestly to promote their spiritual advantage. His influence over them was productive of very happy results, and some of them became exemplary Christians. When Mr. Grant left Malda, he was succeeded by Mr. George Udny, who had been his assistant, and who most worthily carried forward all his plans of Christian benvolence there.

Mr. Grant and his brother-in-law were very anxious to establish an evangelical mission in Bengal, and proposals regarding it, which, they hoped, might obtain the sanction of the Government, were drawn up, and, as opportunity offered, recommended to the notice of those who appeared to be likely to forward the plan. Of the results, more will be said hereafter. Mr. Chambers was Persian Interpreter to the Supreme Court, and a distinguished Persian scholar. He attempted to translate the New Testament into that language ; and proposed to have his translation turned into Bengali by a native scholar. This method of producing a Bengali New Testament must be regarded as singularly unpromising, and it was never more than a project. Mr. Chambers had the work in hand at least seven years ; yet at this death he had translated only thirteen chapters of Matthew into Persian,—of which those containing the Sermon on the Mount may now be seen printed at the end of Gladwin's *Persian Munshi*.

There is yet another attempt to enter upon evangelistic work in Bengal to be spoken of. The Moravian Brethren, who had accomplished so much in many other parts of the world, had missionaries also in Bengal. At the request of the Danish Asiatic Company, two of them settled near Serampore. A few years later, others resided in Calcutta, where they had a mission house in Park Street, and where one of them, Dr. Charles Frederick Smith, died on the 31st of August, 1783. No success appears to have resulted from their labours, and, on the death and removal of the missionaries, the mission was discontinued. In March, 1787, Mr. Thomas was told that in these Moravian missions there had been only one case of hopeful conversion in about thirty years.

Calcutta is still the scene of much gross immorality, of great ungodliness, and of wide-spread unbelief; and its vast population of Hindus and Musulmans is still far from the acknowledgment of the truth of the gospel. The heart of the Christian philanthropist must sink within him as he surveys the evil which the great metropolis of India exhibits even now. Yet who can contrast the Calcutta of the present,—its numerous places of worship of all denominations, well filled with attentive hearers of the gospel, —its many churches of faithful men,—its evangelical agencies,—and its increasing community of native converts, with the city of which we have been speaking, without acknowledging that a great and happy change has been effected? We have much, in our day, over which to lament; but, nevertheless, "the Lord hath done great things for us, whereof we are glad."

CHAPTER III.

Voyages to Calcutta and engagement as a missionary.—1783-87.

THE reader may have made the voyage from Gravesend to Calcutta in a passenger-ship of modern days, and yet know but little of the voyage as it was in the period to which this biography belongs. From the time when the last trace of the English coast fades out of sight, to that when the fringe of trees upon the banks of the great Indian river is discovered, the modern voyager very possibly sees no land. If his voyage be speedy and without disaster, he needs to anchor upon no intermediate coast. It was otherwise when Mr. Thomas sailed in the *Earl of Oxford*, and a few particulars of his first voyage, gathered from the fragments of his journal, may be interesting.

The squadron was composed of the Commodore Morgan's ship, the *Pigot*, the *Duke of Kingston*, the *Vansittart*, and the *Earl of Oxford*, East Indiamen. On the 11th of March, they sailed from the Motherbank, and passed through the Needles at 4 o'clock next morning. When to the westward of the Scilly isles, the captains opened their instructions, and found orders to touch at Santiago, one of the Cape Verd islands, for fresh water. Several troops, with officers, were on board; and, early in the voyage, Mr. Thomas mentions that a court-martial was held upon a man who had in a frolic thrown his comrade's cap overboard. The delinquent was punished with fifty lashes!

Some severe weather was experienced before the squadron entered the tropics; but early in the morning of the 28th of March, the sleepers on board the *Earl of Oxford* were called up on deck to see the high mountains of San Nicolao, which island was so close to the leeward of the vessel, that they dreaded lest they should be driven upon the rocky shore. On the morning of the 31st, however, they safely anchored in Porto Praya. Here a few days were spent very pleasantly in excursions on shore. They left Santiago on the 5th of April.

Another place of anchorage was the island Johanna, or Anzuan, between the northern part of Madagascar and the coast of Africa. Whilst here, Mr. Thomas received most satisfactory evidence of the confidence reposed in his medical skill. His captain had been severely ill for some time, and there was now an opportunity to hold a medical consultation, by calling in the surgeons of the other English vessels. Mr. Thomas strongly urged this; but captain White would not hear of it. He would take no medicine, he said, but that prescribed for him by his own doctor; and his subsequent recovery justified this determination.

When off Ceylon, a terrific disaster befell the squadron. The *Duke of Kingston* took fire, and in a short space of time was utterly destroyed. The *Earl of Oxford* was close at hand, and gave all the assistance in her power. Some of Mr. Thomas's reflections upon the dreadful occurrence may be quoted here.—

The people on the ship expected every moment that she would blow up; they therefore did not stay to take money or clothes out of their cabins; but left her as speedily as they could. Some, who could swim, leaped out of the ship, without waiting for rafts; but the current carried them away, and they perished. Others escaped by our boat and by rafts, and got on board our ship. One man, not contented with his life, returned to fetch away some valuables from his cabin. He secured his treasure, but lost his chance of escape. He perished, reaching in vain after a second opportunity. Captain Nutt, the master of the unhappy vessel, was saved. Many who survived were so burned and scorched, that I was long in soothing their agonies, and they remained disfigured all their days. The most part perished. What struck me most of all was, that those with most skill in swimming perished first, and perished miserably. They were swept far away, beating the fierce current in vain; and at last, hope and strength sinking, were overpowered by the dreary sea, in sight of our ship and of the distant mountains.

SICKNESS AT KEDGEREE.

After a short stay at Madras, the *Earl of Oxford* safely reached her anchorage in the Calcutta river. It is to be regretted that few memoranda concerning this visit to Calcutta have been left by Mr. Thomas. His first impressions of the great city would doubtless be interesting to the reader. Most of his time, however, was spent in his ship at Kedgeree; for East Indiamen were not accustomed to come up to Calcutta, but anchored at Kedgeree or Diamond Harbour, at which latter place they discharged and took in their cargoes. This arrangement seems to have been very unfavorable to the health of ships' crews. The river carried down vast quantities of decomposing animal and vegetable matter, much of which, at low water, lay stranded upon the muddy banks, exposed to the fervid heat of the sun. In the rainy season especially, the malaria from the swampy Sunderbun forests also rendered the anchorage at Diamond Harbour most unhealthy, and the mortality amongst the shipping was very great, almost every year. In 1783, the season was exceptionally sickly. Mr. Thomas says:—

> Vast numbers died; and in some ships there were not enough living to bury the dead; so that without ceremony, coffin, or much grave, the surgeon of the *Lord Macartney*, and others, were buried by black men. I was the only visiting surgeon in the fleet for several weeks, and was preserved in perfect health.

With a very grateful heart, he afterwards looked back upon this time of danger, and thanked God for the preservation of his life, when he ran so much risk of accident in passing from ship to ship, and in ministering to the diseased, escaping as he did " the infection of putrid fluxes, rotting bodies alive; the fury of the tides several times a day; and all the variety of diseases and perils of service at Kedgeree; dangerous vessels in the river; up and down, to and from Calcutta, with all his property; and more instances than could be remembered; besides all the dangers of fire and shipwreck, storms and tempests."

He also had escapes from wild beasts, which abounded in the jungles on shore at Kedgeree, and which his adventurous disposition led him to encounter there. Twice he was confronted by tigers, and his adventure with one of them may be related in his own words.—

One evening, I left the ship to take a walk on shore; and, that I might shoot some jungle fowl, I went into the woods. I found a long strip of grassy land where some deer were feeding, and, having loaded my guns with ball, I pursued them to the bottom of this lawn. Finding the thicket beyond it impenetrable, I waited until sunset for them to come out; when I thought it prudent to return. But, judge of my alarm, when I saw that a tiger had come out upon the grass, and was lying down in the way I had to take. I had a boy with me, of whom I enquired if there was any other path out of the jungle. He said there was not. I primed my guns, and told the boy to escape, if he could: but he chose to remain with me, relying upon my weapons. The lawn was about eighty yards wide where the creature was; and, as he was at the one side of it, I determined to pass him on the other, if he would let me. If not, I intended to reserve my fire till he came close to me. I marched on, or rather crept; and to my great terror and satisfaction, the beast raised his tail, and, with a frightful roar, turned into the woods; when, all of a sudden, I and my companion became quite light-footed.

Of all such dangers he spoke in after-life with suitable acknowledgments of the goodness of God, which delivered him from these imminent perils; but usually his thoughts of this period of his life were burdened with other recollections, which filled him with shame and remorse. At Kedgeree he was thrown into close intimacy with many irreligious men, in the several vessels of the fleet. His hands were filled by his professional duties. His mind was occupied with many worldly cares. In the midst of these adverse circumstances, his watchfulness over his own heart was relaxed, and he fell into sad neglect of his religious duties and into conduct which he felt to be unworthy of a Christian life. That his wickedness was not an open disgrace to his profession, was occasion for much thankfulness. He has left no particulars on record as to these backslidings; but the terms in which he condemned himself were unsparing and most severe. There were many occasions on which he awoke to some sense of his guilty wretchedness; but to little effect, until at length his remorseful terrors culminated in a vision of an unspeakably awful character. The fullest reference of this circumstance is contained in an entry in his journal of July 11th, in the following year. It is as follows.—

On perusing the story of Colonel Gardiner's conversion, I find a remarkably striking similarity between the vision which effectually wrought on him, and that which had little influence,—so very short and little,—upon my hardened cruel heart, concerning our blessed Lord and Saviour Jesus Christ. I remember that before the time of my vision—it may be about two months—I had read Colonel Gardiner's Life throughout; but this part of it had been entirely lost from my memory, in that awful vision at Calcutta, in October, 1783, and ever since; for I never had heard (to my recollection) of any thing, till this day, that was like my own experience in any measure, and therefore should have been extremely fearful of my credit when I offered to relate it. But, alas, the disparity of effects is so great! —His very soul turned!—My heart returned, dog-like! O Lord, I beseech thee, show me my folly.

In another place, he refers to the same thing in the following terms :—

I had my senses brought into the invisible world. I beheld more than one risen from the dead; one whom I knew! free from all the appearance or likelihood of a mistake. If I had heard him speak ever so long, what could he have said more? If he had been more explicit in all I had done, or more particular in describing all my ingratitude, or more plain in setting forth the terrors of the Lord, how could I have been more affected?—how could I have borne more? This instance is enough to teach me that, though a man be enlightened, and not only acknowledges, but has tasted of the heavenly gift,— that, though a spirit, though an angel, come and talk with him,—all will not do. He will not believe to the overcoming of the world,— which is of God only.

If the reader be disposed to deride the weakness which induced this good man to treat an illusion of his disturbed fancy as a supernatural vision contemplated by his bodily eyes, let him call to mind the many similar cases which were current and familiar in the Christian literature of the period of which we write. There was the remarkable example of Colonel Gardiner, to which Mr. Thomas himself adverts. There was also the dream of Mr. Newton, the case of Mr. Hart, that of Mr. Grimshaw, and many similar facts, which, however popular psychology may now explain them, were regarded by most intelligent good men of the former generation as supernatural; and were accounted for as being the extraordinary methods employed by God to awaken conviction, or to convey instruction to those who were the objects of His special favor.

Just after this, Mr. Thomas obtained some release from his duties on ship-board. The rains were over, and a more healthy season had set in, and he was able to visit Calcutta. With a heart reawakened to the supreme importance of divine things, he eagerly sought after some Christian companionship, if that were to be found in the great city. Let him relate his procedure there in his own words.—

On my arrival at Calcutta, I sought for religious people; but found none. At last, how was I rejoiced to hear that a Mr. Reed, a very religious man, was coming to dine with me, at a house in Calcutta;—a man who would not omit his closet hours, of a morning or evening, at sea or on land, for all the world! I concealed my impatience as well as I could till the joyful moment came: and it was but a moment; for I soon heard him take the Lord's name in vain; and it was like a cold dagger, with which I received repeated stabs in the course of half an hour's conversation: and he was ready to kick me when I spoke of some things commonly believed by other hypocrites, concerning our Lord Jesus Christ; and, with fury, put an end to our conversation, by saying I was a mad enthusiast to suppose that Jesus Christ, who was born only seventeen hundred years ago, had any thing to do in the creation of the world! When I returned, he went home in the same ship, and I found him a strict observer of devotional hours; but an enemy to all religion, and horribly loose, vain, and intemperate in his life and conversation.

After this I advertised for a Christian; and, that I may not be misunderstood, I shall give you a copy of the advertisement, from the *India Gazette* of November 1st, 1783, which lies now before me, and the answers I received.

RELIGIOUS SOCIETY.

A plan is now forming for the more effectually spreading the knowledge of Jesus Christ, and his glorious gospel, in and about Bengal. Any serious persons, of any denomination, rich or poor, high or low, who would heartily approve of, join in, or gladly forward such an undertaking, are hereby invited to give a small testimony of their inclination, that they may enjoy the satisfaction of forming a communion the most useful, the most comfortable, and the most exalted in the world. Direct for A. B. C., to be left with the Editor.

The two following answers were received the next day:—

If A. B. C., will open a subscription for a translation of the New Testament into the Persian and Moorish languages, (under the direction of proper persons,) he will meet with every assistance he can desire, and a competent number of subscribers to defray the expence.

ANOTHER.

The Rev. W. JOHNSON, having read the advertisement of A. B. C. in this day's paper, takes the earliest opportunity of expressing his satisfaction at a proposal for the more effectually propagating, and making known the truths of the Christian religion, in this country of superstition, idolatry, and irreligion; and for setting forth the excellence of that holy institution, so replete with the means of rendering mankind happy, both here and hereafter; most cordially offers his services for promoting and encouraging so laudable an undertaking, and will think himself happy, if he can be at all instrumental in bringing it to any degree of success.

Mr. JOHNSON, from the above reasons therefore, wishes an opportunity of conferring with the advertiser, on the occasion.

I have never yet found out who was the author of the anonymous note;* and as to Mr. Johnson, he was chaplain to the Presidency, and I was afraid to answer him, lest I should be scouted; for I had heard him preach, and the sermon as well as the text was, *The unknown God*.† This well-worded note of his was intended, I suppose, merely to find me out; and I have certain reasons to believe that the advertisement gave him offence. The following year, being at a house in London, where the Rev. John Newton had just called, I heard that a gospel minister was going out to Bengal, and that Mr. Newton had reason to think there were religious stirrings in that country, as he had read a certain advertisement in a newspaper

* It has been assumed by some who have mentioned this circumstance, that Mr. William Chambers was the writer of this advertisement. If so, it is very strange that the fact was never known or suspected by Mr. Thomas, who, soon afterwards, was for some time upon terms of friendly intimacy with Mr. Chambers.

† The Rev. W. Johnson returned to England in March, 1788, having been chaplain for thirteen years. He was reported to have amassed during that period the sum of £35,000.

of such an import; which advertisement was, indeed, what you have now read.

Before he left Calcutta, Mr. Thomas made the acquaintance of a pious tradesman there. This was Mr. James Wittit, a very successful "Europe and China shop-keeper," whose "dwelling house, shop, and warehouses," were "near the Bankshall." He had also a garden house "on the road from the Bytaconnah to the burial ground."* From Mr. Wittit, Mr. Thomas heard of Mr. Charles Grant, then residing at Malda. It is remarkable that nothing seems to have been said by him of Mr. Kiernander or of his mission. That mission had reported seventeen heathen of different castes as baptized in 1783.

One of the passengers to England in the *Earl of Oxford*, on her return, was the Rev. Dr. James Burn, who was retiring from his office of Senior Presidency chaplain, in his eighty fourth year! Mr. Thomas says little about him in his journal. It is, however, evident that the aged clergyman regarded the pious surgeon as being very extravagant in his religious opinions, and was looked upon by him as one who had sought and found his portion in this life.

The *Earl of Oxford* sailed for England on the 16th of March, 1784, with a cargo valued at Rs. 12,32,350. Mr. Thomas left Bengal, in a very different spirit from that he had brought with him there. He says, "In Isaiah xliii. I read my character, the patience and forbearance of God, and, what exceeded all, his blotting out my transgressions freely. The rest of the voyage, I ate, and drank, and lived upon the word of God. My breath was chiefly filled with

---

* Mr. Wittit's piety has left some traces upon the advertising columns of the early Calcutta newspapers. In 1784, he invites inspection of his premises and conference as to terms of sale, &c., "any day of the week, except Sunday," a very remarkable exception in those days.

Hicky's Bengal Gazette, for March, 1781, refers to his endeavours to put good books into circulation. A Hudibrastic rhyming list of goods for sale enumerates,—

"Ladies' caps to adorn the head;
Shrouds to wrap them in when dead;
Salves to cure the itch or evil;
Bible books to scare the Devil,
As good as e'er old Wittit did sell."

prayer and praise." A journal which he began to keep at the end of April, very remarkably illustrates this statement. It bears testimony to many transgressions and to the consciousness of much depravity, but no candid reader could fail to discover in it the character of one whose delight was in the word and service of God.

On the 12th of July, the ship reached St. Helena, and, for the first time since the voyage began, he received letters from his family at home. "After many impatient circles of thought," he perused with deep thankfulness that which his wife had sent him, and found that he was now a father. He wrote to her, the same day,—

I am unspeakably pleased with our 'son and heir,' who has entered into a world of affliction, of which he has begun to taste.— 'A world of affliction,' did I say ?—Lord ! I bless thee for my creation ! An eternity of praise to my God for participation in a life, which, though embittered with the effects of a sinful state and nature, yet abounds with mercy and goodness. But what are all these short-lived mercies, in comparison with redemption from sin and all its consequences, communion with a God ready to pardon and full of compassion, and also the hope of glory ?

At St. Helena, he complained much of his want of stedfastness, in allowing "the attraction of shore-fishing" to draw him from the religious exercises in which he found far higher delight. He also encountered very serious danger upon a shooting expedition. Having lost his way, he tried to cross a precipitous part of the mountains, but found himself unable either to proceed or to return ; when the soil under his feet crumbled beneath his weight, and the rock by which he held slipped and fell. Had he himself slid down but a couple of yards further, he must inevitably have fallen and been dashed to pieces. After a little, he succeeded in passing, " where perhaps never human foot had before trod, or ever would again," and so he escaped. When he returned, he was filled with horror at the dangerous aspect of the precipice, all the way, and his heart abounded with thanksgiving to God " for his goodness and help."

After a few days, the vessel proceeded on her way to England, which was reached about the end of September.

In review of his connexion with the *Earl of Oxford*, Mr. Thomas found great cause for thankfulness. His captain, though an irreligious and very profane man, had shown him much kindness. The ship had suffered with the rest of the fleet at Kedgeree, from the prevalence of disease, but in a far less degree; and not one of her officers had died throughout the voyage; all which had been attributed to the care and ability of the surgeon, and he was warmly invited to make another voyage. His endeavours to hold forth the word of life to his ship-mates were not wholly in vain. He felt that he had not always been wise in his attempts to introduce religious conversation on board; yet those he had talked with appeared to be convinced of the reality of religion. In particular, the chief officer of the ship had been brought under deep convictions of sin, and was anxiously enquiring after the way of salvation.

On the 23d of September, he wrote to his father,—

I am restored through the host of perils common to a sea life, once more to my native country in prosperity and safety. I have been in the midst of sicknesses and deaths, but always in health; dwelling amongst a crowd of dangers, yet kept safe from all; living a life often notorious for want and hardships, yet, in my case, abounding with rich supplies of all needful things, with enjoyment. In travels through so many thousand trackless leagues of the sea, and naturally exposed to tempests, stormy winds, and hurricanes, we have never had one hard gale of wind. Separated from all my friends and acquaintances, in the midst of strangers, I yet found favor in the sight of men, and am befriended with many gifts of money and other unexpected presents and assistance; and were I not abundantly convinced that the ways of God are unspeakably far above our ways, I should be at a loss to understand how it comes to pass that I, who have been so preposterously undeserving, should yet be a partaker of so many of His benefits; for I have no sooner tasted than abused them, or received than forgotten them. I have taken small heed to an evil heart of unbelief in departing from the living God; but have gone astray like, though not with, them that go down to the pit. And not only my body, but my soul, with all her fading, dying interests,—He has raised her up from the chambers of death again!—cleansed and robed her again!—brought me from feeding on husks with swine again, and feasted me with the fatness of His house, and covered me with the richest apparel. This is a mercy that transcends all the rest in its unspeakable value and richness. There was one remarkable providence, so uncommon, that happened to me before I was brought up out of the miry pit, that I shall be unwilling, through former experience, to relate it fully as long as I live ; for with eye-witness I have proved the truth of that testimony in Luke xvi. 31. I have been distracted with the terrors of the Lord ; yet His grace only was sufficient for me. This has been sufficient, I trust. It is now sufficient ; and, after all the crimsons and scarlets, I am left with a comfortable hope that it *will* be abundantly so, far above all I am able to think of it.

The reference to his vision here will not be overlooked by the reader. The terms of self-condemnation in connexion with which it occurs, accord with the general strain of his journal. He charges himself with a number of besetting sins: amongst which may be enumerated hastiness of temper, fickleness in his best purposes, sensitiveness as to his own honor, fondness for amusements, and other forms of self-indulgence. Of a sprightly social temperament, and holding, as the ship's surgeon, a position and relation to all on board which naturally led to intimacy, he found it very difficult to preserve that complete holy consecration which constituted his ideal of the Christian life, and which he was continually bringing into unsparing contrast with the actual results of his endeavours to walk before God and be perfect. It is clear, however, from the imperfect records he has left, that he was earnest in his attempts to do good, and that he was zealous and diligent in his study of God's word and in his strife against every disposition which he saw was condemned by it.

The voyage over, he, with great joy, found himself restored to the privileges of Christian society in his native land, and he now desired at once to profess his allegiance to Christ in baptism. But the discredit of his former difficulties was not yet forgotten, and his proposals met with what he felt to be " undue discouragement." At length, he was baptized by the Rev. Mr. Burnham of the Soho Chapel, without, however, any purpose of joining the church under that minister's care. It was on Christmas-day, 1784, that he thus solemnly " put on Christ." His journal records some disappointment on the occasion. He had supposed it would be a season of very lively enjoyment of the divine presence and favor; but his mind was depressed, and his emotions restrained. He was, however, prayerfully desirous that all his future life might bear witness to his true consecration, and that his divine Master's strength might be made perfect in his own weakness.

In regard to the future, his plans were very unsettled. He was reluctant to go again to India, and made another attempt to establish himself in surgical practice, in Great Portland Street, Oxford Road; not, however, with much promise of success. Although his difficulties were very greatly relieved, he was still in debt, and was occasionally sorely harassed by his creditors. The *Earl of Oxford* was not sent out in 1785, so that for several months he had no need to determine whether he would accompany her or not.

After his baptism, he entered upon a course of engagements which probably interfered with his success in worldly business. Ever since his conversion, he had ardently longed to become a preacher of the gospel. His private memoranda exhibit this cherished wish and the constant bent of his mind towards the study and exposition of the word of God. Now, he " began to exhort in private societies and to preach in different places in town and country." In thus employing himself, he was greatly encouraged by some of his hearers, who recognized in his fervent exhortations and addresses " the demonstration of the Spirit and of power." Others of his relatives and friends did all they could to deter him from preaching. Their opposition did not prevail against his determined inclination, although there were amongst them persons of prolonged experience,—" Christians," as he caustically remarked, " of thirty years '*standing*'—not '*running*.' " Their objections, however, had some effect upon his mind. For years afterwards, " the liberty of prophesying" was a subject frequently discussed in his letters, especially in those addressed to his brother, who also had thoughts of the ministry of the gospel. Very probably, the chief reason why such discouragements were put in the way of Mr. Thomas's ministry, was the unsatisfactory state of his affairs. Whilst the dishonor of debt rested upon him, his best friends might well be excused if they desired to see him devoted to his secular business, that he might owe no man anything, rather than to witness public labours which were liable to be carried forward with reproach.

Only a few fragmentary accounts of his first efforts in preaching the gospel are in existence; but these show that he found most exercise for his zeal in parts of Hertfordshire. He mentions Codicote, as a place where he had found "beloved saints and enquiring sinners," and he was at length invited to become the pastor of a small Baptist church at Hoddesdon. This proposal was under consideration for some time. The most wealthy subscriber to the support of the ministry there, a Mr. Thoroughgood, did not unite in the otherwise unanimous request; and at length Mr. Thomas, somewhat reluctantly, took the advice of Mr. Booth, who recommended him, on account of his youth and inexperience, to decline the invitation, and to make another voyage to Bengal in the *Earl of Oxford*, when she sailed in 1786.

In August, 1785, whilst undecided whether to settle at Hoddesdon or not, he was very powerfully impressed by the perusal of Isaiah xlix., and he seems to have regarded the thoughts which then crowded upon his mind as a revelation of the Lord's will in regard to his whole future life.

In his journal, more than four years afterwards, he says of this occurrence :—

After earnest prayer, my mind was unusually impressed, like broad day-light, with many passages in that chapter. Particularly, I understood that, although I had not 'gathered Israel,' yet the Lord had not 'forgotten me'; but had intimated His design towards me when I was a little child. I understood also that the Lord had hitherto hid me; but it should not always be so: that it was a very small matter, in comparison of what He had for me to do, that I should edify a little congregation of Israel; for He would send me forth into the world, afar off among unconverted Gentiles. This God had in view concerning me, who was, He knew, despised in my own country, and abhorred by many religious professors in my own nation. I understood that I had come with an acceptable petition to the Lord, and, in His own proper time and manner,

He had chosen, and would bless and prosper me in preaching the gospel. I understood that by 'desolate heritages' it was intimated that, by my preaching, those who were utterly destitute of the gospel should receive it, and God would Himself lead them, and would bless and cause them to flourish. And as, humanly speaking, difficulties like mountains would lie in the way, He would remove them. And now the scene began to open as broad as daylight from heaven on my mind, with an inexpressible sweetness and composure of soul. So great and extensive were the things shown me, that I drew back, thinking it too much; for how could all these things be? I understood that the Lord had observed my downcast looks and unbelief, as though He had forsaken me; but my particulars were continually minutely before Him. I understood that the Lord would surprise me with numbers, surpassing my crediting powers: that I should stand astonished at it; and that great personages should be among those who would nurse and take care of me and mine, and the temporal affairs of the Lord's sheep. An uncommon readiness to receive the gospel and a running to it were the last thing in the chapter which the Lord shewed me; and I understood also that these words were written concerning Isaiah and concerning Christ, not excluding our instruction;* and the word of God is not bound, his testimonies are everlasting, and no scripture is of private interpretation. Amen, Lord Jesus. Even so; come now, Lord Jesus!

With reference to this, he further wrote:—

I just add that the way I understood it all was this: that I might fix at Hoddesdon, and go and preach to all the country round about Cambridge and Hertfordshire. But this did not satisfy me; because the field was not big enough to hold one of the scenes, which appeared to me to be many and great; therefore, thought I, it may be that the Lord will take me another voyage, and, among the unconverted desolate heathens, he may send me to preach the gospel. Here all things suited; only the impossibility of leaving the ship, my family, &c. So the state of the case was. I abode in surprise and joy, believing that what the Lord had said would verily come to pass; though I did not know exactly how and when, or other particulars. Soon after, going by Tottenham Court Chapel, I dropped in, as Mr. Matthew Wilks was in the middle of his sermon, on

* This is not very intelligible. Mr. Thomas's meaning will better appear from what he wrote to his brother in January, 1787. "From Isaiah xlix. I was made to see the truth of that saying of Witsius: 'Whatever is written of Christ, becomes true in its order and degree, to all that are Christ's.'"

this text: 'Thy testimonies are wonderful.'—Psalm cxix. 129. Just as I went in, he spoke to this effect, 'Sometimes the Lord shows His people in a wonderful manner, by His testimonies, His own secrets; and yet, though they are so surprised and satisfied, they do not know and understand for some years afterwards; but when the things come to pass, then they know clearly.'

Two or three years before this, he had a dream, to which likewise he makes frequent reference in his after-life. This, too, may be quoted here.—

In this dream, I thought I had something in my ear,—very large, but not painful to me; and I picked it out, and it fell down; and, lo, it was a crab-fish! I was afraid of its claws; for it was alive; and I took it up carefully, holding its back, whilst the claws played about, reaching after anything they could lay hold of. While it did this, I looked, and, behold, its legs and claws became lilies, such as I had never seen!—very beautiful flowers!—very fragrant!—and I smelt them with delight, and wondered at their sweetness! And, behold, in one moment, in the twinkling of an eye, these flowers were transformed, and became ears of ripe corn, very large, very full, very long in the ear, with the sun shining upon them in his strength:—and I awoke, and, behold, it was a dream!

These curious extracts are not without importance to the narrative. The reader will, very probably, deem them insignificant trifles; but the impressions and the dream here described were esteemed by Mr. Thomas as having a divine origin. Nor was their influence upon him fugitive. On the contrary, it will be seen that, more or less actively, it wrought upon his mind throughout all his subsequent history.

Nothing of particular interest appears to have happened during this sojourn in England, save that a second son, whom he called James, was born to him in October, 1785. Both this child and John, the first-born, died at a very early age.

When upon the point of embarking for his second voyage, he wrote to his beloved sister Sarah a letter, beginning, with characteristic abruptness, thus:—

Death is disarmed: never fear him. You ask me of the antidotes against the fear of death, and I shall not deny you my thoughts because they are weak ; for there is One stands by me and you who has strength enough for us both, and to spare. The fear of death in a believer may be either a wile of the devil, a shudder of flesh and blood, a dark drapery of a gloomy imagination, or the teeming of a timid constitution. It is a disease that hath many causes, and but one *remedy*, and that remedy is *Christ*, even He who came ' to *deliver* them who through fear of death were all their life-time subject to bondage.' ' In Him is plenteous redemption.'—Psalm cxxx. 7. Now when the soul can realize this text, what can be wished for more ? All fear of death is then taken away. If our trust were wholly out of ourselves, and only in Him, these fears and doubts would be overcome and put to silence ; but the mischief is, we all like to trust in *ourselves*, more than we think we do ; thence it is that, upon finding in *ourselves* deficiencies, immediately the fear of death advances. Courage fails in proportion as that fails in which we trust. But Christ will never fail us : we have need of much, and in Him is plenty.

What would it avail you to plead before God that you had as much moral righteousness as all the holy prophets and apostles ? One spark of Christ's righteousness would as far outblaze it all as the sun surpasses a glowworm. And if one spark is so, and sure I am it is, then what have they to complain of who shall be covered with it,—filled with it ? And what if you were loaded with the sins and blasphemies of a whole age of men ? What would all these be for the blood of Christ to cleanse away ? Not so much as a grain of sand before a boisterous sea. Jesus Christ is an altar which whatsoever only toucheth shall be holy.—Exodus xxix. 37. Therefore I think that an apprehension of Him by an eye of faith is the best antidote ; and you know this. The Holy Ghost expresses diligence as the best cure in the world of a saint's doubt and scruples of his salvation. Let us follow the wise men, who set out and sought Christ diligently ; and, till they had found Him, returned not back. Seek, and you shall find ; for every one that seeketh findeth. Whom did Christ suffer for ? It could not be for Himself : He was the Holy One. It must have been for us ; and let us take the benefit thereof, rejoicing in Him, and having no confidence in the flesh.

My things are gone aboard ; and I leave town to-morrow. May the peace of God be with you. May you labour these eighteen next months for those things of eternal life which overcome temporal death, which the Son of man shall give unto you. Him hath God the Father sealed. And then, when I return, if ever that should be, I shall hear a new song, which Christ can put in your mouth, of praise to God for Jesus Christ, who performeth all things for you.

Few incidents relating to his second voyage to Calcutta are worthy of record. The *Earl of Oxford* sailed from the Downs on the 5th of March, in company with the *Walpole* and the *Berrington*. She called at the Cape of Good Hope. It is interesting to find the following observations, under date of July 6th, just before Mr. Thomas reached Bengal, introduced by the words, " Propose to address this to young ministers and students."

Hath God revealed the spread of the gospel, for nothing? Do not all things revealed belong to us? But how much more especially *these* things?—to us, in particular, upon whom the ends of the world are come? for the time is nigh at hand :—' It shall come, that I will gather all nations and tongues ; and they shall come, and see my glory,' saith the Lord.—Isaiah lxvi. 18. If we live to see the dawn of this day only ; surely it becomes us to leave a mark behind us of our eager expectation, from the trust we have of the faithfulness of God. He that heareth and keepeth fast the testimonies of the Lord concerning these things, in these latter days, is a blessed man, and getteth great good to his soul.

Such sentiments were not a little remarkable when they were penned.; and if the appeal the writer of them intended to make was never put forth, as he originally proposed, his life itself became the means of awakening missionary devotedness in the classes he desired to address.

When the above remarks were being written, another good man had found a home near Calcutta, prepared to devote himself to the promotion of Christian truth there ; and, as he was to exercise much influence over the career of Mr. Thomas, he must here be introduced to the reader.

The Rev. David Brown, late of Magdalen College, Cambridge, was selected by Major Mitchell, on behalf of the Military Orphan Society, as well fitted to take the superintendence of their school for the children of non-commissioned officers and private soldiers, then established at Howrah, on the western bank of the river, opposite to Calcutta.* Mr. Brown accepted this appointment, and

* The school for officers' children was to be under the direction of another gentleman, who was expected from England. Until he came, Mr. Brown had the general superintendence of both schools, which were for some time held on the same premises.

having obtained deacon's orders from the bishop of Llandaff, came out to India in the ship *Juliana Maria*, captain Davidson. He landed in Calcutta on the 8th of June, 1786, and was kindly welcomed by Mr. William Chambers and a few others who rejoiced at the arrival of an English clergyman of thoroughly evangelical principles. For the especial benefit of the numerous young people under his charge, Mr. Brown commenced a Sunday morning service in the school house. He also preached to the troops in the garrison, having been appointed chaplain to the 6th battalion, immediately upon his arrival in Bengal.

The *Earl of Oxford* anchored at Diamond Point on the 14th of July. Throughout the voyage, Mr. Thomas had very faithfully striven to do good to all on board, and a small congregation used to meet in his cabin for religious services. On arriving in Bengal, his great desire was that he might be able to maintain a holy deportment before all men, and to exert a Christian influence upon his acquaintance in Calcutta, whether he discovered any fellow-believers there or not.

The principal officers on board East Indiamen were all entitled to a certain amount of tonnage in their vessels, to carry merchandise for sale on their own account. The Calcutta newspapers of this period nearly always contained advertisements by merchants and shop-keepers, in which the investments brought out by the captain, the chief officer, or the surgeon of some ship just arrived from England, were offered for sale. Mr. Thomas of course availed himself of this privilege of trading. Captain White most kindly became his security with the merchants who entrusted their goods to him; and on the present occasion he was so successful that he reckoned his profits to be upwards of £500. This was much more than enough to release him from all his pecuniary difficulties; but it was also a strong inducement to him to venture yet more freely in the purchase of goods for the return voyage, and thus, as will be seen, his present success brought about a calamity which embittered and most disastrously affected all his subsequent life.

Holding the medical charge of a large ship, which lay at Kedgeree, he could not spend the whole of his time in Calcutta; but when there he eagerly resumed his enquiries after God-fearing men. Mr. Wittit, the only Christian man he could discover in 1784, was now on his way to Europe; but he met with Mr. Robert Udny, by whom he was introduced to Mr. William Chambers and to Dr. James Nasmyth, and a few other good men, and he was soon upon terms of warm intimacy with them all, taking an active part in the meetings for prayer and exhortation which they held in each other's houses. Between Mr. Chambers and Mr. Brown there was at this time some unpleasantness. The young clergyman appears to have been censured for accepting the military chaplaincy in addition to the duties he had been brought out from England to perform at the Orphan House. Dr. Nasmyth, however, who was the surgeon of that establishment, spoke very highly of him, and, after hearing him preach at Howrah, Mr. Thomas strongly urged his friends to attend his ministry, rather than that of Mr. Kiernander and his son, whom they were accustomed to hear at the mission church. He appears also to have done all he could to remove misunderstandings between Mr. Brown and the few persons in Calcutta who could sympathise with him in his aspirations after usefulness. This appeared to be happily effected, when, towards the end of October, fresh discord arose.*

* "October 27th.—This day we had a meeting at Mr. Udny's, in behalf of Mr Brown, whose conduct has been much blamed by us all, and he will not receive our mild admonitions. I therefore proposed this meeting to be held twice a week, that the Lord may be pleased to forgive him and restore his soul. I read the beginning of Luke xi. and xviii. on the encouragement our Lord gives us to pray, and Mr. Udny prayed. I then read 2 Samuel vii. and went to prayer. Afterwards, I read 2 Chronicles vii. 12—22, and Mr. Nasmyth concluded in prayer. Proposed to meet again on Monday.

"October 30th.—I met my Christian friends again at Mr. Udny's, for prayer and reading of the word. Great consolations on the house-top, where I retired a little before we met. We read Jeremiah ii. and Nehemiah ix. shewing the goodness of God to backsliders, and each of us engaged in a lively manner on behalf of our drooping brother and minister of our Lord Jesus Christ. He still seems heady, impatient of reproof, overbearing in his opinions, full of contradiction and dispute, and on Sabbath day preached to us a defensive misquoting sermon, and leant a great deal on our conduct towards him. I feel myself attached to him in

Mr. Thomas evidently enjoyed the warmest esteem and affection of these friends, and was " strangely caressed" by them. His prayers, his addresses, and, whenever absent from Calcutta, his letters to them, were highly appreciated; and their deference to his judgment and counsels encouraged him to use much boldness towards them, in the belief that the Lord would accomplish great good amongst them by his means. He cherished expectations of yet wider usefulness. In the early part of December, he employed his leisure in writing a little book for distribution, which he called, *A Word of Comfort and Encouragement to the Poor Afflicted People of God*. As " a physical man," he wrote, he had often good opportunities of putting such a paper into the hands of his patients. It was printed; but no copy of it has been preserved.

Mr. Charles Grant was now looked for in Calcutta, to make arrangements for removal from Malda to a more important post at the Presidency. He had heard much from his correspondents of the pious surgeon of the *Earl of Oxford*, whose society had so much delighted them, and he came fully prepared to admit the stranger to his most affectionate confidence. On the 16th of December, they met for the first time, and had much " sweet conversation" together. Mr. Grant laid before him his wishes as to the diffusion of the gospel in Bengal, and spoke with him of his own Christian experience. Mr. Thomas found him " harassed with perplexing doubts and fears, jealousies of himself, &c., but with much appearance of unfeigned love, and humble sincerity." On the other hand, the impression Mr. Grant received from the lively spiritual discourse of his new acquaintance was such as to confirm all

---

the midst of all, and, at the bottom, see in him something lovely, and that loveth, hopeth, and beareth, and is not easily provoked.

"November 3d.—Heard of some very reproachful speeches that had been uttered against me by Mr. Brown :—that I am a babbler, and quote scripture without meaning; but he did not instance one particular. Mr. Udny has received a letter from him, wherein he calls him the devil's instrument, and desires him to be open, honorable, and undisguised, and to leave all intrigues to the devil, with several other similar insinuations. He spoke slightingly of Mr. Chambers, and said he would answer his letter off-hand."—*Mr. Thomas's Journal.*

the favorable accounts he had received concerning him. This was clearly shown when, on the evening of the 18th, Mr. Robert Udny informed him that Mr. Grant was very desirous to have him stay in Bengal, "for the work of the ministry."

Mr. Grant put into his hands the proposals he and Mr. Chambers had drawn up, for the establishment of a Protestant mission in Bengal and Behar. These had already been submitted to Mr. Brown, who had entered heartily into the plan, suggesting several details, with the very natural impression that the effort would be under the direction of the Church of England. But now that Mr. Grant had been introduced to dissent in the person of Mr. Thomas, he was willing to include in his scheme the co-operation of pious nonconformists also; and he encouraged his new friend to alter his plan freely, and to forward copies of it to such dissenting ministers at home as would be likely to take a practical interest in the great object they had so much at heart.

The proposal that he himself should become a missionary, was without doubt very gratifying to Mr. Thomas. It was the cherished desire of his heart to be a minister of the gospel, and he firmly believed it to be God's purpose to make him useful to many souls. The noble apostolic work of witnessing for Christ in a heathen country hitherto destitute of any spiritual light, must have appeared eminently attractive; yet, at first, he thought it quite impossible that he could accede to a suggestion encumbered by so many difficulties. The absence of his family, the unsettled state of his temporal affairs, and the labour and difficulty of acquiring the Bengali language before he could preach to the heathen, appeared to be insuperable obstacles, and his reply to Mr. Udny altogether discouraged any endeavours to urge the proposal upon his consideration.

His intimacy with Mr. Grant became closer day by day. On the 29th of December, he was invited by him to address the little company of Christian friends; and, taking for his text Galatians v. 1, he endeavoured to set before them the liberty of the gospel of Christ. In this discourse, which was not delivered without serious apprehension of offending his hearers, he pointed out with much boldness and force several doctrinal and practical errors which he had observed amongst them. But his pointed animadversions were taken in excellent part by them all. In the words of Mr. Grant, all he said " was received with submission and respect : no one gainsaid, no one disputed." He was afterwards repeatedly invited to preach again ; and very much pleasure and profit were acknowledged by those who heard him.

In a letter to his brother, dated January 11th, 1787, Mr. Thomas thus describes Mr. Grant's missionary project, and the part he was taking in giving shape to it :—

I have a piece of news for you. You must understand there is a Mr. Grant here, a man of fortune and consequence, who has projected a mission of gospel ministers to this country from England. The papers are drawn up and are now in my hands, submitted to any alteration I may think necessary. Mr. and Mrs. Grant, with about eight or nine others, dependents, serve God, and he himself is a humble, teachable, strict and zealous man. He is too partial to me, a great deal, and has made an offer for my support with my family, if I would stay here and reside at Malda. He has made several alterations in the proposals of *my* stating, and has now given the papers wholly into my hands. Mr. Brown; a preacher of the gospel here, who has the care of an Orphan House, at first regulated the plan, and named eight young men who are in the Colleges at home, as fit persons to be invited to this work. Here I have objected that *young* men in Colleges are tender and nice, unlikely to endure hardship ; that, besides, from the scarcity of gospel ministers of this denomination in England, it was to be supposed that, if either of these men were likely and promising, he would be taken particular care of for destitute churches there at the disposal of friends of the gospel. Besides I argue that the character of missionaries ought to be settled and known, having been *proved*. So we have spared the young collegians from the undertaking. Brown is jealous of me, and severe ; but I stand as firm as a rock in mind and conscience, and am *too* high in the favor and opinion of Mr. Grant, to whom the Lord has made me useful. Brown is to blame. Mr. Grant proposes to send papers acquainting ministers of the gospel in general of the opening in this country, and he also offers to entertain two missionaries at his own expense, and will allow each a salary of £20 a month; will furnish them with books and teachers besides, whereby they may become acquainted with the languages of the country. A Mr. Schwartz, a Dane, has had great success upon the Coromandel coast, and his converts have suffered shame, exile, and death from their countrymen, and joined the martyrs above. He is a most exemplary man and an indefatigable labourer in Christ's vineyard. I have begun to speak in this country, and with power. Mr. Grant and almost half of the few saints here are shackled, but their bars are almost broken asunder by what is revealed Galatians v. 1, and elsewhere, concerning the grace of the gospel and entanglements of the law. They have received it well, and I have reason to be thankful; only they try me with too much commendation.

Flattered by the admiration of his Calcutta friends and, without doubt, really useful amongst them, Mr. Thomas was under strong temptation to neglect his duties to his ship, which was lying at Diamond Harbour. His "mate," the assistant surgeon, soon felt that he was badly used, in being detained on board through the prolonged absence of his superior, and he wrote to Mr. Thomas with bitterness, and complained of him to the captain. Some other disagreeable occurrences, connected with the ship, combined with these things greatly to annoy him, and the result of them all was a most momentous change in his plans. The invitation given him to remain in Bengal had not been forgotten. It had never been explicitly renewed; but remarks had been dropped every now and then by Mr. Grant and the rest, which Mr. Thomas interpreted as indications of their unaltered desire that he would give it more favorable consideration. These things had somewhat unsettled his mind, leading him often to contrast the pleasantness and advantages of such a life of service to Christ amongst the heathen, with the uncongenial character of his situation as surgeon on board an East Indiaman. But now that actual unpleasantness had arisen between himself and his fellow officers there, he thought it might be that the Lord was showing him that he should quit the ship and give himself up to the work of the mission. The suggestion kindled in his heart a flame of desire for missionary service, and his mind was soon filled with a rapturous persuasion that he had a divine call to undertake it in Bengal. The impressions he had received in August, 1785, when Isaiah xlix. appeared to set forth before him God's purposes as to his career, were now vividly revived, as he contemplated a field of usefulness broader and more fruitful than he had ever before imagined. In the deep emotion thus excited, he spent the night of Thursday, the 12th of January, 1787, "in prayer and meditation, with fear and trembling; and concluded that he was heard of God; and rested satisfied." On Friday morning, he hasted to announce his convictions and plans to Mr. Grant. He and Mr. Udny both appeared to rejoice in his readiness to undertake the mission; and Mr. Thomas immediately went to ask the captain's consent to his release from his engagement with the ship. This, however, was positively refused, "with three hours' pouring out of rage, threatenings, and abusive language." But his confidence that the Lord had sent him to the people of Bengal remained unshaken, and he was persuaded that the captain's opposition and every other obstacle would speedily be taken out of his way.

His journal for January 16th, and one or two following days, may be quoted, to show the reasons why he so firmly believed that he was called by God to become a missionary to the heathen, and the progress of his arrangements.—

When Mr. Grant first asked me to the work, it was both unsought for and unexpected by me, and seemed to be accompanied with warm and continued desires in him that I should undertake it; for though I had some thoughts and tears about the condition of the heathens and my preaching to them, yet there was no probability of it. And when I was invited, although I did not feel at all unwilling, yet the thought about my creditors, leaving the ship, my wife and family, and the people in Hertfordshire, seemed to me most insurmountable objections indeed; and Mr. Grant, being a discreet man, thought it not best to press the matter in that case; but continued showing me the abiding bent of his inclinations by every now and then hinting about my staying in this country. On Thursday, I conceived a most formidable disgust of mind against my ship, partly occasioned by a trifling affront from my mate and other news of rather an imposing and oppressive nature. Still, though it was all trifling, they occasioned a very disproportionate and almost insupportable weight upon my spirits. But late in the evening of that day, near midnight, I had such a powerful persuasion of mind that I was intended to be a messenger of the Lord to the poor heathens, that I could but stand astonied at it. I hurried my servant away, and prayed heartily to God, confessing my sin, and the guilt of it that bore upon me, and after prayer the persuasion grew stronger. I continued, sometimes in tears and in strong cries, till 3 o'clock in the morning, when my mind was so fully satisfied that it was so, that I spent the remainder of the night-time, till half past 5 o'clock, in wonder at my own situation of circumstances and condition in the world. I begged of God that, if it was a delusion, he would be pleased to reveal it to me; but still my persuasion grew stronger and stronger; insomuch that I was fully sure that when I should come to open my mind to Mr. Grant, he would assent to it; which made me long for the morning light, that I might tell him all my heart. And after prayer with him and my well-beloved Udny, they both did soon very joyfully receive me.

The next step was to communicate the matter to the captain; thinking it prudent to conceal from him my purpose of preaching, and only ask his permission to stay, promising him repeatedly that I would not stay without his leave. This seemed at first to produce no visible alteration in him; but at supper-time he broke out into the most passionate expressions against me, telling me that I and all my friends were what is too bad to be mentioned. He threatened to put me under a charge of sepoys when I got up to leave him; but I told him I only made him angry by staying. He mixed his wrath with expressions of friendliness, and paid me the highest compliments as a professional man; but continued in the greatest displeasure notwithstanding. I reasoned with him, offered to go home, or do anything; but all to no purpose. About 1 o'clock, he retired, and so did I, still trusting in the Lord to move his heart to the cause, however much against his mind.

My mate had all along intended to stay in the country; which determination was all against me, having nobody else to supersede me: but much about this time, he changed his mind; for the captain had both shewn and promised him his favor and interest.

Isaiah xlix. which had formerly been so strongly impressed on my mind after prayer, though not understood then, was now renewed to my soul. Enemies of the worst sort who formerly resided here, were all removed away; and the door formerly opened seemed now to be wide open.

The leaving of my few friends in England for ever, the improbability of my ever living any more but among heathens,—poverty, and many other formidable shocks to flesh and blood, did not alter my determination to give up all and follow Christ, but rather excited me so to do.

Though I do find a mixture of base motives, yet these are all weak and despised by me, and, upon the whole, I have cause to think that I am seeking His glory that sent me, and not my own.

Assurances that I could not destroy another man's foundation also encouraged me.

Also, in all this business, my heart has been, by night and by day, like a weaned child. A holy, quiet, assured, peaceable, mild, gentle, forgiving, heavenly, loving frame of mind has possessed me all the while.

I feel as though I could do anything for Christ: go or stay, live or die. I would go and suffer shipwreck and death, to glorify Him but a little, or even to satisfy His desire. But if He should tear my heart from these heathens, there would be a bleeding, for my soul is set upon them.

Psalm xxxix., from the 10th verse to the end, has just afforded me support under the threatening opposition. It is a comfort to me to think that, as to the captain, the Lord seeth his very looks.

January 17th.—Spent the rest of yesterday in great heaviness of heart and grief of mind. Fear and heaviness were my portion for the day. New sources of discomfort this morning, and new reasons to believe that the course of human events is against me, and that the captain will never consent to my staying. His cruelty provokes me; and I have sinned in being angry. The Lord is kind and merciful to my soul in a storm.

I have been pouring out my heart unto the Lord, and recollecting that it is His leave *only*, that I should ask, about staying in this country; and when I rose from my knees, I intended to look in my concordance for this text, 'Wait thou only upon God.' And, behold, instead of what I looked for, these words came before my eyes: 'Pharaoh shall restore thee to thy place,' but I do not —— I was just going to say that I did not understand the Lord's answer, when, in came Mr. White, the captain's brother, and told me that he had been 'working for me at the captain,' and had obtained his consent so far as to say that, as he is bound for me, I must satisfy that demand. O God, who will not fear and glorify thy great name! Thou art faithful, but I am unbelieving!

Mr. White has been telling me, that he has also been treating with Curry's friends; and they all advise him to go home. Oh, in how many ways doth the Lord work to-day!

The remainder of the day was spent in joy and solid comfort, and was closed with social prayer at Mr. Grant's. I spoke a few words from Job xlii. 7, 8, 9.

Wednesday 18th.—I begin the day abundantly satisfied that God is with me indeed, and will bless me.

The captain to-day personally consented to let me stay, on the condition of Mr. Curry's taking my place. I left Calcutta, after taking leave of Mr. Grant and Mr. Udny, with prayer.

The arrangements into which Mr. Thomas and his friends wished to enter involved many very difficult and delicate questions and relations, which ought to have been considered before-hand with much deliberation and care. Mr. Grant was a man remarkable for his great prudence: Mr. Thomas certainly could make no pretensions even to an ordinary share of it; and his precipitancy in this matter is not so much to be wondered at, as that of his friends. To his mind, the arrangement proposed had been encumbered only by the one great difficulty of obtaining the captain's consent, and he believed that the providence of God would certainly secure this, in pursuance of His own purpose, and in answer to his prayers. His "mate," Mr. Curry, had before obtained leave to stay in India; and the vessel could not be left without a surgeon. The captain moreover thought very highly of Mr. Thomas's professional skill, and had a great liking for him. In two or three days, however, all was amicably adjusted. Mr. Curry was induced to alter his plans and accept the promotion on board the *Earl of Oxford*, and captain White laid aside his profane bluster, and consented to his surgeon's application for release. This was regarded by Mr. Thomas as a most signal interposition of God's hand, confirming his call to the mission; of the reality of which, indeed, he was so fully assured that, afterwards, when Mr. Grant and all his Calcutta friends were quite convinced that they had been misled when they engaged him, he found comfort under their desertion of him, in the persuasion that even Paul's vocation to preach the gospel in Macedonia was less distinct and direct than that which now determined him to devote his life to the evangelization of Bengal!

On the 18th of January, therefore, he left Calcutta and

proceeded to Kedgeree to attend to the ship's company, until he should be finally released from his duties, and was for some weeks with the vessel, suffering nearly the whole time from severe illness, having incautiously salivated himself, by wearing " an under-waistcoat which was full of mercury." Mr. Grant also went back to Malda; but finally removed to Calcutta, on the 19th of February, to take his place as fourth member of the Board of Trade, to which he had been appointed by Lord Cornwallis. Mr. George Udny succeeded to Mr. Grant's former position, as Commercial Resident at Malda.

Mr. Thomas returned to Calcutta fully released from the ship, on the 16th of February; but he had not secured his liberty without considerable difficulty and sacrifice. His successor took advantage of his eagerness, to make hard terms with him, and claimed compensation for the relinquishment of his own plans. Mr. Thomas was induced to pay him Sicca Rs. 1000, and to give him in addition a bill upon his London agent for £36. He also had to pay him for the freight of goods he was sending to England, and he made over to him the care of a young passenger, "Mr. Grant's little nephew;" for looking after whom he was, no doubt, very handsomely remunerated. Indeed, Mr. Thomas computed all his "expenses and losses in staying in the East Indies" "to amount to £600, at the least." This was much more than he had to lose; but he had arranged that the ship should carry home a quantity of Indian muslins and other goods, which he believed would sell for at least £2000, and he confidently expected that his profits would clear every liability, and leave a considerable surplus for the support of his family until they could join him in Bengal.

The ship sailed on the 18th of March, and he was left to engage in his new duties, one of the first and chief of which was the acquisition of the Bengali language. He had procured Halhed's Grammar, and applied himself to the study in January, with strong hope that, in spite of all difficulties, he might be able " to preach to the black fellows at Malda on his birth-day." But he could learn little of the language without a teacher. Now, on the 8th of March, he engaged a múnshi, recommended to him by Mr. William Chambers. This man was of the Káyastha or writer caste, and was named Rám Rám Basu, or, as the name is commonly pronounced, Bose. He was said to be a good Persian scholar; but knew very little English. There will be frequent occasion to speak of him hereafter.

Who has not suffered severe disappointment after some long-coveted object has been attained, and especially an important change in the conditions of life? A closer knowledge of new circumstances and associates often falsifies our anticipations regarding them; and, most commonly, we find ourselves self-deceived. We thought to leave evil influences and sinful tendencies behind us in the scenes of our former failures and defeats, and expected to have, in our new positions and surroundings, only incentives to all that is good; but we discover that we have brought with us into our new world our old dispositions, and have greater need than ever to watch and pray lest we enter into temptation.

It was so with Mr. Thomas now. Not that he had looked forward to a life of quiet enjoyment in the service of Christ henceforth. He had endeavoured duly to estimate all the difficulties of the course he was adopting. He was prepared to encounter many trials, to engage in painful and laborious efforts in preaching the gospel, to brave the contempt and hostility of his ungodly countrymen and the hatred and persecution of idolators, and at last, perhaps, to suffer a martyr's death. "None of these things moved him;" but these were not the evils with which he was actually to contend. Dangers more subtle and insidious, and trials more bitter, which he had not anticipated, were, however, close at hand.

When free to live on shore, he soon felt that he stood upon an altered footing with his friends. Before leaving the ship, he had been their much honored guest, perfectly independent of their assistance and support, and able, as all felt, to "help them much who had believed through grace," by his larger knowledge of divine truth, as well as of the opinions and usages of Christian people at home.

Now, he was to do certain work, in which they desired to employ him; and he was to receive from them his support. Possibly neither party at once clearly recognized the change in their mutual relations, but both were instinctively conscious of some difference in the terms of their association. Mr. Thomas began to fear that his friends were not as completely devoted to the service of Christ as he had before supposed. Mr. Grant's position in Calcutta was one of great prominence and responsibility, and he was necessarily closely occupied with his official duties, which also brought him into the society of other principal men in the Presidency, most of whom had no fear of God before their eyes. This was unavoidable; but Mr. Thomas saw it with much dissatisfaction, and with a jealousy which may not have been wholly unselfish. He thought that the character and tastes of the little society he had assisted to build up in Calcutta were undergoing a change, through the familiarity with worldly men which Mr. Grant's settlement in the city had brought about. He wrote in his journal: "Reputation is a snare to those who are called to follow Him 'who made Himself of no reputation.'" And again,—"Our Lord Jesus Christ, his gospel, and his honor are more at stake through Mr. Grant's coming to Calcutta, than through all else that has taken place." He complained that "the glory of the Lord was becoming dim in his house. Little or nothing was ever heard there of the Lord Jesus Christ. Who would know it to be a Christian's house?" These were his reflections as early as the 10th of March. But he did not mourn over the failings of others only. He bitterly deplored the frivolousness of his own spirit, confessing that he found himself frequently betrayed into levity and jocularity amongst his friends, notwithstanding his earnest desires and prayers that he might be able to lay aside all such foolishness, and to have his "speech always with grace, seasoned with salt, that he might know how he ought to answer every man."

Mr. Grant was accompanied from Malda by his steward, Mr. O'Beck. This good man's Lutheran instincts appear to have been immediately affronted by the position Mr. Thomas, a lay-man, had assumed amongst his friends. His early scruples as to his employment as a missionary were, however, for the present overruled, and they occasioned no breach of the harmony which existed in the circle he now joined. Mr. Thomas found great pleasure in his society, and heard from him with much delight details of the self-denying labours and extensive usefulness of Mr. Schwartz and the other missionaries on the coast.

Mr. Brown was still in some measure estranged from the society to which Mr. Thomas was attached, and had been no party to the action Mr. Grant had taken in engaging him as a missionary. He would probably have prevented it, if he could ; and, had his counsels been invited, he could certainly have pointed out difficulties likely to arise between the Baptist missionary and his Pædobaptist supporters, which none of them had been sagacious enough to anticipate. His little intercourse with them was partly due to the displeasure he had manifested in October, and partly, no doubt, to the fact of his living on the other side of the river. Probably his reserved manner and unattractive address in the pulpit also contrasted very unfavorably with the vivacity and affectionate earnestness of Mr. Thomas, who was ever ready to lay himself out for the edification of his friends. Mr. Brown was soon, however, to gain a high position in the esteem and confidence of Mr. Grant and the rest, and Mr. Thomas did all he could to bring this about, in the following manner.

His surgical skill was, of course, at the service of his kind friends. On the 9th of March, he inoculated Mr. Grant's youngest child for the small pox, and, the next day, a child of Mr. William Chambers. The measles raged with great violence during this month at the Orphan House at Howrah, and it was therefore thought best that Mr. Brown's little boy should not be inoculated by the surgeon in attendance there ; and as Mr. Thomas's young patients were doing well, he was asked to inoculate Mr. Brown's child. He most cheerfully consented, and it was done on the 21st of March. On the 9th of April, however, he was suddenly called in to see the child, who had been seized with inflammatory symptoms, and was in great danger. All that could be done to relieve the little sufferer was of no avail, and, on the 20th of April, he expired.

During the intercourse brought about by this sorrowful event, Mr. Thomas discovered the cause of the unpleasantness which had existed for so many months. Mr. Brown stated that Dr. Nasmyth, the intimate friend of both parties, had informed him that Mr. Thomas had written a long letter to Mr. Grant at Malda, very much to his disadvantage. At the same time, Dr. Nasmyth had told Mr. Thomas that Mr. Brown had spoken of him in terms of most contemptuous disparagement. The story of the letter was utterly untrue, as was now confessed; and, when, confronted by both parties, the mischief-maker was constrained to acknowledge the wrong he had done them. With unfeigned delight, Mr. Thomas communicated this explanation of the mysterious discord to his friends in Calcutta, and a cordial reconciliation was the immediate result.*

---

* Mr. Thomas thus related this circumstance: "One of the members of our little prayer-meeting falsely accused me of having written a letter of eight sides to Malda, full of reproach against Mr. Brown. A coolness took place on his part, which I never could account for, till providence one day placed me in company with Mrs. Brown, to whom I expressed my cordial wishes for the welfare of her husband. She rejected these with disdain; and a discovery followed of the charge which had so long lain against me. I denied the fact, having never written to Malda, or to any one anything against Mr. Brown. On seeing Mr. Brown, he brought me and my accuser face to face; and, with many tears, this person acknowledged the whole to be a falsehood, fabricated, without any other inducement than an unaccountable secret urging in his mind so to do."

This accords with the entries in the journal.—

"April 19th, 1787.—Returned from Mr. Brown with a heart full of joy, and all my best wishes fired with a prospect of fulfilment. We all have for a long time considered our friend Brown in a wrong light, and at last I have detected the reason of all our division and strife, and all the disaffection that, to our shame, has been amongst us these five or six months. The 'tale-bearer,' the 'revealer of secrets,' the 'sower of strife,' with 'words as wounds,' is at last, by the mercy of God, discovered to us.

"April 21st.—With much delight, communicated to our friends the happy prospects of love restored, to their great joy and comfort.

"April 23d.—The Lord hath granted peace, love, and unity, according to my prayer, when all was dark, and it seemed to us to be impossible. Nasmyth owned that he caused the separation. He wept, and said that he was afraid he had not the grace of God, that he had acted wrongly; nay, that he had injured the cause of religion; but with the same mouth he told Mr. Brown, that, if he was a man of the world, he would commence a pitch quarrel with him!"

THE MISSION CHURCH. 69

Shortly before this, Mr. Kiernander, now in his seventy-sixth year, was overwhelmed by calamity. The residue of his once large property was involved, and finally lost, in some unfortunate speculations conducted by his son, and his estate was attached for the benefit of his creditors.* The mission church which he had built was seized, with the rest of his possessions, and there was a project to convert the building into a public auction room, when Mr. Grant came forward to secure its continued appropriation to the worship of God. He gave Rs. 10,000, the amount at which the church, with the school house and burial ground, was valued, and so secured the whole from desecration to secular uses. It was supposed that the Calcutta mission would be revived by the Society for the Promotion of Christian Knowledge, under whose patronage Mr. Kiernander had laboured, and that they would send out clergymen to conduct public services in the church; but in the meanwhile a temporary arrangement had to be made in Calcutta.

This occurrence gave a new direction to Mr. Thomas's thoughts. He was secretly wishful that Mr. Grant would make him the minister of the mission church, and a word of invitation to it, would, no doubt, have assured him that this was the purpose of God. All the night of March 28th, he lay "very wakeful, with continual thought and prayer concerning the expediency of abiding in Calcutta; and was all night long much impressed about Kiernander's church, thinking," as he wrote in his journal, "I might be called to speak for Christ there, till I had gained the Ben-

All the entries reveal a disposition of most cordial desire for Mr. Brown's reconciliation with his Calcutta friends, very far from any appearance of jealousy or ill-will. Mr. Thomas would have been more worldly-wise had he left Mr. Brown to fight his own battles. He wrote afterwards:—"He has greatly discouraged me all along, from the first; and was always very cool, except just while I was reconciling him to his friends."

* The statement made above as to the origin of Mr. Kiernander's troubles seems to be well sustained by the best accounts of his history. As was to be expected, in such a case, many unfavorable rumours were afloat as to his conduct. In October, 1788, "Messieurs Kiernander, senior and junior," inserted an advertisement in the *Calcutta Gazette*, in which they cautioned the public against giving credence to "various quite false and malicious reports," "industriously spread about" to their prejudice. They added, "It is very hard when sufferers by a public calamity are still more hurt by false tongues."

galese, and then there might be persons arrive better fitted to fill the station. I leave this before the Lord, hoping that, if it is of Him, I shall hear my friends speak of it, and find His direction in their mouths." He appears to have sounded Mr. Grant's inclinations in this matter; but met with no encouragement to think that his wishes would be realized, and he therefore soon abandoned them.

An extract from Mr. Thomas's journal for Good Friday, April 6th, 1787, may be interesting in its reference to the mission church, and will indicate the arrangement made for supplying its pulpit.

A day of solemn awe on my spirit. Heard Mr. Brown unexpectedly at Mr. Kiernander's church; and rejoiced with the brethren that he has at length been permitted to preach.* I was unexpectedly asked to Mr. Grant's, where, without much previous study, I exhorted them in the words of the apostle, Philippians iv. 6, 7, observing that this precept and promise offered to believers, was not the effect of a start, but of a durable habit of soul, answered by a durable dwelling, and not a transient visit, of the peace of God which passeth all understanding. Glory be to God for liberty, clearness, consolation, and hope. All which was greatly added to by our father O'Beck's devout and fervent prayer.

Mr. Grant's plan for Mr. Thomas, from the time of his engagement, had been, that he should go to Malda, where Mr. George Udny would, for the present, entertain him in the English Factory. There he was to study Bengali, and to preach in English to the Europeans under Mr. Udny's direction. When he had gained an adequate knowledge of the Bengali language, he was to live at Goamalty, where Mr. Grant possessed a large tract of land within the limits of the ancient city of Gour, and had established an indigo factory, under the management of Mr. Henry Creighton. It was thought that the settlement of the mission here, on a spot which was Mr. Grant's own property, and amongst some two hundred families, to whom he had given homes

---

* On the 31st of December, 1806, Mr. Brown reminded his hearers at the mission church of the same circumstance. "It was," he said, "on Good Friday, in the year 1787, nearly twenty years ago, since I commenced my ministry in this place, and I recollect that my text was part of the words which I have now chosen, viz. 'I determined not to know any thing among you, save Jesus Christ and him crucified.'"

and employment, would be an arrangement exceedingly favorable to the missionary's comfort and influence, as well as to his success.

Not without some secret reluctance, Mr. Thomas adhered to these plans. He would have liked rather to continue in Calcutta till he could preach in Bengali. His friends had highly appreciated his efforts, and had warmly acknowledged the benefit they had derived from his instructions. He delighted in his labours amongst them, and was very unwilling to leave them; and though the beginning of April was fixed upon as the time of his departure, he remained fully a month longer, before all his arrangements could be completed.

Before he left, however, he saw reason to believe that his friends were ceasing to defer to his judgment in religious matters as they had done at the beginning. Both Mr. Chambers and Mr. O'Beck had, he believed, brought with them from the Coromandel coast strong Arminian tendencies, upon which he looked with great alarm and aversion. Mr. Chambers had been one of his warmest admirers at the outset of their intimacy, and he was still "kind and loving;" but he would not be argued out of these errors. Mr. Thomas was a firm Calvinist, and felt it to be his duty to warn Mr. Grant of the pernicious tendencies of his brother-in-law's sentiments. Mr. Grant, however, loved peace; and while he assented to his friend's doctrinal theses, he strongly dissuaded him from controversy. Mr. Thomas was intensely uneasy in the restraints thus imposed upon his ministry, and they served to reconcile him to departure to Malda; where he hoped to be able to declare all the counsel of God, as he had himself received it. Before leaving Calcutta, he spoke with great seriousness in reference to some of these difficulties, taking for his text Psalm xviii. 26, "With the froward, thou wilt show thyself froward," yet he appears to have escaped giving offence to his hearers. To the last, they continued upon affectionate terms with him, and he often afterwards called to mind the loving expressions they used towards him, and how Mr. Grant in particular had said, as they walked together up and down his hall, "When you are gone from us, Doctor, I fear we shall go on poorly."

There is no room for doubt that his ministry in Calcutta had been attended with a blessing. Two or three young men were hopefully converted under his preaching. One of these was Mr. Richard Thomas Burney, a brother of the once renowned authoress of *Evelina*, and son of the celebrated Charles Burney, Doctor of Music. Mr. Burney lived in Calcutta for upwards of twenty years subsequently, and was the means of turning many to righteousness.

Apart from such instances of good accomplished by his preaching, there is every reason to believe that Mr. Thomas's sojourn in Calcutta after leaving the *Earl of Oxford* was both useful to his companions and pleasant to himself. Though he found the study of Bengali an irksome task, and had been desirous of escape from going to Malda, it must not be imagined that he ever turned aside from his missionary calling, which he was assured he had received from God. On the contrary, he rejoiced greatly in it, and maintained a spirit of assured confidence that the divine blessing would attend him in the discharge of it. On the 5th of May, when his stay in Calcutta was drawing to its close, he wrote in his journal the following remarkable words :—

Day and night, I meditate on the word of God, both when asleep and awake, and have much fellowship with God, and much confidence of being sent with a message from God to these poor heathens, and that the Lord will certainly bless the preaching of the gospel now at this very time. I have said that the gospel would never depart from this country till the glory of the latter times comes. I have made my boast of God amongst the people, and told them that I had unshaken trust in God; and I do not think of being ashamed of this boasting; but believe what God hath spoken concerning those that wait for Him and put their trust in Him.

The ordinary tone of his letters and journal at this period indicates the same persuasion, and betokens much spiritual enjoyment, and a firm assurance of the love of God in Christ Jesus our Lord.

Perhaps it might have been well to give fuller illustrations of the state of mind in which Mr. Thomas abandoned his secular employment and became a missionary to the Bengalis. It cannot be denied that he was actuated by zeal for the glory of God and ardent desire to be consecrated to the service of Christ, with tender compassion for the perishing heathen and for his godless countrymen in India. These grand motives were, no doubt, mingled with much imperfection and weakness. Considerations of ordinary prudence appear to have been quite overlooked by him, and the requirements of domestic duty seem, in this crisis of his history, to have received little thought. But it is anyhow clear that it was not to improve his worldly circumstances, that he became a missionary. Never had his prospects of pecuniary gain been so bright as when he resolved to quit the *Earl of Oxford;* and the sacrifices he made to purchase the possibility of release, sufficiently prove how indifferent he was to all temporal advantages, as compared with the desire of his heart to be a missionary. This he also clearly shows in a letter to his father, written on the 6th of March. He says there,—

I have written to my creditors, made my will, and consigned the care of all my matters at home, by power of attorney. I have sent home goods and money, to the amount of £2000, computed value here, which may well be expected to fetch somewhat more in England. Also I have sent an account of my old and new debts, directing that all shall be paid. So that my debts are but paid, and I have food and raiment, I care not what becomes of me, I assure you; neither do I desire the riches of this life, nor a quiet death. I care not how or where I temporally live or die. I find the daily comings in of the service of God sufficient. I have placed my happiness in His favor, and enjoy the light of His countenance. He overcometh my follies, and passeth by my transgressions. I have not deserved any of His mercies, nor acquired one of them. But He hath been pleased thus to deal with me.

I reap as I sow. By grace, I am delighted in His service, and that not of myself, it is the gift of God. I am not enthusiastic; neither do I much neglect temporal affairs; and if I do, I choose that fault before a greater, namely, that of neglecting the great salvation.

O for a seeking *first* His kingdom daily! O for the marrow of His word, the energy of His Spirit, and the sober consolations of uninterrupted fellowship with Him. But I do not desire consolations only, seeing it is best sometimes to suffer; therefore I throw the reins to Jesus, not with an air of carnal ease, but with the utmost desire that He should undertake the work of guiding and governing me through a slippery dangerous path.

I want nothing. When I want money, I have a banker in heaven. When I *want* any thing else that heaven or earth can afford, I shall have it. Ask what I will; it shall be given to me.—John xv. 7.

This is a text I have lately considered at large, and, to my no small comfort, have discovered by many days' search, prayer, and meditation, some things which you have learned long ago: as, for instance,—

I.—That the text is a true report.

II.—That the *abiding* in Christ on which this promise rests denotes stedfastness; not mere sincerity, which is its meaning in the previous verse, where it is opposed to the casting forth, the withering, and the gathering to be burned, which are the fate of those who have no root, and a beacon to those who have.

III.—That this *abiding* consists in a steady apprehension of Christ, branching out into close conformity with His will, and so 'bringing forth much fruit.'

IV.—That this *asking* has always four things essential to it, without which our prayers are not asking, according to the text:—

1st.—*Desire*, arising from a knowledge of value and worth in the things asked for,—from a sense of their necessity,—and from a remembrance of the promise of God to bestow them.

2nd.—*Expectation*, that cuts off extravagant and impertinent desires and petitions, and is excited by the truth moving in energy upon the soul.

3rd.—*An estimation and use of appointed means*, without idolizing, and without slighting them.

4th.—*Importunity*, not soon forgetting what we ask, but making unceasing application at the door of mercy.

I must go no further; but eight or ten other things are considered, and have been read in manuscript by my friends here. I intend to investigate this pregnant promise more fully, and to reduce its truth to some practical results; and this I will do in the strength of the Lord and the power of His might.

My moments fly. My life is a vapour. I truly rejoice that there is a bodily death coming. The Lord keep me from desiring it! May I wait patiently till my change come. I am not now under troubles; but I see in death the source of life, and the concealed glories of the world to come, centering and blazing effulgence in Christ.

In a letter to his brother also, he says,—

I tremble to think of my future temptations, because of my own weakness and remains. I am sure if I fall, I shall rise again; but, for all that, I do fear declension exceedingly. There is but one thing that keeps me from being sure that I shall sooner or later fall, as I and others *have* done, to the dishonor of God: namely, my trust in Him who is faithful and able to keep me from falling, and, till that trust fails me, I deny danger. As to health, and money, and friends, I have enough; and if I wanted more, I could have them. The Lord will give me any thing that I ask Him for. But the truth is, we are not fond of asking trifles, when we are in the spirit of His will. Our words and wants are few then, and large. One will serves God and me too. I find when I have no sensible comfort, I can stay my mind a little on Christ. I am beginning to live the life of faith.

Another short extract may be added from his journal, written just at the close of his stay in Calcutta.—

May 1st.—Sweet, sweet, and happy day. How I boast in God to-day! My thoughts rise in multitudes, and the comforts of the Holy Ghost delight my soul. I boast in the Lord without either measure or limit. I therefore become most willing to enter into His vineyard, whatever sufferings may await me there.

Mr. Thomas's departure for Malda took place early in May. On the 2nd, a prayer meeting for the success of his ministry was held at Mr. Grant's house. Messrs. O'Beck, Udny, Chambers, and Grant took part in it, with Mr. Thomas himself. They began their devotional exercises at a quarter before 10 o'clock, P. M., and continued them until a quarter after 12. He left his friends on the 7th, "with an exhortation from Ephesians iii. 13-19, and the blessing of the Lord upon it." The first day's journey was ended at Menampore, a place between Barrackpore and Pulta, where Mr. Chambers had a small country house. Here he tarried more than a week, being delayed through Mr. Robert Udny's illness. He was to accompany Mr. Thomas to Malda; but severe rheumatic disease had so disabled him that it was feared he might lose the use of his limbs. On his account, the journey had to be made slowly; and the care his painful affliction rendered needful was laborious and full of anxiety to his companion. The travellers did not arrive at Malda until the 18th of June.

The circumstances of Mr. Thomas's engagement by Mr. Grant and of his sojourn in Calcutta, have been detailed at perhaps tedious length; but this was needful to explain subsequent events. The reader has now seen evidence of the high esteem in which he was held by his Calcutta friends, and how, in the peculiar circumstances in which he found them, he became their minister and helper in the service of Christ. Just before he left them, to remove to Malda, the purchase of the mission church by Mr. Grant had opened the way for the exercise of Mr. Brown's ministry in the city, and the circumstances of the society in which Mr. Thomas had moved were thereby greatly modified. It would have been wisdom on his part had he more promptly recognised this obvious fact. Instead of this, however, he carried with him to Malda the consciousness of a quasi-pastoral authority over his friends in Calcutta; and, as will be seen hereafter, he was thereby led into very great difficulties. His excuse for this mistake lies in the facts now detailed, and in his sincere, even if mistaken, sense of responsibility in regard to those who, a few months before, had so warmly welcomed all his counsels and admonitions.

CHAPTER IV.

The First Year at Malda.—1787-8.

THE confidence with which Mr. Thomas committed himself to the enterprise he was to undertake at Malda was not unmingled with apprehensions that many new troubles awaited him there. Of Mr. George Undy, in whose household he was to reside, he had heard only most favorable reports, but in view of the instability and imperfection of all human friendships, he told him in a letter, before they met, that much as they expected pleasure and advantage from their future intimacy, "the time might come when they both would wish they had never seen one another." But the arrangement opened with the fairest promise. A most kindly welcome was given to the missionary, and he was soon quite at home at Malda, in the society of the young men connected with the Commercial Establishment. Mr. Udny was unmarried, but was expecting his mother from England in the following year, and Mr. Thomas confidently hoped that his wife and child would be her fellow voyagers. A month after he reached Malda, the following description of his new situation was written to his brother.—

Still among the living, greatly rejoicing in God, through Jesus Christ. This is so strange a part of life to me, that I cannot help likening it to a great calm, after a long and boisterous storm. Psalm ciii. is woven into the texture of my mind, so that it will never be picked out. All I desire or wish below is in possession, save my poor wife and babe, who are yet in the storm. When the Lord has done this; nay, even *now*, I want to be neither greater nor richer. The sorry riches and honors of life, which have cast down many strong men, are now in Agur's scales. I have a pleasant and beautiful situation, and my days are portioned out in the following manner.

The Chief or Governor is Mr. George Udny, with whose brother I became usefully acquainted at Calcutta. He is a mild and beautiful copy of Christian temper; a heart meltable to divine things; an obedient ear; a growing cedar, flourishing in the courts of our God. In his house I live; under whom are about seven Europeans, and sometimes more, who, together with visitors, officers, and people of rank that drop in, compose our family. At 6 o'clock, there is a large bell rung, which calls all the party to a chapel in the house, where a portion of Doddrige's *Family Expositor* is first read, and then prayer is offered up by the mouth of one of us. We then breakfast, and find it half past seven. I allot the following hours till ten o'clock for sweet meditation, reading and prayer; but it is very short. From ten till two, I give to the study of the Bengal language. We rise from dinner before four; then sleep, according to the custom of hot climates; read; ride out in a carriage, (for we have no less than seven carriages, of which two are the Governor's phaetons,) in the cool of the evening; and rise from the tea table at about half past seven. I allow till nine for the study of the language, and till ten for private devotion; at which hour we all meet again. After a hymn, I read, and close with prayer. A refreshment of fruits and wine afterwards completes the mercies of a day.

On the Lord's-day, the same in the morning, and at ten the bell rings. All are assembled, and, before I arrived here, they read the prayers of the Church of England and a sermon. But now, after the first day,—on which prayers were read, and I exhorted,—I give out a hymn, read a striking portion of God's sweet word, call on the name of Jesus, to be in the midst of us, and then deliver my message in His name, and close in prayer, after a hymn. We then, without *one word* spoken, retire to our closets; an example they have steadily followed, and, I have no doubt, to their advantage. We meet again, and I give them an evening lecture; and truly there is One among us whom we see not. I find my poor talent enlarged, and by night and by day, the word of God is as a fire shut up, or breaking out. The Lord says great and many things to me in Isaiah xlix. He made me useful at Calcutta; but I was obliged to cry aloud there. However the Lord opened their ears, and, after one alarm, their whole conduct was altered, and continues so, with thanksgiving, to this day. I wrote a letter to a profane young man in distressed circumstances, on the one thing needful, and the Lord was pleased to raise him from his sepulchre, and he is now come among us, calling on the name of the Lord. We are all young men; and they look to me on all occasions, in matters of duty. I feel how unfit I am in some instances, and perceive much more, with the quellings of Christ within. Considering the kindness of God my Saviour, I am baser than ever. However, the Lord smiles upon me, and makes every man about me join Him. They make too much of me, and sometimes become snares to my soul. But the Lord is my strong tower. I run into it, and am safe from every thing.

The young man to whom Mr. Thomas here says his correspondence had been made useful was Mr. F. Dingley, who had formerly been an officer in the Dragoons, and had come out to India in the *Earl of Oxford*. The kindness of Mr. Udny now found employment for him, so that he continued to enjoy the counsel and help of his Christian adviser, at Malda. Another young member of the family there, was Mr. William Long, a relative of Mrs. Thomas; and, no doubt, he also was entertained out of kind consideration for the missionary, who always mentions him in his journal by the familiar name of Bill. He appeared to be a sincere Christian. A cloud of trouble rested on the Malda family within a month after Mr. Thomas's arrival, in the illness and death of Mr. Forsyth, one of its members. A young civilian, Mr. Harry Verelst Darell, with Mr. William Grant, Mr. William Brown, and Mr. Henry Creighton of Goamalty, made up the company of Mr. Thomas's ordinary associates. Mr. Robert Udny's home was in Calcutta, but he frequently came to Malda. Visitors of high respectabilty were often at Mr. Udny's house, and all his guests were expected to be present at the devotional exercises held there.

Many interesting details as to Mr. Thomas's early ministry at Malda are recorded in his journal. Prayer meetings were regularly held, in which nearly all the young men took their part, and a very lively interest in divine truth was manifested by some of them. Of Mr. Thomas's addresses, a single specimen outline may be presented, out of a very considerable number which have been preserved. It is prefaced by many expressions of self reproach, that he had so imperfectly prepared himself for the labour he had in hand.

2 Kings v. 13, 14, 15. 'And his servants came near, and spake unto him, and said, My father, if the prophet had bid thee do some great thing, wouldest thou not have done it? how much rather then, when he saith to thee, Wash, and be clean? Then went he down, and dipped himself seven times in Jordan, according to the saying of the man of God, and his flesh came again like unto the flesh of a little child, and he was clean. And he returned to the man of God, he and all his company, and came, and stood before him: and he said, Behold, now I know that there is no God in all the earth, but in Israel: now therefore, I pray thee, take a blessing of thy servant.'

Our Lord Jesus hath fitted the leper's case to the sinner's, so that we may here be instructed of—

I. The evil of sin;—for if the prophet had bid this leper '*do some great thing*,' he would have done it; and such a keen sense of the evil of our leprosy, and the value of a cure, becomes us.

II. The means of grace are easy;—'*He saith to thee, Wash, and be clean.*' Christ's yoke is easy and his burden light. The children of grace have not to earn, to buy, to deserve; but to open their mouths and be filled, to eat, and to let their soul delight itself in fatness.

III. In the use of the means of grace, there is always importunity when their success is really known and when the power of God in them is really felt. '*He went and washed seven times;* and his flesh was as a child's, and he was clean.' Thus in the means of grace, as rightly used, our withered frames, withered zeal, self-revenge, contempt of the world, &c., come fresh upon us, and we receive the kingdom again, as it were, as a little child, and by His word of grace we find we are made clean.

IV. As our sense of the evil of our sinning leprosy is great or small, so will be our sacrifice of joy, after profitably using the means of grace;—'*and he returned to the man of God, &c.*'

Improvement 1.—Nothing is to be attributed to chance or the design of men, in the means of grace they may bring to us, or that are with us.—Luke iv. 27; 2 Kings v. 2.

2.—We are unacquainted with our own hearts if we are not afflicted by a sense of the grievous leprosy that remains there still. —Romans vii. 20. Let us compare ourselves with others who excel in their walk:—the difference we may discover all arises from the body of uncleansed leprosy.

3.—If the waters of Jordan so cleansed Naaman, how much more shall the blood of Jesus Christ purge us from our dead services and duties, to serve the living God, in a more lively and spiritual manner!

4.—If we belong to Christ, the means of grace have a power and efficacy in them to us, that they have not for others. If all the lepers in Israel had gone and washed in Jordan, not one of them would have been cleansed; but to Naaman *it was said,* ' *Wash and be clean.*'

It would be easy to multiply examples of such exhibitions of divine truth. Surely this little congregation at Malda, with their minister, formed a spiritual oasis in the midst of the dreary desert of Bengal, where, as we have seen, there was at this time everywhere a dearth of divine knowledge, a famine of the word of God.

Of Mr. Thomas's missionary zeal, many illustrations might be quoted. One passage, from his journal of July 2nd, especially deserves to be quoted here. He wrote,—

I have thought of Thy word by night and by day; and, when I am in sleep and when I awake, I am still by a multitude of thoughts led into and all about Thy word, and I find in the mean time my lusts, and self-pleasings, and indulgences laid low. I fervently desire the good of souls, and that the great name of the Lord Jesus may be magnified, whether by me or by others; and I remember this day out of what a low, gorged and miserable state of body and mind I was called to this service among the heathen; and, after all this, I cannot doubt that the Lord Jesus will be magnified, according to Thy word, on which Thou hast caused me to hope, and I am persuaded beforehand that the everlasting gospel will spread from this time in Bengal.

Frequent references to Isaiah xlix, show that he never lost sight of the predictions in it which had with such peculiar power been impressed upon his heart. He evidently was greatly predisposed to apocalyptic studies, and was fully persuaded that the grand events foreshadowed in divine revelation were swiftly approaching fulfilment, and would in a very few years be developed with an awful rapidity, which would demonstrate the presence of the Lord and the glory of His power.

Several occurrences within the year 1787 were well

adapted to deepen Mr. Thomas's compassion for the people to whose enlightenment he had now devoted himself. Some of these he mentioned in a letter to Dr. Stennett, in the following order.—

The first was the extraordinary breaking in of the sea upon the neighbouring coast, which swept away great multitudes of people, over an extent of almost one hundred miles.

Another was the falling of a vast rock into a great river, which immediately turned its course, so that the stream ran violently and desolated whole districts before it.*

Another event was the great flood of the rainy season, by which the inhabitants of the country have been distressed and destroyed, without any to help or pity them. The thousands who have perished by this inundation are not so much as mentioned among the natives, or at all noticed by Europeans. Add to this, a grievous famine, which has spread almost all over the country. In some places the living were too weak and too few to bury the dead, and the air was poisoned by putrid exhalations from the unburied corpses, so as to threaten a pestilence. The soreness of the famine was to the eastward of us, about nine or ten days' journey.

On the 2nd of November, there was a terrific storm of wind,† such as I never before witnessed, on land or sea. A cold rain fell with it. Many cattle were killed. The rivers were covered with fragments of boats, and the villages with roofs and other scattered materials of native houses. Trees of forty or fifty years' growth were torn up by the roots; and in some places whole groves were destroyed, and the trees laid one over another. I see no spot of the country without some marks of this desolating wind upon it, which may continue for years to come; for the trees which remain are shattered and bent out of their erectness. The number of boats lost upon the river between Calcutta and Murshidábád alone is computed at about five thousand.

* Mr. Carey also alluded to this curious fact in a letter, written in 1795, as follows:—"We have a river, named Atreyi, almost as large as the Thames, into which, a few years ago, there fell an amazing rock, on the borders of Bootan; and though many hundreds of people were long employed to clear the old channel, it was choked up. But this did not stop the river. It took another course, formed a new channel far from the old one, but in the same direction, till it found the sea."

† The *Calcutta Gazette* for November 8, 1787, stated that this cyclone, as it would now be called, "exceeded in violence any that had been experienced in Calcutta for twenty years past," and gave many particulars of its destructive fury.

Add to these things the public and domestic wars and bloodshed among themselves, the heavy oppressions of others, cruel robbers, cities, like Gour, lying waste, with the houses inhabited by all manner of wild beasts, and I cannot but view these people as distinguished from the rest of the world by their weakness and adversity, as much as England is by her power and prosperity. I compare their calamities to the confusion of Egypt, and the people to her inhabitants.—Isaiah xix. 1-17. Truly these men are 'like unto women,' timorous, fearful, feeble, childish. One European might put to flight a little army of them.

During the famine, the natives have sold, and are now selling, their children, to buy rice for themselves. As many such poor children fall into bad hands, it was thought expedient by Mr. Grant, Mr. Udny, and others, to save a few of them by paying for them, and forming them into a school, where they may be brought up in the nurture and admonition of the Lord. Some of them were accordingly purchased for less than an English three-pence each! Blessed be God, great numbers of starving people have been liberally relieved since that time by the flock at Malda; and larger measures are now being adopted by Government for a more general relief.

The children thus saved from starvation were intended to be sent down to Calcutta, to a charity school, which was projected by Mr. Brown. For the present, however, they were gathered into a school at Malda, the oversight of which devolved upon Mr. Thomas.

He also found much employment for his knowledge and skill as a doctor. The natives of the East are everywhere glad to be treated by European physicians, and he was soon beset by a throng of eager applicants for medical relief at Malda. He was very happy to obtain influence with the people by such means, and "never turned aside from man, woman, or child;" but did what he could for them, however insignificant their maladies appeared to be. "No small success in two or three noisy cases" spread his fame to a considerable distance; and his acting also as Mr. Udny's almoner largely contributed to the increase of the numbers who came to him daily for assistance.

Pleasant as, in most respects, his situation at Malda was, it had, nevertheless, its own disadvantages, in addition to his painful separation from his wife and little one. He resided in the same house with those to whom he ministered, and in the intimacy of daily companionship, he found it difficult to avoid the social temptations which were regarded by him as his most powerful and insidious foes. The amusements of his associates, their quoit playing and shooting, sometimes enticed him from the studies to which he had pledged all his strength ; his cheerfulness now and then degenerated into jocularity ; or the discussions which arose out of ordinary conversation were pursued with such positiveness of assertion and combative ardour, as he afterwards feared were very unwise and injurious. As on board the *Earl of Oxford*, so here also, his sensitive vivacious mind too often forgot in familiar intercourse with his daily associates the severe restraints which he had anxiously adjusted to himself in his closet, and this failure to realize and preserve his own ideal of the Christian deportment and spirit was the occasion of frequent and bitter lamentation and repentance.

On the whole, however, his associations at Malda were very satisfactory, and at the end of 1787, he could write of them in the language of grateful love, as follows :—

Thus closes a most important year of my chequered life : full of changes, big with events. I am now separated from all my kinsmen, and friends, and countrymen, in a foreign land, separated from my wife, dropping my profession, and taking upon me the ministry of God's holy word. He that hath fixed the bounds of my habitation hath done this. He hath brought me out of great and sore troubles, and cast my lot in pleasant places. He has raised me up new and valuable friends. He hath watered my soul from on high, and after the storms of sorrow and the floods of care I have been used to all my life, he has made peace in my borders, and filled me with the finest of the wheat. Yea, he hath turned my mourning into dancing. He hath put off my sackcloth, and girded me with gladness, to the end that my glory may sing praise unto my God and not be silent. I am now the leader in worship among six or seven young men, of all of whom, except one, I have reason to hope well. We have no jars or dissensions ; and if there happens a trifling dispute among us, I have more than once observed that it awakens that brotherly relenting that in the end knits and confirms the bands of our friendship. They have obedient ears, and are all willing to forward the gospel, as the greatest work of their lives, and to distribute to the poor and distressed most liberally. The Lord hath been particularly bountiful in raising me up such a friend as George Udny, in whom there is an association of qualities suited to my temper, with no small measure of those spiritual gifts and graces which make him still more valuable; so that I have all I want or wish in this transitory life, except my wife and child. But I have experienced so many fluctuating changes in my past life, that I am ready to think these things will not last long, but that evil is before me. Sufficient, however, unto the day is the evil thereof.

> This God is the God I adore,
> My faithful, unchangeable Friend,
> Whose love is as large as His power,
> And neither knows measure nor end.
>
> 'Tis Jesus, the first and the last,
> Whose Spirit shall guide me safe home;
> I'll *praise* Him for all that is past,
> And *trust* Him for all that's to come.

It is very pleasant to be able to record at least one testimony, given about the same time, by one of Mr. Thomas's associates, as evidence that he did not overestimate their affectionate feeling towards him. We cannot recover the name of the writer, but his letter may be read in the *Missionary Magazine*, for March, 1797. It was written, November 30th, 1787, and says:—

Our society here at Malda underwent a great change about the beginning of the year. Mr. Grant and his family then removed from us to Calcutta; and he was succeeded by a gentleman who has been in the family seven or eight years, and who being, like Mr. Grant, a well-wisher to religion, the alteration has caused but little difference in our way of living. God has, since that time, been pleased to add another man, Dr. Thomas, to our little family, and every one of us has great reason for thankfulness for such a gracious providence. He was surgeon of the *Oxford* Indiaman, but a desire of becoming serviceable to the souls of the heathen here induced him to leave his post on board ship, and to remain in the country. He has been blessed with great gifts for preaching and praying, and gives us a regular discourse, *extempore*, twice every Sunday, and short exhortations frequently on other occasions. He is now busy learning the Bengal language; and, being of a conciliating temper, he may, very probably, through the blessing of God, become serviceable to the natives, as well as to us.

Reference must now be made to Mr. Thomas's relations with his Calcutta friends, for it was of these he especially thought when he wrote at the close of 1787, that he was ready to think evil was before him.

The reader has seen upon what happy terms of intimacy he had lived with these friends, how active he had been amongst them as a minister of the truth, and how well they had appreciated his services in the circumstances of spiritual privation in which he found them. He had " borne his testimony as to what he saw amiss," he had " done what he could to reconcile their broken friendships," and he had " received in writing the thanks, the hearty thanks, of them all," before he left Calcutta. Was it at all strange that, on removing to a distant station, he should carry with him many anxieties on their account, and should earnestly strive still to help forward the good work which he believed he had already promoted in their hearts ? How disastrously his well-meant endeavours issued, will, however, now appear.

The Arminian tendencies he had detected in Mr. William Chambers sorely troubled him. He had been restrained from fully controverting them in his sermons at Calcutta ; but could not satisfy himself with avoiding the further discussion of sentiments which he believed to be fraught with danger to his friend's best interests. He had indeed already said enough to Mr. Chambers to provoke some displeasure ; and, in his journal, before leaving Calcutta, he speaks of him as a " Galatian," who had, at his first coming, " received him as an angel of God, even as Jesus Christ ;" but to whom he was now almost " become an enemy, because he told him the truth." But, at the end of April, he prepared a letter to Mr. Chambers, inveighing against the tenets he held in terms so authoritative and severe that it must have been grievously offensive. Be it remembered, however, that this act of imprudence was committed in an age when the amenities of religious controversy were little understood, and when many holy and good men saw nothing more than godly zeal for the truth in the most acrimonious and offensive epithets with which Augustus Toplady and others could assail the apostle of Arminian Methodism, who, on his side also, lacked not bitterness in his treatment of doctrinal opponents. "There is no doubt at all," Mr. Thomas wrote, "that your error ranks you with the Arminians of this day; a sect which, as Rutherford says, 'throweth Christ on his back, in his weak servants; and oppresseth truth!'" "No man," he added, "ever stabbed election and perseverance, without going all through the heart of Christ and the promises of God." He went on to say that the error would be of less consequence anywhere else than at the beginning of the Gospel stream in Bengal: there, it would empoison every attempt his friend might make to do good; and he significantly told him, "Perhaps there will be a Bible from a quarter that none of us expects. As to your translation, I shall so far pray against it, as I love Christ." He concluded this strange epistle in the following terms:—

I earnestly entreat you to be careful what use you make of this friendly letter; for if the Lord is not in it, He hath not spoken by me. I humbled myself before you in red ink,* on purpose that you might freely discharge me from setting up myself as some great one. I abase myself; but the Spirit of the Lord is upon me, and Christ's people shall, by and by, acknowledge me, that I am among the seed which the Lord hath blessed.—Isaiah lxi. 9.

In all this, Mr. Thomas had not the excuse of haste. Made ready in April, his letter was not despatched from Malda until the end of June. Mr. Chambers seems to have thought

* He refers here to a note he had written to Mr. Chambers, in which he disclosed the most discreditable facts of his own history,—a piece of gratuitous candour which did him considerable harm in the estimation of his Calcutta friends.

He thus explained his motives to Mr. Grant: "After much prayer and many fears, I determined to do thus: I would first abase myself, and show him and you my own error and wickedness; then I would speak home to all your consciences on the lesser blemishes I now saw in your conduct, knowing that He that ruleth in His Gospel had taken the beam out of mine eye, that I might the more plainly see how to take the mote out of my brother's eye; and, this done, I determined to tell him plainly that he actually was in the error of the Arminians."

it undeserving of any reply; but, a month later, Mr. Thomas wrote to him again; and then, as he obtained no answer, he wrote to Mr. Grant, begging for his interposition with Mr. Chambers. Mr. Grant seriously remonstrated with him upon the arrogance and indiscreetness of his letter, and advised him to withdraw it. In reply, Mr. Thomas was ready to admit his imprudence, in not having sought out more acceptable words, but still affirmed the substance of his epistle to be according to the will of God. He, however, did all he could to bring about the restoration of Mr. Chamber's friendship, and on the 28th of December, 1787, wrote him a letter, from which the following extract may be made.—

Before the year shuts up, allow me the hindermost place among them that bring you the compliments of the season. You and I have had some severe weather between us; but when we get into our harbour, we shall forget our sorrows, in the joy of finding it was a right way by which the Lord led us. You are sensible that I meant to do you good, and not evil, in what is past, and also that young beginners generally do mischief before they do good, in most trades and callings, and sometimes it is the same in the gospel; and though I hope I have done no material mischief, yet I would wish you to avail yourself of that supposition, and, even then, conclude in yourself, whether I ought not to be forgiven, or at any rate released, after having been so long punished with the loss of your company and conversation, in a country where such company is scarce, and such conversation precious. Therefore let us not be rigid towards one another, especially as this is the first offence, but tender-hearted, forbearing, and forgiving one another. The matter now must have been sufficiently considered, and the result is by no means at all necessary to be made known. If you cannot benefit by what I wrote as an *exhortation*, take profit out of it as a *trial;* and I will not fail on my part to lecture myself on all parts of our past disagreements, so as to be more wary and wise in matter and manner another time.

Say, are we never any more to help one another on in the way? Shall we no more weep together with them that weep, and rejoice together with them that rejoice? Shall we never mourn together any more over the world's coldness to a crucified Saviour, nor rejoice over those things which discover an accepted gospel, and the saving of a soul? The worldly fall out with one another, and fall in again; and why not we? Have we not hoped for it, longed for it, and prayed for it? Have we not said within ourselves, When shall it once be? Have we not spoken well of each other concerning other matters? and approved each other in other things? and profited each other on other occasions?

Let the shadows flee away then, and let us say, The winter of our friendship is past, and the time of singing of birds is nigh. True it is, that, like many others, we have fallen out, we neither know how nor why; and it will be a virtue to fall in so too.

But this affectionate overture was made in vain. The result of it may be given in the words of his journal for January 17th, 1788.—

Received a letter from Mr. Chambers, pretending to forgive me, but, at the same time, discharging all acquaintance, and forbidding future correspondence, on account of the inconsistent behaviour he has observed in me ever since I have been in this country!

Here was a wretched termination to a once pleasant and profitable friendship! Mr. Thomas was very deeply wounded. He could only solace himself with the assurance that indignant resentment only, and not calm judgment, had found expression in words at once so harsh and so inconsistent with Mr. Chambers's many former professions of affectionate esteem for him.

His correspondence with the Rev. David Brown was almost equally unpleasant. With him there had been repeated misunderstandings from the beginning of their acquaintance. In his situation at the Orphan House, upon the opposite side of the river, Mr. Brown was very much out of the way of intimacy with his Calcutta friends, and his ministry was available for them only when they were able to cross over to Howrah to hear him, or to join the congregation of troops of his battalion. There was nothing at all attractive in his preaching or personal address. He was a very sensible scholarly man, quite evangelical in his opinions; but devotedly attached to the Church of England, and, in particular, a resolute Pædobaptist, and a strong admirer of the Book of Common Prayer. Mr. Thomas had attempted to lead his friends to a higher level of Christian privilege than that represented by the formularies of the Establishment. As they had hitherto known these, they were indeed lifeless things; and the lively stimulating addresses of the pious surgeon, and their pleasant meetings with him for reading the Scriptures and offering heartfelt prayer to God appeared to be far more edifying, than attendance upon the services held by the Calcutta chaplains. His dissent, and even his opinions as a Baptist, did him little harm in their estimation in those early days. It has been seen already that at the close of his stay in Calcutta, his personal relations with Mr. Brown were quite friendly. He had become a frequent visitor at the Orphan House, and held long conferences there regarding the prospects of Christ's cause in India. On leaving Calcutta, he carried away an injunction from Mrs. Brown to send her down a supply of the mangoes for which Malda is so famed, in the ensuing season; and from Mr. Brown he had received a more serious commission, to get for him from the ruins of Gour, a slab of black marble which might serve for a memorial tablet to be placed over the grave of the child they had so recently lost.

But religious affairs in Calcutta were greatly altered after the mission church became the property of Mr. Grant. The Kiernanders had left the city, and no new missionary of the Society for the Promotion of Christian Knowledge could be expected for more than a year, to occupy the deserted sanctuary. Mr. Brown was the only clergyman available for the immediate necessities of the church, and he was willing, notwithstanding the opposition of the Managers of the Orphan Establishment, to undertake regular services there. Accordingly, about a month before Mr. Thomas's departure from Calcutta, Mr. Brown commenced his disinterested ministry at the mission church; and on the last day of October, 1787, Mr. Grant executed a deed which transferred the church and the property connected with it to three trustees,—the Rev. David Brown, Mr. William Chambers, and himself,—that it might be for ever appropriated to religious uses, for the benefit of the Protestant inhabitants of Calcutta.

With the occupation of the mission church, Mr. Brown

passed into a new relationship to the members of the circle in which Mr. Thomas had moved. He now became their pastor, and possessed the great advantage of combining in himself the unquestioned status of a clergyman of the Church of England, with a sincere attachment to those views of Christian truth which they had been previously taught of God to hold dear.

In these arrangements, Mr. Thomas naturally took an intense interest; but he was by no means satisfied with them. He thought that Mr. Brown's ministry was lacking in simplicity, and destitute of warmth and power, and he had no expectation that any considerable success could attend it. He believed that Mr. Brown's influence for good was impaired by a too easy compliance with the habits of Calcutta society, whilst he anticipated nothing but evil to himself from his prejudices as a churchman, and from his natural dislike to dissent, and to the outspoken nonconformity of the Baptists in particular. Mr. Brown was, there is very good reason to believe, a lover of all good men, and his later history exhibits him in most friendly relations with the Baptist missionaries at Serampore; but, at the present period, he evidently regarded it as a very grievous mistake that Mr. Grant had attempted to give effect to his mission scheme by engaging the agency of a Baptist,* whose presence in a ministerial capacity, whether in Calcutta or at Malda, appeared to him to threaten disturbance and disunion amongst the very few godly people at that time to be found in Bengal; and, feeling thus, it was no marvel if his free strictures upon the missionary's proceedings contributed not a little to aid the development of the mischiefs he foresaw.

The position of Mr. Thomas in such circumstances was

* Mr. Thomas wrote to Dr. Stennett at the beginning of 1788 :—" Mr. Brown, a minister of the Church of England, at Calcutta, is far from showing himself friendly to the Baptist cause. Mr. Grant and his friends had agreed to send the mission papers to you also, as well as to Mr. Newton and others; but, in my absence, by various arguments about the danger of mixtures, he overruled this measure; and they are gone home to Mr. Newton and other clergymen of the Church of England." Mr. Brown, however, himself sent a copy of the Proposals to the Rev. Robert Robinson of Cambridge.

evidently one of great difficulty, and the exercise of the utmost prudence would hardly have secured him from unpleasantness in the conscientious avowal of the sentiments he held; but he was constitutionally imprudent, and perhaps nothing could have been more unguarded and unwise than his actual procedure.

He wrote letters to Mr. Brown which, though affectionate and well-intended, immediately affronted him by the tone of fraternal equality they maintained, and by the animadversions they conveyed, when any thing appeared to the writer to call for the exercise of Christian faithfulness. Mr. Brown at once indicated his dislike of such correspondence; but, in reply, was told that Mr. Thomas "must for ever differ" from him as to the principles which should regulate Christian intercourse, and he was desired to peruse the offending letters again, since they contained a blessing not as yet recognized. Mr. Brown in his rejoinder, unsparingly animadverted upon Mr. Thomas's presumption, and charged him with many defects of character: using reproofs much more severe and caustic than his own, and he thus completed a breach between them, which was never healed.

Mr. Grant must have suffered immense vexation in the differences we have now adverted to. To him Mr. Thomas wrote most frequently and voluminously, and although for several months his friendship was preserved, it was very sorely tried. His brother-in-law and Mr. Brown complained of the character of Mr. Thomas's letters to them. Mr. Thomas on the other hand appealed to him against them both, complaining of the unchristian manner in which they had received his "brotherly reproof," and also sent to Mr. Grant himself admonitory epistles, which he must have found it hard to take in good part. Mr. Thomas saw with grief that, under Mr. Brown's influence, Mr. Grant was becoming a more thorough churchman than before. He also thought him less zealous for the spread of the gospel, and feared that he had become more "conformed to this world." Having been his intimate friend and adviser in spiritual things, he very naturally wished to be so still, and wrote him pungent exhortations adapted, as he supposed, to the state of his soul. Two very lengthy letters upon "Laodicean Christians," in which the evils of lukewarmness were forcibly described, were amongst these, and the busy Member of the Board of Trade must have sighed over the bulky documents which, almost every week, came to him from Malda. Mr. Thomas also ventured upon topics which prudence would most certainly have counselled him to avoid. Thus when Mr. O'Beck, of whom Mr. Grant thought so highly, was invited by the trustees to occupy the school house, next door to the mission church, and to assist Mr. Brown in looking after the poorer and more ignorant members of the congregation, Mr. Thomas expressed his strong disapproval, in terms which must have been very offensive to the good man's friends. Mr. Brown himself fared but little better at his hands. Mr. Thomas said he could hope for no success as the results of his labours, and told Mr. Grant, " I fear that the mission plan is ruined ; for who ever prospered who was like him ? But I am not afraid : the Lord Jesus Christ will Himself send out labourers in a way not sought for or expected."

However such asperity may have been provoked by the bitterness which had been manifested towards him by some of his former friends, it is to be deplored that anything should have induced Mr. Thomas to write of God-fearing men so severely. The consequences to himself were most painful and disastrous. His excuse must be that he fearlessly spoke out his honest convictions, upon subjects in which he thought that the interests of truth were deeply involved ; and let it ever be remembered that he did it in the full knowledge that he was acting so as to endanger and impair his own private advantage. He believed that " necessity was laid upon him" in these things : that God had made other men's sins a burden to his heart, that he should reprove them in the spirit of Jeremiah, Ezekiel, and Ezra, " whether men would hear or whether they would forbear." He felt sure that God was for him, in the opinions he held, and he therefore resolutely avowed them ; not fearing what man could do unto him.

It is time, however, that the history of events at Malda should be resumed. Early in 1788, Mr. G. Udny gave Mr. Thomas a very pleasant proof of his confidence. He put into his hands the sum of £200, to be distributed in England amongst the poor of Christ's people, as he thought best. Accordingly £100 was sent to Dr. Stennett, for indigent Baptist ministers, and £50 each to two other faithful almoners. Nor did Mr. Udny's "voluntary bounty" cease with this donation. Another £200 was sent again towards the end of October, 1788, and other such gifts subsequently; and when Dr. Stennett died, in 1795, Mr. Thomas wrote that his generous friend was very deeply affected, and that he had sent the good Doctor at various times " several hundred pounds," to be disbursed for the relief of poor Baptist ministers.

A very considerable part of the young missionary's time at Malda was daily devoted to the acquisition of the language in which he was to preach to the heathen. This was a pursuit not at all congenial to his natural disposition and his dislike to the close application it rendered necessary afforded him abundant occasion for bitter self-reproach in his journal. In after years, however, he recognized the kind help of the Lord in the perseverance and success with which, notwithstanding all drawbacks, his studies were now carried forward. Never before did he succeed in learning a foreign language. The mastering of the Bengali tongue, when he learned it, was not an easy task.* Standard books in it were then unknown; and its

* The Bengali language had been very little cultivated by Europeans at this time. In 1778, Mr. Nathaniel Brassey Halhed had printed his Grammar, having obtained Bengali type for the purpose through the extraordinary mechanical skill of Mr., afterwards Sir Charles, Wilkins, who cut the punches with his own hands.

This Bengali Grammar Mr. Thomas had, but no Dictionary or even Vocabulary of the language was then in existence, nor were there any printed Bengali books to help his studies. The urgent need of a dictionary was set forth by natives anxious to learn English in the following advertisement, which appeared in the *Calcutta Gazette* for April 23d, 1789.

"CARD.

" The humble request of several Natives of Bengal.—We humbly beseech any Gentlemen will be so good to us as to take the trouble of making a Bengal Grammar and Dictionary, in which, we hope to find all the common Bengal country words

colloquial dialects differed widely in different places.* Hindustani was mixed largely with them all. The Moravians had pronounced Bengali to be inadequate to the statement of Christian doctrines,—an opinion which Mr. Thomas strongly combatted. He had a clever teacher in his múnshi, Ram Ram Basu, but found very little help from books. His journal thus relates one of his earliest attempts to preach :—

Friday, December 7th, 1787.—Went round the road to-day, after visiting the children, whose school began last Monday, and when I came to the high place, under the green tree, where an idol is worshipped, I stopped, and began talking to a few people. The sum of what I said was, the experienced inefficacy, both in good and bad men alike, of worshipping idols. But that the true worship of the true God is accompanied by such effects, so similar and so great, as give an unquestionable proof that it is accepted by God. This appears in its changing the inclinations of the heart, which none ever did but God. One blood in all nations—one law for all—one work prepares all men to enter into heaven.

I found this a pleasant and profitable work. Oh, that I had more words. When shall I speak again ? Oh, for seriousness, spirituality, and meekness of spirit!

The following Tuesday, he relates a conversation held with people who had brought an offering to their idol. He was encouraged by their apparent ability to understand him ; but the priest was greatly provoked by his address.

A few weeks later, he was able to inform his father that he "had held straggling conversations with the people, and had spoken, for twenty minutes or so, about the first things of religion ;" but was not able yet to "deliver himself handsomely, or, in other words, to preach to them."

made into English. By this means we shall be enabled to recommend ourselves to the English Government, and understand their orders. This favor will be gratefully remembered by us and our posterity for ever."

* Mr. Forster, in the introduction to his *English and Bengali Vocabulary*, published in 1799, says,—" There never having been a native Bengali grammarian, nor indeed any author of note (I speak of the vulgar Bengali), who might be considered a standard, the orthography has, consequently, never been fixed; and being current over an extensive country, and amongst an illiterate people, almost every word has been, and continues, in one district or other, to be variously spelt, and not unfrequently is so disguised as to render it difficult to recognize it when met in its genuine form in the Songskrit."

Very soon, he was anxious to attempt a translation of the Gospels. His journal says,—

"Tuesday, March 4th, 1788.—This day, after having desired the prayers of others, and after earnest prayer to God, I began translating the book of Matthew into Bengalese, that I may have it in my power to read the word of God to myself and others in that language. O that I may labour and not faint, and may the blessing of God be in it. If ever I did show perseverance in any thing, I should think it would be in this. One means of continuing this good work will be a regulation of time in it, not to be trespassed upon by any other work whatever; and, that I may not fall short or exceed, I appoint two hours in the morning and one in the evening, and a faithful register to be kept of my proceedings in a book made for that purpose.

Not very much was to be expected from so premature an effort to translate the word of God; but who can wonder that, in Mr. Thomas's circumstances, this was one of the first things he attempted? and what friend of Bengal will look back upon the purpose here recorded without gratitude to God for all the successful labour in the translation of His word which was begun in that feeble attempt, and which has been carried forward to the present day by men evidently fitted by God to accomplish it?

On Lord's-day, April 20th, he records his anxiety to promote the better observance of the day, and the following resolution is entered in his journal :—

To give all my servants, my múnshi, harcará, boy, washerman, and tailors positive orders to attend me at the school bungalow every Lord's-day, where by the blessing of God, I intend to read a portion of God's holy word in Bengalese, and offer such things for their instruction as I may be able to prepare from Sabbath to Sabbath: beseeching them to save themselves from this untoward generation.

The following Sunday, April 27th, he writes :—

Having placed all my servants and the forty children, I delivered in Bengalese an exhortation, for the first time, from Isaiah ii. 2-6, 8, 17-20, and lv. 1-9.

I told them that the Lord's house was any place where two or three met together to hear His word and to worship the true God. I spoke of the happy days coming; and explained to them that the thirst, the wine, the water, and the milk here spoken of were for the soul, not for the body; and told them that God spake to them, for the wicked to turn, and He would pardon and receive them,—and for the thirsty to come to His word, and He should and would satisfy them. I told them that God was the Friend of friends,—that *their books* taught them how the rich and the wise should enter into the kingdom; but *this* how the poor also, and the ignorant, and the repenting sinner should be received. I besought them to pray to God when they came again, &c. Great pleasure had I in this service, and blessed be the God of all comfort!

Encouraged by the success of this first attempt to preach in Bengali, he wrote to Mr. Creighton, and arranged for a visit to Goamalty on the following Friday, that he might repeat his discourse there to the people employed at the factory. This he was able to do, and had about two hundred hearers on the occasion.

On the 9th May, the journal contains the following entry, about a sermon at Goamalty.—

I must needs take my notes to-day and read them over in English to Mr. Udny, and thus I got myself considerably disheartened; for he would have it at once, that it was what they could not understand :—that I ought to preach more against their idols, and less about eternal life.

গোনার মাহিনা মির্তু কিন্তু খোদার দিয়া চির প্রমাই জিজহ কাইট হইতে।*
এই মির্তু এখন অরহ, তখন ——

The above text was preached from to about one hundred and fifty natives, and the text itself I caused to be written in red ink on twenty pieces of paper, for them that could read. Before I began, I dealt out about four, and they asked me who Jesus Christ was, and I told them that they should hear presently. While I was preaching, to my great surprise, there was several times an involuntary groaning among them, and that out loud.

I told them particularly to observe that the death was *wages*, but the life was not so: the life was a *gift*. No good work could deserve such a blessing, especially from a sinner all full of sin. It was a free gift. To whom? To sinners,—the vilest of sinners. It had in it the pardon of all sins and offences whatsoever. This is the gift of God.

* This is given as a specimen of Mr. Thomas's earliest Bengali. The text is Romans vi. 23.

I said that it began in this life, with joy, and peace, and love toward God; which joy I had; and that I now wished to lead them to this Saviour, that they might have the same. I said, This night God has sent His word. Hear, and your soul shall live.

I fain would have said much more concerning a precious Saviour; but concluded by saying that he that had got this gift of God, his soul would fully partake of life after death. When the body died, he would be cleared at judgment, and the soul and body coming together again, as they are now, would go up into heaven to be happy in the presence of God, without end. I besought them to remember and believe what I had said, else these eyes would see them in the lake of fire.

Many were pricked in their heart, and unitedly sent forth a sort of involuntary groan, appearing to be ready to say, 'Sirs, what shall we do?' The strips of paper with the text in red ink were caught at, like so many bank-notes, and eager were they for more when the last was given. I observed also that, when I had done, they did not all get up immediately, as before; but sat astonished, till I had spoken to them repeatedly to go.

This extract is long, but the records of first endeavours in a great work are always interesting; and what work is greater than to bring the gospel of our Lord Jesus Christ to the ears and hearts of a people who for many ages had been sunk in heathen ignorance and misery! Mr. Thomas was one of the very first to speak of the great salvation in the Bengali tongue. He now began a mission which has been carried on by a goodly company of preachers since, and not in vain; but to the glory and praise of God in the salvation of many hearers. Great results of the work so imperfectly and feebly commenced have been already achieved, and results beyond these will every day accumulate, as the Lord more abundantly acknowledges the labours of his servants in Bengal.

But in the midst of these beginnings of missionary effort, things were taking place which rapidly led on to the completion of that alienation from his friends which he had seen reason to anticipate.

In August, 1787, Mr. Thomas suffered very severely from boils, so that he could scarcely walk, or even use his hand to write. While thus afflicted, his thoughts were directed to the practical neglect of the Lord's Supper in which he and his frends at Malda were living. Here is the conclusion to which these reflections brought him.

Having had very sharp impressions on my mind about my boils and other remarkable diseases of body, which bring to mind the saying that is written of this ordinance abused or neglected, '*for this cauſe many are sick*,'—1 Corinthians xi. 30, I intend thus to commemorate Christ's death, once a month, and to signify it to some of the brethren, of whom I find reason to believe they trust in His blood, and make His word the rule and governing of all they do.

From this it may be concluded that, up to this time, the communion question had suggested no difficulty in the way of Mr. Thomas's ministry among his friends. Probably he had thought little about it. Now, however, it became a question of no small interest ; and, remembering the practice of most of the Baptist churches he had known in England, his convictions gradually grew stronger and stronger that he ought to insist upon the immersion of all those who claimed to partake with him in the fellowship of the body and blood of Christ.

But even after this, for some time, the matter does not appear to have come into actual debate amongst his friends at Malda. The next entry bearing upon the subject is dated April 12th, 1788 :—

O Lord, forgive the things that are past !

This day some movings of conscience urge me to speak boldly to all concerning their baptism and partaking of the Lord's Supper. Lord, grant me wisdom and discretion how to walk, when thou hast delivered me from this half-hearted way and frame of mind. As to the word of God, I know more than I practice.

Convinced that he ought to speak out plainly upon the subject of baptism to his friends, Mr. Thomas proceeded to do so with the utmost confidence, not only in the scriptural authority of the opinions he himself held, but in his ability to bring others to accept them. It was not in his nature to do things by halves. He was not content with insisting upon the necessity of immersion, at Malda, but he wrote largely upon the same subject to Mr. Grant and others in Calcutta. The consequences which resulted may be seen in a later entry in his journal.—

Sunday, May 24th.—This day, I saw that Mr. Udny received two books from Mr. Grant, with Mr. Brown's name, on the subject of baptism. This is ominous. They show secresy. I have no doubt, these books are sent up in consequence of the letters I lately wrote to Mr. Grant, declaring my sentiments in favor of adult baptism, with my clear convictions and settled determination.

If the tiny pins of a watch are of so much value and use, notwithstanding their smallness, and if it be essential that they are rightly placed, who can say that the ordinances of God's house are less so ?

I will give myself unto prayer. The lion roars. Lord, be thou near at hand.

Monday.—This evening, I had a very long conversation with Mr. Udny about baptism, in which we greatly disagreed. I avowed my sentiments clearly, and was grieved. After prayer &c. we were quiet, and I finished the evening with a few reflections upon the opposition I had met with in Calcutta, and, from the length it has gone, concluded that some providence will overtake us, and show itself strong on behalf of them that fear God, and a swift witness against others, &c.

Whatever the causes and instruments used in this affliction, let me not forget that it is a rod, and cometh not from the dust. Oh for *meekness* of spirit and patience ; then who or what can hurt me !

Wednesday.—I praise the Lord with great joy and thanksgiving for the recruited strength and spirits he has given me, in writing a reason why I would not baptise infants, but immerse adults. Now I begin to think that, though I am become as the offscouring, and have many troubles all around me, yet the Lord will certainly bring me so out of them, as may work together for my good. So surely as, after the longest and darkest night, the sun arises, and seems brighter than it was before, to them that see it, so surely shall the Lord make my enemies to be at peace with me.

Thursday.—Proclamation of peace. Mr. Udny sent me a letter.

I resolved to publish my pamphlet, if God gives me wisdom to finish it, and if Dr. Stennett approves of it, and to give the sale to the poor Baptist ministers in Europe.

Friday.—All this week I have been labouring night and day about the controversy on Baptism, and I have prepared, as I suppose, an unanswerable refutation of infant sprinkling and a defence of immersion. Special help from God has surely been bestowed. Truth is on my side, and I fear not ; though I am like a sparrow alone.

My confidence is strong, and I am persuaded that I shall convince every one of my hearers. If so, I will publish it, and give the proceeds to poor Baptist ministers in England, &c. I think I *shall* convince, because God seems on my side.* For my own part, as my arguments rise up, they astonish me with their simplicity and clearness, as though the Lord had heard my prayer indeed. I prayed it might be useful to thousands, and who can tell ? My confidence is free, easy, and clear, that I shall indeed convince beyond the power of any to answer to good purpose. How many times I have thanked the Lord for it, as though it was already done !

Lord's-day evening.—Mr. Udny having heard all these arguments, seems to fortify himself and the rest by saying he would hear what others say on the matter, and by quoting Nebuchadnezzar's dew, and the children of Israel being baptized into the cloud and into the sea, which he thought favored the idea of sprinkling. I thought otherwise. However, give me, O my God, meekness, patience, and love to those that differ.

Friday.—I leave all in thy hands, O God of truth, and may no wrath be used to work the righteousness of God.

June 2nd.—Mr. Udny this morning read Romans xv., and I incline to think he judges me to be pleasing my own self, and thinks that I fail to please my neighbour for good to edification. An expression or two in his prayer still further convinced me that the opposition awakes again.

Now, being thus arraigned secretly, I thought it my duty to write him plainly—yet as peace is to be followed, I have torn up the letter and declined it. In controversy, let him that thinketh he is on the right side be mild ; and now I will betake myself to prayer and the word, thinking I have some right and title to the following texts :—

2 Timothy i. 8. 'Be not thou therefore ashamed of the testimony of our Lord ; but be thou partaker of the afflictions of the gospel.'

1 Corinthians iv. 3-4. 'It is a very small thing (how I wish it were !) that I should be judged of you, or of man's judgment ; yea, I judge not mine own self. For I know nothing by myself ; yet am I not hereby justified : but he that judgeth me is the Lord. Therefore judge nothing before the time, until the Lord come, who both will bring to light the hidden things of darkness, and will make manifest the counsels of the hearts : and then shall every man have praise of God.'

'I know nothing by myself,' but from the Holy Spirit, whose gift knowledge is ; 'yet am I not hereby justified,' either from

---

* A note in the journal against this says,—"That is no proof! Remember Jesus ! !"

error or mistake, of myself or others. But I shall be brought into judgment, after all; and He that judgeth me is the Lord.

After I had delivered my sermon last night, Mr. Udny prayed as usual, and in his prayer quoted a text of scripture, and expounded it contrary to what I had been saying. In my discourse, I said that the believer was directed to look back to his baptism as an incentive to holiness of life.—(Romans vi. 3, 4.) 'We do,' said Mr. Udny in his prayer, 'O Lord, look back to the time when we were dedicated to thee (in infancy).' All this is so marked, and so far from edifying, that I know not what to do. It seems to me as though all I said now would be brought into judgment and condemned. Oh what a leaven is this that is come up from Calcutta!

I have determined to go to Goamalty; thinking there to be at peace. Our Lord did not do many mighty works because of men's unbelief; and how is it possible I can edify? It seems to me, in my heart and conscience, impossible. Mr. Udny's influence is very considerable, on account of his high station. I therefore proposed by letter to remove to Goamalty. Mr. Udny expressed his surprise. Afterwards, we both lamented our disputes; and I agreed to defer the step for one week.

These extracts exhibit the feverish impatience and excitableness of Mr. Thomas's character, and its sensitive petulant weakness. He had begun a controversy, full of unpleasantness to his friends, and had, no doubt, used the strongest and hardest arguments he could find to make good his position. When they, however, defended their long cherished opinions, he was immediately sore and offended! If he was touchy and weak in some respects, however, he was bold and strong in his assertion and defence of truth as he had received it in the word of God, and was quite resolute to dare all the issues which his unwelcome avowal of it might provoke. "If the consequence should be that I am to be cast out, and become a vagabond, or if I come to a morsel of bread, I will still stand up for the Lord, and against them that receive not His word in meekness and love." Such was his determined resolve, and to this he stood firm.

But even now he hoped for better things from his beloved hearers. Poor simple man! his tractate on baptism *must* convince, first them, and then all the misguided Christian world besides; and the profits of its publication should fill the empty pockets of poor Baptist ministers! He could have known little of the world, when he thought the work of persuasion so easy. Perhaps, however, some who now read of his disappointment may be reminded of their own similar failures. What assured Baptist has not at some time felt that, with a command so explicit, expressed in words so simple and intelligible, and which, in its obvious import, is so perfectly and beautifully in harmony with all the analogy of the Christian faith, he *must* be able to convince every candid opponent that his practice was in accordance with the ordinance of God? And who has not found upon experiment that nothing is so hopelessly obstinate as theological traditional prejudice?

It would be unjust to Mr. Thomas to omit from this account of his controversy the remarks upon it which he recorded upon the 12th of June.—

Whether the wrath of man intermingled may prevent the efficacy of my simple arguments, I cannot tell; but I greatly fear it. I pray thee, O Lord, to preserve me from this evil, and to give us one heart and one mind, and suffer us not to hinder or forbid one another; because we follow not with them that differ in such respects. Confirm them that are in the truth, and loosen and lessen our mistakes for us.

Surely hitherto I am deceived. I may stand on good ground, so far as baptism is concerned; but I have certainly acted ill upon it. My confidence, my self-sufficiency, my assurance of success, my anger, my uncharitable walk towards my brethren, all seem to be too glaringly uppermost, as I look over my diary of the last few days. I desire to cease from anger and forsake wrath, to humble myself before God and man. Oh that I may do this wisely, O Lord, give me true repentance, I beseech thee.

Two of the young men at Malda, however, Messrs. Dingley and Long, professed to be convinced that the Baptists were in the right, and, in the face of all opposition or displeasure, he determined to baptize them at once, according to their desire. As the appointed time drew near, however, Mr. Dingley first wavered in his purpose, and then altogether abandoned it. This was a severe mortification to Mr. Thomas; but the other young man,

Mr. William Long, persisted in his wish, and we must extract from the journal an account of probably the first administration of the rite of baptism, according to scriptural example, in Bengal.

Friday, June 13th.—Went early to Goamalty, and enjoyed a calm and delightful day in prayer and meditation. In the evening, having well arranged and studied my Bengali address, I was able to deliver it with freedom and delight, and that in an uncommon measure.

We then proceeded to the river; but the sun being set, I was in too much haste. I read and commented all the way, which was half a mile. After a short exhortation by the water's side, we went down with these words, hand in hand, 'And they went down both into the water, both Philip and the eunuch; and he baptized him.' The water was of a proper depth and gradual descent.

Having pronounced the words first in Bengalese, I then repeated them in English, in the usual manner, and so baptized him. On the bank of the river, I offered a short prayer and an exhortation, both in English and Bengalese, in the midst of which Mr. Udny came, with Mr. W. Brown and a few natives. After dressing in the house, I continued exhorting him against self-sufficiency, as in Peter's case, forewarning him of troubles, persecutions, and much tribulation: but spoke also of the good Master. I insisted also upon the necessity of watchfulness and prayer, and the power of indwelling sin, and warned him of the inexperience of young converts. Herein also were mingled remarks upon the benefits into which he had been baptized.

I enjoyed much solemnity and liberty. Lord, teach me what to do about the Lord's Supper.

And now Mr. Thomas had witnessed for truth before his Christian brethren, in a manner which he believed must deeply displease them; and he certainly did this with a clear persuasion that many severe trials were likely to arise out of his procedure. For the present, however, nothing took place to disturb his position.

Up to this period, he was quite uncertain whether his wife was coming to join him in India. At the beginning of June, he heard good tidings of her improved health, and that a daughter had been added to his family. The letter of his sister-in-law announcing these mercies gave him unspeakable joy. He had suffered a thousand tender anxieties for his delicate wife; and it was delightful to him to be assured of her safety, and to read of his little James, whose " face was like a peach, fresh, fair, and ruddy," and of the babe Betsey, " one of the finest girls in the world." The faded pages which told their father this have long survived those whose early bloom they described. The little boy died in his infancy, but his sister lived to suffer the infirmities of old age.

Mr. Thomas's religious experience during this first year at Malda exhibits the same unevenly ardent aspirations after holiness, and the same bitterness of disappointment in the consciousness of a strong tendency to sink down to the level of a mere pleasant associate of the cheerful young men around him, as he had experienced in his former situation : the same lofty standard of self-denying consecration, and the same failures in the attempts he was continually making to attain and preserve it. No mention is made here of any new vision, but he appeared to live as if always in anticipation of disclosures from the unseen world. He was persuaded that God still spake with men in dreams and visions of the night; and often recorded his nightly fancies, as though they were intended to be vehicles of instruction to his mind. They may, perhaps, inform us as to the inmost desires and most secret thoughts of the dreamer, and it is interesting to notice that they were almost always "employed on the word of God," or in imaginary translating or preaching in Bengali.

The enthusiasm of his nature appears also very particularly in relation to prayer. He took such promises as Mark xi. 24, in their strictest literalness of interpretation. In the confidence that their prayer of faith would save the sick, he gathered his companions around the death-bed of Mr. Forsyth, and earnestly besought his recovery; which, as we have seen, was not granted. In another case, he was most keenly distressed and disappointed. A poor child afflicted with disease of the spleen was brought to him for treatment, and the medicines given, acting upon a very feeble constitution, resulted in most dangerous symptoms. Mr. Thomas fasted, wept and prayed, and endeavoured to obtain the child's recovery by most importunate supplications, which he tried hard to assure himself must prevail; but the issue disappointed his desires, and covered him with sorrowful humiliation. These incidents are related as not unimportant contributions to the understanding of his character and history. How many of the mistakes and disasters of his life were traceable to his premature confidence that God would bring to pass the desires he laid before Him in prayer. By his sanguine excitable mind an assurance of this kind was regarded as almost a special revelation, in reliance upon which he ventured upon things which in the end disappointed his hopes and seriously augmented his difficulties.

It is matter for more pleasant observation that none of these things moved him from his firm confidence in the fidelity of Him who has promised. He was ever ready to attribute all error and failure to himself; and with abasement to acknowledge that, if his requests were not granted, it was only because he had not fulfilled the express conditions of his Lord :—" If ye abide in me, and my words abide in you, ye shall ask what ye will and it shall be done unto you." Never did his trust in the truth and divinity of God's word seem to waver. He had been sceptical in his younger days, as has been seen; and now he was continually encountering sceptical arguments and sneers from visitors at Mr. Udny's house. But no such argument had weight with him, and no sneer made him ashamed of his hope. He had too truly " tasted the good word of God and the powers of the world to come" to be ever disposed to question the foundation of his faith.

CHAPTER V.

Controversy and Disaster.—1788-89.

THE variance which arose between Mr Thomas and his friends and supporters, some of the causes of which have already been indicated, must now be more fully written of. He conscientiously thought, and he thought truly, that God had given him ability to do much good by letter; and now that he had left his Calcutta friends, and could no longer admonish them by word of mouth, he felt it to be his duty to write to them with a frequency and copiousness which were, to say the least, imprudent and ill-judged. Think of a letter to Mr. Robert Udny, upon "the divine story of Jacob's wrestlings," extending to eighty-eight pages! Mr. Grant was more usually the object of this *cacoethes scribendi*, and he received the elaborate treatises which came to him from Malda, with dismay and with ineffectual remonstrance.* These letters dealt with whatever their author considered a failing with almost epigrammati-

* In addition to letters, Mr. Grant received other proofs of the missionary's desire for his edification. Amongst these were copies of verses, much more correct in doctrine than in metre and expression. How Mr. Thomas spent some of his leisure, the following extract relates.—"I have been five or six weeks about a work for you and Mrs Grant, and I have just discovered that you have it in print. It will nevertheless be acceptable and useful to those who have it not. It is that incomparable work, *Dr. Clarke's Promises of Scripture*, drawn out to the full." He commonly wrote negligently, and sometimes very illegibly, but he could display remarkable neatness of penmanship. We have now before us, in his Common Place Book, a compendium of doctrines, compiled in Scripture texts, all written out with such exactness and care as to be a very beautiful specimen of caligraphy. Its interest in this respect is, however, far surpassed by that which it inspires as a monument of the writer's profound reverence for the word of God, and of his patient, diligent, and loving cultivation of the knowledge of it.

cal severity; and could not but provoke antagonism in those who felt themselves treated with most uncompromising plainness of speech by a man whose advice they had now no disposition to seek.

But his procedure in this respect cannot, perhaps, be more fairly stated or better defended than in his own words, addressed to Mr. Grant, upon this subject, at the end of February, 1788.

He that writes letters in the fear of God, with an aim to edify, must stedfastly pursue 'the old man' and his deceits, by warnings, cautions, charges, and loud and plain personal cryings out, and rebukes against secret or open evils; and, on the other hand, he must follow 'the new man' with cordials, refreshments, consolations, and praise, according to the unalterable prescription revealed of the will of God: and who is sufficient for these things? And in this course, if he writes personally and faithfully, he will surely involve himself in manifest contradictions, to a carnal eye; but they are none other than spiritual consistencies in the analogy of faith and according to the mysteries of godliness; and therefore it is, that, in the inspired writings, the propositions and arguments offered are frequently directed to him 'that hath an ear,' that is able to understand, 'to him that is wise,' &c. whilst others secretly reject the good counsel of God, being wise in their own conceits; and, being accounted of God 'rich' in carnal wisdom, are 'sent empty away.' For the word of God itself will not profit any man, if it is not mixed with faith and simplicity in him that receives it. Now what I have said may be clearly illustrated and proved by what is found in the Holy Scriptures on this very subject, and the kind of contradiction in letter writing that I chiefly allude to is such as is often found in Paul's writings: full of ease, and simplicity, and plainness to the eye of faith, but seemingly inconsistent to the carnal eye, were it to be found anywhere else than in the Holy Scriptures. Instances to my purpose are to be found in Romans, Corinthians, and Galatians: particularly, to mention the first I come to, and that only, 1 Corinthians i. 7, where Paul says to that church, 'In every thing ye are enriched....so that ye come behind in no gift;' yet to the very same people he also says, (iii. 1,) 'I could not speak unto you as unto spiritual, but as unto carnal.' &c.....' For ye are yet carnal.'

I find enough to mortify me for ever, and enough to make me blush whenever I read it, among the remarks on my letters from various correspondents; and this would be enough to persuade me to write much more seldom, and, like the merchants of this world, three lines at a time; were it not for other considerations, such as these:—God has been pleased to own and bless some extracts, overlooking and pardoning the rest, to the conviction, conversion and edification of some; and I have also, now and then, received a very supporting, animating, and strengthening word, from the wisest, most holy, and circumspect men I ever had the honour of being intimate with.

The gold, it must be acknowledged, bears no proportion to the dross; but I am not going to affect any very humbling expressions, neither would I avoid them, for fear of being suspected of affectation; neither am I at all afraid to speak moderately of any gift or endowment God has granted me, for fear of being accused of boasting; for the wise will always distinguish, and the foolish will always be prating. David said, 'Thou hast made me wiser than all my teachers.' Now I am as far from that as the North Pole. Yet I am not at all afraid to think or to say, that God has made me wiser than some men. And I cannot but wonder at, and wish to correct, what I find among many good people, a habit of abusing themselves without mercy, with the odium of ignorant, weak, &c. when they are speaking with persons of acknowledged comparative inferiority.

On the other hand, there is nothing so pleasing and gratifying to a holy self-revenge as the epithets of filthy, vile, foolish, ignorant, beastly, &c. which the *private* meditations and prayers of good men are therefore filled with on particular occasions.

In such matters then, let us pray for wisdom to discern between men and things, ourselves and others, according to the station God has placed us in, to the honour of the gospel, the edification of souls, and the glory of God.

I should like to know which character is to be more avoided by him that would walk in the strait path of wisdom:—such excess of faithfulness as to have no appearance of tenderness, or so much of tenderness as to have no appearance of faithfulness.

I know by experience that those who stand most in need of faithful rebukes, as well as those who are over-tender, cry out against the want of tenderness; and those who have the gift of boldness are apt to make a great noise about the want of faithfulness. When I think much of such things, I conclude that we are all of us made up of inferiority and ignorance.

On the 24th of June, after the news of Mr. Long's baptism

had reached Calcutta, Mr. Thomas received a letter from Mr. R. Udny, in which he said :—" It struck me that you had no authority for baptizing ; as I always supposed it was *a minister* who performed that service." " I wonder," said Mr. Thomas, " what he thinks '*a minister*' to be! I have been *ministering* to him these twelve months, and yet he is unwilling to allow me the same authority as a poor uncalled, unsent, unconverted, but ordained gownsman!"

Without doubt, this was a very important point in the dispute between the missionary and his friends. They charged him with presumption ; and he convicted them of inconsistency with their avowed evangelical principles. He was deeply conscious of a very special call to the ministry he was exercising—a call something like that which laid " the burden of the Lord" upon the ancient prophets. They disputed this call, because it was certified by no human authority, and indeed came into collision with the ecclesiastical system to which they had been taught to bow. Could any association be more incongruous, or more fully fraught with elements of discord than was the engagement between them and himself? He could only quiet himself with such reflections as the following :—" Let me not murmur ; but rather be a partaker of the sufferings of Christ ; for even His mission was constantly questioned with a 'Who is this fellow?' Why should I think so much of it, who am a sinful worm, when He, the Lord of glory, bore it ? Let me rather take up my cross and follow Him, rejoicing that I am counted worthy to suffer with Him."

About this time, he thus reviewed his present relations with his Calcutta friends and others :—

The Lord hath indeed put lover and friend far from me. Mr. O'Beck opposed my coming, and hindered my work ; but Christ did forward my coming here, and blessed my work. When I spoke a word of needful remonstrance to our friends in Calcutta, Mr. O'Beck rose up, like ' the princes of the assembly, famous in the congregation, men of renown,' who withstood Moses and Aaron. Mr. Brown, from whom I should have expected great encouragement, has veered like a weather-cock, and failed me like a breaking bridge. Mr. Chambers, who professed such piping-hot love and thankfulness, turned away because of one unwelcome letter, cast me off from his acquaintance, and deliberately declared me to be a person of a false profession! But 'doth our law condemn a man before it hear him?' He has never yet told me wherefore he condemns me, nor has he heard my defence. O Lord, let me not fall into the hands of men! Mr. Grant has defended Brown, Chambers, and O'Beck, and has never once said a word about their faultiness; and he has grown slack and shy in writing. But, what is worse than all, Robert Udny is working, and Dingley also. Both have opposed me on baptism; and Mr. Grant sent up books whereby our peace has been disturbed, and those even who before seemed to hear me with candour and acceptance are risen up against me. Mr. Frushard has ceased to correspond; and even Burney grows cold and indifferent. All this is like cold lead in my bosom, even while I eat, drink, or sleep.

He was cheered amidst these discouragements by the hope that the Spirit of God was powerfully working in the heart of his múnshi, Rám Basu. This man told him in June, 1788, that he had found Jesus to be the answerer of his prayer. He had cried to Him in sickness, and a speedy cure had been granted. Towards the end of the same month, he brought Mr. Thomas, "a gospel hymn of his own composing, the first ever seen or heard of in the Bengalese language,"—a lyric which still holds its place in our collections of Bengali hymns.* Rám Basu's daily

---

* This hymn deserves preservation in its original form. It has not been much used of late years; but a few of the older native Christians remember the air, and still occasionally sing it. The Bengali original and Mr. Thomas's translation are given side by side.

কে আর তারিতে পারে	O who besides can recover us,
লর্ড জিজছ ক্রাইষ্ট বিনা গো।	O who besides can recover us,
পাতক সাগর ঘোর	From the everlasting darkness of sin,
লর্ড জিজছ ক্রাইষ্ট বিনা গো।	Except the Lord Jesus Christ?
সেই মহাশয় ঈশ্বর তনয়	Lo! that Lord is the Son of God,
পাপির ত্রাণের হেতু।	The intermediate of a sinner's salvation:
উঁারে যেই জন করয়ে ভজন	Whosoever adores Him,
পার হবে ভবসেতু।	Will get over his eternal ruin.
	O who besides can recover us, &c.

conversation betokened also a deep conviction of the truth of the gospel, and there was reason to hope he might soon be an acknowledged follower of Christ. Brainerd's interpreter in the Indian language was one of the first converts made by that celebrated missionary, and Mr. Thomas rejoiced in this parallel with his own experience. Similar hopes were entertained as to Mr. Long's múnshi. The Bengali preaching at Goamalty and elsewhere also was listened to with great interest; and thus it appeared that "a door of faith" was being opened to the heathen of Bengal. In the confidence that God was indeed granting His blessing, Mr. Thomas found consolation amidst all his troubles, and trusted that, notwithstanding all his failings and disappointments, the issue of his engagement in the

এই পৃথিবীতে নাহি কোন জন নিষ্পাপি ও কলেবর । জগতের ত্রাণকর্ত্তা সেই জন খ্রীষ্টছও নাম তাঁহার ।	In all this earth, There is none free from sin, Except the Saviour of the world, And His name is Jesus. O who besides can recover us, &c.
ঈশ্বর আপনি জন্মিল অবনী উদ্ধারিতে পাপি জন । যেই পাপী হয় ভজয়ে তাঁহায় সেই পাবে পরিত্রাণ ।	That Lord was born into the world, To redeem sinful men : Whosoever has faith to adore Him, That is the man that will get free. O who besides can recover us, &c.
আকার নিকার ধর্ম্ম অবতার সেই জগতের নাথ । তাঁহার বিহনে স্বর্গের ভুবনে গমন দুর্গম পথ ।	With and without form, a holy incarnation, That is the Lord of the world : Without faith in Him, the road to heaven Is inaccessible. O who besides can recover us, &c.
সে বদন বাণী শুন সব প্রাণী যে কেহ তৃষিত হয় । যে নর আসিবে শুদ্ধ বারি পাবে আমি দিব সে তাহায় ।	The words of His mouth, hear, O men, For His sayings are very true ; "Whoso is thirsty, let him come to ME, "I will give him the living water." O who besides can recover us, &c.

অতএব মন কর রে ভজন
তাঁহাকে জানিয়া সার ।
তাঁহার বিহনে পাওকি তারণে
কোন জন নাহি আর ।
	Therefore adore, O my soul,
	Having known Him substantial ;
	And besides Himself
	There is no other Saviour.
	    O who besides can recover us,
	    O who besides can recover us,
	    From the everlasting darkness of sin,
	    Except the Lord Jesus Christ ?

mission would be found unto praise and honour and glory in the day of Jesus Christ.

Another source of trouble at this time was his uncertainty whether Mrs. Thomas would arrive, as he had requested her, by the ships now due. Every arrangement he could make for her comfort on the passage had been made, letters were sent to Madras, to await her arrival there, and the anxious husband had ventured to assure himself that he should soon receive her and his little ones. Then a report reached him that she was not coming. The disappointment was a sore one; but, after a few days, a letter was received which spoke of her coming as sure, and intimated that his beloved brother James was coming with her! A former dream of the múnshi's was thought to corroborate this delightful news, and sorrow was turned into joy. But, at the end of July, news arrived that Mrs. Udny had reached Calcutta, and that Mrs. Thomas was not with her. The tidings filled him with anguish; but he had been preparing to go to Calcutta to meet her, and he resolved still to go. She might yet come, perhaps, by some later ship. He therefore left Malda on the 29th of July, and, after a journey made difficult and sometimes even dangerous by contrary boisterous winds, reached Calcutta on the 8th of August. Before arriving there, letters reached him from his wife which destroyed all hope of seeing her soon in Bengal, and filled him with unspeakable sorrow. But he had arranged to visit Calcutta for other reasons. He hoped that a little personal intercourse with his friends there might destroy the unpleasantness which had arisen between them. His relations with them had been very happy whilst he was near them: might he not, if he could speak with them, re-establish himself in their affections and restore that Christian fellowship which had been so delightful only a few months previously? He was full of hope that it would be so. He longed to address them once again as he had so often done before.

All such expectations were signally disappointed by the issues of his visit. If he was not already convinced that he had utterly lost the favor of his once admiring friends, his experience, when he again met them, established the fact only too clearly. Perhaps, he might have had better success, had he come to the interview with a disposition less resolute to maintain the right of his cause. But he fortified himself before entering upon it by reading passages in Ezekiel, and he wrote in his journal, " As the above word says, whatever I have said or written against them, was for the Lord; and, if so, He will own it at last, and make my enemies to be at peace with me."

Some of the entries in his journal during his stay in Calcutta, will best show the results of this unhappy visit.

August 8th.—Saw Mr. and Mrs. Brown, Mrs. Udny, Mr. R. Udny, and Mr. Grant. I dine by myself: they with Mr. Chambers.

Saturday, 10th.—I discoursed with Mr. Grant on Mr. Chambers's letter, Mr. Brown, and baptism. I was neither abashed, nor confounded, but my face was like a flint; yet with modesty. I boldly professed to differ. Cleared up some mistakes made by too critically examining words. Confessed want of manner in the letter to Chambers, and uncouthness in writing. Mr. Grant seemed to speak angrily and menacingly—also he said my wife's not coming out would alter the case: as though he would insinuate I ought now to go home! His ideas differ vastly from what they were once! He seemed to draw back his warmth as I urged facts.

Lord's-day, 11th.—I went to church, and took my mûnshi; but they would not let him in! I heard Mr. Brown preach to a very thin congregation of eight or ten Europeans, with others; and if there was the smallest demonstration of the Spirit, it was utterly unperceived by me. Mr. Grant was very slow in asking me to dinner; and on my getting into the carriage, he behaved forbiddingly. At his house, after a little strife of words, he left me to stay in a room by myself down-stairs. At dinner, Mr. Brown remained sulky, and continued so all day. There was an unsavoury asking of blessings, and an unmeaning giving of thanks. In the evening, he read a hymn; but there was no singing, nor word of singing. He then read, without prayer, the parting discourse which he had just delivered at the Orphan House over the water. 'If it was of no use to any one else,' he said, 'it might be of use to the children.' He then concluded with a long prayer, the whole consisting of fine things finely spoken. Our conversation was dry, dull and restrained; in fact, I have not had such a lost Sabbath a great while, and I hope never to spend such another. I am sick of greatness, sick of Calcutta, and sick of human friendships!

Tuesday, 13th.—I had a great deal of conversation with Mr. Grant again, concerning our late differences. He expressed several fears concerning my being 'heated in imagination,' given to 'carnal zeal,' 'bigoted to the Baptist persuasion,' 'thundering out threatenings,' &c., &c., all which things are particularly noticed in a letter which he put into my hands at the same time.

I fully intended to call on Mr. Chambers, but, waiting for Mr. Grant till it became late, and being discouraged by the pains he took to avoid me, in not coming to Mr. Grant's, and not even coming to church on the Lord's-day, I thought that evil rather than good might be expected to result from an interview.

I told Mr. Grant that, respecting Mr. Brown, I really fear, till his contentious spirit is subdued, and cast out, there will be reason to dread a fall and to despair of any gospel success. His technical terms abounded; and yet the bulk of his congregation were people of the middling complexion, and black; for, besides our friends and myself, I could number no more than eight white faces in the body of the church, and I confess I was grieved all the while to hear a good sermon delivered in words not easy to be understood. He talked, as he used to do, about *antecedents*, &c. of which I once told him to his face, and he received it as a godly man should. These things I thought proper to mention. I parted with Mr. Grant in an affectionate and loving manner, and seemingly we were both determined not to judge one another any more.

Mr. Brown had just been dismissed from his appointment at the Orphan House, because he would preach at the mission church; and Mr. Thomas found him fully established in clerical dignity at Mr. Grant's house. *His* voice, once so pleasant and instructive to his friends, was now silenced; and everything seemed to confirm and deepen his humiliation.

He did not see either Mr. Burney or Dr. Nasmyth. The former had offended Mr. Grant, by what he considered an imprudent marriage; and Mr. Thomas was told of "the ill conduct of both, and especially towards Mr. Brown, their minister." He therefore did not visit their houses, but, after dining with Mr. Robert Udny at the Export Warehouse, on Tuesday, the 13th, left Calcutta, feeling that " to its religious society, he was more of a Michaiah than ever."—1 Kings xxii. 8. "I seem," he wrote, "to have had two temptations of the devil in this country: in the first, he attempted to lift me up by praise; in the second, to cast me down by reproach; and he used the same instruments; for he can use Peters as well as Judases."

In leaving Calcutta thus, he must have very painfully contrasted his present relations with his friends with those which existed when he first went to Malda, only fifteen months before. Then he had left them with an exhortation that they would not faint at his tribulation for them, which was their glory:—now he had reason to think that they would very gladly be rid of him, if he could be induced to relinquish his engagement in the mission. He seems, indeed, to have felt that he had special occasion for thankfulness that his withdrawal from his missionary work had not been peremptorily insisted upon. He had yet greater cause for joy, on turning his face towards Malda, in the persuasion that things there were "upon a very peaceful loving footing, and as happy as any society he had ever known, notwithstanding their determined differences about baptism."

He had preached with much encouragement on his way down, especially at Bhúlaháth, a village containing "more than five hundred houses," about six miles from Malda, and at Cutwa, Nuddea, and several other places. Now that he was returning, against the stream, he had many more opportunities, and was deeply interested in speaking of Christ to crowds of hearers who had never before heard of the gospel of salvation. At Nuddea, he parted very affectionately from Rám Basu, who was going to see his family for some weeks.

Perhaps no more striking proof of Mr. Thomas's lack of common prudence could be given, than that which appears in the fact that he employed himself as he went back to Malda in writing to urge his brother to come and join him in his mission! He had said how much he should like such an arrangement when he was himself first engaged by Mr. Grant, and he then believed that his influence would suffice to ensure his brother's support as his fellow worker. But now, everything was disastrously changed. He well knew that his own engagement was no longer regarded with any satisfaction by his principal patron. How could he, in such circumstances, without a word of encouragement even from Mr. Udny, have endeavoured to bring his brother, with a wife and young family, out to Bengal? It can only be said in reply that he believed the mission to be so directly the Lord's work, that he might safely rely upon Him to meet all the wants he incurred in the methods employed to accomplish it.

Malda was reached on Thursday, August 28th, with great gladness at rejoining his companions there. "Bless the Lord," he wrote; "I heard and saw on my arrival many things to rejoice my heart. I am made exceedingly welcome indeed by my beloved friends here. Oh, how different is my reception here, from that which I found in Calcutta! The Lord has surely watered them in my absence from them."

The letter which Mr. Grant put into his hands when they parted engaged much of his attention as he travelled from Calcutta. A copy of the principal part of his reply has been preserved, and his journal contains a much more diffuse rejoinder, noted down as the thoughts occurred to his mind. Some of the principal paragraphs may be extracted. They will, with sufficient clearness, set forth Mr. Grant's charges, to which they were the answer. Mr. Thomas wrote,—

He that is *really* right in anything commanded does not appear to me to be the cause of a division, however the church may be rent by his holding fast his integrity. He that differs from him is the real cause of the division, and not he that abides in the doctrine he has learned. 'Now, I beseech you, brethren, mark them which cause divisions and offences contrary to the doctrine which ye have learned, and avoid them. For they that are such serve not our Lord Jesus Christ, but their own belly; and by good words and fair speeches deceive the hearts of the simple.'—Romans xvi. 17-18. Here we have a case of controversy, with division and separation; but all the censure falls on him that was in the wrong, and he that was on the side of truth is acquitted of blame. And in all controversies it is the same; though it is impossible *now* for those that are on the side of truth in any controversy so to prove it as to convince all the enemies of truth, or of any part of truth. Happy is the man who enters into no controversy but such as he knows to have the truth of the Most High for its foundation. He is a happy man, although he be now never so much contemned.

You remark that I said in some letter that I was not given to bigotry; and I think in my conscience, I am not; but if you inferred thence that when I have to speak publicly to my own converts or any others, I should conceal my own opinion, or, what is worse, conceal the truth, because I determined to bear with those who err, you certainly carried my words a great way beyond their natural meaning; and I particularly remember my asserting in that same letter the very contrary, intending to apprise you directly of my fixed intentions. But your remarks on this occasion may serve to balance the censures of some other good men, who have thought me too charitable with those that differ, and too relax in asserting the duty of baptism according to the Scriptures.

When I retire within from all the censures of men, and view and review the actings of my inmost soul towards them that differ, *I* am at once satisfied that I am not a bigot: but how shall I persuade my brethren, with whom I differ, of this?

I am greatly surprised to see you disown your having called me to my present office, in these words,—' Nor did I give you a call of any kind. I only accepted your overture to preach.'

I can only repeat now what passed at the time, which I accounted a call. One evening, without the slightest inducement or encouragement from me, Mr. Robert Udny told me that you had expressed a desire that I should stay with you, for the purpose of preaching to the heathen. This seemed to me then a most improbable and unlikely thing, especially on account of my family; and accordingly I so expressed myself to Robert Udny. And the difficulties in my way rose and increased by consideration, so that I gave Mr. Udny reasons enough to think that no such thing could ever happen. After this, it now and then recurred to my mind, with fresh impressions that I could not get rid of, and thus I continued for twenty-five days, during which time you yourself personally several times expressed to me an expectation of my staying in the country, though without ever saying anything particularly as to what it would be for. You know partly what passed in my mind to bring me to determination. That morning, I spoke to you to this effect:
'Mr. Udny told me, Sir, some time ago, that you expressed a

wish that I would stay in this country to preach to the heathen?' 'So I did,' said you. 'Well, Sir, I now wish to know if you are still of the same mind?' 'Yes, I am. I see no reason to alter.' And so, after prayer, the matter was settled, provided that providence favored me in regard to the difficulties that presented, concerning the captain's consent.

I believe that all the rest of you were of the same mind, except Mr. O'Beck. As for Mr. Brown, if the Lord had not been pleased to put him aside while I came in, I think verily he would most heartily have opposed it: nay, he did, as it was, and sent a letter written by Major Mitchell for Mr. Chambers to read, in order to draw him to his own opposition. This, with the letter that accompanied it, I read myself, and so saw the truth of what I here assert.

So that you have certainly forgotten that you called me, although you own that you sent me; and I hope and pray, and will watch and labour too, that you may never repent it here; but rejoice over me and others, at the coming of our Lord Jesus Christ,—for I am not without hope of obtaining mercy to be faithful.

Concerning the Common Prayer Book, I may add something to what has been said already. When I earnestly entreated you not to mention it, I had never yet heard Mr. Udny's sentiments on his laying it aside, and I supposed if you did mention it, it would be mentioned fully, and might, for aught I knew, influence him to use it again. As a lover of peace and concord, I dreaded the consequences. I should be obliged in my conscience to declare that it was contrary to the word of God: abounding with vain repetitions and tending to formality: not to say how often the 'holy and reverend' name of God is lightly used, especially when most irreverently bawled out by a parcel of boys and girls, and other most thoughtless people. Whether this opposition to it would be according to truth or not, I must stand or fall to my own Master. But I could not but entertain apprehensions of new differences that would be as unavoidable as undesirable. But since that, I learned that Mr. Udny acted on full conviction. As to any thing of a serpentine, indirect, unfair handling of any of these subjects, as you insinuate in various parts of your letter, I do not know it. Excess of frankness is more like my fault. Such craft does not belong to me, and I am only sorry that you should think otherwise.

Were the Church of England not the established religion of our country, it would be called a sect; and indeed, a small one. Nay, when we consider that there are but about two hundred enlightened ministers in it, according to the estimate of one of the very best of them,* I reckon it a very small sect; and we have no substantial reason to speak 'of the great body of the Establishment,' unless we mean all the people of England, good or bad: and if we do; even then it is but a sprig to the Church of Rome, from which, in short, it sprang, leaving many uncleannesses behind, but not all.

You say, 'I would ask, where is the authority for a dissenter, a Baptist, to denounce evil?' I answer, I have never denounced evil against you; and what I have said that answers to this strong expression was according to the word of God, as far as I am capable of understanding it, and was offered in love to souls, 'for edification, and not for destruction,' and always bears in all my letters more of the form of warning by quotation, than threatening, denouncing, predicting, &c.

Thus I have endeavoured to say something by way of explanation, and although I may not be so happy as to satisfy you, it has nevertheless been my intention and desire to do so, if it can possibly be done, in this clear discharge of, and in consistency with, the dictates of my conscience.

I have now to answer sentiments and opinions as to myself, which you tell me you have expressed after *due deliberation.*

The first thing is the 'want of solid judgment,' and 'a heated imagination.' I have often thought that the faults I have seen in others, existed also in myself with some aggravating circumstances; and so I dare say you might think of yourself, if you were at leisure, for you have censured me for using too strong expressions in my letters, whereas you yourself are not quite free. For instance, 'disturbing the church,'—'awful conjuration,'—'awful threatening,' —'delivered yourself so vehemently,'—'on pain of the most serious consequences,' (what I really said was: If you would avoid

---

* This statement appears to be taken from the writings of the Rev. William Romaine. Although, in his own way, a sort of High Churchman, this eminent minister entertained the very lowest opinion of the spiritual character of the clergy of the Establishment. On one occasion he told his congregation at Blackfriars that he and three others had agreed to spend one hour every week in prayer for the revival of the power of godliness in the Church of England; for that, out of twenty thousand ministers, she had not twenty who preached the truth as it is in Jesus! It is said, however, that, before his death, Mr. Romaine had in his possession a list of more than three hundred of whose piety he had reason to think well. It may surely be believed that He who "knoweth them that are His," had, even in the worst times of religious declension in England, a larger number of faithful and enlightened servants than some of His people were able to discover or acknowledge.

&c.)—' I mistrust the solidity of your judgment,'—' the great warmth of your imagination,'—' exalting thoughts,'—' a violent overbearing spirit increased,'—' self-seeking visible,'—' situation at Malda too much for you.'

Now, if you have done rightly, and judged your neighbour with righteous judgment and truth, undoubtedly I am not only an unworthy person, but pernicious; for the fruits of character you have applied are such as mark a man out for no ordinary degree of contempt and disgust in every line and order of society. On the other hand, if I have obtained mercy to be faithful, and if I am ' a labourer together with God,' and if His Spirit is in me, if I labour in our Lord Jesus Christ in sincerity, and in my very heart abhor these evil things,—then you have not done well. Your language bears the complexion of anger and resentment. And why? Is there any substantial reason even for this?

I may be allowed to remark, that in all this catalogue of bad principles you have not adduced one single illustration or corroborative fact.

The want of solid judgment is rather one of a man's infirmities, than a culpable fault. I do not suppose you expect me to prove to you that I have a solid judgment. Your allegation is that kind of charge against a man which of all others is generally avoided, however just. I know not indeed, what to say in my own defence; and therefore, admitting this reproach, I beg you will tell me how I shall mend it, how I shall forsake this sin, and where and how I shall obtain a solid judgment, and get my imagination cooled. It is seldom, I say, that a man is told this, especially a young man, a beginner, just entered upon a laborious and difficult work. Solidity of judgment is generally looked for among the aged, and expected amongst those who are putting the harness off, not those who are putting it on. As I am, however,—if it is to be had, and indispensible,— I would buy it at any price: or strive after it at any cost of labour, if I knew how. At present, I know of no better way than that of David,—which was to pray,—' Teach me good judgment.'—Psalm cxix. 66.

We might find some difficulty in determining what solidity of judgment is, and it may be more safe and easy to say what it is not. It is not every cloke of solemnity that passes for it; and many things besides may be said of what it is not; but we have only a few words, but those are of great authority, to describe what it is!—' A judgment according to truth,' or, in other words, ' righteous judgment;' but that is often very far from the decisions of wise, and cool, and critical men. However, if you excel in it, be thankful, and pity me.

As to 'a heated imagination,' have you well considered my natural temper, my religious education, the time I have made a profession of religion, with the suddenness and changeableness of heated imaginations? Have you well and maturely considered the vast difference that the Almighty makes in men's gifts, and that this is His wisdom;—that every man hath his proper gift of God, some after this manner, and some after that?—that He alone knows why this man is more slow and solid, and that man 'heated in his imagination,' or, suppose we say, in his affections? Have you considered that the Lord can make His word a fire in our bones? Have you well considered the sin and folly of men, and watched and guarded against them, in despising the gifts of others, because they differ from their own? This is the very course of a proud spirit, that values itself on judgment, to contemn and despise others, just like the sage Pharisees did. If you *have* well considered all these things, I will say no more on the subject, but yield this point also, desiring to know how I may be cooled.

I must take the remaining things into a little closer consideration: and the first is 'exalting thoughts.' How do you know what my thoughts are, Mr. Grant? Can you safely say they are such as 'the Lord abhors?' You speak 'with due deliberation!' If I have endeavoured to help others to abase themselves, does it necessarily follow thence that I have lofty thoughts of myself? I am persuaded you can have no other grounds for this charge against me. But what God has humbled, call not thou exalted! If you only mean that exalting thoughts have existence in me: show me a man in whom they have not. But if you mean to draw this as a predominant feature in my character, you should have taken more care not to trespass against one of your poor brethren, who trembleth at his own condition, as well as weeps over that of others.

'Overbearing spirit.'—It often is the misfortune of those who obtain mercy to be faithful with men about their sins, to fall under the censure of those around them, as well as those who urge and push forward for the things which they hold near and dear to their own and others' souls, and against their opposites in others. It is not Moses' case only, but every labourer's, to have his hearers rise up and say, 'You take too much upon you!'

If a man were to call me a rascal and a villain, I should be under much the same difficulty in justifying myself from his aspersions as you see I find in answering yours; but if you had 'duly' annexed several facts to each of these charges, then I might have denied or owned, admitted or refuted, as I saw occasion. But here, as you simply say, 'You have an overbearing spirit,' I can only say, as simply, 'I have not.'

Is my 'situation at Malda too much' for me, in a lucrative, or religious, or honourable, or pleasant view?—for you have left me at a loss to guess which you mean. As to the first, the situation I left was five or six times more profitable, for the time being, and always would have been superior. And so of the second, since I had greater numbers, a more public charge, greater and better reception in doctrine, offers, and hearty, unsuspected, undissembled love from the brethren. I say as much for the third, and more in a worldly point of view. The fourth is the only one upon which I have not so much to say. But even this, when you consider the absence of my wife and children, need not be considered 'too much for me;' especially if you remember the efforts that have been made to render it uncomfortable. However, if you think it is still 'too much,' you might lessen some of its advantages for me. But indeed, had you entirely forsaken me, and induced Mr. Udny to do so too, the justice of my cause and the consciousness of my injuries, would help me still to be a happy man, hoping in a faithful God; and I had determined on a lowly support in the Gospel, which I could, and, I believe, should, have had, even in that case.

Thus I have endeavoured to answer you; and oh! that I may be preserved from all these evil things, however I may be filled with the reproach of them.

I have written for your satisfaction only; for I verily think I am nothing altered in spirit, in temper, in conduct or imagination since I came to Malda. I am a man who fears God, loves our Lord Jesus Christ in sincerity, mistrusts himself, and is looking and waiting for the coming of Christ, having His authority to comfort myself and others with His word.

This spirited letter is unhappily not at all conciliatory in its tone, and, as may be supposed, it and other similar communications accomplished no reconciliation between the writer and his displeased friends in Calcutta. But no particular reply was made at the time by Mr. Grant, and Mr. Thomas hoped that his vindication of himself had been effectual.

The encouragement he had received in preaching at Bhulaháth, when going down to Calcutta, led him to renew his visits there, and many hundreds of people came together to hear him. They set up a rude platform for him to stand upon in preaching, brought him gifts of plaintains, and in other ways expressed the pleasure they felt in listening to his addresses. All this appearance of extraordinary interest in the gospel soon abated; but amongst his most regular hearers was a man of whom some special notice must be taken. This was Mohan Chandra Adhikári, a Bráhman, who had a great number of disciples, and was supported by their offerings. When he first attracted the preacher's attention it was in no very promising manner. How often first impressions are justified by after-events! "He constantly came, and heard me from the first," wrote Mr. Thomas, in his earliest reference to him, "but I always thought him a sour, ill-looking fellow, with the most unfavorable, forbidding countenance of them all; so that I felt myself quite discouraged whenever he appeared in sight." But at the end of October, this man came forward with several questions which seemed to indicate a strong desire to know the truth, and he was soon regarded as a very hopeful although in some respects an unsatisfactory enquirer. It may be feared that he was never anything but an unscrupulous and crafty impostor; but he long succeeded in hiding from Mr. Thomas his true character. After a few weeks, he wrote him some letters, which have been preserved, in two of which he professed to relate legends of the gospel history current amongst the Hindus. The deceitfulness of the attempt is most palpable, and the very forms of the names and the expressions he used show that he had simply recast in a Hindu form the facts the missionary had told him, and was now claiming for his version of them the character of Bengali folk-lore. That his motives in attaching himself to Mr. Thomas were selfish and impure, was speedily made evident by his solicitations to be helped in various secular matters. From this time, he is frequently spoken of in the journals as "the Brahman," and his character will be developed in the progress of this narrative. Other apparently very hopeful hearers were found in neighbouring villages, and Mr.

Thomas felt the strongest confidence in the success of his mission.

His munshi returned at the beginning of October, "full of the sweetness of the gospel," and Mr. Thomas was very anxious that his apparently sincere faith should be confessed, according to the commandment of the Lord Jesus. Carefully and patiently did the missionary expound to this supposed convert the nature and design of Christian baptism, hoping that an example of native consecration to Christ would speedily be exhibited in Bengal. But this was an issue to which Ram Basu was not at all willing to be brought. The call to decision led him to discover many insuperable difficulties in the way of his being at once baptized; and Mr. Thomas soon found that all his fair speeches were of very uncertain value, "he was such a halving soul." Still it was hard to surrender hope of success in such a case. Some of Christ's earliest followers were timid and undecided at first; and who could say but that this poor irresolute Bengali, and others who were like him, if once the restraints of caste were overcome, might, in the strength of Jesus Christ, endure the loss of all things, and emulate the zeal and fortitude of the apostles and martyrs of old?

The work of preaching to the European congregation, now containing thirteen persons, also proceeded prosperously. Mrs. Udny proved to be most kind and religiously disposed, though Mr. Thomas still thought that the influence of a lady at the head of the household tended to the increase of worldliness at Malda, since it led to visits from persons of high social position, but destitute of any satisfactory Christian principle. The controversies which had arisen were, for the present, quieted, and the discouragement of a too profuse correspondence with Calcutta issued in the avoidance of causes of agitation like those which had been so frequent in the former part of 1788.

There was, however, to be no revival of that happy intimacy which once existed between Mr. Thomas and his friends in Calcutta. He might for the present be left undisturbed at Malda as a missionary; but they would no more acknowledge him as a minister, or desire instruction from his lips as they once had done. Mr. Brown was now preaching regularly in the mission church, and he was their pastor. And indeed the circumstances under which he maintained this ministry recommended him much to the sympathy and confidence of his flock. His determination to preach at the Old Church, as it was called, cost him his situation at the Orphan House, from which the Managers dismissed him in August, 1788;* and although he took charge of the church with the sanction of the Presidency chaplains, he yet seems to have encountered some official difficulty in the discharge of his disinterested labours. The *Calcutta Gazette* of January 8th, 1789, published the following "Ecclesiastical Order," the point of which it is hard to understand, if it does not relate to the services Mr. Brown was holding in the mission church. Possibly the object of it was to make the continuance of those services clearly contingent upon the approval of the Presidency chaplains.†

* The reasons which induced the Managers of the Orphan House to deal so decidedly with Mr. Brown do not very clearly appear. They acknowledged "a just sense of the laudable motives which influenced him in forming engagements to officiate in the ministry of the mission church." Probably they considered that his position in the Orphan House, demanding, as he admitted, "all his zeal, perseverance, and affection," could not be efficiently maintained if, together with it, he attempted to discharge not only his duties as Garrison chaplain, but also the ministry of the Old Church. They do not appear to have treated him ungenerously. They had brought him out from England at an expense of Sa. Rs. 5336, and of this he seems not to have been required to refund any part.

† It is only fair to state that no hindrance to Mr. Brown's ministry at the mission church seems ever to have been offered by Messrs. Blanshard and Owen, the Presidency chaplains of that period.

But, *O si sic omnes!*—Towards the end of 1808, the Rev. Thomas Thomason, appointed to the mission church by the Court of Directors, commenced his useful and faithful ministry. After Mr. Thomason, on his arrival, had preached once at the Presidency church of St. John, the Rev. Dr. Ward, the Junior chaplain there, found means to prevent his reappearance in that pulpit, and afterwards presented a petition to the Governor General, Lord Minto, urging that the mission church should be opened for divine service only when the doors of St. John's were shut, since the congregation there was thinned by Mr. Thomason's preaching! At the close of 1813, after Mr. Brown's death, this ineffectual opposition to Mr. Thomason's ministry was revived. The Presidency chaplains then memorialized the Court of Directors, stating "that the population of Calcutta was not large enough to fill both churches," and they proposed, if

In order that the intention of Government may be without the possibility of mistake, relative to military chaplains doing occasional duty within the limits belonging to the Chaplains of the Presidency,—

It has been resolved that it be published in General Orders for the information of Military Chaplains, that they are prohibited from doing this duty except at the request of the Chaplains at the Presidency.

Mr. Brown, on being dismissed from the Orphan House, lost, of course, his salary and residence there;* but he was now Chaplain to the Garrison of Fort William, having been promoted to that post from the chaplaincy of a Battalion, in March, 1788, when the Rev. J. Owen vacated it to become Junior Presidency chaplain. Mr. Brown was also employed by Mr. Grant as tutor to his sons; and after Mr. Grant's departure to England, he established himself as a school-master in Calcutta.† In 1794, he became Junior Presidency chaplain, on the retirement of Mr. Owen; early in 1797, Mr. Blanshard's departure left him Senior Presi-

a substantial increase were made to their own salaries, to hold an additional service at St. John's, when the mission church might advantageously be shut up altogether, and Mr. Thomason could be removed to some military station up the country!

* The "salary and allowances of Mr. Brown as school-master, and Mrs. Brown as school-mistress," at the Orphan House, were together, Sa. Rs. 246 8 0 per mensem.

† Here is the advertisement which he published in the Calcutta newspapers.—
"ADVERTISEMENT.

"THE Reverend Mr. BROWN is willing to undertake the Education of a few Children; and hopes the Attention he shall be able to bestow on those who may be put under his Care, will give Satisfaction. He wishes to board such only as are under the Age of Twelve Years; and to take others as Day Scholars. He has rented, with this View, the House known by the name of Major De Glass's Garden, in Durrumtollah; the Situation of which, in respect to Healthiness and Convenience, is well known.

"His Terms, which he trusts will be deemed moderate, will be communicated, on Application to him, by Letter.

"*Calcutta, 10th June,* 1790."

This school was very successful, and, in a few years, Mr. Brown was able to purchase the house in which it was held.

For a Calcutta chaplain to supplement his income by keeping a school was no novelty at this time. At the beginning of 1786, the Rev. T. Blanshard, Junior Presidency chaplain, and the Rev. J. Owen, Garrison chaplain, jointly established a school for young gentlemen, under the patronage of some of the principal merchants in Calcutta.

dency chaplain; and, in 1800, he was made, in addition, Provost of the newly-established College of Fort William.*

No such career of well-paid service lay before Mr. Thomas. Amidst all these unhappy disputes, he must have felt keenly his dependent position and the precariousness of the income allowed him by Mr. Grant, of which an augmentation of displeasure might at any time wholly deprive him. A terrible aggravation of this painful dependence was now ready to befall him.

It has been already stated that he sent home in the *Earl of Oxford*, in March, 1787, a large consignment of Indian goods, by the favorable sale of which he expected to be relieved from all debts, and to be provided with a considerable surplus for the benefit of his family. Of the successful results of this speculation he had ever since been fully confident. In June, 1788, he heard that the goods had safely reached England, but no particulars of the sale were received until towards the end of January, 1789. Then word came from his agent in London that his muslins, &c., which were to have sold for £2000, had realized no more than £924, and so "he was plunged in debt, and his family in distress, and he saw no way of recovery." This great disaster arose from the state of the market at home. It was overstocked with such goods: the demand for Indian muslins having been impaired by the recent introduction of English manufactures. The effect produced by this intelligence may be readily imagined. Mr. Thomas was overwhelmed with grief, and ready to abandon himself to despair. He was, however, soon cheered by the goodness of his friend Mr. G. Udny, who wrote him "a very tender, kind, and genteel

* Such a career must be pronounced eminently successful. It had, of course, its drawbacks. Perhaps the chief of these was an attempt made in September, 1805, to obtain his dismissal from his chaplaincy. Three or four other chaplains united in this, urging that as he had received only deacon's orders, he was not qualified to hold the office to which he had been promoted. Especially, they accused him of unjustifiable presumption, in having taken upon him to administer the communion at the mission church,—a deacon being ordained only "to assist the priest in divine service, and specially when he ministereth the holy communion, and to help him in the distribution thereof." But this dangerous attempt to injure Mr. Brown did him little harm. The Government of that day did not concern itself with ecclesiastical discipline, and the matter came to nothing.

letter," offering "to advance half whatever was needed, and to ask Mr. Grant to advance the other half." The generosity of this promise deeply affected him, he acknowledged the offer most gratefully, and Mr. Grant was accordingly written to. He, however, was still seriously displeased with Mr. Thomas, and was little inclined to bestow upon him so large a sum of money,—at any rate unconditionally. The request led, therefore, to a renewal of those imputations, which had been felt to be so odious and unfair, and which Mr. Thomas had already, as he thought, satisfactorily replied to. Mr. Grant at length yielded a reluctant consent to provide the money, but stipulated that, if he did so, the missionary must at once remove to Goamalty, which would, of course, hinder his preaching in English at Malda, and that, further, he must no more trouble the good people at Malda and Calcutta with his Baptist notions. Yet another condition was added. Mr. Thomas had finished the translation of Matthew into Bengali, and was eager to print it. Mr. Grant, who probably thought that this translation had been undertaken in unfriendly rivalry with Mr. W. Chambers, and who concluded that it was a very imperfect version of the word of God, insisted that it should on no account be published.

Baptist translators of the New Testament within the present century have offended Christians of other denominations by their pertinacity in translating *all* the divine record; since it has been contended that it is desirable to leave some terms in the obscurity of the original Greek. It may be remarked of Mr. Thomas's version of Matthew, that it was charged with the opposite offence of retaining some words, not indeed from the Greek, but from his own vernacular! Despairing of any suitable Bengali renderings, he had introduced such terms as *gospel*, *Lord*, and *Holy Ghost*, by mere transliteration of the English words in Bengali characters, an arrangement which was justly regarded as very unsatisfactory.

Upon Mr. Grant's terms, Mr. Thomas conscientiously could not, and he would not, accept the help his circumstances so urgently needed. He lamented, he said, the unhappy consequences of his having spoken the truth as he had received it, but, nevertheless, as a faithful minister of Christ, he could not consent to be put to silence: he felt that he must, if occasion arose, "do the same again."

As to Goamalty, the reader will remember that, in June, 1788, he had been eager to go there at once, to escape the unpleasantness which had arisen out of the baptismal controversy at Malda. That purpose, he had thought better of, as soon as the irritated feeling out of which it arose subsided, and he had now come to the conclusion that the plan which would make him a resident at Goamalty was one he could in no wise adopt. It is not difficult to discover his reasons for this change of opinion and purpose.

The factory and village of Goamalty were built upon a grant of waste land, within the limits of the ancient city of Gour, which lies a few miles from Malda. The ruins of this city are not less than fifteen miles in length, extending along the old bank of the Ganges, and are two or three miles in breadth. At the time written of, villages had sprung up here and there within this area, and the land around them had been brought under cultivation. The remainder was covered with thick jungle, the habitation of wild animals. Bears, buffaloes, deer, wild hogs, monkeys, snakes, and pea and jungle-fowl abounded. "At night, the roar of the tiger, the cry of the peacock, and the howl of the jackal, with the accompaniment of rats, owls, and troublesome insects," were familiar to the ears of the few inhabitants who dwelt amidst these desolations.* For centuries, the ruins of Gour had been regarded as an immense quarry, whence bricks had been carried to Malda, Murshidábád, Rájmahal, and other places, and many majestic and beautiful edifices of great antiquity had been thus destroyed. Marble and stone, being rarities in Bengal, were the objects of constant de-

* See *the Ruins of Gour described and represented in eighteen views, &c.* by H. Creighton, 1817. Mr. Creighton died in 1807, and this book was published for the benefit of his family.

predation, which was so ruthlessly carried forward, that some noble structures were defaced or undermined for the sake of a few blocks or slabs of marble built into their brick walls. At the suggestion of Mr. Charles Grant, St. John's church was paved with stones taken from these ruins, and sent down by him to Calcutta, at a cost to the church building fund of Rs. 1258. Materials for floors, chimney pieces, and sepulchral monuments, were thus appropriated and carried off by any one disposed to take possession of them. At the time now written of, some of the gateways, mosques, and royal tombs were still tolerably perfect. The principal mosques were visited by pilgrims from the surrounding districts. Mr. Grant thought that these poor people, as they passed by Goamalty, might, with great advantage, be discoursed with by the missionary there, who would instruct them concerning the more excellent way; whilst the factory people, who had settled in the village for the sake of employment, to the number of about two hundred families, would very naturally attend to the teaching bestowed upon them by a missionary sent thither by the owner of the estate.

To all this Mr. Thomas had assented at the outset, and he went to Malda intending to carry out the plan. When, in July, 1787, he paid his first visit to Goamalty, however, he was very unfavorably impressed by it. He pronounced it "a miserably desolate and unwholesome place," and whilst he was "ashamed to be so tender" in regard to his abode, he greatly disliked the thought of living there.

As soon as he could speak a little in Bengali, he began to visit Goamalty regularly, and had a large company of apparently attentive hearers. He soon found, however, that many of them were Musulmans, who understood Hindustani much better than Bengali. This was a great obstacle in the way of his usefulness; and he saw other reasons to disapprove of the original plan. The character of the people settled here seemed to him very much to resemble that of the refugees in the cave of Adullam, wherein were gathered from all the country round "every one that was in distress, and every one that was in debt, and every one that was discontented." " I consider Goamalty an out-of-the-way place," he wrote, " and little better than a pent up harbour of thieves and the lowest order of the people ; and I regard my going there, though formerly designed, as *unfit* and *improper.*" On the other hand, he had found at Bhulaháth, Cossimpur, and other places upon the Mahanuddy river, regular and attentive audiences; and his work seemed to him to lie amongst the people who continually flocked about him at these villages. In this opinion, he stedfastly refused to yield to Mr. Grant's peremptory demand that he should now make Goamalty his home. He felt most strongly in the matter. " I *did* think," he wrote, " that I was to go there; but not *strictly* and *irrevocably*. I *did* intend to go there; but providence and changes led me to relinquish the design, and Mr. Grant's letter has now made me *abhor* it, since I perceive that Goamalty is neither friendly nor hopeful ground." He contended for some freedom of choice in a matter so closely affecting his own comfort and missionary usefulness, and pleaded apostolic example.—" Even the great apostle gave up his own wish and opinion, when he saw a mind which was more immediately concerned about the right or wrong, than his own, strongly bent against it.—' As touching our brother Apollos, I greatly desired him to come unto you with the brethren ; but his will was not at all to come at this time ; but he will come when he shall have convenient time.'— 1 Corinthians xvi. 12."

Thus no concession was made by either party. Mr. Grant would give the help required only upon the terms he laid down.* Mr. Thomas felt that those terms oppress-

---

* The following extract from the will of Mr. Charles Grant shows that his desire to have a mission established at Goamalty was never extinguished.—

" Further,... I give and bequeath... to the Protestant mission in Bengal, conducted, at present, by the Rev. Dr. William Carey, and others, in token of my esteem for their labours and desire for their further success, £200. And I also bequeath, to the said mission, a parcel of land which I possess in fee, at Goamalty, in the neighbourhood of Malda, in Bengal ; the said parcel, exclusive of the ground whereon certain Indigo works, belonging to me, stand, which ground I do not make over to the mission, may be about 900 or 1000 bigahs in measurement (equivalent to about 300 of our acres). This land I do not give as being likely to procure much annual rent, but to be useful as a missionary station."

ed his conscience and robbed him of his freedom as a Christian missionary, and he would not accept them. The correspondence irritated feelings which were already unduly excited; and at length he allowed his indignation to guide his pen. Mr. Grant had persisted in his former charges as to "self seeking," &c., which Mr. Thomas considered so odiously unjust, and which he thought he had abundantly refuted, and the latter now wrote rejecting his conditions, and even declining his further acquaintance, unless Mr. Grant would do him the justice to soften the terms of his animadversions upon his character.

This renunciation of his patron's correspondence, whilst he did not renounce the support he received from him, does not appear to have struck Mr. Thomas's mind as being any thing anomalous or extraordinary. He was indeed very sensible that Mr. Grant's assistance would probably be withdrawn; and he soon saw that, with Mr. Grant's favor, he was losing his hold upon the help and regard of his Malda friends. To them Mr. Grant wrote, complaining of Mr. Thomas's conduct in the matter; and the missionary also addressed them, in defence of himself, with much warmth of feeling. He says in this letter,—

Mr. Grant being called a brother, and having vilified me, the Scripture prescribes to me the steps I have taken concerning further acquaintance; but this I do, not for any personal affront; for except what he has done among my hearers, I never feel any personal opposition or offence; but I mourn for a hindered gospel and wounds which now seem to be incurable.

No 'untempered mortar' can I use to build up the desolate breaches. That which I have received of the Lord *is* awfully resisted. I rely upon my God now to bring forth my cause as the noon day; and I know He will do it, although many must take leave of me. I am content now to wait patiently for the Lord, and, declaring to Israel his sins, to endure the contempt and forsakings of all; and, if it should please God, a broken heart, to finish a short pilgrimage, which I have made to heaven, ' without golden slippers, but with wet feet and pain and sorrow,' as Rutherford expresses it.

The pecuniary bequest "was generously doubled by Lord Glenelg;" but, perhaps in consideration of that arrangement, the gift of the land at Goamalty seems never to have been carried into effect.

I am ripe for forgiveness of friends or enemies; but I must uphold my cause, as a good one.

I find the God who hath so humbled and abased me among you, is 'a God at hand,' and 'the God of hope;' 'the God of patience,' and 'the God of consolation,' and next to my own soul, if not before it, I desire fervently for you all, nearness to Him. Thy will, O Lord, be done! In writing this, I have just given the simple thoughts that came uppermost. I see myself destined to a sorrowful life and everlasting joy. By taking thought, I cannot add one cubit to my stature. Therefore the will of the Lord be done.

Notwithstanding the kindness he continued to receive at Malda, his relations there were now greatly disturbed. Mr. Udny was naturally influenced by Mr. Grant's view of his proceedings, and as Mr. Grant would not accede to the proposal to pay his debts, Mr. Udny also finally withdrew his generous offer. It would have been far better for the unhappy debtor had that generous offer never been made. In that case, he must have grappled with his difficulty as he himself could; and he must have done it at once. But, comforted as he was by Mr. Udny's promise of aid, and by his prompt assurance, "We can both very well do it," he wrote off to his creditors, engaging that they should speedily be paid,—an engagement not to be fulfilled. He was also encouraged to think that his Indian friends *ought to* extricate him from his debt, as he believed they could most easily do; and the expectation that sooner or later they would do it took possession of his mind. Unreasonable as this expectation may have been, he justified it by the considerations that his calamity befell him *after* he had left his more lucrative profession to become a missionary,—that the payments and sacrifices he had made in order to obtain his release from the ship formed a considerable part of his deficit,—and that, if he had gone home to manage his own affairs, much of the loss he suffered would have been escaped.

But, although Mr. Thomas was determined not to live at Goamalty, he was quite willing to have his habitation away from Malda, in some spot favorable to the prosecution of his work amongst the natives. Such a spot he believed he had discovered, in December, 1788, at Harla

Gáchí, about six miles from Mr. Udny's residence, and near to Bhulaháth. This was a piece of ground containing about fifty bigas, belonging to the Factory at Malda, "a beautiful and fit place for a bungalow." After some hesitation, Mr. Grant consented to the proposal that the missionary should make this place his home, and gave Rs. 500 to build him a bungalow there. Mr. Udny generously supplemented this by as much more as sufficed to erect a very small brick house instead, and it was made ready for occupation by the end of October, 1789.* From the time the place was selected, Mr. Thomas constantly visited it and endeavoured to make it the centre of his missionary efforts.

From the middle of February, till towards the end of August, 1789, Mr. Thomas's diary, if he kept one, has not been preserved, and only a few particulars can be recovered. That the history thus lost was a painful one will appear but too plainly in the following extracts from a letter written to Mr. G. Udny in March, 1790. In this epistle, after acknowledging his former great kindness and courtesy, Mr. Thomas said to him.—

It pleased God to impress my mind and heart with some inevitable evils approaching to try us all to the utmost. I gave warning repeatedly, and am sorry to see the issue of all. I could by no means think at that time that the preaching of any part of the gospel which you well understood I had received, would ever give you such offence, especially Baptism by Immersion, for I had heard you say, that, if you had children, they should all be immersed. But, when I had occasion to baptize, you were quite incensed; which fact I have no need to dwell upon, because you furnished me with a very becoming confession in writing. Soon after, I endeavoured to convince you that it was necessary for you also to be immersed, and to consent to the practice of the apostles, if you would come to the Lord's-table: and this I did without heat or passion at any time, and it is my comfort that I have a faithful and true witness in God.

* This first Mission House contained a hall, 21 feet by 15, and a bed-room, 15 feet by 15. The rooms were 16 feet high. The verandas at the sides of the house were covered with straw; but were enlarged, and one of them rebuilt of brick, by Mr. Thomas, which cost him "about Rs. 700."

Besides all this, the society at Malda seemed to me to be making swift approaches by worldly compliances and carnal prosperity to the very state of the people of Laish, 'who dwelt careless, after the manner of the Zidonians, quiet and secure; and there was no magistrate in the land, that might put them to shame in any thing; and they were far from the Zidonians, and had no business with any man.'—Judges xviii. 7. You yourself had greatly impaired the efficacy of my ministry and the force of all my earnest endeavours to build and edify you, by bringing a part of my labours into contempt, and, with wealth and power on your side, what was I that I could withstand you? and, yet, I did not see you decline quietly, but boldly urged in a close warning. In the same manner as I feared, all is come to pass, and more also. Our disagreements were inflamed to such a degree, that at last you even took the greatest offence where I thought you would have have great pleasure and profit, and what was preached to you in meekness and love, in the sincerity of my heart, for your everlasting benefit, and of the greatest moment, served only to cavil at, and quarrel over at your dinner-table; and, by a very bad example, you openly and passionately dishonoured yourself.... Thus being, to the very last extremity, opposed in one city, I fled to another; but surely I staid as long as ever an ambassador for Christ ought to stay. I determined to leave you; at least for the present. As soon as I was gone, you sent me a letter, and, soon after, another, which seemed very sincerely to signify your repentance, wherein also it was evident that you knew I had not withdrawn without just cause, that I had conducted myself in all other respects to your satisfaction, and that you yourself had behaved very ill, and knew it. These are your own words:—

'My love to you is fixed upon a foundation which I am sure cannot be moved. As I love Christ, so I must love every one who bears His image. I have always been forward to declare that I esteemed your ministration amongst us a blessing: that I was benefited by it, and so were others. I wish I had spoken my apprehensions in private, and with more of the temper and moderation which becometh the gospel. I do not think I am warranted to hinder myself or others from the benefit of your preaching, and therefore request you to come back to us.'

I returned, forgiving from the heart, and not once suspecting it possible that you could have called me back to have the pleasure of turning me out so soon afterwards. By Mr. Grant's letters, I was astonished to perceive that he had been told quite a different story.

He was complained to that I had left you in sudden violent resentment. What a comfort it is to look up and calmly say, 'Lord, thou seest: thou knowest!' I preached again amongst you, but the destroyer had not left you. He very soon after aimed another head-stroke at my ministry, and, on my preaching from Revelation ii. 20-22, Mrs. Udny took that character to herself, hardly spoke for three days, and the whole family was in an uproar again. Your brother was now come, whom I had but just before restored to the use of his limbs, and he entered into this confederacy, and carried you on in it with spirit. I saw his countenance fallen, and inquired into it, and was not only given so to understand, but that he himself believed that the devil was in me,—that I had been impudent in staying so long with you,—and he would not wonder at what I did!

Whilst his relations at Malda were thus unsettled, Mr. Thomas made another journey to Calcutta, where he arrived on the 18th of August, 1789. He went to the city again in the hope that his wife and children might arrive in one of the ships then due. He received, however, only letters informing him that Mrs. Thomas had again declined the much dreaded voyage. He took with him his múnshi and the Brahman Mohan Chand, of whose conversion he now felt confident, and he hoped that Mr. Grant and others in Calcutta might be excited to renewed interest in the mission by the evidence these persons afforded that the word of God was taking effect upon the natives of Bengal. Another principal object of the visit was to remove, if possible, Mr. Grant's displeasure, and to effect the withdrawal of what he regarded as his very mysterious opposition to the publication of the translation of Matthew, and in any case to arrange for putting the book at once to press. He hoped too that some way of deliverance from his terrible load of debt might be opened before him.

But the visit only increased his mortifications and difficulties. He went to stay at the Orphan House, where Mr. James Mackay was head-master of the school for officers' sons, and Mr. Burney assistant-master of the school for the children of private soldiers and non-commissioned officers. A few extracts from his journal will show how full of discomfort his visit must have been.—

Lord's-day, August 23d.—I heard Mr. Brown preach from the words,—'And when he is come, he will reprove the world of sin.' —John xvi. 8. I was little delighted. The congregation was very small. He preached about thirty-six minutes, which was said to be unusually long.

I arrived last Tuesday, and have been ever since with Burney and Mackay: little, I fear, either to my own profit or to their's. I find sad jarrings and disgusts, complaints and disputes, among all at the Orphan House. These, however, are not so high and uncommon as those I am involved in; as the following little incident will show.

When I asked Mr. Burney to come to church with me this morning, he called me aside, and begged me to excuse his accompanying me! The disputes between me and other friends ran so high, he said, that he, who took no part on either side, did not wish to compromise himself by appearing in public with me! I reasoned with him to no purpose, and he went on to tell me that the Rev. David Brown, having heard I was coming down, sent him a note, in which he besought him, *for the honour of the gospel*, not to associate with me! I was surprised, and still dissuaded him from absenting himself from church; but without effect.

I preached in the evening at Burney's house, from—'We know that all things work together for good to them that love God.'—Romans viii. 28.

Monday.—I left the Orphan House, and wandered about. On my arrival in Calcutta, I wrote to Mr. Grant, and told him all was well at Malda, &c. He replied, acknowledging my note, and expressing his good wishes for my welfare, notwithstanding my having acted in opposition to his judgment and advice, and in departure from my agreement with him. To-day, I replied, deliberately and meekly, and besought reconciliation with him.

Tuesday.—Having slept last night at Moore's, thus inadvertently depriving a young man of his bed, and having dined there to-day, I departed, heavy and sad, to my boat again, in a most depressed condition of mind.

Wednesday.—Moved up the river, hoping to find a quiet place to anchor my boat. I attempted to speak to the people; but found myself so dejected, I could not.

Thursday.—This day I hoped to spend in quiet meditation and prayer; but was sadly disconcerted last night by distressing tidings from Malda, by which it appears that Bill Long has incurred Mr. Udny's displeasure.

In the evening, went to preach on the shore. After tea, several natives gathered near the boat. We sung a hymn, and, desiring them all to sit down, múnshi and Brahman, of their own accord, began religious conversation with the strangers. I silently heard them zealously contending for some time, and then addressed the people myself; especially I endeavoured to deal with a very knotty cavil of one of them, who asked *if sin and all evil did not proceed from God Himself*." In this belief, they often take occasion to make light of the evil and danger of sin. After speaking to them with much fervour, we prayed and sung. Altogether we were about two hours with them. They eagerly asked if they might come again on the morrow.

O my God, I desire to thank and bless Thee for restored liberty and utterance, with which I have now been enriched and helped. The joy of this hour has cancelled my cares and sorrows of many days past. Give me, O my God, a clean heart, and renew in me a right spirit, and prepare my way before these poor people. Oh bear witness, enlighten, and confirm.

His journal shows how keenly he felt the loss of the high esteem and love in which his Calcutta friends once held him. It shows too how, even in "dishonour" and "evil report," he was constant and fearless in rebuking profaneness and sin, in whatever company he found himself; and he saw reason to believe that in this conflict with the common vices of Calcutta society, the Lord gave him a tongue and wisdom which his adversaries could not resist or gainsay.*

* An extract from a letter written to Mrs. Powell, Mr. Thomas's aunt, in September, may illustrate this remark.

"I have lately been at Captain White's, but the dreadful oaths and curses I heard there made his house loathsome to me. When I dined there, I always called them up to ask a blessing. The old captain did not like it; but, afterwards, conformed. He is near his last end, I fear; and my opinion of his case put him in fear also. They said I was *worse* than I used to be; but, though that means *better*, yet I cannot say that it is true. Upon the whole, from the greatest to the least, all through Calcutta, with few exceptions, there is such drinking, lying, blasphemy, deceit, hypocrisy, and every unclean and hurtful lust, with hardly any good people to save them, that I should not wonder if it was to be burnt with lightning or swallowed by an earthquake. Their tenets are deism throughout; hardly a man free. One person had the indecency to swear several horrid oaths before me at table, in a large company. He was a perfect stranger to me; but I was determined to reprove him. Opportunity soon offered. I heard the same man speak of one Williams, and say he was a good man. 'Only,' said I, 'he used to swear so horridly, that it was a misery to be in company where he was.' He answered 'He might be a good man for all that.' 'That is impossible,'

His attempts to conciliate Mr. Grant were productive of no success, and the little further intercourse he had with his once affectionate patron was full of unpleasantness. As to the unfortunate translation, Mr. Grant had sent the MS. of the Bengali Matthew to Mr. Grassman, a Moravian missionary, who was supposed to know the language, and he had reported unfavorably upon it. Mr. Thomas therefore went to Serampore to see this critic, whose chief objections he was able to remove, whilst he saw reason to think that Mr. Grassman was ill qualified to give counsel in the matter which had been submitted to his judgment.* As, however, Mr. Grant continued unalterably adverse to the printing of the translation, Mr. Thomas applied to Mr. Cooper, a printer in Calcutta, for an estimate of the cost of its publication, and determined, if possible, to accomplish the work by a public subscription.

His debts lay heavily upon his mind, and, in despair of help from his friends, he was, for a day or two, inclined to listen to proposals made him by Mr. John Moore, a commission agent in Calcutta, that he should enter into

said I. It went home; and he said at last, 'Why, I myself swear!' 'Then, Sir,' said I, 'you are in a lost condition, though you will not believe it.' The conversation continued about three hours, in which I had a fine opportunity of pouring out my witness against their unrighteous deeds, and that before a large number of profane persons. They were still and silent, and the man in question, who is an opulent tradesman, asked me to come and dine with him, acknowledging his fault before the company. So much to his credit; but he is still the same."

Captain White died on the 10th of October, 1789. His tomb-stone commemorates the "Christian fortitude" with which he bore his "long and tedious illness." He had been in the service of the East India Company from the time he was twelve years old.

* He says in his journal,—

"It is remarkable that Mr. Grant should make so much of Mr. Grassman's opinion of my translation. My múnshi asked his sircar if his master understood much of the Bengal language: he answered, No; very little: he always spoke to him in Portuguese. He then asked him how many months he had been with him? and he said, Six or seven years, off and on. He asked if he knew the word of God? or Bible? No: he had never heard of it. Had he heard of one Jesus Christ, a Saviour? No, never. Mr. Grassman himself told me that he kept no múnshi; and that to the man that was with him to examine my translation, he paid only 5 rupees a month. I conclude from all this and other things which he himself said to me about the conversion of the natives, that if twenty thousand such men were to come and spend their lives here, there would never be one convert among them all."

partnership with him. He speedily rejected this project, however, and resolved to devote himself more completely than ever to his mission work. In the painful alienation which had arisen at Malda, he was almost ready to abandon that neighbourhood, and to make Calcutta his home; and he had thoughts of trying to support himself by the publication of a weekly paper, to be called *The Friend*: a project which he soon saw reason to abandon.

In the meanwhile, he lived in his boat, moving up and down the river, and preaching constantly to the people he met upon the banks. The múnshi and Brahman assisted him in this work with much apparent earnestness, and his confidence in the reality of their conversion grew stronger daily. An extract from his journal may interest the reader, as describing a suttee, one of those scenes of horror which were often before the eyes of men sojourning in India, when he began his mission.* The occurrence related took place at Báli, half way between Calcutta and Serampore.

* It is pleasant to know that this horrible practice was never so frequent as was supposed, even by the best informed enquirers, before the matter was investigated by Government authority. In 1787, the Rev. D. Brown wrote to the Rev. Robert Robinson of Cambridge,—" My very learned friend, Mr. William Chambers, has computed that about 50,000 widows are, in these provinces, burnt annually with their husbands!" That must have been a mere conjecture. "In 1803, an enquiry was set on foot by Dr. Carey; and, by an actual enumeration, it was found, that, in a small district round Calcutta, 275 burnings took place within six months; and it was therefore estimated that in all the Bengal provinces no fewer than 10,000 persons were thus consigned to death in the course of a year." This number was therefore confidently assumed to be about the truth, and was used by the Baptist missionaries in their public statements. Enquiries made by order of the Supreme Government, however, showed that, from 1815 to 1818, the average annual number of widows burned and buried alive, in the Bengal Presidency, fell below 600! Mr. Charles Lushington, Chief Secretary to Government, on the strength of these returns, designated the estimate of the Baptist missionaries as "one of the most preposterous misrepresentations that ever proceeded from credulity or ignorance." There was, however, some reason to doubt the completeness of the official returns. In 1815, only 378 cases were reported, but in 1818, 839; an increase which the authorities themselves were willing to ascribe to "greater vigilance on the part of the police in ascertaining and reporting suttees." The enquiry also showed that the custom was to a great extent local, —some districts being nearly or altogether free from it. It is strange that this fact was not more considered by the missionaries. Dr. Carey had been in India more than five years before he witnessed a suttee. During this period, he had lived chiefly in the Dinájpur district, where they were infrequent.

Lord's-day, August 30th, 1789.—I was called up this morning upon the bank, to see a woman who was going to be burnt alive with her dead husband. I found a great concourse of people gathered together, and the pile preparing. The dead body was close by; and the unhappy woman was a little on one side, being daubed over with turmeric, which is used in their superstitions. The Brahmans being all around her, I asked for the chief; who seemed excessively confident that he was doing right. I talked with him of the crime of murder, and of self murder; and of the great wrath of Almighty God revealed against all murder. He and others pleaded, first the shastras, then their custom, and, last of all, caste. Some present assisted me by saying there was no commandment to do so in the shastras. I argued that, if there were, it must be a shastra of men, or devils, and not of God. And, as to custom, I said, it was the custom of thieves to steal, and of murderers to kill, and it was the custom of many men to ruin themselves in soul and body for ever; but was that any just reason why we should do so too? These and other arguments they assented to, and said that my words were very good. But, last of all, they came to the miserable motive which was chief with them, and that was, they said, if she did not burn, the family would lose caste. All her relations seemed to me influenced by this; and rather than they should suffer disgrace, they were glad that she should suffer a cruel and untimely death.

Moreover I told them that inasmuch as it was the Brahmans' duty, according to the shastras, to forbid all evil among the common people, and they were present, aiding and assisting in this murder, they must be obnoxious to punishment,—every one of them for neglect, and how much more such of them as were active in such a horrid cause.

They had now been hindered for some time in their ceremony, and they entreated me to depart. I was determined to stay, and be at least an eye witness of the whole, so I refused. They became clamorous, and some of them violent; but I told them I knew I was amongst murderers, and they might murder me if they pleased; but I would rather lose my life than go away. And so I was determined to do; but I really had no apprehension of their doing more than lift me out of their way. Then others persuaded them to be quiet, and begged me to remove a few cubits from the pile. To this I yielded, and, after repeated and gentle entreaties, removed further and further by degrees.

Before this, I should say, the woman had gone off to a little distance. I insisted on speaking with her; but this was strongly objected to. I told them I certainly would, if I died for it.* They said that she could not speak to me; and I replied, I only wanted to speak to her, and would not require her to give any answer to what I should say. At length they yielded, and the Brahmans themselves made a path through the multitude, down to the river, where the poor woman was. She was an elderly person, at least fifty years old. Her attendants withdrew, and left her standing in the water, about two feet deep. I asked her, whether or not it was of her own will, or by persuasion of the Brahmans, that she was going to do this violence to herself. She answered, it was of her own will. I endeavoured to prove to her, that no law of God ever required any such thing. I told her that she and I were both sinners against God already;—that we were in this world for a short time, and that there was another state prepared for us. I added, 'You are going to die; or rather, to kill yourself. This is a great sin. God will be very angry with you. Have pity—have mercy on yourself and your children.—Consider what you are about. Your pains of body will soon be over; but your soul will fall into hell-fire, and suffer the punishment of self-murderers.'

She seemed to be ready enough to converse. She pointed up to the heavens, and, with seeming composure, said something that I could not hear; but this I understood plainly, pointing to her forehead, she said it was all written there. The bystanders also told me, that she said she had died six times before with this same husband. She was not only infatuated with the dreams and superstitions of the country, but was evidently intoxicated, either with opium, bhang, or spirits. Her speech was thick, and her tongue and eyes heavy, while there was a merry cast upon her countenance. In fact, had I seen her in the field, and on any other occasion, I should have said, That is a drunken woman.

I found all I said was of no avail, and returned to the pile, with my soul in uproar. I alternately looked and tormented my own spirit, and then cried out, and told them their hands were imbrued

* Interference with the rite, and especially any attempt to lay hold on the victim, who was thereby defiled and rendered unable to burn, was most angrily resented by the Hindus. The Dutch Director Sichterman—already referred to on page 26—paid a heavy penalty for his humanity, which led him to interfere on such an occasion. He was compelled to appease the popular commotion thus raised by giving Rs. 25,000 to the Brahmans! The redoubtable Job Charnock, the founder of Calcutta, however, boldly rescued a young widow, and is said to have made her his wife. His violence easily prevailed, where the kindly-intentioned Dutchman's entreaties issued only in loss and disgrace.

in innocent blood; and that in the account of God they were murderers. Some said my words were very true. The dead body was then laid on the pile, and a little rice and curry set before its mouth. Then, after being washed, the woman was brought from the river, with a basket of *koey*, or parched rice, in her hand. This she scattered about; and, seeing the people scramble for it, she, looking down beside her basket, actually laughed, as though she had not been the victim. I do not think she was suffered to walk alone. I am sure it would have been very crookedly, had she done so. She was now immediately laid on the pile; in their doing which she showed some reluctance, by objecting to the placing of the wood, or some other trifle, which they overruled with a great deal of noise. Her right arm being placed under the head of the dead body, and she lying by its left side, dry *tál* or *toddy-tree* leaves were thrown over them both, and upon these a quantity of oil or *ghí* was poured. On the side where the woman lay, two long bamboos were fastened by ropes to a stake, driven into the earth at the edge of the pile; and the leaves having been laid over the bodies, these bamboos were bent over the pile, and, a man taking hold of each, they were pulled down, so that they must have compressed the bodies like a lemon-squeezer: only the slender bamboos were too flexible to crush her, being intended only to secure her, and to restrain her dying struggles. The nearest relative then set fire to the pile beneath her head, and, with a great shout, they drowned all her expiring shrieks. The flames began slowly to consume, and so ended this horrid scene. I would have made yet more strenuous attempts to save the unhappy victim, but I was well assured that all would be in vain.

I wonder that the Government has never done any thing to put a stop to this most inhuman practice. I am persuaded that if a smart fine were laid on the surviving family, it would effectually prevent it throughout the whole country; and the money might be given to the poor, or to imprisoned natives, This would very well accord with their own notions, and it would be such a close and strong inducement to the family to dissuade the widow from burning, that the custom would soon become obsolete. So several intelligent natives whom I have consulted also think. Other methods might be devised by more able counsellors. Surely every upright mind must so revolt against this detestable and useless practice, as fervently to wish that something may be done to abolish it.

Almost any thing, possessing the sanction of Government, would have a good effect; for now it is believed that the Government approves of it; and indeed the people quoted Mr. Hastings's conduct on such occasions to convince me that it really was so.*

The building of the little mission house at Harla Gáchí was meanwhile proceeding, but not without obstructions. The zemindar of Bhulaháth first disputed the title to the ground, and, when the authorities set aside his claims in that respect, he endeavoured to hinder the spread of the gospel by petty persecution of any who were disposed to join themselves to the missionary. Mr. Thomas saw in this conduct a daring defiance of Him whose messenger he felt himself to be, and had ventured to say to his converts that he was afraid this enemy of the truth would suffer a visitation of God's awful judgment. On reaching Calcutta, he heard of the sudden death of this man, and immediately concluded that sentence had gone forth against him according to his word!

Mr. Thomas's debt must have been a source of great vexation to Mr. Grant, and to Mr. Udny also. They had shown their anxiety for his release from his pecuniary difficulties by the generous proposals which had unhappily become abortive,† and they thought, since Mr. Thomas had practically declined their help, he ought now to give up his missionary work, and go back to his former profession, in order, if possible, to meet the demands of his creditors. When therefore Mr. Grant found that he was in treaty with Mr. Cooper to print his translation of Matthew, he was very seriously displeased, since he saw in this arrangement, not only utter disregard to his own wishes, but an increase of hopeless debt. He wrote therefore a letter of severe remonstrance, the extraordinary

---

* Mr. Thomas sent an account of this suttee to the editor of the *Calcutta Chronicle*, and it appeared both in that paper and in the *Calcutta Gazette* of September 3d. From the latter, it has been reprinted in Mr. Seton-Karr's *Selections*, vol. ii. page 224.

† Mr. Grant had actually complied with Mr. G. Udny's proposals, and had sent him, as his share of the sum which was to be remitted on Mr. Thomas's behalf, £550, when the matter was set aside by the missionary's persistent refusal of the conditions his friends as firmly laid down. He wrote to his brother,— "When the money was offered me, some injunctions that very much affected my religious liberty, and which I would by no means consent to, were laid upon me; and therefore the kindness intended was repaid."

effects of which will be best exhibited in Mr. Thomas's own words.—

September 15th. Mr. Grant sent a messenger after me to Nuddea, with a letter, telling me that he had heard of my being about to print my translation of Matthew's Gospel,—advising me against it, and intimating that he is not obliged to afford any countenance or aid to it. In plain English, he threatens to punish me for it by discontinuing his support.

This is one of the most extraordinary things I ever heard of. A missionary threatened by his supporter with severest punishment, for translating a Gospel! I was half-distracted; but went to prayer with my people at night. Still I found myself so utterly dejected that I got up, and departed, alone and in the dark, to a solitary place, and there prayed, or rather groaned, to Christ. I besought Him, if I was His servant, and if God had not forsaken me, that, at this extraordinary moment, He would grant me extraordinary help, and would answer and direct me, before I returned to my people. I felt assured that He was able to send to me,—to use a voice, or by some other method, even before I got back to my boat. But there seemed to be no reply: my dejection continued: I was come within a stone's-cast of my boat, still praying and expecting that the Lord would help me,—or else I must despair and die,—when, lo! I heard a voice, from out of a boat full of people, say distinctly in Bengalese, *Jemíndár jor kare;* and, presently after, *Kál jáibe!**

On hearing these first words, my mind was immediately impressed with a sense of God's wonderful power, in having stopped, by a sudden death, the persecution and threatenings of the late zemindar at Bhulaháth; and the thought followed, that He was undoubtedly able to help and deliver me again, in any way He saw good. From the other words, I understood that I was not to send Mr. Grant's messenger away now, with the short note I had given him; but on the morrow, with a bold and deliberate reply.

I returned comforted, and with my mind fully made up! It was remarkable, though the man was talking very fast, that these were the only words I could at all distinguish or understand. I know that illusions happen; but this was no illusion, but a gracious interposition of providence.

The reader may well be startled at such a wild conclusion. Two little unconnected Bengali sentences, reach-

---

* জেমীদার জোর করে।—" The Zemindar uses violence." কাল যাইবে।—" He will go to-morrow."

ing his ear amidst the din of a crowd of vociferous natives, suggest to his mind thoughts as to God's purposes and his own duty, in a most serious crisis in his history, which he thereupon accepts as divinely communicated, and he ventures his very means of support upon the belief that they were really so!

The journal proceeds,—

Wednesday, September 16th.—This morning, I called my beloved mûnshi and the Brahman, and told them all; asking them what I had best do? They advised me to carry on the translation, and not to fear Mr. Grant, but to fear God. We then all prayed. Múnshi said in his prayer, 'Who these are, O Lord, or what they are, that hinder this work, whether good or bad, we do not know. Thou alone art Judge; but, Oh, send us Thy help!' &c.

I prayed in Bengalese also, and had very great liberty and strength poured into my soul. Afterwards, I rose up, and in ten hours finished a reply to Mr. Grant, telling him the work would go on and be printed,—even if a press and types had to be made on purpose for it. I said we feared no threats; but would fear God, and 'at destruction and famine we would laugh.' I concluded with quotations from *Luther on the Galatians*, concerning false brethren, who opposed, after a time, those whom at first they received with great love.

But now, if the Lord look not down, and with His own omnipotent arm work our deliverance, we are undone. If He prevent not, Mr. Grant will now forsake me, and that will not satisfy him, but he will write to Mr. Udny, and influence him to do the same. Enemies enough there are, and afflictive providences too; so that in a little while I may become a very *fakír*.

This evening, I went ashore, dejected to the back-bone. I could not lift up my head; but, constraining myself, I sent for my bible, and, with a view to the profit of the Brahman and mûnshi, I read the commencement of John viii. As I read those gracious words, my spirit revived within me, and great was my refreshment and liberty in expounding and praying; so that mûnshi also took particular notice of it. Afterwards, we walked through the bazar, and preached Christ, and one man in particular seemed affected. I returned to my solitary boat, and read of the distresses of Jeremiah with wonder and comfort.

Friday.—By reading the Scriptures, and especially the prophets, I am comforted and strengthened. Since Mr. Grant has threatened to abandon me if I persist in publishing St. Matthew's Gospel, I find my mind vastly encouraged and incited to do it. I believe also that it will be best to persevere boldly, and not draw back; and that the Lord will indeed 'strengthen the spoiled against the strong,' and bless the poor and afflicted, and 'feed the poor of the flock with Beauty and Bands.'—Zechariah xi. 7.

Saturday.—'*Whosoever shall lose his life, for my sake, shall save it.*' —I see then nothing so tremendous, in the friendships, the salary, the comforts and conveniences of my life being lost, for Christ's sake, since, under all, He has put His promise and protection, and I am able to lay hold of it; and out of all these afflictions, I doubt not but there will be a furtherance of the gospel: and be that my only desire.

I feel sure that my debt happened to me, in part, to try those who were quite able to deliver me, but they delivered me not; and also to chastise me, and to humble and prove me; and, if so, in due time, the Lord will remove it; for He will not always chide. Let me be patient and submissive then, and wait till it is the good pleasure of God to deliver me. If I knew all, perhaps I should see that these afflictions are the best things that ever befell me.

The tendencies of Mr. Thomas's mind to crave supernatural interpositions, and his confidence that his own conclusions were authenticated by special divine direction, have again and again appeared in this narrative. A few months previously, he wrote about Goamalty, in a letter to Mr. Grant, "The Lord's dealings with me of old, have taught me to look to, and understand, His directions in all such matters, and never swerve. The issue has ever hitherto proved, and always will prove, how 'blessed is the man that trusteth in Him.'" He acted now in the same confidence, and proceeded with a conscientious, however ill-founded and headstrong, reliance upon his best judgment of the Lord's will.

On the 21st of September he returned to Calcutta, and was a witness of another suttee fire, at which he arrived too late to interfere with the performance of the cruel rite. He could only warn and exhort the Brahmans as they dispersed from the dreadful scene.

The arrangements for printing Matthew in Bengali, unhappy as the consequences arising out of them had been, came to nothing. Mr. Cooper wrote to Mr. Hay, the

Secretary to Government, to ascertain if the publication would be regarded with disapproval by the Governor General; and he was told in reply that Lord Cornwallis would neither hinder nor encourage it. But, in the lack of funds to meet the great expense of printing, the work was for the present postponed; and, on the 3d of October, Mr. Thomas left Calcutta to return to Malda, if indeed he was to be permitted any longer to reside in that once hospitable home. In passing Serampore, he again called upon Mr. Grassman, who examined part of his translation whilst he remained there, and "found no fault but what was presently overruled."* He had, he said, written to Mr. Grant, and not to the translator's prejudice.

But, after the defiant letter he had received from Nuddea, Mr. Grant was sufficiently assured that Mr. Thomas would in nothing be directed or restrained by his wishes and advice, and his anger was very unhappily aggravated at this time by the following circumstance.—After some delay, the Society for Promoting Christian Knowledge had found a successor to Mr. Kiernander, in the person of the Rev. Abraham Thomas Clarke, who was to take charge of the mission church in Calcutta, and to revive the Protestant Mission there. Mr. Clarke arrived in the ship *Houghton*, which reached Calcutta about the same time as the *Earl of Oxford*, whilst Mr. Thomas was still there. Some of his old fellow-officers from the latter vessel, knowing the severity of his religious views, maliciously amused themselves by giving him a sad and very untrue account of Mr. Clarke's morality, at hearing which he was greatly concerned; and he, innocently, but most imprudently, mentioned what he had heard to one of his Calcutta friends, who carried the story to the displeased ears of Mr. Grant, and thereby excited his deeper indignation against Mr. Thomas.

With a troubled and heavy heart, therefore, he proceeded towards Malda, not knowing what things await-

---

* In this interview, Mr. Thomas says, Mr. Grassman contended that ৱ, not ব, was the proper equivalent of the English *d*. Also that the proper sound of ব was *v*. The munshi pronounced him quite ignorant of the language. "What a fool was I," wrote the translator, "to be discouraged by his remarks!"

ed him there. To his brother he wrote, "Those who were my friends, are not so now; and I shall become a beggar soon, if the Lord help not." His múnshi again left him, to visit his family; and Mohan Chand went on before him to Bhulaháth; so that his journey was made alone, and in great sadness. His leisure was occupied in extracting from the Scriptures, and writing out, at length, " close points and characteristics of a state of grace, and also those of the reprobate." In this "awful and delightful work" he found much instruction and encouragement. He preached constantly, and had encouragement everywhere in the eagerness with which he was received by the people. There was something most attractive and winning in his address and manner of preaching; and now that he spoke the language freely and intelligibly, he readily met with hearers in almost every place. His conferences with those who came around him were not indeed all cheering. Often was he cast down and distressed to the last degree, and especially when the pantheism of the Hindus came to light in their attempt to find the origin of all evil in the Supreme Being. "This," he wrote, "is the fatal thought, that God is the author of sin, by which the devil incites them to lay all the blame and filth of sin on the pure and holy God, and not on themselves; and he also tempts them thus to commit sin, as being that which God himself excites to! Oh dreadful, soul-destructive sin! Of 'all filthiness of the flesh and spirit,' this thought seems to me to be the most loathsome. He that charges God thus, seems to commit an act of infinite filthiness. The utterance of such blasphemy rends my ears. Poor creatures! Oh that God may give me grace to think well of this matter, and to write and speak plainly and effectually against this battery of the devil."

It is interesting to look back upon these early missionary efforts, carried forward without the aid of those appliances which are now at the disposal of any one who desires to recommend the gospel to the people of Bengal. In the lack of printed gospels and tracts, Mr. Thomas was accustomed to copy out portions of his translation for distribution, and to prepare slips of paper upon which striking texts of the gospel were written in his own admirable Bengali caligraphy. These he gave away, after preaching, in the hope that they might prove to be good seed unto life eternal. Often, when his hearers left him, he was " in a transport," overwhelmed by the thoughts he had striven to communicate to them ; and often did he, before his boat conveyed him out of sight, watch the dispersing audiences, and pray that the emotions they had displayed might not leave them quite unchanged. Thus he describes them :— " Now they would point at the book given to them ; then lift up their hands toward the heavens ; then proceed ; then stop and look at the departing boat, indicating by some motion of the hand their sorrow at parting." On one such occasion, after witnessing the very deep interest displayed by his hearers, he wrote :—

I never saw the like ! What a power has God's word over the natural conscience ! Credulity and faith are exceedingly different, and these people are very credulous ; but, whatever they be, it makes nothing for my discouragement as long as I see something of 'the Lord working with me, and confirming the word with signs following.' Surely one such sign is, 'The common people heard Him gladly.' When Christ Himself preached, joy only was produced in the minds of some, the stony-ground hearers ; but in the case of others, fruit, by the same word. My courage had fled away, and left feeble knees, and hands hanging down ; but now, thanks be to God ! my drooping heart is lifted up, my hopes are revived and quickened, this morning. I would not change the pleasure I have now enjoyed for all the wealth in the world. Oh for a watchful spirit, a single eye, a single heart, that I grieve not that Holy Spirit, whose wonderful power I have just seen, and tasted, and handled, and felt, and on whose energy all my success depends. I wonder at it. I am astonished that His power should accompany anything I say ; but it has been so. I dare not say otherwise. Glory be unto thee, O Lord.

So, at another place, on the same day.—

Went to a village where I met a few people. I began to talk with them upon some trifling matter, so as to engage their attention : but soon there came others who remembered me. I preached to them about two hours ; and afterwards wrote upon slips of paper,

'*The blood of Jesus Christ alone cleanseth from all sin,*' this being the substance of what had been said. I made them read and understand it, and desired them often to think of it. I warned them against false worship, and, after prayer, left them. At last, there were fifty or sixty of them. They besought me to stay, longed to hear more; and, methinks, I could be well content to stay with them; but that I know how much the inclinations of such hearers are like 'the morning cloud' that soon vanisheth away. I returned to my boat, prayed with my people, and sat down, solidly comforted, though a little weary. Glory be unto God! These people seemed to be free from the common blasphemy. I questioned an old Brahman about that and other things. I could see clearly that they all desired me to continue with them; and their hearts were so moved and stirred, that I feel sure my visit will not be quite forgotten even for years to come.

CHAPTER VI.
Harla Gáchí.—1789-90.

ON the 26th of October, Mr. Thomas arrived at Bhulaháth, and was welcomed by many of his hearers there with great joy; but his mind was oppressed with dread as to the reception he had to expect at Malda. Without going there, he found his forebodings of evil verified. Mr. Udny sent him a letter requesting him to discontinue preaching at his house, and to regard the connexion which had existed between them as dissolved. He was invited to come to the Factory as a guest, but his official labours there were to be carried on no more. Mr. Udny avoided any censure of Mr. Thomas's conduct; but said he thought that the Malda family might derive spiritual benefit from the use of printed sermons, and that he believed they would enjoy greater tranquillity if the missionary resided elsewhere. Mr. Thomas therefore went to the cottage prepared for him at Harla Gáchí, and took up his abode there, on the 31st of October, "deserted and lonely," not being sure that he would be able to continue even here, since the new zemindar of the estate to which it and the neighbouring ground belonged was very hostile to the gospel, and was disposed to trouble the missionary and his adherents with vexatious and exorbitant demands. His work for the present, however, lay before him. The day he took possession of his new home, he had "a pretty large company in the evening for hearing and prayer," and he arranged with the Brahman for regular Bengali services every Lord's-day. He was much comforted by the sympathy of the young men to whom he had been accustomed to minister, nearly all of whom, in "heartfelt, kind, and brotherly" words, assured him of their deep regret that he had been removed from the Factory. He paid a few visits to Mr. Udny's house; but chiefly to prescribe for some who were sick there; and he felt that he was no longer a welcome guest. Then, on the 7th of November, "a letter came from Mr. Grant, utterly cutting off all his allowances, and advising him to return to his old profession." Mr. Udny also declined to be at all responsible for his support. The poor deserted man wrote :—

Such is this great day of rebuke! I am cast down, and can hardly eat my food. What shall I do? Except the Lord help quickly, I know not what to do. While there are rebukes and discouragements here, there seems to be a call below, at Calcutta. Which way to take, I know not. '*The Lord will provide*.' Many are my sins. Great my troubles. As Frazer says, 'Persecution may be at once a correction for sin, and a testimony for Christ and His truth.'

Such trouble as that in which he was now placed was well adapted to induce most searching self-examination, and the effect of this was to fill him with abasing thoughts of himself. He most humbly deplored his defects and backslidings; but, whilst he was willing to admit that the least favorable opinion his late friends entertained of him, was better than he deserved, he stedfastly maintained his confidence that in the specific points which led them to cast him off, he was altogether in the right, and had only done as his duty before God required of him.

Troubles, if possible, still more acute and discouraging threatened him. His múnshi, as has been related, was again gone to visit his family. He had left with prayers, and tears, and many protestations of sincere and undying attachment both to the missionary and to the gospel. Now, however, the Brahman Mohan Chand insinuated that this supposed faithful and loving servant and disciple was capable of all manner of deceit and wickedness. At that very time, he said, he was trying to secure other employment; and would only return in case of failure to obtain it. He had, the Brahman declared, cheated his master in every commission entrusted to him, and, far worse still, had been guilty of crimes so heinous that the details given were utterly revolting. This disclosure was full of misery. Either the múnshi was a wretched hypocrite, or the Brahman a lying calumniator: and these were the two men over whose happy conversion he had rejoiced in all his afflictions; and who had together prayed with him, and stood by him as he declared the way of life to their countrymen! His soul had taken comfort in them as "the first-ripe fruits" of his mission to the Bengalis; and now, was this the result of his hopes and prayers? Their unwillingness to abandon their caste and to be baptized had often before led him to question their sincerity, but he had made large allowances for the influence of family affection and of timidity, and had always been ready to hope that they had really received the truth, and that it would soon more irresistibly assert its authority over them.

The return of the múnshi at the beginning of January, 1790, when he brought with him several people who professed a desire to become Christians, led to explanations which relieved Mr. Thomas's mind of the suspicions the Brahman's charges had engendered. He was, indeed, only too willing to believe the statement whereby the múnshi exonerated himself; and both Rám Basu and the Brahman were soon almost as highly thought of as before. Nor did the hopeless condition of his affairs keep him in continual depression. His spiritual joys were at times almost extatic: he felt his lonely little cottage to be a Bethel; and, in commemoration of this happy experience, he gave it the name of Bethelpur.

All things appeared to be against him, but he looked back upon the bright expectations of usefulness with which he had left England in 1786.—Isaiah xlix. and his interpretation of it, with his dream of the lilies and wheat, all came vividly to his mind, and he had, even now, a "lively hope and assurance that there would be a fulfilment of those things" which he had been led to look for, in the future.

Mr. Grant left India on the 23d of February, in the ship *Berrington*. Before his departure, he empowered Mr.

Udny to make some final overtures to Mr. Thomas, whose account of them is as follows :—

Mr. G. Udny told me that Mr. Grant wished not to be unfriendly; but, if I wanted assistance to go to England, he would readily give it. My answer was, that I had no reason at all to doubt that the Lord had called me to this work, and therefore I could not leave it upon any account whatever ;—that I looked upon it as an insult, after wronging me so much, to talk about my leaving my work ;— that Mr. Grant *had* wronged me very much ;—that the charges he brought against me could not condemn me, if they were all true ; but they were not true ;—that nothing had happened to me but what was common to men in my situation ;—that I should be glad indeed if Mr. Grant would help my creditors ;—that Providence had brought me into my present state, and would in due time bring me out of it ;—that I had hope in the Lord.

Poor man! He assumed a bold front in the presence of his opponents; but it contrasted strongly with the dismay and almost despair which only too frequently assaulted him in his solitude. After making the above entry in his journal, he adds,—

I think I never *cried* more from the bottom of my soul for help, than I have now, in this affliction. I do hope that, notwithstanding I am so forsaken now, yet the Lord will appear. David had great troubles, but they issued in great blessing. David sinned, and the Lord visited him and his people for his sins ;—not for ever, —but for a season. 'A little wrath,'—'for a moment.'—Oh for David's heart: humbly, penitently placing myself at the feet of His grace and mercy, till He arise to my help; for I know the mercies of the Lord are *very great*. Therefore I hope ;—but the time is excessively dark.

The details of this unhappy separation of Mr. Thomas from his supporters have been, as far as they could be recovered, fairly represented. The reader will review the relations of the two parties from the outset of their association, and will form his own judgment upon the case. He will not, it is believed, conclude that because Mr. Grant was a prosperous and a great man, and Mr. Thomas a needy and unfortunate one, therefore the blame must have been altogether with the latter. He, it may be, expected too much from his opulent friends, and exaggerated his claims upon them. That, in another way, they did the same by him, may also appear from the foregoing facts. The world's verdict has long ago been given against the poor missionary. There may, even yet, be some grounds for appeal in his favor to the higher court of conscience.*

From his letters to his father some interesting notices of himself may be gathered. One, dated November 5th, 1789, says :—

I am afar off from riches, reputation and worldly pleasures. Many are they who rise up against me. Some are displeased with me for preaching at all: others are displeased with me for preaching to the natives. Others threaten me if I should print my translation. Others are angry because I preach the baptism of Christ and his apostles. Others that I will not administer the bread and wine to them, because they were never rightly baptized. Others are angry with me for personal reproof, &c. But the greatest question of all is, whether *He* be angry or no, in whose name I continue to say and to teach these things. I am getting farther and farther away from all my countrymen, and am more intensely and entirely engaged with natives, about twenty of whom have left their idolatry, flower offerings, and vain ceremonies ; read the scriptures, pray, and sing Gospel hymns. Only two, however, afford me any satisfying signs of a saving work in their souls ; but, for these two, surely the Lord hath done great things.

My wife and family not coming out, is a grief to me. My circumstances are another source of trouble ; but I believe that, by my poverty, the Lord is trying those who are rich and able, and on whom it is very incumbent to relieve me ; and in due time I hope to be relieved. But, if not, I had rather be as I am than as they are ; and blessed be God always, that He has afflicted and tried me, and, by some indiscretion of my own, brought me into a state of

---

* It may be well to introduce here Mr. Carey's opinion on this matter, written after three years' companionship with Mr. Thomas, with sufficient knowledge of his constitutional peculiarities and defects, and after close intimacy with Mr. Udny and other Indian friends of Mr. Grant. He wrote, June 17th, 1796,— "Mr. Grant's opposition to the work, I think abominable. The fact is, as can be proved by a long correspondence between him and Mr. Thomas, now in preservation, that Mr. Thomas left a much more lucrative employment, and the society of his family, at Mr. Grant's desire, to preach the gospel among the natives ; who afterwards, because he would not conform to his peremptory dictates, in matters which he could not conscientiously do, cut off all his supplies, and left him to shift for himself in a foreign land."

poverty and dependence. Blessed be the Lord, I am more safely wrapped up in reproach; while some are exposed to the dangers of fame and reputation.

I begin to get old, and this country will quicken my pace. It cannot be much longer; I may safely begin to take leave. Adieu, vain and empty world, vile and sinful body, frail and fluttering friends, kind and sterling brethren!—Adieu.

But where I am going must be considered, and, alas, I cannot well say. I cannot truly constantly think. I am betwixt two opinions of myself. I have too much hatred of sin, and too much love for that which is good, to think myself still in the bonds of iniquity; and I have too many of those things which grow on corrupt trees, to think steadily that I am a child of God. Sometimes I find my hopes are beyond all painful scruples; but never find my despair and doubt beyond any comfortable hope.

The foregoing extract speaks of his hopes of success amongst the natives. A passage from his journal of the 3d of January, 1790, may serve to illustrate this.—

I preached to-day from Matthew iii. 2, describing the three kingdoms on earth,—that of men,—that of hell and the devil,—that of heaven and Christ. I had great enlargement. My congregation increases. I had thirty volunteers in all, and they were very attentive. After I had done, they sat and heard me relate several stories of remarkable conversions. When they were gone, I heard them, to my great delight, singing hymns on the other side of the water. I did not know that so many of them could sing. Some voices I never heard before. They sang, 'Who besides can deliver us?' and 'O sinful heart, go and worship at Jesus' feet.'

On the 9th of February, 1790, he says in a letter to his father,—

By the grace of God I continue to this day in exceeding good health of body and consolations of soul; yet in a field of coldness, difficulties and troubles, inwardly and outwardly, through which I am obliged to wade on. I know you will have no difficulty in reconciling this seeming contradiction:—there is hardly a happier man in Bengal, and hardly a more unhappy one, excepting only those who stop not at desperation. I have read somewhere that many of David's Psalms are so written, that we might think one person had begun, and another finished them; and those who are in the warfare are exposed to such opposite principles that they must be permitted to speak like two different persons, if they are to express outwardly what passes inwardly. I am more indebted than ever, and less able to pay. Yet I have not less hope than I had; for God is able to deliver me, let my case be every way bad. One prophet had his creditor to pay after he was dead, and the Lord paid it.—2 Kings iv. 1-7. I am also in the hands of those who are very well able to pay me clear. £20,000 a year is supposed to be the income of two who profess highly to be related to the Lord Jesus Christ, and who have also professed to love me. If I am their brother, then, you will say, 'Are they therefore obliged to pay your debts?' Why, I must confess, I fully believe they are; for 'we ought to lay down our lives for the brethren,' how much more our superfluous money! And the holy apostle makes this a determining point, you know, and condemns him who 'seeth his brother have need, and shutteth up his bowels.' Methinks, sometimes, whatever chastisement this affliction is to me, still it is the trial of the Lord to them, as much perhaps as 'Go, and sell all,' was to the ruler: only the ruler's was '*all*;' this only a little; for £500 or £800 is much to me, but mites to them, and not so much. A renewed heart, money-clenched!! I can never believe it; especially when the anathemas of scripture come to mind, which are written to the point, and are like so many aimed thunderbolts, directed personally to the unpitying, sordid, rich, lucre-craving, covetous and money-loving mind. It is hard to speak, out of an unlearned mouth like mine, without uttering unmollified, ill-shaped, and hard-carved things. It looks like a bitter spirit, and like forgetfulness of home faults, to be much taken up with other people's; yet I do not know what a man is to do, who is a defender of truth and grace, and an opposer of error and wickedness, by profession, if he does not often dwell upon other people's faults; and he may possibly do this from a principle directly opposite to that of the censorious:—from a principle of love, and not of hatred; and with a design to do good, and not evil. I am glad I am a poor, afflicted, despised man; not that these things are at all pleasant; but, for such a wretched man as I, this is the safest posture my heavenly Father could put me in, and the fittest and wisest of measures concerning me. He knows what sort of a man I am. My heart is all window to Him, and His eye covers it. Wherefore let it not altogether vex and fret you that you have a son in such circumstances; but rather hope that when grace grows, and makes him able to bear a little prosperity, then his heavenly Father will be at no loss to find means for his deliverance.

As to my reputation, it is worse than my circumstances; for I never was rich, and then became poor; but my character and reputation have been very high, but are now become very low indeed. I hardly know how to describe to you in few words whereabouts I stand; but it is something of this kind of sketch that represents your son to the view of the religious folks hereabouts :—*A bigot intolerable,—and a selfish, obstinate, overbearing, insolent, stubborn sectarian!* As to what your son thinks of himself, that is of little importance; else *he* thinks attachment to evident truths, firmness in a good cause, and a heart fearless towards the sons of men, have contributed something towards this unhandsome collection of hard words. But what does his Master think of him?—Is he a vessel or not?—Is he His messenger or not?—Was he sent to say these things or not? This is the grandest question of all; and we have a copy of His mind and decisive judgment in the written word. I esteem all things right which I find testified there.

Of your son's success, he can say very little at present. Sometimes an enquirer starts up; and sometimes two or three together vanish away, to the grief of his very soul; but this is a work that requires a broad bottom, and a length of time *to begin* to begin. 'All that the Father giveth me shall come to me;' and whether these dry dead bones can live, the Lord knows. I believe I must needs go and call them, and say, ' Stand up !'

I have finished a translation both of Matthew and Mark, into the Bengalese; and am forming a catechism out of Mr. Beddome's; but I am afraid I have many projects that will never ripen into anything. Death hastens on, time dissolves so fast, difficulties and interruptions are so thick : and it is seldom that inclination, leisure, ability, and execution, meet together; and more seldom still that they stay.

Another letter, written on the 11th of April, says,—

Your son is in disgrace ; but he believes it is not on any account that would give you pain, if opportunity allowed him to rehearse all the particulars. I hope the Strict Baptists, as they are called, have the good cause and the right side : if so, I shall never repent in the end. I am in good health and spirits, though I have suffered a sad windfall of friends, and am now without any support : having nothing, and yet it is quite sufficient; freed from the gloomy veil of black and lowering despair, by the common light of the gospel. About two months ago, I was in very great heaviness, but my calling to this work seems to have been renewed since that time, and I am fully persuaded, although the work goes on through a forest of difficulties, and with such gradual progress, yet it hath a blessing in it. The Lord is able to deliver me from my temporal difficulties; and, if worst comes to worst, I have reason to be thankful that they permit pen, ink, and paper to be used in a jail, and the Bible also.

In this letter he says that he made all the use he could of Dr. Doddridge's *Family Expositor*, adopting its renderings as far as they commended themselves to his judgment, and especially " preferring them where they were most analogous with the idiom of the Bengalese."

In March, 1790, Mr. Thomas found no small relief and encouragement in a visit to Mr. Samuel Davis, a civilian at Bhaugalpur. He had met this gentleman at Malda in 1788, where he had him for some time under medical care whilst recovering from injuries received in a dangerous encounter with a bear, and he had often striven to bring him under the influence of the gospel. Although such efforts had proved fruitless, the missionary was delighted with the amiable character and many " lovely virtues" of his patient. Mr. Davis also possessed considerable literary and scientific attainments. He was one of the first of our countrymen to investigate the principles of Hindu astronomy; and his essay upon the *Surya Siddhánta* and the Indian method of calculating eclipses, and other papers, may be seen in the earlier volumes of the *Asiatic Researches*. His deistical prejudices were too firmly rooted to yield to Mr. Thomas's arguments; but the evident sincerity and warm enthusiasm of the missionary left a most favorable impression upon his mind; and, now that trouble had arisen, Mr. Thomas had a very cordial invitation to the civilian's house. Indeed Mr. Davis did all he could to help him. Finding that the new zemindar of the property upon which Harla Gáchi and the neighbouring villages stood, was, like his predecessor, making many illegal and vexatious demands, he issued such orders as effectually frightened him and his agents, compelled them to desist from their exactions, and brought them to entreat pardon in a very abject and submissive manner. He also most kindly offered to find employment for Mohan Chand, at Rajmahal, and very warmly encouraged Mr. Thomas to put forth proposals to print his translations of Matthew and Mark by public subscription, and "did of his own will begin it, and that after some very hard arguments," putting down his own name as a subscriber to the amount of forty guineas.*

Shortly after Mr. Thomas's return from Bhaugalpur, he used much affectionate importunity with Mohan Chand and the múnshi to confess their faith in Christ by baptism. Towards the end of April, both seemed to be quite willing. They, however, found means to postpone the event, by saying that they wished to be baptized in Calcutta, whither Mr. Thomas was intending very soon to go.

He had, indeed, now come to believe that it was his "plain duty" to make Calcutta his home. During the months he had spent at Harla Gáchi, he had been without pecuniary support, awaiting help which never came. His friends at Malda all appeared to grow weary of him, except Mr. Long, who, having lost his situation in Mr. Udny's service, was glad to find a home at Harla Gáchí, and was trying to support himself there by breeding silk worms. Mr. Thomas had much confidence in his piety, and was thankful for his society and fellowship in prayer. His own debts, of course, increased, and necessity called

* In July, 1795, Mr. Davis was appointed Judge and Magistrate of Benares. On the 14th of January, 1799, after the assassination of Mr. Cherry by Vizier Ali, the deposed Nawáb of Oudh, that unscrupulous murderer directed his followers to put to death all the Europeans in Benares. Captain Conway and Mr. Evans were slaughtered at Mr. Cherry's house, and Vizier Ali then led his band to Mr. Davis's residence, killing two other gentlemen upon the way. A sentinel at Mr. Davis's gate opposed the entrance of the party, and by shooting him they gave notice of their approach and design to his master. He instantly armed himself with a hog-spear, and took refuge with his wife and children upon the flat roof of the house. His assailants rushed after him; but the narrow staircase would only admit of their passing one by one. One by one, Mr. Davis was prepared to encounter them, and with the utmost coolness and courage, for the dear lives of his wife and children who stood behind him, he kept them at bay. Two or three of his assailants were killed, and others were desperately wounded. For more than one hour and twenty minutes, this fearful strife was maintained. Then a body of cavalry rode in to the rescue, at the approach of which the assassins took to flight. Mr. Davis had the high satisfaction of knowing that his bravery saved not his own family only but several others. He detained the murderous party by his unexpected defence, until their time for doing further harm was gone. To him it was, under God, due that "the Benares massacre" numbered so few victims.

DISTRESSING CIRCUMSTANCES.

upon him to do something for the relief of his affairs. In his forlorn condition, some strange methods of succour suggested themselves to his bewildered mind. Thus, in May, he wrote in his journal :—

With the few Rupees left I intend to put into the Madras Lottery, accounting that very lawful in exigency which would be otherwise questionable and sinful. 'The lot is cast into the lap, and the whole disposing thereof is of the Lord.'—Proverbs xvi. 33. I intend also to exercise my profession, encouraged by the example of Barnabas and Paul, and by the thought that natives, seeing me manage both temporal and spiritual things, may have an example before them, shewing that true religion leads no man into a jungle, or out of society.

The very dangerous doctrine, enunciated above, that the morality of an action depends upon the exigency of the circumstances in which it is performed, is not to be defended. The temptation to invest in the Lottery was not, however, at this time yielded to. As we shall see, it reverted at a later period, and was then acted upon.

With regard to his proposed removal to Calcutta : there, he thought, " he might, if called on, exercise his profession, and do any thing he could invent for his creditors and family ; not doubting that the one would be paid and the other provided for." If such a change of plans bore the appearance of " lightness" or fickleness, he fortified himself against that charge in the belief that he " was born to wander from place to place," according to Isaiah xlix. 21, in which chapter he still read his missionary commission. But it would be unfair to overlook all the painful apprehensions and mental struggles which issued in this determination to leave Harla Gáchi. He says to his brother, in a letter written on the 14th of May,—

I have often looked forward to some happy day when the Lord should bring me out into a fine, wealthy, easy place for body and soul. But, alas, I find ten-fold trouble, affliction, vexation and sorrow of heart. I am an older man by ten years than I was two years ago. I am in troubles that make me feel their weight : as though I should never, never, rise again. But God, who raises the dead, is able to bring me out of all my afflictions ; and if, being able, He yet desists, He is like a wise and tender physician, and father too, who lets this caustic remain, otherwise something else, which He sees, will not go away from me. It is a hard thing in troubles to think that God is much wiser in His management of us than we should be in managing for ourselves. It is harder still to believe that humbling mortifying dispensations proceed out of His loving heart. It is a shame to think how we *do* think. Sometimes I am so unspeakably full of joy, that my troubles disappear, and the Lord is praised for not giving me up to perish in my own way; and for stopping me, and curbing my pride with such dispensations as these: the hardest of which is a mercy disguised. My translation and mission work has gone on very slowly this year.

But this intention to remove to Calcutta was very soon afterwards set aside by occurrences which seemed to indicate that the work near Malda was being signally blessed by God. The sequel to the letter above quoted will show this, and in it Mr. Thomas will relate his own story. Thus he proceeds, under date of July 10th,—

Many things have happened since I wrote thus far. I am now in good hope, and have many reasons to assure myself that the Lord is among us in truth. Enemies of my own country; friends turned into enemies; enemies and scoffers among the heathens; no salary; no friends appeared, but slunk away when they saw the storm,—all this, my dear brother, was the true state of my affairs when I wrote you the first page. Since that, God has plucked His hand out of His bosom. I have been astonished to see our persecutors come and catch my servants by the feet, imploring mercy, driven by inward fears. Some have turned friends who were very much displeased, and some who were great enemies. Some particulars I must relate to you. A Brahman was going to be baptized, and this becoming known to his family and friends, they consulted together concerning what should be done to turn him from 'this way,' and fixed upon an old man at Gopálpur named Nanda Lál, who had been one of his father's disciples, to come and set all his strength against the gospel, to persuade him not to embrace it. Nanda Lál accordingly came, and sat down for five or six days, urging the folly of turning from the path of their fathers and fathers' fathers, &c. The Brahman said he would read to him the books he spoke against, and if he was able to point out any evil thing in them, he would abandon them. Having thus secured his attention, he read and prayed in the name of the Lord Jesus Christ to God the Judge of all; and, lo, the old man was quite silenced, and was afterwards prevailed on to come and hear me. Nay, he was effectually convinced that the gospel was not an error, but the word of God. He eagerly heard me several times, with wonder, and then said he would return to his family, consisting of about thirty or forty persons, and convert them all! I preadvised him of disappointment; but he said that he had so much influence over them, that they would all see with his eyes. But, poor old gentleman, he found that, by embracing this new doctrine, he had lost all his old credit, character, influence and all. They abused him, and cast it in his teeth that he had gone to turn others from error; but had fallen himself. His wife and all his nearest friends waged war with him. After two days, therefore, he sent for the Brahman, and my mûnshi went with him; and they found the Hindu scribes and doctors assembled together, with a pile of human traditions, held by them in devout esteem. Seeing this, the converts were afraid, feeling conscious of their ignorance and inferiority in point of rank and learning; wherefore they proposed to retire and pray to God, who often gives to them that know Him a mouth and wisdom which no one is able to gainsay or resist. Having committed themselves to Him, they met the assembly, and, in a little while, silenced every opponent. They then read to them at one sitting, Matthew and Mark throughout, and all were constrained to confess that it must be the word of God. Nanda Lál was hereby greatly strengthened, his family reconciled to him, and indeed the Spirit of God seemed, throughout the whole assembly, family, opposers and all, to move on the face of the waters. I have gone and preached there since, several times; yet I cannot say that I see the Lord's hand satisfactorily, any further than in that full assent and liking which falls so short of solid conversion. However, the old man seems to be an exception, with one of his sons. I am in expectation of seven or eight being added to us, and about sixty or eighty nominally, who will all lose caste, forsake heathenism, and become stated hearers.

These things happened in May and June; and before the latter month expired, another case, which appeared to be full of remarkable interest, called forth Mr. Thomas's surprise and thanksgiving. This was the supposed conversion of Párbati Charan Mukerjea, a Kulin Brahman of the highest class. He was a most strict observer of Hindu ceremonies, rising early every morning, and repairing to the distant jungles to gather particular flowers, superstitiously valued by the Hindus. These were offered with all the details of Hindu ritualism in the river Mahanuddy, which was near; and, at particular seasons, he repaired to the yet more sacred river, the Ganges, whose waters are believed to cleanse from sin. There was scarcely his equal in all the neighbourhood for zeal and exactness; he was a thorough devotee. Párbati heard with great displeasure of the new religion which some were receiving, and, calling upon Mohan Chand, who was connected with his family by marriage, on the 28th of June, he reproved him for apostasy from Hinduism. Finding that Mohan had just been to visit Mr. Thomas, a *mletchchha*, he demanded that he should bathe and change his clothes; otherwise he was unfit to speak to a pure Hindu like himself. Mohan said that filthy men did filthy deeds, whereas this Englishman was good and pure in his behaviour. Párbati was indignant that his words were thus rebutted, and, by a significant act, intimated that he regarded Mohan Chand as a man who had forfeited his caste:—when the hooka which Mohan had been smoking was handed to him, he emptied out the water, in the presence of several other persons. Mohan Chand, deeply aggrieved, went out and laid his complaint before God; and afterwards, as it was evening, he did not return to his company; but retired with his family to rest. At two o'clock the next morning, there was a great cry outside Mohan Chand's house, and, the door being opened, Párbati was found lying there, apparently in the greatest perturbation and agony of mind. He implored Mohan Chand to tell him the way of salvation by Christ, and to pray for him. Mohan replied as well as he could, and took him over to Rám Basu's house, where they passed the time till day-light, in reading, praying, and singing. Párbati forthwith abandoned his flower and river worship, and, about noon, returned to the múnshi's house. When asked to explain his great emotion, he told them that he had had a wonderful and terrific dream. In it he had seen the Lord of all, seated upon a throne of dazzling brightness, and He had demanded of him how he dared to persecute His servant? and had ordered him to enquire from Mohan Chand what he must do to be saved. Mr. Thomas, in the account from which these particulars are taken, says, " The effects were visible upon his body and mind for several days. I found it very difficult to administer any consolation to him, and was afraid the consequences might be fatal; but he continued to hear the gospel daily, and began to join the rest in singing and prayer. He confessed all his former folly, and professed to believe that the Bible was the only word of God, and Jesus Christ the only Saviour." He was a sensible man, appeared to abhor idolatry, became a great and rapid acquirer of Scripture knowledge, seemed likely to be made very useful, and he greatly animated the missionary and his disciples by his company and conversation.*

* Mr. Thomas was deeply convinced of Párbati's sincerity—and has given the following example of the profound feeling he manifested. He says,—" You must know that we were on the river, going to Calcutta, and we had a prayer meeting on setting out. Ram Ram Basu having made his intercessions, I called upon Párbati, whom I had never before heard; and though the múnshi's prayer was more judicious and orderly, yet that of Párbati, both in manner and matter, was at that time inexpressibly sweet and awful to my spirit.

"The following are my recollections of this unparalleled prayer, as I wrote them down, several days afterwards, August 19, 1790.

"'I performed the rites of the Ganges; I called this good. I worshipped wood and stone; I called this good. I heard the shastras of men, that are all false and vain; I called this good.—Lord, I am a most wretched creature to this day: I know nothing—nothing. I have spent all my days in wickedness, and have not obtained the least knowledge of God. O put far from me these evil things! O make them depart far from me. I have hearkened now to thy word. I will hear them no more.—I will not the least regard those idols of wood and stone any more!—Vanity: lies. Lord, I will hear no more at all these shastras of the Hindus; they are all false and vain. Wretched sinner! Save me! O save—save, save me. Give—Give—O give—Give, O Lord! Give me to know—Hell! what? Heaven! what?—Without the blood of Christ I shall never be saved. Without the flesh of Christ I shall never live.—Lord, what is the meaning of this? I know not what it is.—How can I get the blood of Christ?—O teach me. I will do any thing thou sayest.—Caste! what?—Home! what?—Friends! what?—Life! what?—What is any thing? All is nothing, without thee.—I want no money, I want nothing but thee. O what a wretched sinner am I! O tell me thy way! O tell me by múnshi; tell me by the Sahib. We are going to Calcutta. Many, many wicked things are there. O keep us all while we stay there.

"'O that I had but love! O that I had but faith! O that I had forgiveness! O that I had but those things which thy people have. Like them—O make me like them,—like them. O Lord, how many evil things are in my mind every day! I am a wicked blasphemous wretch! I have shame in me.—Wicked shame

All these occurrences naturally produced a considerable stir. Bhulaháth and Gopálpur were full of talk about Párbati's marvellous vision and conversion, and it is no wonder that Mr. Thomas was greatly cheered by what he witnessed. Yet there was an aspect of his success which might well fill him with anxiety, and which indeed should have led him to question its reality and worth. Poor as he was, all his converts looked to him for help and support. The múnshi was, indeed, his salaried servant, and often needed additional assistance to clear off debts which he was somehow continually contracting. Mohan Chand, ceasing to be the *guru* of a circle of disciples, required to be supported by an equivalent from the missionary. Párbati also had to be helped with money; and no sooner did Mr. Thomas visit Nanda Lál, than he too " talked with considerable anxiety about food and raiment for his large family." " A recommendation to trust in Jesus Christ, and to read often Matthew vi. 25-34," was, it may be feared, not felt by the old Bengali to be of much practical worth. Thus the poor missionary's anxieties were sorely aggravated by his apparent success. " Destitute of any salary" for many months,

before the people, and wicked fear of men!—Far, O far away from me, put far away my sins. Forgive me; and teach me what I shall do. I will do any thing. O that I did but know what to do : O give—give—give—Lord, what shall, what can I do ?'

"'Here he burst into a flood of tears, with now and then such fervent cries, as I never before heard. He continued in prayer about half an hour. I read and explained the faithful promises of God to supply the poor and needy, and to satisfy the thirsty soul with living waters. I spoke of the mind, and the inner man, delighting in God manifested in the flesh, and crucified for sin; that this was eating the flesh and drinking the blood of Christ. After concluding, he retired to his boat, and, as the múnshi tells me, wept there over his own sinfulness, a long time.' Thus far my diary.

"Considering that this took place several weeks after his dream, and observing the deep concern of mind, which is but imperfectly expressed in this written account, you will agree with me, that it is a very extraordinary affair; and the loss and shame among men with which it has been ever since followed, put it beyond all doubt, with me, that it has pleased God to awaken this man. He continues, [this was written in 1793,] a living witness to thousands, of the vanity of paganism, and the reality of the Christian religion. The Brahmans and relations of these people, who find their interests shaken, have raised reports, stirred up enemies, and brought accusations against them, evidently false; but they behave, on these trying occasions, like Christians, who have their trust and hope in God."

he wanted " to put up a place of worship for his hearers, and to purchase types and a printing press, which they might work for themselves, and print the translation" as it advanced ; whilst the burden of finding daily support for his converts pressed heavily upon him ; for it was with difficulty sometimes that he could supply his own wants.

In regard to Mohan Chand, the burden became still more intolerable. In June, a claim for Rs. 300, for money borrowed on the occasion of a marriage, was put forth against him by another Brahman; and, this sum not being forthcoming, his creditor sat down before his door, "heavily complaining, in a manner which was supposed to be the prelude to imprecations of the worst evils upon the unhappy family." Mohan ran off in terror; his wife gave way to frantic distress ; and Govinda, their son, shortly afterwards began to complain of symptoms of fever. The effect upon Mr. Thomas was quite as painful, and, it may well be suspected, more real. He dreaded lest the superstitious fears of his converts should be followed by actual disease, to the injury of the gospel ; so he sent for the creditor, paid him one fourth of the money at once, and gave him a promissory note for the remainder, payable after twelve months ! " The family were restored to great joy ;" but the misery of the poor impoverished missionary was enhanced proportionately. He had already been compelled to borrow from his friends at Malda, and was keenly feeling the humiliation of the debt. Rs. 650 was owing to one of them, who came, on the 5th of July, as Mr. Thomas feared, to demand the amount. Having no money left, he offered his creditor any thing he had, even his boat, if he would take it, in part payment of the sum. What was his surprise to hear that it was no longer owing ! Mr. G. Udny had paid it all ! He blessed God for this great instance of His favor. A kind letter followed, in which his relenting friend " lamented the distance which had come between them," and expressed hopes that happier relations might be restored. A few days afterwards, Mr. Thomas went to the Factory, and found a most affectionate welcome. Good Mrs. Udny, who had long been distressed by reports of his difficulties, received him with tender sympathy; and he wrote, " Kind and attentive was Mr. G. Udny, to a very great degree. The Lord forgive all our faults, and receive us together, as His dear children."

With a heart greatly relieved, Mr. Thomas set out on his annual visit to Calcutta on the 2nd of August, taking with him the múnshi and Párbati. Mohan Chand pleaded inability to leave his home, through illness; having probably in mind his promise to be baptized when he next went to Calcutta. The journey down was turned to excellent account in preaching, wherever people could be gathered together. At Nuddea, in particular, the missionary and his companions remained nearly a week, finding repeated opportunities for preaching to the pandits there, with apparently very favorable results.

Calcutta was reached on the 21st, and a letter from England told Mr. Thomas that his wife was not coming. He found little to encourage him in the great city, especially as he was distressed for want of money; and his most needful business was soon despatched. He was particularly employed in preparing for the press a prospectus of his translations of Matthew and Mark, with some supplementary works he intended to print together with them. Before leaving Calcutta, it occurred to him to write to Sir William Jones regarding these proposed Bengali publications. In reply, he received a very kind invitation to visit him at his country house at Kishnagur. This place is near Nuddea, and was upon Mr. Thomas's route in returning home, so he left Calcutta on Friday, September 9th, and proceeded thither. The following is an account of his visit.—

Sir William gave me great encouragement and important assistance, and spoke very highly in favor of my plan. He subscribed for thirty copies, Rs. 480. He told me that if one word could be obtained from the king to the Board of Controul, the Company would certainly encourage the work; and said that he would send copies of my proposals to Lady Spencer, and to one of the Bishops, and was quite confident of success. He repeated a saying of Barrow's, in one of his sermons, that he did not doubt that if any one were ever to attempt the conversion of the Hindus, he would certainly have divine assistance.* 'We must take care, however,' added he, 'that we be not enthusiastic.' He told me I should be most likely to meet with great success amongst the deists, who tear their *poitás*, and leave their *shástrás*, caste and all. He gave me some lines of the *Vedas*. He also showed me their greatest mystery;† and let me see a beautiful and extensive Shanscrit vocabulary, in the Deb Nagri character, most elegantly written, I suppose, by his pandit, &c.

Mr. Thomas, ever sanguine, expected very great things as the result of Sir W. Jones's recommendations. He thought he might possibly obtain even royal patronage to his undertaking, "and so nursing fathers and mothers to Israel might be kings and queens."—Isaiah xlix. 28. Such lofty expectations were soon laid low. Encouraged by the great cordiality shown him at Kishnagur, he wrote to the learned jurist for permission to mention to Lord Cornwallis his opinion that the translation was accurate. Sir William sent back a somewhat distantly worded refusal, saying that he made no pretensions to a knowledge of Bengali.‡ Mr. Thomas concluded that the "uncomfortable letter" which conveyed this unexpected reply was another evidence

* The passage to which Sir William Jones referred was most probably the following. Having spoken of the miraculous powers displayed in the first age of Christianity, Dr. Isaac Barrow says :—

"Neither, perhaps, is the communication of this divine virtue so ceased now, that it would be wanting upon any needful occasion. The frequent performance of such works among them in whom faith by abundance of other competent means may be produced and confirmed, unto whom also the first miracles are virtually present by the help of history and good reason, is indeed no wise necessary, nor perhaps would be convenient; but did the same pious zeal for God's honour, and the same charitable earnestness for men's good, excite any persons now to attempt the conversion of infidels to the sincere Christian truth, I see no reason to doubt but that such persons would be enabled to perform whatever miraculous works should conduce to that purpose; for the Lord's hand is not shortened, the grace of Christ is not straitened, the name of Jesus hath not lost its virtue."— Sermon xx. on the Apostles' Creed.

† This must mean the *Gáyatri*. Mr. Thomas does not seem to have recognized its importance. A few years later, as will be seen, he was deeply interested in discovering this mysterious text.

‡ Sir William Jones, in a memorandum regarding his attainments in languages, professes to have studied *Eight* "critically," of which English was of course one;—*Eight* others he had "studied less perfectly, but all were intelligible with a dictionary,"—and amongst these Bengali is named;—*Twelve* others are mentioned as "studied least perfectly, but all attainable."

of the unfriendly influence of Mr. William Chambers, Master in Chancery in the Supreme Court.

Meanwhile the proposals for the publication had been printed in Calcutta and were being distributed. No copy of them has been found; but the following particulars appear in his journal. The projected work was "to consist of seven parts. 1.—*Promises and Prophecies.* 2.—*Matthew.* 3.—*Mark.* 4.—*Texts and Precepts of the New Testament, for Newness of Life.* 5.—*The Ten Commandments, and a Dissertation on Scripture in general.* 6.—*An explanation of the three first chapters of Matthew.* 7.—*A Glossary.*" The price of the work was to be a gold mohur, or Rs. 16, per copy, to Europeans; and the natives were to receive it gratis. The first four parts, "being scripture only, were to form one volume; and the rest another." He was expecting to find subscribers even amongst infidels and those who had no love for the gospel. "The dry terms of my proposals," he wrote to his father, "are adapted to dry people, who are considered to be chiefly addressed: deists, infidels, and all sorts, who fancy to subscribe. I intend to face them into duty."

The reader will not be surprised to find that this too extensive project was never realized. The proposals met with small encouragement; and even the portions of the translations which were ready for press could not be printed. Rs. 3000 was the amount thought needful for the purpose, and this was far beyond Mr. Thomas's ability to raise.

CHAPTER VII.

Reconciliation and Return to England.—1790-92.

BUT closer reunion with his Malda friends and some relief from utter destitution were now at hand. The stir amongst the natives excited an interest in the minds of their European neighbours, and they at length consented to a monthly contribution for the missionary's support as a preacher to the Bengalis. The two brothers Udny promised to give Rs. 70; Mr. Darell, Rs. 20; Mr. W. Brown, Rs. 10; Mr. Creighton, Rs. 15; Mr. Dingley, Rs. 15; Mr. W. Grant, Rs. 10: in all Rs. 140 monthly. Another friend, Mr. Grindly, became a subscriber some months later. The first Rs. 100, for September, was paid in the middle of October, and on his return to Bethelpur, Mr. Thomas wrote, "Very much enjoyed relieving the Brahman out of my new salary."

From the time of his visit to Calcutta, he had suffered severely from illness; and, towards the end of October, it was so aggravated as, for a short period, to threaten a fatal issue. In the prospect of death, his self-scrutiny was close and unsparing. Of the results of this introspection, he wrote,—"I thought myself a Christian, indeed, though a lame one; or else I am a deceived man. If I am a hypocrite, I am like a believer. If I am a believer, I am like a dog, and a swine, and a hypocrite." In the midst of these unhappy uncertainties, he was, however, conscious of "a hope worth all the world, and its riches too."

Having recovered from this illness, towards the end of December, he was invited to resume English preaching at

Malda. He was full of joy on this occasion. " The Lord has restored me," he wrote, " by a wonderful and unexpected change, unsolicited, unlooked for, yet not unprayed for to God. This goodness of God to me gives me intense pleasure, and subdues my soul in a sweet and thankful frame."

A sermon on the angel's message, Luke ii. 10-11, preached at the Factory on Christmas-day, 1790, commenced his new ministry there, which was continued uninterruptedly as long as he remained in the neighbourhood, and was conducted with a most anxious and prayerful desire for the edification of his hearers.

On New Year's day, he preached from " Thou crownest the year with thy goodness."—Psalm lxv. 11. His diary of January 4th, 1791, contains the following entry.—

Last night, being the first Monday of the month, we had a meeting for prayer, and were very happy with consolations from the word. Messrs. Brown, Creighton, and Udny, with myself, prayed. Several texts were first read to encourage us in the duty of social prayer. I hope that the Lord is about to bless us now more than ever. He has cast me down and raised me up. It was very gracious, and at a time when, most unworthy, I had feebly prayed for it, but was not now looking for it. O the grace and condescending goodness He hath showed toward me in this! O Lord, my God, without desert, thou hast crowned the past year with thy goodness. Thine it is to crown the next. To thee I look. Be thou—thou alone—the glory and crown of this year to me for Jesus' sake.

A very characteristic letter to his brother, dated 7th March, must be introduced here. He says,—

I am restored to my congregation of English hearers. I have not yet baptized the natives, but still expect to do it shortly. My constitution fails. My temporals are better; but I am still in debt. Spirituals are worse on the whole; but better lately. Jesus Christ is still the life and briskness of all the joys I have, worth the name. Very, very precious is the Saviour to a sinner of my magnitude. His word still rejoices this heart, as though it had found treasures and spoil. Afflictions are my choice mercies; though I hardly say so cordially, while I feel them. Grief refines, and prepares us for our places, else we should never have so much of it. Let us kiss His rod, and say, ' He has punished us less than our iniquities deserve.' That man I intended to be,—that work I intended to do, when last we saw each other, is not yet accomplished—nor anything like it;—and I am far off from being, in good earnest, the Christian indeed. I am defiled, nonplussed, and baffled; with sad slips and slides the backward way; but with no thorough turning back yet. Neither my heart, my life, my lips, my hands, my feet, my conscience, my memory, my judgment, nor any one of my affections at all performs what was expected; but every one fails, and disappoints all expectations. Yet expectations return. I shall never be convinced of my nothingness, thoroughly, till this body of sin and death is brought to nothing. Thus, my brother, polluted and cast down, I weep, I mourn, I despair almost,—until the Lord Jesus Christ speaks, and a ray of light, life, love and liberty, is shed abroad in my little heart, and I rejoice in Christ Jesus again. But I am so feeble in faith, such a little Christian to this day, that I distress myself if I have no sensible enjoyments, mingled with favorable views of myself. O dear self, how close thou art! Yet there are moments, when I seem as though I was in heaven, out of all fear and troubles; and this happens when my eyes have been just anointed to see that all my sins were utterly abolished, and my soul for ever sanctified, by virtue of what Jesus Christ did *at once* for me,—independent of my faith, my sorrow, my lively joy, my sanctification, or any other gifts, or graces, wrought in me, or done to me. All these are after-consequences. 'He that believeth shall be saved: he that believeth not shall be damned.'—Very true. But, again, he that believeth should take notice of the following things in Christ, as well as of what passes in himself :—Jesus Christ, 'by Himself, purged our sins;' not Jesus Christ and another.— 'This He did once, when 'He offered up Himself.'—And again, 'By His own blood, He entered in once into the holy place, having obtained eternal redemption for us.' 'He offered Himself.' 'Now once hath He appeared to put away sin by the sacrifice of Himself. 'By the which will we are sanctified, through the offering of the body of Jesus Christ, once for all.' 'By one offering, He hath perfected for ever them that are sanctified.'—Hebrews i. 3, vii. 27, ix. 12, 14, 26, 28, and x. 10, 12, 14.—*Now* I have 'a heated imagination,' if could but retain it! These truths fire my soul, and clear my eyes; and I look forward to the joy that is set before me, and consider, if a face of flesh and blood can inspire me with confidence, joy, and delight, and impart, with the same glance, its own love and complacency, then what will *that* inspire you and me with, and what will be imparted, when we indeed see the glory of God in the face of Jesus Christ, face to face? 'For we shall see Him as He is, and we shall be like Him!' Riches, honours, delicious things, will only whet the edge of all the pains in hell; and poverty, for Christ's sake and conscience sake, and also pain, and heaviness, and reproach, and sufferings, and dying, endured now, will heighten the pleasures, and enrich the recompense of the reward in heaven. Never forget we have a freehold estate there. 'So much as she glorified herself, and lived deliciously, so much torment and sorrow give her.' 'Rejoice and be exceeding glad when men speak evil of you; for your reward shall be great.' 'I will give to every man according as his work shall be.'

The arrangements he had entered into, for the resumption of regular preaching at Malda and for the oversight of the professing Christians there, appeared at first to promise much advantage. Mr. Udny's restored friendship was the source of great comfort. In Mrs. Udny's delight in God's word and prayerful spirit, he also saw much to assure him that his labours were attended with a blessing, which he trusted would issue in the happiest results. Under the same date as the foregoing letter, he wrote to his father,—

I am recalled to my former station, and continue to preach in English, as well as Bengalese, to a very loving little flock, whose affection is improved and refined by tribulation and experience. The natives still increase in numbers; but we have not come to the expected revolution among them by baptism. Wait for another letter, and then, perhaps, you will see what the Lord will do.

May the precious things of the everlasting hills be the pasture of your souls, and may our lips be filled with freewill offerings of praise and thanksgiving, for all that Christ has done *for* us, and *in* us, and *to* us; and for the lively hope yet *before* us. When I first heard the gospel effectually, I learnt to 'labour for the things of eternal life;' and that 'the Son of man would give' them. And if He did not do the same to this day, my profession would quickly come to nothing. As to my salvation, I know it is wholly effected for me, independent of repentance, faith, or anything wrought *on* me or *in* me. These are all after-consequences. But for these I long, I faint. I long to be more sanctified; and am burdened with such things as persuade me, like so many fresh evidences, that the Lord has not given me over: no, nor ever will. I entreat you to pray that your son may be divinely instructed, guided and upheld from falling, and finally presented with you faultless before God.

But the hopeful appearances over which he rejoiced in March were sadly dissipated in April. Facts came to light which compelled him to believe that Ram Basu, his too well-trusted múnshi, had been "guilty of lying, defrauding, and adultery!" Nor was this all. One of his younger English hearers, whom he had regarded as a fruit of his own ministry, was convicted of almost the same sins, and Mr. Thomas's heart was sorely cast down. He wrote to his brother some months later :—

My work among the heathen has gone on slowly since December last, for I have been constantly preaching in English at Malda. I have seen with my own eyes, the true thorny ground, stony ground, and infested hearers, great falls, total apostasies, great recoveries, and all in a little society. As to myself, I have been kept, thus far, from forsaking my ministry. I am kept alive from the dead ; but my field of corn, which was so green and promising in appearance, and vigorous in blade, is so infested with rats and mice, and other devouring vermin, and so dry for want of rain, and so pale and sickly and feeble, that were it not for, now and then, a little reviving shower to fill up the holes of the rats and mice in dry places, and make it bud a little, I should ere now have given it all over for lost. Many tares, also, have lately appeared, which, while young, I took to be blades of corn.

The discouragement, arising out of the unhappy facts above adverted to, was never fully removed. Other unpleasantness also arose, and Mr. Thomas felt that his prospects of usefulness amongst his countrymen at Malda were become very poor. He saw reason too to mistrust those appearances of the progress of the gospel amongst the natives, which were so fair in the middle of 1790. His faith was evidently to be put yet more severely to the test.

In the latter part of July he accompanied Mrs. Udny and her son on an excursion to the Rajmahal hills ; but the weather was stormy, and he appears to have returned in somewhat impaired health.

He had now begun to think of returning to England. Mr. Udny wished him to remain a few years longer, and then to go home with him ; but, as the year 1791 advanced, he became more and more impatient to rejoin the dear ones he had left behind him. If his intentions and wishes be rightly considered, it will be seen that he who refused to give up his work among the heathen and return to England in the beginning of 1790, was quite as little disposed to abandon his missionary calling now that he found himself compelled to revisit his native land, two years later. In August, he wrote to his brother,—

> I am going to tell you some news. You need not be surprised to see me in England, perhaps about the middle of 1792; for I intend to take my passage this season. My intention is to make types, procure a press, also a fellow-labourer; and, if I can, establish a fund in London for the support of this work, and also to regain my family, and return after eight months' stay in England. Come, what say you? Will you take heart, and come along, bag and baggage?—Ezra viii. 21, 31. I shall have good news to tell you by and by, as I said before. We must wait the Lord's time; for, after all, He is everything, and all in all.

Rám Basu's guilt did not lead to his dismissal, even now. Mr. Thomas could not bear to think that all his hopes of him were futile, and was only too ready to accept his professions of penitence and a new heart. The discouraged missionary, however, began to feel that all his pretended converts, by their avoidance of baptism and by the pertinaceous preservation of their caste, had given him much reason to discredit their sincerity, and he was at length weary of all excuses and postponements.

What was the real character of these men, of whom Mr. Thomas had so confidently believed that they were new creatures in Christ Jesus, whilst their inconsistencies and unwillingness to profess themselves Christians in baptism, so often, and so sorely, disappointed his hopes? It is most difficult even now to form any satisfactory opinion of them. Some of them had evidently felt very deeply the truths announced to them, and their emotions went far to satisfy Mr. Thomas of their genuine conversion. They also did much as avowed believers in Christianity, which must have compromised them in the eyes of the people who formed their world; and they did this at a time when the missionary was so deserted by his friends, as to be apparently able to do very little for those dependent upon him. It is therefore difficult wholly to deny their sincerity. Probably the judgment of truth would regard them as men halting between two opinions, in whose minds the lower, baser, motives of action gained strength by the indecision and delay in which they persisted. " The latter end was worse with them than the beginning." Perhaps, too, it should be acknowledged that they were not very wisely treated by their instructor. That he was indulgent to their failings ; and, to the extent of his ability, yea, far beyond it, lavish in his generosity towards them, has been intimated above. How constantly and carefully he taught them in Christian truth, appears from his journal. But his too sanguine temperament no doubt misled him in judging of their spiritual state ; whilst his impatience betrayed him into occasional fits of displeasure, which must have greatly disturbed and damaged his influence over them.

Now that he was leaving Bengal, he determined to bring them to decision, one way or the other. "I declared," he wrote in the middle of September, "in the most solemn manner, that if they did break their promise with me, I would not keep any one of them all, nor give them one more Rupee, by any means whatsoever, so long as caste was observed. This has thrown them into great consternation, tears, and supplication, with catching hold of my feet ; also with a plain intimation that they would drown themselves ! 'What,' said I, 'had you rather drown than obey Christ, and be baptized ? If it is come to this, I am more than ever determined to keep my word, whatever be the consequence.' Then they said they would never leave me, though I gave them nothing. They now say, they will see what will be done at Nuddea."

This was followed by meetings for special prayer to God, by affectionate exhortations, and the reading of some of the most striking texts of the gospels appropriate to the circumstances, and the men all wept, and at length declared themselves resolved to be baptized at Nuddea. But when the time came, they drew back, and after repeated efforts to bring them to a sense of their often acknowledged duty, not one of them would confess Christ in the manner of His appointment. Mr. Thomas regarded Mohan Chand as much more in fault than the rest; but it is difficult to see wherein the múnshi and Párbati showed themselves any more worthy of his confidence.

On the 13th of September, he left Malda and his house at Bethelpur, hoping to be able to carry out his design, and go to England at the beginning of 1792. But how was he to manage this, overwhelmed as he was with debt and surrounded with difficulties? After leaving India, Mr. Grant "showed some favor:" probably it took the form of a contribution which Mr. Udny might apply towards the expenses of the homeward voyage. Mr. Grant evidently felt that as he had been instrumental in inducing Mr. Thomas to remain in Bengal, he ought to assist him to leave it. Mr. Thomas's debts, the same entry shows, were now estimated at £1000! His hope of discharging them appeared to be smaller than ever! In his thoughts of going home, it was by no means his wish to forsake his mission work;—he wanted indeed to take Rám Basu home with him, so that the translation might not be interrupted;—but, if nothing better could be done to arrange his circumstances, he intended "to appease his creditors, to regain his family, to come out again, and to go into practice." Then he would "take twelve native medical scholars, and twelve European children to educate, and so work himself free of debt!"

The temptation to try what a lottery ticket would do for him reverted under these perplexities; and this time he yielded to it. The counter-check for *No.* 6457, *Madras Exchange, Fourth Lottery*, is pasted into his journal, opposite the date, October 4th. Calcutta was all astir with Lotteries and Tontines at this period, and when, towards the end of April in this year, Mr. Charles Weston, a wealthy and very benevolent East Indian member of Mr. Brown's congregation, drew the chief prize in Mr. Tiretta's Lottery, consisting of the Bazar in Calcutta which still bears his name, valued at Rs. 1,96,000, Mr. Thomas was probably irresistibly inclined to believe that this method of relief from his difficulties would be effectual. Experience taught him, however, that this was not according to God's will.

He had begun to learn Sanscrit, in the hope of thereby increasing his missionary efficiency; and he resolved to improve some of the months yet remaining to him in Bengal by carrying forward this study at Nuddea, the most celebrated seat of Hindu learning in Bengal. From that place therefore, he wrote to his father, at the end of October, as follows :—

I said in my last that I had thoughts of coming to England; and I had determined on doing so this year; but such things have come to pass contrary to my expectations, that I had partly laid aside my design. Your letter has revived my purpose. If the Lord please, difficulties that yet remain will be removed, and I shall come home, and once more see my dear father. You must know that if I come home without a native, the translation ceases, and my labour on this work must be suspended. He who was to come with me finds his heart utterly fail him; because he would thereby lose his caste, and none of his nearest relations and countrymen would ever eat with him again; but would account him unclean, as they do us. It is astonishing to see how tenacious they are of their caste.

I am now set down here in a house I have just erected, made of bamboos, twine, and straw. It is on a large plain on the banks of that celebrated river the Ganges. I sleep in my boat, for warmth at night, and dwell in the house, for coolness by day. Every morning, the bank of the river is covered with the lame, the halt, and the blind; every one to be cured gratis, and paid a few cowries for food besides. My heart aches every day to behold their helpless state in body and soul.

This Nuddea, you must know, is our Hindu Oxford, where all the learned pandits dwell, and where disciples come from very remote parts of India to be taught their shastras or laws.* I am

---

* An interesting paper on the present state of the Nuddea "Toles," from the pen of Professor E. B. Cowell, may be found in the *Proceedings of the Asiatic Society of Bengal*, for June, 1867, p. 36. Their condition in Mr. Thomas's time is perhaps more exactly described in the following extract from the *Calcutta Monthly Register*, for January, 1791.

"The grandeur of the foundation of the Nuddea University is generally acknowledged. It consists of three colleges,—Nuddea, Santipore and Gopalpara. Each is endowed with funds for maintaining masters in every science. Whenever

quite a prodigy amongst them, and they are very apt to bestow upon me such blasphemous titles and names, as I cannot endure to hear. Whereupon, I too often convince them that I am but a frail mortal; for they hold that a man of real holiness can never be angry. Sometimes I remonstrate with them so sharply for their behaviour and speeches, that their blessings are turned

the revenue of these lands proves too scanty for the support of the pandits and their scholars, the rájá's treasury supplies the deficiency: for the respective masters have not only stated salaries from the raja, for their own support; but also an additional allowance for every pupil they entertain. And these resources are so ample and so well administered, that in the college of Nuddea alone, there are at present about eleven hundred students, and one hundred and fifty masters. These numbers, it is true, fall very short of those entertained in former days. In raja Rudra's time, there were at Nuddea, no less than four thousand students, with masters in proportion.

"The students that come from distant parts, are generally of a maturity in years, and proficiency in learning, to qualify them for beginning the study of philosophy immediately on their admission; but yet they say, that to become a real pandit, a man ought to spend twenty years at Nuddea, in close application.

"Any man that chooses to devote himself to literature, will find a maintenance at Nuddea, from the fixed revenues of the University, and the donation of the raja.

"By the pandits' system of education, all valuable works are committed to memory; and to facilitate this, most of their compositions,—even their dictionaries,—are in metre. But they by no means trust their learning entirely to this repository: on the contrary, those who write treatises, or commentaries on learned topics, have, at Nuddea, always met with distinguished encouragement and rewards.

"The time of attending the public schools and lectures, is from 10 o'clock in the morning until noon. Their method of teaching is this:—two of the masters commence a dialogue, or disputation, on the particular topic they mean to explain. When a student hears any thing advanced, or expressed, that he does not perfectly understand, he has the privilege of interrogating the master about it. They give the young men every encouragement to communicate their doubts, by their temper and patience in solving them. It is a professed and established maxim at Nuddea, that a pandit who loses his temper, in explaining any point to a student, let him be ever so dull and void of memory, absolutely forfeits his reputation, and is disgraced.

"The Nuddea rajas have made it their frequent practice, to attend the disputations. On all public occasions especially, the raja assists, and rewards those who distinguish themselves. But, instead of cup-fulls of gold and silver, as formerly; all that this prince can now afford to bestow is a *lotá, dhoti,* i. e. a brass cup and a pair of drawers. These, however, from the raja's own hand, are considered by no means a trivial reward.—No emperor's *khelat* communicates a higher pleasure, or inspires a nobler pride.—Nothing can be more characteristic of philosophic simplicity and moderation, than the value which they set upon it: 'Is it not,' say they, 'the dress and furniture which nature requires?'"

into a volume of bitter curses; but, in general, I am in very great favor. Yesterday evening, three of their divines, whom I had never seen before, came to my cottage, and sent notice that they were come to judge shastras with me. I immediately ordered a mat to be spread on the ground; on which they sat down after their custom, and I in the chair. I spoke first, and said, 'In *this* world, we judge shastras; but in *that* world shastras will judge us.' I asked one, who seemed chief, what books he had read; and I happened to know them all; for they were a Sanskrit Grammar and and Dictionary! He confessed that he had read only one holy book, and that not throughout. I told him he must read *two*, before he could possibly be a judge! The rest had read no book on religious subjects. Then we entered into a conversation, which ended in their repeated request to see a Bible. I brought it, and read it, till it was grown quite dark; and they departed, filled with wonder. Many and many such interviews I have with them; yet does it all pass away; and they are so highly prejudiced in favor of their own books, that I think sometimes it is all in vain to persuade them. They hold the Bengalese language in great contempt, as soon as they become acquainted with the Shanskrit, in which all their religious stuff is written. Wherefore I am now at this place on purpose to acquire a knowledge of the Shanskrit language.

Great dejections trouble and haunt my spirit continually because I am made no more successful in my ministry to these heathens. I have been a minister of the New Testament to them; but, whether of the letter or the Spirit, I hang in doubt. I have been greatly humbled also; but not enough. '*Our* sufficiency is of God,' says the Apostle. Self-sufficiency is of the devil. I mourn, I sigh, I grieve. Still I find a cold, hard, desperate heart, and if God enter into any thing else but pure mercy, *I* am sure to perish. My soul groans and cries out for God.

Mr. Thomas soon became popular with the Nuddea pandits. One of them, "Panchánan Bidyálankár, a most agreeable melodious teacher," found for him a good Sanscrit tutor, whose name was Padma Lochan. By his aid, the missionary was soon initiated in the introductory mysteries of the *Mugdabodh Byákaran*. He studied very diligently, and laboured constantly to set the truth of Christ before the learned pandits he daily encountered at Nuddea. Every day too he was busy attending to the sick and the indigent, who flocked to him for relief.

During the early part of his stay at Nuddea, he renewed his acquaintance with Sir William Jones, who was enjoying his long vacation at Kishnagur. This place was chosen for his retreat, because of the facilities it afforded him for prosecuting his Sanscrit studies, with the aid of the Nuddea pandits. He now showed Mr. Thomas great kindness, was always glad to see him at his house, and took much interest in his engagements, especially in his translations. He discussed with him the exact meaning of Bengali terms, which occurred in the version, and greatly encouraged him in his endeavours to acquire a knowledge of the Sanscrit language. The missionary also found a friend in Mr. Redfearn, the energetic judge of the district, who was very helpful to him; but he went little into their society, and passed "weeks together without seeing an English face or using his own language, except in prayer."

On the 10th of December, he finally left Nuddea, having been utterly disappointed in the refusal of his people to be baptized. He now made arrangements to go home in the ship *Il Nettuno*. She did not leave until the end of January, 1792, and meanwhile he was actively engaged in preaching to the villagers on each side of the river above Calcutta.

Mr. Thomas's profound reverence for the Scriptures has often appeared in the foregoing narrative. On Lord's-day, January 8th, 1792, he recorded some observations upon the word of God which may be read with interest. They seem to have been suggested by his recent experiences of Calcutta infidelity.—

Amongst the proofs commonly given of the divine origin of the Scriptures, I do not find this grand one, which is adapted to the understanding of the most uncultivated mind, viz.—*We are sure that the Scriptures are from God, because God is now dealing with every man according to the Scriptures.*

For instance,—Some, ' when they know God, they glorified Him not as God,... wherefore God also gave them up to uncleanness and a reprobate mind !'—Romans i. 21-28. Some who had been labouring under guilt of conscience and the sense of their past wicked lives, and had been heavily laden at heart, have come unto the Lord, and He hath given them rest, and peace which passeth all understanding.—Matthew xi. 28. Some are blind and see not, nor own any thing of spiritual truth, however evident, according to 1 Corinthians ii. 14. Some are turning at God's reproof, and He is pouring out His Spirit upon them, 'as the dew,' 'as the gentle rain,' 'as the showers,' or 'as floods;' and God is making known to them His word in a manner they had no conception of before: according to Proverbs i. 23. Some are wise, great, and good in their own eyes, but God hides His communications from them in His displeasure.—Matthew xi. 25.

Now if this be true, that God is dealing with every one according to the Scriptures, then any man upon the face of the earth, who has access to the sacred oracles, may have within himself, if he pleases, the most lively proofs, not only that there is a God, and that the Bible is His word, but that God is dealing with him himself, at this very instant, and every day of his life, exactly according to that word. The predictions of God, there written, were not only fulfilled a thousand years ago or more, but now: not only in the wide theatre of the world, but in the little narrow compass of every man's heart. There are different degrees of evidence of this affecting fact. The dealings of God are more observed and searched out by some than others; and therefore more manifest to some than to others. Every thing that can be met with in experience is really described in Scripture, but some understand not. We see and know that the effects of idolatry, as we witness it amongst the Hindus, and of false doctrines, such as we find amongst the Mahommedans and others, are in the world exactly what is said in the word.

There are many things which, if rightly considered, fully account for the general carelessness of mankind as to the interesting subject above written of, and particularly in this country. Take this in particular.—It is the happiness of a good man that God is what He is, and that His word is a living truth, with all power within it. But this is also the ungodly man's greatest misery. To blasphemers, free-, and foolish-thinkers, deists, theists, and all sorts of infidels and libertines, there is no woe greater than that conveyed by those two utterances—' I am that I am,' and ' Thy word is truth.' As the guilty prisoner cannot but wish the jury may bring in a false verdict, so, in like manner, these cannot but wish to refute the ' holy apostles and prophets.'

We see characters amongst men which we never should have thought of, perhaps, if they were not in various ways marked out to us in the Scriptures. Who, for instance, would have expected to find amongst mankind 'haters of God?' All men pretend to love Him, or honour Him,—even those who hate or dishonour Him most of all. But who can think of what God is,—holy, just, and an avenger of all sorts of wickedness,—and then see how men drink down iniquity like water, 'make a mock at sin' and every thing that relates to God and eternity,—who can hear their malignant speeches against religion, and its acts and professors,—who can see their aversion to God's word, attributes, worship and servants,—without beholding, as in high noon-day, their hatred to God and all His ways?

As it is impossible to prove to an ignorant rustic in half an hour that the sun is larger than his head, or a fixed star bigger than the moon, so it is impossible to prove to these gainsayers, that God is worthy of their thoughts and infinitely more lovely than any thing they have either knowledge or experience of; or that the Bible is of divine authority, and infinitely more worthy of their attention and perusal than all other business cares or books in the world. You cannot make these sinners against their own souls believe this. Their consciences are so hardened that common strokes leave no impressions. Nay, worse, the gospel and all good counsel not only fails to do them good, but leaves them the worse for it. 'Death unto death.' As the swine trample upon the pearls, and fiercely turn upon those who offer them, so do these rise up with fury, if any godly advice, precious counsel, or reproof tending to their reformation, is offered to them. This is another living proof of the truth of the Bible in all countries and companies, but especially in this.

Little has hitherto been said of Mr. Thomas's methods of preaching to the heathen. His journals contain many such particulars of great interest; but few of these have been inserted lest the book should be unduly expanded. One illustration may, however, be introduced, to show the tact and ability with which his labours were conducted. It is in its proper place here, having occurred on the 10th of January, 1792. The name of the place has not been preserved; but it seems likely that Pánihátí, a village between Serampore and Calcutta, was the scene of the narrative. Mr. Thomas says,—

I was returning from a journey on the Ganges, and expected in one more tide to reach Calcutta; but was obliged to come to, about seven or eight miles short of that place. Dinner not being ready, I went to take a walk on the bank. On landing, I saw no town or village near; but, conversing with a poor native, I understood that I was within half a mile of a Hindu college, where two famous pandits and several students, the Brahmans, resided. I determined to go and pay them a visit, and the poor man directed me, pointing to a large grove of trees, among which they all dwelt. I proposed to myself to go among them as an enquirer, and to say little or nothing to them directly like a teacher. On my arrival at one of the outer buildings, I met with an elderly Brahman, who asked me what I did there? and, while I was satisfying him, another Brahman came up, of a more open countenance and intelligent manner, with whom I began to converse. I told him, I had in my heart a very great anxiety; that I was a sinner, that I had but a little time to stay in this world, and when I should die, my soul would depart to heaven or hell, and dwell there for ever and ever. 'You are a Brahman,' said I, 'can you not tell me what I shall do to escape the wrath to come, and to obtain forgiveness of sins and admittance into heaven?' He replied, 'You must give to the poor.' I thanked him; but asked how *much* I ought to give, so that I might be sure, and not fail of escaping that wrath and obtaining this felicity? He then said I must give one-fourth of all that I possessed. 'But,' said I, 'Brahman, if all I possess should amount to four rupees only, then by giving one rupee to the poor, shall I certainly escape hell? Can heaven be obtained for one rupee?' Here the poor Brahman felt himself involved in an unexpected dilemma: for it is by no means a notion among them that many will get to heaven. I desired him to speak again, and he then directed me to do holy deeds; but when we came to discuss the quantity and quality of these deeds, he abruptly broke off, at the dread of another dilemma, and said he would take me to the college close by, where the pandits and more able Brahmans would answer me better than he could. The buildings were mud walls, covered with straw, and surrounded with cocoa-nut and other trees, which made a pleasant grove, and afforded an agreeable shade. Their several houses are all round about it, at different distances. As you stand opposite the front of it, you see a large open shed, considerably raised, where the pandits give lessons to their students every morning. On each side, is a row of toles,* or cottages, joined to each other,

---

* Mr. Thomas appears to use the word "Tole" in an incorrect manner. Properly, the whole college was a tole: not each cottage. Professor Cowell, in the paper already referred to, upon page 181, says:—

"A tole is generally a mere collection of mud huts round a quadrangle, in which the students live in the most primitive manner possible. The pandit does

all exactly alike, and these are habitations for the students, who come from distant countries, and partake of the bounty allowed by the rájás or other persons who contribute to their support. On our arrival there, they seemed to have heard of my coming, for the students poured out from their toles on each side, and assembled themselves under the large shady trees. Thither they brought mats, and spread them underneath the shade, for the Brahmans to sit on; a chair also was brought for me; and they all sat down. After a little time, one of the venerable pandits appeared, and all rose up to receive him; some paid him homage by prostrating themselves at his feet, and others, who perhaps had already seen him on that day, offered him less tokens of veneration and respect. All now waited for my taking my seat; but I professed to honour my elders, and requested the pandit to be seated first. At this they were the more astonished, because it is not the custom of Europeans to suffer natives to be seated in their presence. After much persuasion, the pandit seated himself in the front of the Brahmans. I then took my chair, and all the Brahmans seated themselves on the mats, in the posture which tailors commonly use at their work. I now began to rehearse the questions and conversation that had passed between me and the Brahman I brought with me, to which they listened with all avidity. I then asked them what I could to do obtain the great ends in question. Some said I ought to apply myself to the name of God. By this they meant, that I should perform the *Jap*, which, in its greatest latitude, consists in pronouncing the name of God millions of times, without speaking any other word; and some whom I knew have continued this vain repetition for whole days and nights together, till their mental faculties were quite deranged. I replied after this manner, 'How can the infinitely great and holy One be pleased to hear His name pronounced so often by these polluted lips?' I enquired if the Supreme Being was wise and good; to which they yielded ready affirmatives. I then fixed my eyes on one of the nearest Brahmans, and asked him if he had a son?

not reside with them, but comes to teach them on the lawful days. Each student has his own hut, with his brass waterpot and mat, and few have any other furniture. Most make their own copies of the books they use, and a large part of the year is vacation, during which they wander over the surrounding country on begging expeditions; but during the reading months much hard mental labour is undoubtedly gone through. On one side of the quadrangle there is a 'lecture hall,' usually on a raised platform, some three feet from the ground. It is open on one side, and just sheltered on the other three from the rain and wind. In some toles, it is only a thatched shed; in others, it is a little more elaborate."

He said he had. 'Whenever you return home,' said I, 'suppose your son were to come running to meet you, and falling down at your feet, should call out, *Pitá,** *Pitá, Pitá, Pitá*, incessantly, without ever saying another word, what would you think of him?' 'I should think,' said he, 'that he was become demented.' 'So, I fear,' said I, 'would the wise and good One, if I were, in the same manner, to call over His holy and reverend name.'

I continued my enquiries, and they directed me to wash in the river Ganges, and the water of that sacred river would cleanse away my sin. I asked them such questions as these: 'Does not sin, according to the shastras, defile and darken the mind? If sin were taken away, would there not be a great change of mind, as from light to darkness, and misery to happiness? and then would not the renewed enjoy sweet communion with the Supreme, who is all light? Does washing the body cleanse away pollution of the mind? Do you yourselves, who wash in the Ganges daily, find this great change? Do you go down into the water with a mind darkened by sin, and come up with a mind enlightened by the Ganges?' It is difficult for me to express their utter confusion and astonishment; for, it is probable, they had never before heard any of these things questioned. But their candour compelled them to speak freely from their own experience, which immediately reflected the condemnation of their doctrines.

Others directed me to worship the gods. I then enquired if it was not written in their shastras, that without faith no worship or ceremony could be acceptable to God? They said, 'Yes.' 'Then,' said I, 'my worship and ceremonies never can be accepted; for I have none of that which you call faith. No caste, no faith. How shall I worship? how shall I be accepted?' The question then was, whether or not I could obtain faith, and how? '*Faith*,' they said, 'was obtained by reading the Vedas.' 'But,' said I, 'the words of the Vedas are reputed so holy, that if any man should read them who is not a Brahman, he would commit sin. I am not a Brahman; neither can I become a Brahman if I would give ten thousand worlds. Besides,' said I, 'do you believe the words of Judhisthír?' 'O! yes, certainly, certainly,' said they, from every quarter. Now Judhisthír is a very great personage in their grand poem, the Mahábhárat; and some think the account there given of him is a mutilated tradition of Jesus Christ. Be that as it may, they say of him, in this poem, that he was not born by ordinary generation, but of Dharmma, the Holy One: that when he was born, all the

* Father.

hills of the earth were enlightened: that, whilst a child, a
great king sought his death: that, as he grew up, he went about
doing good, and diffusing blessings wherever he came. Judhisthír
had several younger brothers, who had not the knowledge of the
Holy, like himself; and on a certain day, his mother sent one of
her younger sons to fetch water from a tank, or pool. On his
coming to the tank, he saw Dharmma, the Holy One, sitting on
the water's edge, in the shape of a bird. Dharmma asked him four
questions, of which the third and chief was, 'What is the way to
heaven?' The lad said he could not tell. Dharmma then forbad
him to take water till these questions were answered. The lad,
however, heedlessly went to take the water, and, in doing so, fell
down dead. The mother, finding her son did not return, sent
another; and the same thing happened to him. She sent them all,
one after another, except Judhisthír, and they all died in the same
manner. Last of all, she sent Judhisthír. When he came, he
readily answered all the questions; and to the question, What is
the way to heaven? he answered thus:—'*Vedá bibhinná;* the
Vedas are discordant: contradictory, one points this way to heaven,
another that. *Shmritayo bibhinná;* the shastras are also discordant. *Náshou munirjashya matang na bhinnang;* none of the rules
of the ancients, but what are discordant. *Dharmmashya tattwang
nihitang guháyáng.* The way to heaven is different from all these.
Mahájano zena gatah sha panthá. The path which the great person
walks in, that is the way.'* Judhisthír having satisfactorily replied,
Dharmma was well pleased: in token of which, his brothers were all
restored to life, and, taking water, all went home with him. 'Now,
Brahman,' said I, 'I ask you the way to heaven? You direct me
to the Vedas. Judhisthír says, The Vedas are discordant. But nothing that is discordant could ever come from God, you know. I
ask you the way to heaven? and you direct me to the sayings of
the shastras; but Judhisthír says, The way to heaven is different
from all these. Which am I to believe?—You or Judhisthír? You
cannot be both right.' Here they expressed their wonder, how I
came to be acquainted with what was written in their shastras;
and they knew not what to say; but continued to declare, they

---

* The original Sanscrit is as follows,—

वेदा विभिन्नाः स्मृतयो विभिन्नाः
नासौ मुनि र्यस्य मतं न भिन्नं ।
धर्म्मस्य तच्वं निहितं गुहायां
महाजनो येन गतः स पन्थाः ॥

never saw or heard of the like. Another question arose concerning who this *Mahá Jan* could be ? Some said, God ; but I objected, that he was never called *Jan*, or a person, in their shastras. Others said it must mean any holy man. I asked if ever they heard of a holy man who walked differently from the Vedas and all the shastras ? They said 'No.' Besides, I said, it was the superlative term here used, and not to be applied to any but One.

At last, they asked *me* who this *Mahá Jan*, this great One, was ? and though I had planned to assert nothing, but only enquire, I could now restrain myself no longer, but began to unfold to them the word of God, which, at sundry times and places, and in divers manners, was sent to men in past ages by the prophets. I particularly spoke of the prophecies of the Great One who was to come, of the time, the tribe, the place, and the manner of His coming,— of His conception, his birth, mysterious person, miracles, life, death, resurrection, and ascension, and of His shedding down the Holy Ghost in the first times ; and of His giving that rest, and peace, which passeth all understanding, to poor sinners, even to this day, of whom I myself was one ; and that He would do so in all parts of the earth, wherever His saving health and holy name were known.

I told them that the *Mahá Jan* had come thus, 'according to the Scriptures.' That while on earth he wrought, and, while he wrought, the glory of Omniscience, Omnipotence, and Omnipresence sparkled through all His doings, 'according to the Scriptures.' He died and rose again. He ascended and shed down blessings 'according to the Scriptures.' I said that I,—a miserable, lost, wretched, and undone soul, labouring in mind, day and night, finding no rest or peace, heavy laden with guilt and wretchedness, distracted by the terrors of the Lord,—I myself had fled to this Jesus and found rest, and received blessings from Him, 'according to the Scriptures ;'—that millions of great sinners of my country had also fled to Him and found great mercy. He saved them all, 'according to the Scriptures,' and never cast out any. That He would come again, to judge the world in truth and righteousness, and for that purpose would raise up all the dead from their graves, 'according to the Scriptures.' That, till then, all the weary and heavy laden sinners of any country that flee to Him shall certainly find rest and peace, pardon and blessings of grace, '*according to the Scriptures.*'

It would not be easy to describe the affecting emotions of mind which my hearers expressed in different ways. Some ran and climbed up the cocoa-nut trees, gathered the nuts and broke the shells, that I might drink the sweet water out of them. God

Almighty grant that I may break the shell to many of them, that they may drink of living waters, out of the inexhaustible fountain in Christ! Others brought sweetmeats, fruits, milk, and the like, and laid them at my feet, saying it would be a sin to suffer me to go away and not eat; for the day was now declining. We had been six hours and upwards in conversation, and I began to take leave; but they continued to follow me even down to my boat. There I shewed them a BIBLE, the first they ever saw; and reminded them of a saying in their shastras, that all nations of the earth should one day become of one caste, and one religion. To this they assented. Also I told them that it was said that there should come a little book, and eat up all their great books. Yes, they all knew this saying to be current. Then, holding up a BIBLE, of Pasham's edition,—which, as you know, is very small,—I said, '*This* is the little book! This is the book of God!' I also very much pleased them by showing them some parts of it translated into their own language, and by telling them of the awful and delightful effects this book is to have upon all nations, when it shall be 'come abroad into all the earth.'

The evening came on, and we parted. Never, methinks, did a people show more reluctance to part with a man who was a perfect stranger. They stood upon the bank, watching and looking, as long as I could see them from the boat. Three weeks later, I sailed for England.

A review of all the facts this history has recorded must surely convince every reader that Mr. Thomas's missionary life, thus far, had been full of painful anxieties and distresses. Nor will it be overlooked, that, in his work amongst the Bengalis, he had enjoyed no true sympathy even from the kindest Christian friends who had in any way helped him. They valued his preaching to themselves, but took no steady interest in what he did for the natives. They suspected—he thought, most unfairly,—the motives of his converts, and gave him little assistance in sustaining the burden he bore in caring for them. He was really *alone* in his attempts to bring the Bengalis to the knowledge of Christ: the one man in all Bengal who practically cared for the people perishing there "for lack of knowledge." How great the discouragements under which he laboured were, has been seen. Yet, notwithstanding all, his longing for the salvation of these poor heathen continued unabated. He would not, he *could* not, abandon the work to which he believed God had called him, and which he loved even as his life. And now that he was about to leave the country which had witnessed his discouragements and difficulties, he had no stronger wish than to return to it again, with such help as would enable him more efficiently to pursue the noble calling he had accepted when he left the *Earl of Oxford*. All his trials and disappointments, great as they had been, could not destroy his confidence in the ultimate success of the gospel in Bengal. Thus, at home, after speaking of what he had witnessed of the convictions produced by the gospel in the hearts of many of his hearers, he declared :—" And if these were dead, I should go over to the Hindus with all joy and confidence of hope, assuredly gathering from these tokens, and many others, that the Lord hath called me to preach unto them 'the unsearchable riches of Christ :' and I hope and pray that He will yet enable and call others more fit for, and worthy of, this delightful work than myself."

The paper from which the foregoing extract is made refers in very affecting terms to the circumstances in which he gave himself to the mission, and to the mistakes and other painful experiences which had succeeded that period of consecration to an arduous and hitherto untried service. —" Waters enough," he wrote, " have risen since to damp, but will never utterly extinguish, what was lighted up at that time !"

Rám Rám Basu and Párbatí accompanied him to Calcutta when he was about to set sail. They knew that he corresponded with the Rev. Dr. Samuel Stennett, one of the most influential ministers in the Baptist denomination in England, and they were anxious that their message of entreaty that the spiritual wants of Bengal might receive due attention should be conveyed to that excellent man. Mr. Thomas suggested to them that they themselves should write to Dr. Stennett whatever they wished to say. They did so ; and he took home with him a letter from them, of which the following is a translation. Its English date is January 18th, 1792.

GREAT SIR, *7th Mágh*, 1198.

We sinful heathens for a long time have used worship and ceremonies according to our paganish shastras and customs, and we have been accustomed to think, that different kinds of people, having different kinds of shastras, would be saved by the words thereof. The deeds of the shastras of this our country, you will become acquainted with on conversing with Mr. Thomas.

O great sir, though we thought that many nations had many kinds of shastras, yet in the country of the English we thought there was no shastra at all; for, concerning sin and holiness, those who are here have no judgment at all. We have even thought that they were not men, but a kind of other creatures like devourers. Within these six years, it is our mercy and praise that Mr. John Thomas came into this country. Such an excellent kind of person we had neither seen, heard, or known of, at any time. On his coming here, he employed me as his múnshi; and after I had taught him a little Bengalese, he asked me, 'Múnshi, if you were to die now, whither would you go?' 'How can I tell, Sir?' said I; 'I shall go where God takes me.' 'True,' said he; 'but men in general, when they die, where do their souls go?' I answered, 'All men go to a place according to their works: the holy go to heaven, and the sinner goes to hell.' He asked me what heaven and hell, what sin and holiness were? to which I replied particularly. He, smiling, said, 'How can a man be freed from his sins by such superficial works as these?' But none of us could answer him, only that it was written so in our shastras, and that our forefathers, from generation to generation, were thought to have thus obtained salvation: this was all we knew. Mr. Thomas knows the drift of our shastras, and will describe them to you.

When he began to tell us how men could be saved, then we greatly wondered, and we thought within ourselves, These English are the unclean; they have never had any shastras, and how should this man know the way of salvation? But we said, 'Speak, Sir, and we will hear.' He began to read to us the glad tidings of salvation out of the Bible; and as we heard him speak, we were amazed and rejoiced. Now we know certainly that this is the shastra of God, and the way of salvation. This will stand, and all others are utterly vain. O great Sir, we are now very thoughtful, and bethink ourselves what have we been doing all this time? We deserve the depth of hell as the fruit of our doings; at the thoughts of which we were greatly troubled. But the gospel is begun to be published. The books of Matthew, Mark, and James, are almost ready, and the gospel is coming into our country. Our Sahib has preached in many places; and wherever the people have heard, there they have been amazed and glad. Several of us who were before workers of iniquity, have now understood the evil of it; all which our Sahib will make known to you.

Now it is our wish that this great word was translated into Bengalese. As we hear, we make it known: but we are only a poor people, and cannot do as we wish. But we hope, great Sir, you will have compassion upon us, and send preachers into this country, and those that will help forward the translation; and that we sinful people may walk according to this word, for whosoever has faith in the Lord Jesus Christ, will be cleansed from his sins by his blood, and we do hope that He will help us in all these particulars. Our hope rests in Him.

Great Sir, we have never before seen the excellent people; the first we ever saw was Mr. Thomas; and by him we know that the greater people will shew compassion. Of other things we will write hereafter. This is all.

SHREE PARBATI, BRAHMAN.
SHREE RAM RAM BASU, KAISHTHA.

The ship *Il Nettuno* was bound to Ostend. Her commander captain Angelo Borgo, was a Roman Catholic, and the passengers were all irreligious people, in whose society Mr. Thomas could find little pleasure. One of them, however, must be specially noticed,—Captain James Wilson. He was retiring to England after a life of strange adventure, involving almost incredible hardships and dangers. He was an able navigator, and as commander of one of the Hon'ble East India Company's country ships, had distinguished himself by the daring and success with which he conveyed supplies to the troops under Sir Eyre Coote, when hemmed in by the forces of Hyder Ali. Captain Wilson several times most cleverly escaped the French squadron employed in intercepting all relief to the British army; but at length his vessel was captured, and he was carried as a prisoner of war to Cuddalore. Having vainly attempted to escape, he and his fellow-prisoners fell into the hands of Hyder Ali; and, refusing to become a Mussulman and to enlist in Hyder's service, he suffered a long and frightfully rigorous imprisonment at

Seringapatam, until the triumph of the British arms led to his release. Upon his recovery from the effects of his captivity, captain Wilson resumed his former employment, and after some time became commander of the *Speke*. By his skill and enterprise, he had thus gained a competency, upon which he was now intending to live quietly at home. In his religious character, he was only too much like the generality of his countrymen then in India. Mr. Thomas called him "a rank deist of the profaner sort." He held many a stubborn dispute with him about religion, and so badly did the missionary think of his opponent, that he one day told the chief officer of the *Il Nettuno* that he had far better hopes of the conversion of the ignorant lascars on board than of that of captain Wilson!

But this daring disbeliever in the word of God was, two or three years afterwards, brought to surrender himself most completely to its authority; and in the fervent love of his renewed heart to the Redeemer, he was eager to know how best he could devote his strength and ability to His service. A course of usefulness opened up before him. The newly formed "Missionary Society" was preparing to send forth a number of missionaries to the islands of the South Seas. Captain Wilson heartily sympathised with the enterprise, and volunteered to command the ship which should be freighted with these messengers of the truth. His offer was gratefully accepted by the Directors, and the exemplary prudence, piety, goodness, and ability with which he fulfilled his responsible undertaking were beyond all praise. Having, with the utmost care, arranged for the settlement of the missionaries, captain Wilson took the *Duff* on to China, whence the East India Company had chartered her to bring home a cargo of tea. This was shipped with prompt despatch, and landed in perfect order. The freight thus earned, £5,000, was somewhat more than the sum paid by the Missionary Society for the ship. In 1796, on captain Wilson's appointment to the command of the *Duff*, he sent word to Mr. Thomas of the mighty change wrought in his convictions, and the news was "as cold waters to a thirsty soul."

But, to return to the *Il Nettuno*. She left Calcutta on the 30th of January, and, sailed for Europe, after some days' delay at Kedgeree, touching at Vizagapatam, Coringa, Pondicherry, and St. Helena on her way. Mr. Thomas found himself and his religious opinions regarded with great contempt by his fellow passengers at the beginning of the voyage, but he was always intrepid in the defence of what he believed to be the truth, and, as time passed, he won his way to the esteem of his companions. At the commencement of April, he induced some of them to listen on Sunday to a sermon which he read in a cabin below, This was so well approved that, on the third Sunday and afterwards, he usually preached sermons of his own to all on board who could understand English, assembled on deck or in the ship's cuddy. His discourses seem to have been discussed with remarkable freedom by his hearers; but if they were "complained of by some," they were "approved by more;" and he was not without hope that God's blessing would make the word spoken effectual to the salvation of his hearers. The voyage passed with the usual experiences. He found many opportunities to make himself serviceable to the sick on board, and had much time for devotion, and self-improvement in reading. Towards the close of the voyage there was the excitement of being chased by Algerine cruisers. On the 8th of July, he was happy to stand once more on English soil, at Dover. It was the Lord's day, and, with gladsome heart, he joined the congregation worshipping under the ministry of Mr. Porter. The next morning he was on his way to London, and the same day happily rejoined his beloved family at Hampstead Heath, where his wife had been living "at the back of Jack Straw's Castle," since he last saw her in 1786.

Here, for a little while, Mr. Thomas's personal history may be left, whilst the attention of the reader is directed to other matters of interest to this narrative. It may be imagined with how much joy he found himself restored to the society and Christian privileges he had longed after in a distant land. With great delight, he once more resorted to the sanctuaries hallowed in his memory by so many sacred associations; and listened to the preaching of Dr. Stennett, Mr. Burnside, Mr. Beddome, and the then youthful Mr. Jay, who was visiting London at the time. He was also himself invited to preach for Dr. Stennett and others, and he lost no time in urging his plans for the establishment of a Baptist mission to Bengal upon the good Doctor's attention and that of Mr. Booth.

CHAPTER VIII.

Missionary Projects for Bengal.

SOMETHING has already been said of the Calcutta Protestant Mission and of the results ascribed to it down to the time when Mr. Kiernander's misfortunes led to his removal from the post he had so long held, and brought about the transfer of the mission church to Mr. Grant, who purchased it, and the two trustees he associated with himself in the custody of the property.

It may be well here to trace the further history of this mission, as far as it can be thought to have survived in the associations of this church or otherwise.

The trustees, on assuming charge of the property Mr. Grant rescued from the wreck of Mr. Kiernander's affairs, put themselves in communication with the Society for Promoting Christian Knowledge, which had so long aided the Calcutta Mission, and confidently expected that they would immediately take steps to supply Mr. Kiernander's place. Mr. Brown and his co-trustees besought the Society to lose no time in sending out to Calcutta an English clergyman, who might preach in the church and revive the other operations of the Protestant mission. Long as this Society had been engaged in supporting East Indian missions, it had never yet been able to employ an Englishman in the work, but depended wholly upon the the selection made for it, by Professor Francke of Halle and others, from the young German theologians who were eager to labour in the East. It was indeed a reproach not unfrequently alleged against the venerable

Society at this time, that it could give any thing to the good work of evangelizing the heathen, except a man to preach the gospel. To the Calcutta mission, in particular, it had sent books, a clock, bells, paper and a press, and printing materials, an organ, and even an organist,—but not a missionary from amongst its own countrymen.

Mr. Brown and his colleagues directed the attention of the Society to the Rev. T. Lloyd, of King's College, Cambridge, who, they hoped, would accept the charge of the Calcutta mission. In urging his engagement they stated that the mission church was "the only place that the native Portuguese had to look to for deliverance from the slavery of the Popish communion, and that it promised to be a convenient place of instruction to the lower class of Europeans, and although the church was situated in a large town, they judged that a missionary on the spot, besides instructing the English and Portuguese, might have opportunities of addressing himself to the conversion of the natives, and of aiding any views that might be entertained of that sort."

Mr. Lloyd was, however, unable to accept the post offered to him; but, to the great joy of the Society, a young English clergyman was at length found ready to undertake the work of the mission. This was the Rev. Abraham Thomas Clarke, B. A., formerly of Trinity College, Cambridge, who was solemnly set apart to the duty in March, 1789, and shortly afterwards sailed for Calcutta. His arrival there, in August, was, however, productive of little benefit to the cause he was sent out to sustain. In addition to the charge of the mission church, he, soon after his coming, became Head-Master of the Calcutta Free School, and, in December, 1790, he altogether abandoned the mission to become a Government chaplain.*

* This circumstance may be noted as a curious illustration of the irregularity with which affairs were conducted in the early days to which this history belongs. The Rev. Thomas Clarke was announced by the Court of Directors as having been appointed a military chaplain upon their Bengal establishment. The Rev. A. T. Clarke thereupon concluded that he was the man, and that he was indebted for the appointment to the kind interest of some unknown English friends. He

Many fruitless attempts were made to replace him in the mission till, in the middle of 1797, the Rev. William Tobias Ringeltaube, from Halle, was sent out to Calcutta. After his arrival there, in October, he announced that "the school which was instituted in the year 1758 for the instruction of children, European and native, in English, writing, and arithmetic, would again be opened on the first day of January, 1798, for day scholars." As a preacher, Mr. Ringeltaube seems to have been much liked by the congregation at the mission church; but he speedily became dissatisfied with his very narrow income, and "did not see the prospect of usefulness before him." At the close of 1798, therefore, before the Society could reply to his complaints, he quitted Calcutta and returned to Europe.* This gave very sore vexation to those who sent him to India, and they stated that they could "only hope, and pray God, that their expectations might not be so disappointed in any future missionaries that might be sent out." Thus the charge of the mission church was again and again thrown back upon Mr. Brown, who was, however, very much aided in it now by the Rev. Dr. Buchanan. The Portuguese congregation was still under the ministry

therefore applied to the authorities in Calcutta for admission to the post, and, upon the strength of his own mistaken representations, he was sent as chaplain to Chunar, at the close of 1790. After several months, however, the other Mr. Clarke arrived, and took the place of his disappointed namesake, who returned to Calcutta. He then, at the end of 1791, made an attempt to introduce "the voluntary principle" into the Presidency church. The chaplains allowed him the use of the building for evening services, and a subscription list was circulated in order to support him as Sunday Evening Lecturer. The project soon came to nothing; and Mr. Clarke set up a school, in which Mr. Foley was afterwards his partner, "at No. 75, Cossitollah." His health having failed, he went to Malacca, where he kept an English school, and was engaged to officiate as chaplain to the British garrison. It appears also that, whilst at Malacca, he acquired a knowledge of the Malay language, and endeavoured to speak of Christ in it.

* This was not the termination of Mr. Ringeltaube's missionary career. After associating in Europe chiefly with the Moravian Brethren, he offered his services to the London Missionary Society, and, in 1804, arrived at Tranquebar as their missionary. He was a most eccentric man; but his missionary labours were unremitted, his abilities great, his enthusiasm undying, his self-denial almost unexampled, and his success wonderful. In 1816, he quitted India and went to Java. It is said that he left behind him in Travancore, as the fruit of his labours there, six missionary stations and nine hundred baptized Christians.

Mr. Frenzel, who had been Mr. Kiernander's assistant. Nothing more was done to revive the old Protestant mission; and, at the close of 1808, a new character was given to the church by the appointment to it of the Rev. Thomas Thomason, as a chaplain upon the Bengal establishment, by the Hon'ble the Court of Directors. His able and faithful ministry attracted to the Old Church the élite of Calcutta religious society, and while the least cultivated hearer was instructed by his preaching, the congregation generally was no longer made up of "the lower class" of citizens.

These facts sufficiently show that, at any rate after the departure of Mr. Kiernander, the Calcutta mission sustained no operations especially designed to accomplish the conversion of the heathen to the knowledge and obedience of Christ. Services were held at the mission church in English and Portuguese, and the school was revived for a few months by Mr. Ringeltaube; but nothing else deserving the name of a mission seems to have been carried on. A number of poor Protestant Christians, some of whom had been reclaimed from Romanism by Mr. Kiernander and his colleagues, appear to have received stipends from funds at the disposal of the mission. Mr. O'Beck was employed to look after these persons, and, as Dr. Buchanan informs us, "his office" was "the distribution of four or five hundred rupees a month to the poor." Help to the mission seems to have been directed into the same channel of expenditure. An advertisement, in the Calcutta papers for 1792, announced the publication of *Ostervald's Abridgment of the History of the Bible*, in English and Persian, "to be sold for the benefit of the Protestant mission in Bengal," stating that the proceeds would be devoted to "the support of indigent Protestant families in Bengal."

But what of the *Proposals for establishing a Protestant Mission in Bengal and Behar*, drawn up originally by Mr. Grant, and spoken of in the earlier pages of this volume?

It is hardly necessary to inform the reader that Mr. Thomas's influence in modifying those proposals, of which he wrote so complacently in a letter quoted on page 58, was very short lived. The papers speedily reverted to the hands of the Rev. David Brown, and the "eight young men who were in the colleges" reappeared in the MS. scheme, which he urgently recommended to the interest and support of the most influential men in the Church of England at home, likely to favor such an undertaking. The Rev. John Newton, the Rev. Thomas Scott, the Rev. Charles Simeon of Cambridge, W. Wilberforce, Esq., and others, were entreated to do all they could to carry it into effect, and all were cordial in their promises of assistance. Mr. Simeon, in particular, regarded all the details of Mr. Brown's scheme as displaying "the most consummate wisdom, combined with the most ardent zeal." The eight young missionaries, Mr. Simeon tells us, with a salary of £350 per annum each, were to "reside in the eight grand divisions of the country, (as it is existed at *that* time,) namely, at Calcutta, Murshidábád, Patna, (or Benares,) Monghyr, Dinájpur, Dacca, Burdwan, and Ramgur;" and they were, "at their respective stations, to set up schools, employ catechists, and establish churches."

If any reader is at a loss to comprehend this territorial allotment, let him seek the key to it in the Index Map to Major Rennell's *Bengal Atlas*. There the relations of the eight principal maps, one to another, are exhibited; and Bengal and Behar are, for that artistic purpose only, divided into eight sections, a principal town in each of which was selected by Mr. Grant and his friends for missionary occupation. The plan, at any rate, looked well upon paper; and Mr. Grant anticipated the most magnificent results, if it were fairly carried out. His regret was that it had not been inaugurated by Clive or Warren Hastings. "Had this subject," wrote he, "been attended to twenty years ago, our religion and our language* might have been diffused throughout these provinces. Late as it is, this great object still remains within reach."

* The above extract is taken from Mr. Marshman's *Life and Times of Carey, Marshman, and Ward*, (vol. 1, page 33,) with an important conjectural alteration. Mr. Marshman gives the passage, "one religion and one language." If Mr. Grant really wrote that, he must have been capable of greater extravagance than Mr. Thomas himself.

This projected mission had no inconsiderable advantage in the willingness of Mr. Grant to pay the salaries of two missionaries immediately, "until a public fund could be established." Mr. G. Udny and others also would, no doubt, have contributed liberally; and the reader may ask why, with such encouragements, nothing was actually done? The reason was this: Mr. Brown and his friends wished to move in their undertaking with the full consent and, if possible, even with the positive support of the Government. He emphatically declared, "IN EVERY MISSION SCHEME FOR BENGAL, THE PROTECTION OF GOVERNMENT IS INDISPENSIBLY REQUISITE. It requires only to live a week in Bengal, to become convinced of this point." This may have been, as Mr. Simeon thought it was, "consummate wisdom," but what if Paul and his companions had adopted such a principle of action?

Meanwhile nothing that could be done to obtain this protection for the mission was neglected by its projectors. The two Calcutta chaplains, the Revs. T. Blanshard and J. Owen, were induced to recommend it to the notice of Lord Cornwallis. The address they presented to his Lordship was framed by Mr. Grant, who dexterously put forward the plan of native schools, rather than proposals of any immediate attempts to give Christian light to the heathen.* Lord Cornwallis was thus approached by "very gentle gradations," and the scheme was so framed as not to alarm any apprehension he might have of work in earnest for the kingdom of Jesus Christ. The chaplains, however, could make no impression upon the Governor-General. He said, after listening to their representations, that "he had no

---

* In May, 1797, the Rev. J. Owen thus stated his recollections of this missionary scheme.

"A few years ago a letter subscribed by four or five clergymen resident in Bengal was presented to the Government, proposing the establishment of free-schools for teaching the English language to the natives, and with it the first principles of the Christian religion. The Hindus are extremely desirous to learn the English language for the purposes of business. They were to be informed that in the progress of teaching them our language, we wished to give them some notion of our religion. They know that with Englishmen they have nothing to fear from wrong-headed zeal. They who wished for the language only, might know what our religion is without receiving it."

faith in such schemes, and thought they must prove ineffectual; but he had no objection that others should attempt them, and promised not to be inimical." Then Mr. Grant himself, enjoying, as he did, in a very high degree, his Lordship's confidence, ventured, in a private interview, to entreat his patronage for the mission. All he had to say was heard with patient civility, and a copy of the proposals was most politely accepted at his hands, but the utmost the Governor-General could promise was that he would not oppose the plan.

It was then urged by Mr. Brown that a beginning might be made; and that two young clergymen should be at once sent out to India. After a short stay in Calcutta, they were to go to Benares, for about three years, to study Sanscrit, and "furnish themselves with languages." Then they might "begin their glorious work, of giving the Gentiles light, with every probability of success." Mr. Simeon was entreated to find the men. But they could not be found; and this step forwards could not be taken.

When Mr. Grant returned to England, the mission was still an object pursued by him, with constant endeavours to remove the obstacles which prevented its establishment. He waited upon the Archbishop of Canterbury, and engaged his good will to it. He was assured by his Grace that he had already spoken of the matter to the king; and he did so again after the interview with Mr. Grant. The Archbishop also mentioned it with commendation to Mr. Pitt and Mr. Dundas; who were reported to be, "on the whole, favorably disposed."

In 1793, the India Bill, brought forward by Mr. Dundas, afforded an opportunity for action in the direction of this long talked of mission. Mr. Wilberforce undertook to bring forward Resolutions in connexion with the Bill, committing the House of Commons to an acknowledgment of the duty of seeking the religious and moral improvement of the inhabitants of the British possessions in the East, and particularly of providing religious instruction for all persons of the Protestant communion in India. These Resolutions were carried; and Mr. Grant and his friends were overjoyed at their easy triumph. Mr. Wilberforce thought that "the hand of Providence was never more manifest than in this Indian affair." But technical hindrances to the introduction of the new element into the provisions of the Bill arose; the now alarmed East India Directors bestirred themselves in opposition to the dangerous innovations proposed; the new clauses were struck out; and matters were finally left in the same condition as before.

Meanwhile, Mr. Brown in Calcutta was doing what he could to keep alive the hope of the mission there. Sir John Shore became Governor-General, in October, 1793, and his approval of the enterprise was strongly hoped for. He, however, did almost as little to encourage it as his predecessor had done; and the expectations of any such sanction as the projectors of the mission thought indispensible to success, appeared to be as remote as ever.

Here then was the failure of wealth, combined with all the political influence and Indian experience which could then be enlisted upon the side of the gospel. The friends and promoters of Mr. Grant's scheme were defeated in all their attempts to give effect to it; and were obliged to content themselves with the addition of a few chaplains to the Bengal establishment, whilst their special anxieties for the evangelization of Bengal were finally merged in the more general enterprise of "the Church Missionary Society for Africa and the East."

Another, and a much more vigorous, attempt to enter Bengal with the gospel was made in 1796, which was so remarkable in its character, that although it belongs to a later date than our narrative has yet reached, we must give some account of it here, in order thereby to exhibit the immense difficulties which stood in the way of missionary enterprise in the East at the close of the last century. Mr. Robert Haldane became deeply impressed with a sense of the spiritual destitution of Bengal, and resolved to devote himself and all the resources God had given him to the work of its evangelization. Mr. Haldane inherited the estate of Airthrey, near Stirling. He was most happily married; and for ten years had occupied his fine mansion, and employed himself in improving and ornamenting his property, when an all-controlling desire to live for Christ and for man compelled him to exchange a life of elegant retirement and affluent ease for one of vigorous self-sacrificing Christian activity. In his project of a mission to Bengal, he found a band of devoted men ready to co-operate with him; and, especially, the Rev. Messrs. Innes, Bogue, and Ewing, who were eminent for Christian usefulness then, and whose after-lives abundantly fulfilled their earlier promise, undertook to share with him the apostolic labours to which he was eager to consecrate himself. The combined contributions of no associations or special Society were desired or needed for the support of this mission. Mr. Haldane sold Airthrey: and the proceeds were all available for the maintenance of himself and his companions in their noble undertaking. They proposed to establish themselves at Benares, where, with a staff of printers, catechists, and school-masters, they would carry forward the preaching of the gospel, the translation and publication of the Scriptures, the Christian instruction of the young, and every other department of evangelical effort which the providence of God might render possible and desirable. "Probably above thirty persons" were ready to employ themselves in these various labours in co-operation with Mr. Robert Haldane.

It was a truly magnificent instance of Christian devotedness! Mr. Haldane kept back nothing; but would consecrate his large property and himself also to the propagation of the gospel in India. Nor was this a mere project. As far as the steps needful to carry out the design could be taken, he took them. He then sought to obtain the sanction of the Board of Directors and of the British Government. Mr. Dundas, then at the head of Indian affairs, was visited, and in repeated private interviews was made acquainted with the plan, and his acquiesence in it entreated. On the 29th of December, the Court of Directors was petitioned by the intending missionaries to grant its consent to the enterprise. A reply was soon given, to the effect that "weighty and substantial reasons" induced the Court to decline compliance with their request.

The missionaries did not readily abandon hope of success. New Directors were to be elected in April, 1797. They resolved to await the formation of the new Court, and then to renew their application. Meanwhile their plan was published in the *Missionary Magazine*, and the prayers of all God's people were besought in favor of those who were striving to carry it out. In May, the intending missionaries again addressed the Board, "urging them by every motive of policy and duty to review their decision." They appealed "to all the principles likely to operate upon the human mind: to their justice, their interests, their humanity, their love of literature, their philanthropy, their religion, their hopes and fears for this world and the next." The extent of the missionaries' petition was thus stated:—

If we obtain leave from your Honourable Court, we propose to go out to Bengal, with our families; to take a few persons with us as catechists, and to settle in a part of the country which may be found most convenient, both on account of a healthful situation, and for furnishing opportunities of communicating instruction to the natives. When we have made ourselves masters of the language, we design to employ our time in conveying the knowledge of Christianity to the Hindus and Mahommedans, by translating the Sacred Scriptures for their use, by conversation, and by erecting schools, to be kept by the catechists, for teaching the children the first principles of religion. Such is our object, and we have sufficient funds for its support.

The favor we ask of you, Gentlemen, is leave to go out to Bengal, and protection there, while we demean ourselves as peaceable subjects of the government, and good members of the community.

A memorial was first presented to every individual Director, and also to many of the leading Proprietors. Then, some three weeks after, the petition was sent in to the Court, "supported by letters from many hundreds of clergymen and ministers of England, Scotland and Ireland, earnestly urging their compliance with the request made to them, and entreating them to allow the gospel to be preached to their poor heathen subjects, by every consideration of duty, humanity, consistency and propriety." The petition and letters were received, and much more deliberate attention was given to them than to the former application.

But the result was the same. The permission asked was refused; and, most reluctantly, the plan was finally abandoned.* One of the Directors was reported to have said

* An extract from a letter from the Rev. Andrew Fuller to the Rev. W. Ward, dated May 23d, 1801, will supply some interesting particulars as to the remarkable results of the failure of Mr. Haldane's project. Mr. Fuller says :—
"Many of the Circus people at Edinburgh are turning Baptists. They are a sort of Scotch Methodists. Their origin, I believe, may be traced to brethren Carey and Thomas going to India. That undertaking seems to have deeply impressed a young Scotch gentleman, Mr. Robert Haldane. Not that it was the occasion of his conversion to Christ; but, when his heart was already turned to Him, it occasioned his giving up himself and all his property (some thousands a year) to the name of the Lord Jesus. He is a nephew to Lord Duncan; and his lady and himself are of one heart. After providing for their only daughter, they agreed to sell all their estates, and put the money into the funds, and to go into the East Indies with two or three ministers. There he resolved to spend his life and fortune in labouring to disseminate the gospel among the Hindus. Application, with all possible interest, was made with the Directors for leave to go; but he was repulsed! Being so, he resolved that his life and property should nevertheless be the Lord's. He and Ewing and Innes, with a number more, formed a *Home Mission* for propagating the gospel in all those parts of their own country where it was not preached, and setting up Sunday schools. He had a brother also, Mr. James Haldane, a Captain of an East Indiaman, whose heart was reached and renewed. He came home, quitted his command, and preached the gospel. A Circus or riding school, in Edinburgh, which would hold 4000 people, was hired by Robert; and his brother James preached in it. Rowland Hill and many other English preachers went down, from about 1797. A church was soon formed on the Independent plan, of which James was pastor. I preached there in October, 1799, to about 4000 people. Robert, intent on his great object, purchased an oblong riding school in Glasgow, and converted it into a place of worship. There brother Sutcliff and I preached to about 5000 people. The General Assembly of the Church of Scotland, alarmed at his progress, wrote a pastoral letter in 1799, warning the nation against him. But this disgusted the people; who saw and felt the purity of Haldane's motives, and the meanness of theirs. The consequence was, no sooner did Haldane open the place at Glasgow, and station Ewing at it, but it was immediately filled; and might have been filled if it had been twice as large. Ewing being stationed at Glasgow, undertakes the instruction of twenty or thirty young ministers, who are to itinerate in Scotland and Ireland. Another large place is built at Stirling, where Innes is placed. The young ministers are going out continually. There is now a large church at Edinburgh and some of them are turning Baptists, which grieves the good men. I do not know any remedy; unless it be that they turn too! Robert is a man of a cool head and a warm heart. His lady is a most amiable Christian."

that "he would rather see a band of devils in India than a band of missionaries;" and nothing would move these resolute opponents of the gospel from their determined hostility to the preaching of the truth in their Indian possessions. It was in their power to withhold a license to proceed to the East Indies from any applicant; and any unlicensed person found residing in India was liable to arrest and to deportation to England for trial, the offence he had committed being punishable with fine and imprisonment.* That was the key to Bengal and to all India; and with it they resolved to lock the door against the entrance of all true missionary enterprise.

In the case of the two missionary projects we have now commemorated, the Directors were completely successful. But another attempt must be now written of, which issued very differently. The men who conducted it were too insignificant to hope, like Mr. Grant and Mr. Brown, to influence and persuade an unwilling Government; and were too poor to apprehend, like Mr. Haldane, the forfeiture or waste of wealth, the expenditure of which, might effect great results under more propitious circumstances elsewhere. With nothing to expect, and as little to fear, from men in authority, they had the resolution to do that which they were assured God had commanded; and their very weakness proved to be their strength. Towards the close of his life, Mr. Grant wrote,—

Many years ago, I formed the design of a Mission to Bengal; and used my humble endeavours to promote the design. Providence reserved that honour for the Baptists.

Both the brothers Haldane were baptized some years later. See the joint Memoirs of these admirable men, published in 1852.

* 33 George iii. c. 52 § 132. "Be it further enacted, That if any subject or subjects of his Majesty, &c., not being lawfully licensed or authorised, shall at any time or times, &c., directly or indirectly, go, sail, or repair to, or be found in the East Indies, or any of the parts foresaid, all and every such person and persons are hereby declared to be guilty of a crime and misdemeanour; and, being convicted thereof, shall be liable to such fine or imprisonment, or both fine and imprisonment, as the court in which such person or persons shall be convicted shall think fit."

CHAPTER IX.

The Baptist Missionary Society and its First Enterprise.

I HAVE been lately told that the light of the glorious gospel is breaking forth in the East Indies, at Calcutta. May it spread far and wide, and bring on that glorious time when all Jewish, papal, pagan, and Mahometan darkness will be removed, and the kingdom of Christ appear with great glory.*

So wrote, on the 15th of August, 1780, John Gill, Baptist Minister at St. Albans, and nephew of the celebrated Dr. John Gill. It may be supposed that some accounts furnished by Mr. Kiernander, and published in the reports of the Society for Promoting Christian Knowledge elicited his missionary aspirations. They are quoted as showing that such desires had their seat in the hearts of good men of the Baptist denomination, long before any plans for missionary effort in heathen nations had been organized by them.

That it was so, a yet more interesting proof is furnished by the pen of the Rev. Samuel Pearce, who was one of the principal founders of the Baptist Missionary Society. Writing of events which immediately followed his own conversion in 1782, he says,—

It is very common for young converts to feel strong desires for the conversion of others. These desires immediately followed the evidences of my own religion; and I remember well they were particularly fixed upon the poor heathen. I believe, the first week that I knew the grace of God in truth, I put up many fervent cries to Heaven in their behalf; and at the same time felt an earnest

* The Sutcliff Correspondence MSS. in the library of the Baptist Mission House, 19, Castle Street, Holborn, London.

desire to be employed in promoting their salvation. It was not long after, that the first settlers sailed for Botany Bay. I longed to go with them, although in company with the convicts, in hopes of making known the blessings of the great salvation in New Zealand. I actually thought of making an effort to go out unknown to my friends; but, ignorant how to proceed, I abandoned my purpose. Nevertheless I could not help talking about it; and at one time a report was circulated that I was really going, and a neighbouring minister very seriously conversed with me on the subject.

Whilst in India, Mr. Thomas had corresponded frequently and even voluminously with Dr. Stennett, Mr. John Ryland, Senior, and some other principal men in the Baptist ministry. His letters to his family also, as we have seen, contained many interesting notices of his plans and labours. In those days, however, information travelled slowly; and his communications excited so little general interest, that few persons, besides his correspondents themselves, knew any thing of him or his doings.* Meanwhile, however, there was rising up in the minds of a few influential men in different parts of England, an anxious desire for some aggressive action upon the heathen world, which had been so long neglected by the professing church of Jesus Christ.

This desire appears to be, in part, traceable to the influence of the writings of Jonathan Edwards, and, particularly, of his *Life and Diary of David Brainerd*, and his *Humble Attempt to promote Union in Extraordinary Prayer for the Revival of Religion*, upon some Baptist ministers.

* One curiously inaccurate notice of his missionary efforts, extracted from an English newspaper, was reproduced in the *Calcutta Gazette* for July 19th, 1792, as follows:—

"*The following ludicrous paragraph we have extracted from an English Paper, which evinces how readily every article of Intelligence from this Country is credited.*

"A private letter, lately received from Calcutta, mentions that, in consequence of the opening of a new chapel at Malda, a settlement 250 miles from that place, two eminent Bramins had been converted, one of whom has become a teacher, and is translating the Evangelists into Persian; a chapter of which, with a comment, he gives his hearers at a time. Another person, a Mr. Brown, from England, has also learned the Persian, and has several hundred hearers, who have formed a church; some of these persons are of rank and fortune in the service of the Company."

As early as 1784, the members of the Northamptonshire Association urged upon those connected with it, to hold "meetings for prayer to bewail the low state of religion, and earnestly implore a revival of their churches, and of the general cause of the Redeemer, and for that end to wrestle with God for the effusion of His Holy Spirit, which alone could produce the blessed effect," spending an hour for this purpose, "on the first Monday in every calendar month." They entreated those who responded to their appeal that they would "not confine their requests to their own societies, or to their own immediate connection," urging, in the true spirit of missionary zeal,—

Let the whole interest of the Redeemer be affectionately remembered, and the spread of the gospel to the most distant parts of the habitable globe be the object of your most fervent requests. We shall rejoice if any other Christian societies of our own or other denominations will unite with us, and do now invite them most cordially to join heart and hand in the attempt. Who can tell what the consequence of such an united effort in prayer may be? Let us plead with God the many gracious promises of His word, which relate to the success of His gospel. He has said, 'I will yet for this be enquired of by the house of Israel, to do it for them. I will increase them with men like a flock.'—Ezekiel xxxvi. 37; Surely we have love enough for Zion to set apart one hour at a time, twelve times in a year, to seek her welfare.

This was the beginning of those monthly meetings for prayer which are now held in many parts of the world. As the immediate result, not a few minds appear to have become impressed with the responsibility of believers to make known the way of life to those who were in ignorance of it. It was no transient accidental impulse which was expressed in these proposals. They are referred to again and again in the proceedings of the Association for the subsequent years; and in 1786 it is recorded, as matter of encouragement,—

We learn that many other churches, in different, and some in distant, parts of the land, and some of different denominations, have voluntarily acceded to the plan.

The events which led to the formation of the Baptist Missionary Society shall be here recapitulated chiefly in the words of two of its original founders. We give first the narrative of Dr. Ryland. He writes :—

As to the immediate origin of a Baptist Mission, I believe God himself infused into the mind of Carey, that solicitude for the salvation of the heathen, which cannot fairly be traced to any other source. When he went to Birmingham, to collect for the meeting-house he had built at Moulton, he mentioned the proposal there. A friend urged him to write and print upon it, and offered to give ten pounds towards paying the printer. On his return, he met brother Fuller and brother Sutcliff in my study at Northampton, and then pressed one of us to publish on the subject. We approved much of what he urged, yet made some objections, on the ground of so much needing to be done at home, &c. However, when he could not prevail on either of us to promise to undertake the work, he said he must tell the whole truth; that, in the warmth of conversation, at Birmingham, he had said, that he was resolved to do all in his power to set on foot a Baptist Mission. 'Well,' said his friend, 'print upon the subject: I will help bear the expense.' That, he replied, he could not do. 'If you cannot do it as you wish,' said his friend, 'yet do it as well as you can. You have, just now, bound yourself to do all you can for this purpose; and I must keep you to your word.' Being thus caught, through his own zeal, he could get off no other way than by promising that he would write, if he could not prevail on any one more competent to undertake it. We then all united in saying, 'Do, by all means, write your thoughts down, as soon as you can; but be not in a hurry to print them. Let us look over them, and see if any thing need be omitted, altered, or added.' Thus encouraged, he soon applied himself to the work, and showed us the substance of the pamphlet, afterwards printed, which we found needed very little correction. So much had this young man attained of the knowledge of geography and history, and several languages, in the midst of the pressures of poverty, and while obliged to support himself and his family,—at first, as a journeyman shoemaker, and, afterwards, as a village-schoolmaster; since his people could raise him but ten or eleven pounds a year, besides five pounds from the London fund!

Between Carey and Fuller there never was a moment's rivalship; and I have no bias on my mind to take a grain of praise from one, to give to the other: but, wishing to regard both with impartial esteem, and truth beyond both, I consider the Mission as having originated absolutely with Carey; and Mr. Fuller's acknowledgement, that he had, at first, some feelings like the desponding nobleman in 2 Kings vii. 2, is a confirmation of my opinion. This, however, is of small consequence. Some time after the conversation in my study, occurred the Ministers' Meeting at Clipstone, in April, 1791. An uncommon degree of attention seemed, to me, to be excited by both sermons. I know not under which I felt the more,—whether brother Sutcliff's *On Being Very Jealous for the Lord God of Hosts;* or brother Fuller's *On the Pernicious Influence of Delay.* Both were very impressive; and the mind of every one with whom I conversed, seemed to feel a solemn conviction of our need of greater zeal, and of the evil of negligence and procrastination. I suppose that scarcely an idle word was spoken while I stayed; and, immediately after dinner, Carey introduced the subject of beginning a Mission, by enquiring, If it were not practicable, and our bounden duty, to attempt somewhat towards spreading the gospel in the heathen world? As I had to preach at home that night, fourteen miles off, I was obliged to leave the company before the conversation ended. At the ensuing Association, held at Oakham, it was announced, that these sermons would be immediately sent to the press. The next Association was at Nottingham, May 30th, 1792; when brother Carey delivered a most impressive discourse from Isaiah liv. 2, 3, chiefly endeavouring to enforce our obligations to *expect great things from God*, and to *attempt great things for God*, If all the people had lifted up their voices and wept, as the children of Israel did at Bochim,—Judges ii. 4,—I should not have wondered at the effect: it would have only seemed proportionate to the cause; so clearly did he prove the criminality of our supineness in the cause of God. A resolution was printed, in this year's letter, 'That a plan be prepared, against the next Ministers' Meeting at Kettering, for forming *a Baptist Society for Propagating the Gospel among the Heathens.* Brother Carey generously engaged to devote all the profits that might arise from his late publication, on this interesting subject, to the use of such a Society.'*

This Society was actually formed at Kettering, in Mrs. Beeby Wallis's back parlour, October 2nd, 1792. As all the friends of the Baptist Mission know, we began with a subscription of £13-2-6;

* *An Enquiry into the Obligations of Christians, to use Means for the Conversion of the Heathens. In which the religious state of the different nations of the world, the success of former undertakings, and the practicability of further undertakings, are considered,* by William Carey. Leicester, 1792. Price One Shilling and Six-Pence.

but, at a second meeting, at Northampton, October 31st, brother Pearce brought the surprising sum of £70 from his friends at Birmingham, which put new spirits into us all. Still, we knew not how to proceed, whom to send, nor where to begin our operations.* Brother Pearce had read the account of the Pelew Islands, and was inclined to propose them for the object of our first attempt.† But, just at this time, Mr. John Thomas returned from Bengal. He had repeatedly written thence to Dr. Samuel Stennett, to my father, and to Mr. Booth, and had given some account of his conferences with the natives. We found he was now endeavouring to raise a fund for a mission to that country, and to engage a companion to go out with him. At a meeting held at Northampton, November 13th, therefore, it was resolved to make some farther inquiry respecting him, and to invite to him go back under the patronage of our Society.

The collection of £13-2-6 as the first Baptist missionary fund has often been spoken of, and not always with a true appreciation of its significancy. So also strange use has been made of "the widow's mite." A well-to-do contri-

---

* Great anxiety for direction how to begin their great enterprise appears in the following memorandum of the Committee, recorded at this meeting, November 13th, 1792.

"N. B.—The following articles we wish to be examined and discussed in the most diligent manner.

"What qualifications are especially requisite in missionaries? What persons are known, or supposed, to be both suitable and willing to be employed in this business? What advice should be given the missionaries, or what regulations adopted concerning them?—Also, In what parts of the heathen world do there seem to be the most promising openings? What information on this head may be obtained from any late books of travels, or from Christian merchants, or from such persons as would at least favor the design of converting the heathen?"

† On the 9th of August, 1783, Captain Henry Wilson of the *Antelope* packet was shipwrecked upon Coorooraa, one of the Pelew Islands. He and his ship's company were treated with great kindness by Abba Thulle, the king; and, when they left, captain Wilson took with him Lee Boo the king's second son, to be educated in England. The prince, as he was called, was a youth of remarkably gentle and ingenuous character, a shrewd observer in the new world to which he was thus introduced, and full of affectionate regard for all who in any way shewed him kindness. After living very happily in captain Wilson's family for little more than five months, he died of the small pox, in the 27th of December, 1784, aged twenty years. His interesting and affecting story attracted much attention. The Pelew Islands were visited by the *Duff*, in November, 1797, but the weather did not admit of delay there, and nothing of interest arose out of the attempt to reopen communication with the islanders.

butor now-a-days calls his gift his "mite," believing himself to speak modestly, because he gives such a name to gold or silver. But when the widow gave her "two mites, which make a farthing," she "cast in all that she had, even all her living." How easy to give much more :—How hard to give as much! In the case before us, the eloquence of missionary orators has often urged an affluent congregation of perhaps two hundred people to emulate at any rate the original collection of £13-2-6; and that small amount has by dint of effort been made up; but how unlike is such an effort to the quiet contribution of this sum by those few Baptist ministers at Kettering in 1792.*

A word must also be said of "the surprising sum of £70," brought from Birmingham by Mr. Samuel Pearce. His ardent zeal for the increase of Christ's glory had led him "to preach much upon the promises of God concerning the conversion of the heathen nations," and, "by doing so, and always communicating to his people every piece of information respecting the present state of missions, they soon imbibed the same spirit." Hence his deacon, good Mr. Potts, had been so prompt to encourage Mr. Carey to publish his pamphlet, and, now that a fund was commenced for a mission to the heathen, many eager contributors came forward to support it. Surely

---

* The particulars of this collection deserve to be put on record. They are,—

John Ryland, Northampton, ... £2-2-0
Reynold Hogg, Thrapstone, ... 2-2-0
John Sutcliff, Olney, ... 1-1-0
Andrew Fuller, Kettering, ... 1-1-0
Abraham Greenwood, Oakham, ... 1-1-0
Edward Sharman, Cottisbrook, ... 1-1-0
Joshua Burton, Foxton, ... 10-6
Samuel Pearce, Birmingham, ... 1-1-0
Thomas Blundell, Arnsby, ... 10-6
William Heighton, Road, ... 10-6
John Eayres, Braybrook, ... 10-6
Joseph Timms, Kettering, ... 1-1-0
A contributor whose name was not recorded, ... 10-6

£13-2-6

Birmingham deserves remembrance and honour amongst the places which first helped the mission.

In pursuance of the resolution, Mr. Fuller, the Secretary, was to make enquiries concerning "Mr. Thomas's character, principles, abilities, and success." "We did so," he wrote to a friend at Colchester, " and received upon the whole a pleasing and satisfactory account of him. Mr. Booth, who had corresponded with him during his residence in India, indulged us with a sight of the letters; at the same time expressing a gladness that we had taken up the business, and his opinion of Mr. Thomas being a suitable person to send." Mr. Fuller added :—

We have not gone about this business in a hurry. We have been praying for it by monthly prayer-meetings for these eight or nine years, and now we wish to do something more than pray. We have solemnly bound ourselves to God and one another, at least to make an effort, by individual subscriptions and congregational collections.

Surely the reader must admire the providence of God, so wonderfully working towards the formation of our Indian mission in all these particulars. Here was Mr. Thomas, who for several years had been "separated from his brethren," now again in England to accomplish the formation of a Society to support the labours he was anxious to carry forward. Here too was the very Society he needed, formed, as it were, in anticipation of his coming : men's hearts engaged in the project of a mission to the heathen, and plans organised for the collection of the needful funds,— only needing determination as to the direction in which the first missionary effort should be made. But for Mr. Thomas, it is to the last degree unlikely that this Society would have thought seriously of India as their field of labour. But for the Society, it is more than probable that Mr. Thomas would have failed to evoke the sympathy and support essential to the continuance of his work. The concurrence of events issued in that practical success and blessing, which all should regard with grateful acknowledgments to Him who is "wonderful in counsel and excellent in working."

But we must resume the history of events in the Northamptonshire Association. Mr. Fuller related them, in a letter to Mr. Ryland, thus :—

We had a very solemn meeting on the 9th January, 1793; but your absence, and brother Sutcliff's, who was detained by indisposition, threw a great weight upon me. I invited several ministers, besides the Committee. Mr. Thomas had hurt his foot, and, therefore, was not at Northampton; nor at Kettering, till Wednesday night. We met in the morning for prayer, and read over all Mr. Thomas's letters to Mr. Booth; by which we had a perfect idea of the man and his communications. Towards night, we resolved, not expecting him to come, 'That, from all we could learn, it appeared to us that a door was open in India for preaching the gospel to the heathen :—That, if a union with Mr. Thomas were practicable, it was to be desired :—That the Secretary write to Mr. Thomas immediately, and enquire whether he be willing to unite with the Society, &c.—That, if Mr. Thomas concur with this proposal, the Society will endeavour to procure him an assistant, to go out with him in the spring, &c.'—After the prayer-meeting, Mr. Carey preached from, 'Behold, I come quickly, and my reward is with me.'—Revelation xxii. 12. In the evening, Mr. Thomas arrived, accepted the invitation of the Committe, and gave us all the information he could. He thinks, after missionaries have been there a while, they may maintain themselves; but this could not be at first. Brother Carey then voluntarily offered to go with him, if agreeable to the Committee; which greatly rejoiced the heart of Thomas. You see, things of great consequence are in train. My heart fears, while it is enlarged. I have, this day, been to Olney, to converse with brother Sutcliff, and to request him to go with me to Leicester, this day se'nnight, to conciliate the church there, and sound Mrs. Carey's mind, whether she will go and take the family, that we may know for what number of passengers to provide, and how many to apply for to the Directors of the East India Company. Our subscriptions, I think, amount to £130. We advised Mr. Carey, if he be decided about going, to give up his school this quarter, that he may prepare for his voyage; and we must make up the loss to him, If his family should go, they must have, I think, £100 or £150 a year, between them all, for the present. If, not, we must guarantee the family, as well as support him in the mission. Mrs. Thomas goes. Mr. Thomas preached with us, on Friday evening, a very good sermon. He was so lame, on

Saturday, that I went for him to Biggleswade, and write this at Wellingborough on my way home. He is now at Kettering, where he was to have a public collection on Lord's-day night. I believe we may have another at Bedford, if he goes next Lord's-day. He hopes he can get £100 among his connections. He should go and preach and collect wherever he can.

We read the letters which had passed between Mr. Thomas and a very respectable gentleman, who had employed him in India. It seemed to us that he had been rather too warm; yet this difference did not sink him, in any considerable degree, in our esteem.

I am much concerned with the weight that lies upon us. It is a great undertaking; yet, surely, it is right. We have all felt much in prayer. We must have one solemn day of fasting and prayer, on parting with our Paul and Barnabas. I suppose it must be at Leicester, a little before they go; which, it is supposed, will be about April. I hope you will be there.

Mr. Fuller's proposals as to the support of the missionaries should not pass without remark. If Mr. Carey's family went to Bengal, the missionaries "must have," he thought, "£100 or £150 a year, between them all, for the present." Those he represented had small knowledge of the necessary expenses to be incurred in supporting two such families, even in the simplest manner, in the East Indies; and they no doubt thought £75 for each a rather generous allowance. Mr. Thomas perhaps despaired of their ability to do more; but he could have told them that this amount was utterly insufficient.* The subscription made at the

---

* Mr. Thomas is very probably to be held responsible for some misconception as to the expenses of living in India. To his fervid mind, any thing was enough in anticipation; and he was now only anxious to urge on the missionary project to some practical results. In his remarks upon expenses therefore he spoke with most incautious assurance of the little cost of living in the East. His remarks upon housekeeping in Bengal deserve to be introduced here. The scale of prices given can only be wondered at, now that the cost of living is so greatly enhanced.

"It may appear a very formidable undertaking to go and preach among these poor, destitute, perishing, souls. Perhaps the heat of the climate, and the barbarous manners of heathens in general, may operate, in part, as a discouragement to some who would otherwise cordially engage in this service; but where God *makes willing*, obstacles will speedily disappear. One part of the year, the weather is cold enough: at night we can bear two or three blankets, and should be unable to sleep for cold without them. In the day, we use warm clothes and fires, especially in the upper parts of Bengal, which lie in latitude 26° N. The

end of 1790 by his few Malda friends, for his own support, was considerably larger than the amount now proposed by the Society as the annual allowance for himself and his colleague with their families! And this was to be given only "for the present." It had, however, been an essential object in Mr. Carey's missionary plan that "the first expense might be the whole." The missionaries were to be set down in the country to be evangelized, and supplied at the outset with some means of establishing themselves there, and should thereafter support themselves by agriculture, &c. Mr. Thomas was consulted upon this matter, and gave an opinion somewhat adverse to Mr. Carey's plan. He wrote, on the 23d of December,—

country abounds with provisions at a cheap rate; so that thousands of the natives maintain themselves and families, pay rent and customs, out of an income not exceeding 10s. sterling per month.

"Near Malda, at which place I resided, the prices of provisions in common were as follow; but at Calcutta they are much dearer:

	s.	d.
30 Fowls,	2	6
16 Ducks,	2	6
A Hog,	2	6
A Deer,	2	6
A Sheep,	2	6
A Kid,	0	8
A Lamb,	0	8

Pine apples, mangoes, plaintains, limes, melons, peaches, vegetables, and fish, very plenty and cheap; and other things in proportion. But if a European must have a great house, a palanquin, a number of servants, and eat and drink the unwholesome food brought from Europe: as hams, tongues, claret, porter, &c. Bengal may prove both an expensive and unhealthy place to him; otherwise the country may be enjoyed, and several servants kept, at a small expense. Some servants are necessary there, who would be quite superfluous here; such as a person to carry a *chhátá*, or kind of umbrella; a cook, a washerman, and perhaps more. The most expensive of these is the cook, and his whole wages will amount to no more than 15s. per month, at farthest, and he find himself. House-rent is the most expensive article; for the lawful interest of money in that country is 12 per cent. and the Company allows eight. But for my part, I have lived in a boat for six months together, as comfortably as any prince in Europe; and for 16 or 18s. a missionary may build an excellent house, with mud walls and straw covering. I have done this also, and lived more comfortably than I do now in England: so that the difficulties attending a gospel mission are not insuperable. If they appear so, it is only at a distance; and should they be ever so great, in a service of this kind, we expect, through God, to do valiantly."

There are many ways whereby a missionary might gain a livelihood and a fortune, that would take less of his time and labour than cultivating land,—but not less of his heart and affections, which are soon carried off too far to be comfortable to himself, or profitable to others, when the getting of money begins.

"An employment of some kind, however, was on all hands agreed to be necessary" for the missionaries; and, when this was obtained, the money given for their support was to be employed in other missionary efforts.

But notwithstanding the smallness of the proposed allowances, the worthy Secretary of the mission and his brethren felt the weight which lay upon them heavily. That "weight," however, was very imperfectly appreciated when he wrote the words above quoted. With £130 only in hand, they were going to send out a party to India, whose necessary expenses they computed at about £550. To get so much money together in three months was, to them, a stupendous undertaking. How would they have felt, however, if they had known from the first that just double that sum would be needed, and must be expended, before their brethren could sail? But they all set to work to collect with hearty good will. Mr. Fuller wrote,—

The Committee frankly stated to the religious public their plan, requesting that, so far as it appeared deserving of encouragement, they would encourage it. Letters also were addressed to the most active ministers of the denomination throughout the kingdom, requesting their concurrence and assistance. The result was that more than twice the sum which had been asked for was collected; yet, when the work was finished, the actual expense had so far exceeded the estimate, that there were only a few pounds to spare.

It is matter for not a little surprise that Mr. Thomas's unhappy pecuniary difficulties did not lead the Committee at Kettering to decline co-operation with him. Andrew Fuller and his colleagues were the very men to feel that hopeless debt was a most serious disqualification for usefulness in the ministry of the gospel. Mr. Thomas was, however, trying to make an arrangement with his creditors, and although he told the Society that he was deeply involved, he no doubt spoke confidently of early deliverance from his perplexities; and they, who perceived the hand of God so plainly leading him to become their fellow worker, were ready to hope all things with him. They probably also thought with him that his debts had been incurred by no positively blameworthy conduct. He had only done what his best friends at the time considered to be well-judged and safe; and the unfavorable issue of his arrangements arose out of circumstances which could not be foreseen when his plans were laid. His debts therefore were matter for regret, but not for censure. Some shades of doubt Mr. Fuller afterwards acknowledged he had felt. Would that the good men who were now to send Mr. Thomas back to Bengal could have cleared him from the distressing embarrassments in which he had become involved. How different his after career might then have been!

Mr. Fuller was anxious that his new friend should advocate the mission cause as extensively as possible. On the 7th of March, Mr. Thomas tells his father,—

I have been out three weeks preaching and begging in behalf of the three societies of Northampton, Birmingham, and Halifax, under whose united patronage we are going out as missionaries to Bengal. That excellent companion, Mr. Carey, whom the Lord has given me, you will have heard of. A man wonderfully fitted for the work. I collected large sums at Birmingham, although they had given £70 towards it before. I preached and collected at Alcester £5-18; at Evesham, £6; at Worcester, £9-9; at Tewkesbury, £8-1; at Bath, £22; and at Bristol, £46, to begin with. The first gentleman gave twenty guineas. Thus you see the Lord lifts up those who are cast down, and surprises the desolate, with money, friends and favor. Mr. Pearce of Birmingham is a very successful preacher, and the hand of the Lord is so much revealed in him that hardly a Sabbath passes without some being called out of darkness into the light. He is with me at Bristol, and is going to London with me on pressing business, for we have but a few days to stay. Our last solemn and occasional association will be at Leicester, the 20th of March. Mr. Ryland and your son are to preach. Many ministers will be there, and very glad indeed should I be to have you there too, if possible. I walked yesterday from Bristol to Bath; then rode to Bradford, preached and returned. We want £550, and have almost got it.

A more detailed account of his experiences at these places was sent to Mr. Fuller:—

You will wish to know how we came on since we left Birmingham, I passed through Bromsgrove, and saw Mr. Butterworth, left him some papers, told him my tale, and he seemed quite pleased with it. On my arrival at Worcester, I had poor encouragement, and began to be cast down. Mr. Evans, who was there on occasional supply, said there were about thirty hearers, even on a Sabbath day. Others told me I was come to the wrong place; that they and several others could not be there; that the house was damp &c. But it got wind that an East Indiaman was to preach, and I suppose the pleasure of expecting a black face and broken English drew more than usual; for we had almost all the seats full, which they had not seen a great while before. And we had a good time also, for my chief aim was to promote their spiritual interests, which seemed rather low; and after I had done, my tongue was ready oiled to run smoothly over my tales, agreeably to myself, affectingly to them, and with interest to us all. They say they never knew so large a collection there. One good woman, who had put 5 shillings in the plate in the evening, came next morning with tears in her eyes and blessings in her mouth, and willingly gave 10s. 6d. more. I asked her name; but she would not have it used: 'But set me down as *Worthless Dust and Ashes!*' So I did. She thinks prayers will ascend, legacies will be left, and the work will go on and prosper. Thus we see, they who lie the lowest in their own eyes have the nearest at heart the cause of the Most High. I met with a willing mind and an active hand in Mr. Willoughby. I called on Mr. Osbourne, who is a Baptist Minister, though he preaches to an Independent congregation. He heard me preach, took one of Carey's pamphlets, and was very desirous of hearing more of it. I was asked to preach at Lady Huntingdon's chapel by one of their people who heard me. I tell you all these things, out of gratitude to our friends, and for information to you. I brought away in all £9-9 from Worcester. I walked to Upton, and preached there next night to a very thin congregation indeed; for, not having received due notice, very few attended. I met with nothing very pleasing here. Mr. Trevor thought it quite unnecessary to have any collection then, and most expedient to defer it till the following Sabbath. Mr. Davis of Tewkesbury preached there on that day and promised to urge our necessity. The money collected there will be sent to one of the treasurers.

The same evening I went to Tewkesbury, where a sister of mine lives; and the next day, Thursday, I preached there and collected £8-1. On Friday evening, I arrived at Horsley, and spent the evening with dear Mr. Francis, at a Mr. Erskine's, in high spirits, with hearty friends. Mr. Francis would have had me stop and preach on the following Sabbath day; but I could not. He has two or three guineas, and will have a collection for us, to be sent to one of the treasurers. The coach came by on Saturday evening at 6 o'clock, quite full inside. I took my dreary seat on the top, and it rained all the way to Bath, where I arrived, dripping with wet and benumbed with cold, at 11. After seeing my brother and all my relations, it was 2 o'clock in the morning before I retired. I preached for them; but as they had made it a rule not to have more than one or two cases a year and no collections, I thought I should have nothing there: but a woman, after hearing the case, sent in a penny! I thanked them, and said I should set down, '*Bath, One Penny!*' On further thinking of the emergency of the case, &c. they agreed to have a collection, and at my brother's table a plate was handed round and £7-7 collected, which, together with what was given at the door, amounted in all to £22-8-6¼. I went out of the pulpit into a return chaise, and arrived at Broadmead meeting just as worship began. I preached there, but my tongue clave to the roof of my mouth, both literally and spiritually. My sermon was like so much cold lead in my bowels all night. I was revived in the morning by the coming of brother Pearce; and on our going round to our friends. The first subscriber was a countryman, who heard me and supped with me at Mr. Harris's. He put down twenty guineas, to begin with, and promised as much more at another time. His worthy name is Newcomen, of Barnstaple, Devonshire. 'One of *my* countrymen, tell him,' says brother Pearce. Mr. Hughes, who desires his love to you, has been with us from house to house to a few places, and we have received about £10-10 more, and hope for twice as much as we have in all, besides a collection at the door next Lord's day evening. Mr. Francis is to preach.

And now, having finished all business for the present, I may talk about myself. All the success in the world in money matters would not raise my spirits; for I am not got over that heavy stroke on my pride! My text was, 'Without me ye can do nothing,' and my sermon was a practical exemplification of the truth! The people expressed no small dissatisfaction; at least, one of them. 'O turn unto me, O Lord, and have mercy upon me, for I am afflicted and desolate.' 'To thee be all glory,' I said, and why should I want any myself? O that I could be contented every moment to see my honour trampled in the dust, if Christ be but honoured and magnified.

Brother Pearce continues indefatigable in desires and exertions for promoting the good work. £5-5, more, since I wrote the above.

Our sum total last night at Bristol was £44, and upwards. We are in distress for time: disappointed of your letter. The words, *Particular Baptists*. seem to stand so very much in our way, that brother Pearce was minded to print a few papers at Bristol. Time fails!

Mr. Carey also visited a few places in the north of England and as the result of these endeavours, which were the commencement of those "missionary deputations," now so familiar to the churches at home, together with the liberality excited generally in the denomination by the enterprise, the sum in hand was augmented to upwards of £800 before the end of March, and a very hearty desire for the prosperity of the mission was excited. Mr. Fuller wrote to Mr. Stevens of Colchester,—

O my dear brother, it would do your heart good to see the love to Christ and the souls of men, discovered in many parts of the country, in readily contributing to this business. Good old Mr. Crabtree, of Bradford, in Yorkshire, upwards of seventy, could not sleep for joy. He laboured night and day; went to the vicar and curate, who cheerfully gave him a guinea each; obtained in the whole upwards of £40, and a great deal of respect from the neighbourhood into the account. 'My heart has been so much in this work,' says the venerable man, 'that it has almost been too much for my poor old body.' 'Blessed be God,' says dear Mr. Fawcett, of Brearly Hall, near Halifax, 'that I have lived to see so much love to Christ. I account it one of the greatest blessings of my life, to have assisted in so glorious and disinterested an undertaking.' Birt of Plymouth Dock, Steadman of Broughton, in Hampshire, and many more, all write in the same strain. I feel an exquisite satisfaction that we have made the attempt: the issue is in His hands, whose cause it is.

Amidst all this enthusiasm and generosity, it does not appear that the ministers and churches of London very greatly distinguished themselves. There were some most honourable exceptions; but the strength of the missionary cause lay in the provinces. Dr. Stennett did not even give a donation to the Society's funds, and he counselled his metropolitan brethren "not to commit themselves." Mr. Fuller wrote,—

Dr. Stennett predicts, I am told, that the mission will come to nothing; from this cause,—people may contribute, he supposes, for once, in a fit of zeal: but how is it to be supported? For my part, I believe in God; and have not much doubt, that a matter begun as this was will meet His approbation, and that He who has inclined the hearts of our brethren hitherto, so much beyond our expectations, will go on to incline their hearts 'not to lose the things which they have wrought.' I confess I feel sanguine in my hopes; but they are fixed in God. Instead of failing in the East India enterprize, I hope to see, not only that, but many others accomplished. I hope the Society will never slacken its efforts, while there are such vast numbers of heathens in almost every part of the world.

Surely the Christian philanthropist will delight to turn away from the avarice and practical infidelity of the East India Directors and the leading politicians of that day, who, as we have seen, were obstinately set against the introduction of Christian truth into Bengal, to contemplate the generosity, love, and zeal, of these poorer, but far nobler, representatives of our beloved country.*

* The Circular Letter of the Northamptonshire Association, for 1793, contains the following grateful acknowledgment of the sympathy and help the mission had called forth.—

"With gratitude to the God of all grace, and to our dear brethren in various parts of the kingdom, we acknowledge that He has stirred up their hearts to concur with our design, and to send us generous aid from the distant extremities of the land. You know already how early and how liberally we received encouragement from *Birmingham;* where a corresponding society was immediately established in aid of the mission; and by the instrumentality of our active friends, we soon derived further assistance from several churches in *Warwickshire, Shropshire,* and other adjacent counties.—From *Yorkshire,* and its borders, where our brethren, unknown to us, had chosen the same subject of *Christian Zeal* for their last year's letter, we soon received a noble evidence that they had not been meditating on a topic they did not feel. The establishment of a society there, which sent us *two hundred pounds* in proof of their fraternity, caused our hearts to rejoice in that union which flows from the love of CHRIST.—From many of our sister churches, both in the neighbourhood of this association, and in more remote parts of the island, we have received substantial succour; in some

On the 20th of March, the friends of the Mission came together at Leicester, that they might solemnly commend to God the beloved brethren so soon to leave them for the distant East. The forenoon was devoted to prayer. In the afternoon, Mr. Thomas preached from Psalm xvi. 4. In the evening Mr. Hogg took for his text Acts xxi. 14; and when Mr. Fuller addressed the missionaries from the Saviour's commission to his disciples in John xx. 21, the impression produced was profound. The athletic form of the speaker was tremulous with his deep emotions; and his hearers were greatly affected. How much more so those to whom his words were addressed, as he developed the analogies between the mission of the Saviour and their own,—in their objects, their divine direction, their difficulties and trials, and in their promises and rewards, concluding with the words,—

instances unsolicited, and in many beyond our expectations. From *Newcastle* and *Plymouth*, *Cambridge* and *Luton*, *Devizes*, and *Bath*, and *Frome*; from several places in *Hampshire*, *Suffolk*, *Essex*, and *Kent*, have kind and considerable donations been transmitted. *Bristol* and the great *Metropolis* of our land have lent assistance in this good work, with a generosity for which the inhabitants of those cities have long been renowned; and which the sad shocks given to commerce and public credit, before their benefactions were solicited, could not suppress. Nor has this encouragement been received merely from our own denomination. Though this Society honestly acknowledged that its founders were of the *Particular Baptist* persuasion, we are sure it was not the interest of a party they wished to promote, but the glory of our divine Lord, and the salvation of immortal souls. Hence it was proposed at first, if no opening was soon found for a Baptist mission, to have requested the *Presbyterian* and the *Moravian* brethren, who had been already employed in labouring among the heathen, to accept some assistance from our subscriptions: for by the leave of the God of heaven, we were determined to do somewhat toward propagating his Gospel in pagan lands. The providence of God pointing out so speedily a sphere of action sufficient to require all our exertions, prevented this testimony of *our* brotherly love for the present; but He who knew our hearts in this request, has inclined our brethren to show *us* favor. Our *Pædobaptist* brethren have not looked upon us with a jealous eye; but *evangelical Episcopalians*, as well as different classes of *Dissenters*, notwithstanding their difference of judgment and practice respecting one of the positive institutions of the New Testament, have befriended our design; and some friends belonging to the people called *Quakers*, who suppose the ordinance from which we are denominated has ceased, have sent in unsolicited aid. One of the ministers of the *Unitas Fratrum* sent us pecuniary assistance; and another in a most friendly letter expressed his earnest wishes for our success, and with great candour and piety, answered some of our printed enquiries respecting the needful qualifications of missionaries, and the advice proper to be given them."

Go then, my dear brethren, stimulated by these prospects. We shall meet again. Crowns of glory await you and us. Each, I trust, will be addressed in the last day by our great Redeemer, 'Come, ye blessed of my Father;—these were hungry, and you fed them: athirst, and you gave them drink: in prison, and you visited them. Enter ye into the joy of your Lord!'

Not the least interesting engagement of this solemn day was the business of adopting a letter to be sent to the Hindu enquirers of whom Mr. Thomas had told them. The letter was read before the assembly, and received the signatures of the ministers and several other Christian friends who were present on the occasion. It was as follows.—

The Society for Propagating the Gospel among the heathen, to Rám Rám Basu, Párbati, and all in India who call upon the name of Jesus Christ our Lord, both theirs and ours.

DEARLY BELOVED BRETHREN,

We rejoice that we have an opportunity of addressing those as fellow-christians, who till lately were lost in heathen darkness and superstition. The accounts which our beloved brother Thomas has given of you have greatly refreshed us. For many years we have been praying to God on your behalf. We knew but little of what our dear brother Thomas was doing among you, but had united together, before we heard of his being in England, for the purpose of sending the gospel into heathen countries. It was by the special providence of God that we heard of him, and of the state of things among you. We thankfully embraced the opportunity, and have ever since been heartily engaged in promoting the good work. From Asia sounded out the word of the Lord into Europe; glad shall we be to have that joyful sound reverberate to Asia again, and extend to every other part of the earth!

You requested in your letter, sent to the Rev. Dr. Stennett, that 'Missionaries might be sent to preach the gospel among you, and to help forward the translation of the word of God.' For these purposes we recommend to you our much esteemed brethren Thomas and Carey, men who, we are persuaded, are willing to hazard their lives for the name of the Lord Jesus; men who will seek not yours, but you; men who, though not pretending to infallibility, we doubt not will labour to translate the Bible as fast as they are able; who will teach you the word of the Lord in truth, and adorn the doctrine they preach by a life of holiness, righteousness, and goodness. Receive them in the Lord, and strengthen their hands by uniting with them in every good word and work.

We hope that upon the arrival of our brethren, you will be solemnly baptized in the name of the Father, the Son, and the Holy Spirit, the one living and true God, thereby putting on the Lord Jesus Christ, and making an open profession of His name. Expect persecutions and reproaches. All that will live godly in Christ Jesus must suffer persecution, because the hearts of men are by nature at enmity with God and true religion. But be not disheartened; tribulations will turn to your advantage and the furtherance of the gospel, through the blessing of your and our God, who will be with you to support you in all your afflictions. Only let your conversation be as becometh the gospel of Christ, that the enemies of godliness may have no evil thing to say of you. Shun all evil company, and all idolatrous assemblies and customs: 'Come ye out from among them, and be ye separate, saith the Lord, and touch not the unclean thing, and I will receive you; and will be a Father unto you, and ye shall be my sons and daughters, saith the Lord Almighty.

Nevertheless, though you have no fellowship with the unconverted in their evil works, yet be courteous, kind, affable, pitiful, and ready to do good to all men, even to your enemies, as occasions may offer. Be faithful and just in all your dealings, speaking the truth, and acting with uprightness. Pray for those that persecute you. Consider who it is that maketh you differ, and pray that the same almighty love which hath conquered your hearts may conquer theirs. Let unchastity, and all manner of uncleanness, and all intemperance in eating and drinking, be unknown among you. Put far away all lying, and deceit, and treachery, and double dealing. Be subject to the laws of your country in all things not contrary to the laws of God. Be obedient to your superiors, and compassionate to your inferiors. Be faithful in all your relative connections. Cultivate love, meekness, gentleness, goodness, and mercy. If any of you be overtaken in a fault, be ready to reclaim and forgive, as Christ also has forgiven you. You have read the eighteenth chapter of Matthew on this subject. If any turn back after professing the name of Christ and are not to be reclaimed, be not stumbled at it, but withdraw yourselves from all fellowship with them. Such things will be permitted to try your sincerity. In short, in your spirit and conduct, let your countrymen behold the tendency of the doctrine of Christ, and we doubt not but God, your own God, will bless and multiply you abundantly.

SPECIAL MESSAGES.

Dear brother Ram Ram Basu,

Thousands in our solemn assemblies have read and sung your gospel hymn, with joy, and hope, and brotherly love!* Your sentiments and feelings are ours! We feel that we are brethren! Though wide oceans divide us, we are of one spirit! We have heard of your labours of love. Go on, very dear brother, and by every means in your power, disseminate the knowledge of Jesus Christ. Teach the gospel which you have heard and learned. Teach your countrymen, by psalms, and hymns, and spiritual songs, to make melody in their hearts to the Lord.

Dear brother Parbati,

We have been made acquainted with the affecting circumstances of your conversion to our Lord Jesus Christ; and we greatly rejoice with you and for you. It does our hearts good to hear of your readiness to avow your attachment to Him; and that you have declared yourself ready to encounter all the difficulties and persecutions that might follow your being baptized in His name. Go on, dear brother. Eternal life is before you! Be you also a helper of our brethren. Endeavour by every means to teach others what you know of Christ; and adorn your profession by an unblemished conversation.

Might we add? (surely we may,)

Dear brother Mohan Chand!

We have heard of your serious attention to the preaching of the gospel, of your being convinced by it that you were a great sinner before God, that there was no refuge for you among all your shastras, and that the gospel alone was of God, discovering the way of salvation; and further, that you had disused the idolatrous worship of your countrymen; had forbidden the vain homage paid you by the deluded people, and had subjected yourself to temporal loss for Christ's sake: yes, we have heard of your adherence to the gospel when visited by Párbati previous to his conversion, and how when threatened by him respecting losing caste, you left the company, and went and poured out your complaint to God in prayer. And moreover, when he came to you in the agony of his soul, requesting to hear the gospel, you directed him in the way of eternal life. O brother Mohan Chand! can you think how it grieved us to hear, after all this, that your heart failed you in a time of trial: that you dissembled for a piece of bread! Surely

---

* Rám Rám Basu's "Gospel Hymn" had been "imitated in English verse" by Mr. Fawcett and also by Mr. Samuel Pearce. The original has been given at page 111.

your heart has ere now smitten you! Our Redeemer is merciful! Remember Simon Peter! But He also is holy, and jealous of His honour. He who denieth Him before men, and repenteth not, him will He deny before His Father and the holy angels!

Dearly beloved brethren, farewell! Thousands of prayers have already been offered up on your behalf! Thousands more will follow! Let us have yours for us in return! The grace of our Lord Jesus Christ, the love of God, and the communion of the Holy Spirit be with you all. Amen. Amen.

Signed at Leicester, March 20, 1793.

ANDREW FULLER.	E. SHARMAN.
REV. HOGG.	C. BRIGGS.
J. SUTCLIFF.	T. EDMONDS.
S. PEARCE.	R. WATTS.
R. HOPPER.	T. TRINDER.
J. RYLAND.	J. YATES.
ROBERT MILLS.	J. CANNER.
T. BLUNDELL.	J. PURSER.
J. W. MORRIS.	T. PROWITT.
W. STAUGHTON.	

Mr. Fuller wrote of the proceedings of the day to Mr. Fawcett,—

I need not say it was a solemn and affectionate meeting. Thousands of tears of joy have been shed on this occasion. We love Christ better: we love one another better. A new bond of union subsists between the churches and ministers who have embarked in this cause. How many names will now be embalmed in our remembrance for ever! When we review the shortness of the time, and the magnitude of the object, we seem 'like them that dream.' It seems to be too great to be true; but 'the Lord hath done great things for us.' May He yet do greater things by us. We fasted and prayed and trembled, when we set out. It seemed to us that we were launching a vessel that required superior ability to stir it. —At length we ventured; and hitherto we have succeeded. Surely the Lord hath been our pilot! Perhaps the greatest storms are yet to come. Be it so! Our eyes shall be up unto Him! When Christ was on board, the vessel could not sink; and those who doubted were reproved for their want of faith.

Mr. Pearce went with the missionaries to London, to arrange for their departure; and quiet enquiries were made as to the possibility of obtaining leave from the Court of Directors. To this end, Mr. Newton and Mr. Scott were asked to use their influence with Mr. Charles Grant. They did so; but quite in vain. He might, he said, have aided Mr. Carey; but he would be no party to the return to India of Mr. Thomas. All their endeavours were alike unsuccessful.

If, however, Mr. Thomas met with dislike from a former friend, he had many evidences that his own brethren regarded him most affectionately. The portrait of him which now hangs in the Museum of the Baptist College at Bristol was painted at this time by Mr. S. Medley, and a warm interest in his missionary labours spread itself throughout the denomination in England.

Most unwillingly, Mr. Fuller and his brethren abandoned the hope of obtaining formal sanction for their missionaries; but they saw clearly that no such sanction would be given by the Board of Directors. Men in power discouraged or forbad their enterprise: in this respect they were in a position similar to that of the projectors of " the Bengal Mission." But they believed that they had divine authority to go forward in their undertaking; that it was right to obey God rather than men; and that therefore they ought to go on. Captain White's brother William had succeeded him in the command of the *Earl of Oxford*. He knew Mr. Thomas intimately, and though well aware that the missionary party had no license from the Board of Directors, he was quite willing to take them in his vessel, upon advantageous terms. £250 was to cover the cost of the passage for Mr. and Mrs. Thomas and child, and for Mr. Carey and Felix. Perhaps, Mr. Thomas was to earn his passage by medical service to the ship. Mrs. Thomas had somewhat reluctantly consented to go, with her little Betsy. Mrs. Carey was expecting to give birth to a child at the beginning of May, so that her going seemed to be impossible. She was besides very unwilling to leave England, having no sympathy with her husband's missionary aspirations. It was therefore arranged that she should remove from Leicester to her former home at Piddington, near Northampton, and should, with her little ones, be supported there by the Society on an allowance of £50 per annum, until Mr. Carey, after three or four years, could return to fetch her. Their eldest boy, Felix, a child of between seven and eight years old, was to go with his father now. There were two other members of the party about to sail: Samuel and Sarah Powell, first-cousins to Mr. Thomas.

And so every thing appeared to be finally settled. The 3d of April was the day appointed for sailing, and Mr. Carey thought they would then leave England. He had no foreboding of the delays and difficulties which were to arise! They embarked, and "sailed off with great joy to the Motherbank," between Portsmouth and the Isle of Wight. There the *Earl of Oxford* anchored to await convoy, and her passengers had to live on shore until she was ready to proceed upon her voyage to Calcutta.

The missionary party took lodgings at Ryde, in the Isle of Wight, and longed for the termination of all their anxious preparations by the departure of the Indian fleet; but terrible perplexities and unexpected troubles were still in store for them.

Mr. Thomas's debts were the first cause of disquietude. He had tried in vain to come to a settlement with his creditors. Always sanguine in his expectations, he had proposed to make them a payment on account, which afterwards he found himself quite unable to do. Unquestionably, he ought then to have met them with a candid statement of his case, and should have accepted the consequences; but he neglected to do so, and was soon beset by the disappointed creditors with clamorous importunity. He then declared his present inability, but full purpose, to pay them all; but there was little disposition to receive his assurances. The fact that he and his family were now going out to India seemed to the creditors proof that he could pay them if he would. The consequences were most humiliating and discreditable. "They began to hunt; and I," wrote Mr. Thomas, "to flee as a partridge; yet still continuing to preach publicly wherever I was asked. Every day I had fears without that I should be arrested, and hopes within that I should escape; till at length the happy day was come when I was relieved by a chain of providences, and embarked, with my family and fellow labourer, on board the *Earl of Oxford.*"

Having some things yet to arrange in London, Mr. Thomas left Mr. Carey and his own family at Ryde, and went there. Just after his departure, one of his creditors called at the lodging, "with a writ and bailiff, to arrest him for £100 or less." This circumstance and the threats of the disappointed visitor greatly distressed them all, and Mr. Thomas endeavoured to escape arrest by remaining in London. A letter which he wrote to his father from that city on the 1st May, speaks of the "hurry and confusion," the "stagnation of all enjoyment in heaven and earth," "without retirement, peace or quietness, or any such thing as meditation," through which he had latterly passed. His complaints related to circumstances for which he was himself answerable. He broke open this letter to say that, after writing it, he had gone to the House of Commons, and had heard Pitt, Fox, Dundas, Sheridan, and Grey speak, with many others. He was "vastly pleased" with Mr. Pitt's oratory. Petitions for a reform of Parliament were presented, which were to be followed by many others, and he expected that "these things would issue in great changes." He adds, "I was at the trial of Hastings yesterday; and, a few days ago, in the House of Lords, and heard the debates there. They speak not quite so well there, as in the Commons. The Duke of Leeds and the Chancellor spoke well; but are, I find, men of like passions."

He was trying to arrange for clearing off his debts, by again taking out with him "a number of things for sale," but though sure of being able to obtain these when he wrote to his father, he, perhaps happily, failed to accomplish this purpose; and on his arrival in Calcutta he had no goods to dispose of on his own private account, except a few English dogs!

Thus, with many sore anxieties and troubles, April had slowly passed by, and the ship still lay at anchor. At the beginning of May, Mr. Carey was made glad by tidings from his wife, which made him feel that this unwelcome delay had yielded comfort in the end.* Then May advanced, and when, about the middle of it, some more definite prospect of departure was gained, the mis-

---

* The letter written by Mr. Carey in reply, may interest the reader.

"*Ryde, Isle of Wight, May 6th,* 1793.

"MY DEAR DOROTHY,

"I have just received yours, giving me an account of your safe delivery. This is pleasant news indeed to me; surely goodness and mercy follow me all my days. My stay here was very painful and unpleasant, but now I see the goodness of God in it. It was that I might hear the most pleasing accounts that I possibly could hear respecting earthly things. You wish to know in what state my mind is. I answer, It is much as when I left you. If I had all the world, I would freely give it all to have you and my dear children with me; but the sense of duty is so strong as to overpower all other considerations; I could not turn back without guilt on my soul. I find a longing desire to enjoy more of God; but, now I am among the people of the world, I think I see more beauties in godliness than ever, and, I hope, enjoy more of God in retirement than I have done for some time past.

"Yesterday, I preached twice at Newport, and once in the country. This place much favors retirement and meditation; the fine woods and hills and the sea all conspire to solemnize the mind and to lift my soul to admire the Creator of all. There are no serious persons at the place where we are, but many on the island. To-day I dined with Mrs. Clark at Newport, and Felix found Teddy Clark one of his old play-fellows, which pleased him much. He is a good boy, and gives me much pleasure. He has almost finished his letter, and I intend to add a little to it before it comes. He has been a long while about it; and I question whether you can read it when it comes.

"You want to know what Mrs. Thomas thinks, and how she likes the voyage. She is a very delicate woman, weak and very nervous, brought up very genteel, and cousin to Squire Thursby of Abingdon, near Northampton. I believe, a good woman. She goes in good spirits, and the sea agrees with her very well. She sends her love to you, and is glad to hear the good news concerning your delivery. She would rather stay in England than go to India; but thinks it right to go with her husband. A young gentleman and his sister, cousins to Mr. Thomas, go with us. They have been brought up under the gospel. Mr. Thomas and I act as masters of the family, and maintain religious exercises.

"I shall be glad to hear of you, and how you do, as often as possible. We do not know when we shall go, but expect it will be in a week at farthest. My love to all of you. Tell my dear children I love them dearly, and pray for them constantly. Felix sends his love. I look upon this mercy as an answer to prayer indeed. Trust in God. Love to Kitty, brothers, sisters, &c. Be assured I love you most affectionately. Let me know my dear little child's name.

"I am, for ever,
"Your faithful and affectionate Husband,
"WILLIAM CAREY.

"My health never was so well. I believe the sea makes Felix and me both as hungry as hunters. I can eat a monstrous meat supper, and drink a couple of glasses of wine after it, without hurting me at all. Farewell."

sionaries thought that the end of their distressful suspense was at last nearly reached. Mr. Thomas ventured to rejoin his family, and all were in readiness to embark, when, four days before sailing, captain White received a letter from the East India House, signed *Verax*, stating that it was known that " a person" was going out in his ship without the Directors' leave, and that if this passenger were allowed to proceed to India, an information would be laid against him. Now this would inevitably have deprived him of his command. Mr. Thomas felt sure the letter did not refer to himself or Mr. Carey; and he took it with him to London, hoping to find out the writer, through his friend, Mr. James Savage, of the East India House, and so to clear up the difficulty. But his attempt was unsuccessful; and on returning to Portsmouth, he found Mr. Carey in tears, with the news that the captain insisted that they should both take out their things at once, and quit his ship. There was no help for it; and, with a third passenger similarly situated, they had to comply. Mrs. Thomas and her child, Mr. S. Powell and his sister, and Mr. Thomas's "black boy Andrew," were allowed to proceed, "for they had the Company's leave," and they did so. " My dear wife," Mr. Thomas wrote, "had uncommon supplies of fortitude. She proceeded on the voyage willingly; and endured the day of adversity better than I." This, he felt to be providential and very remarkable, since it was not without much difficulty she had been induced to consent to leave her native land.

The baggage was taken out of the ship; and Mr. Carey "with a heart heavier than all, came away" with his companion. Their "venture," that is, the packages of goods for sale in India which made up the investment of £150, intended for their support during the first year after their arrival in India, had to go on with the ship. It would otherwise have been " seized by the Custom House officers." With unspeakable distress, they saw the *Earl of Oxford*, with her consorts, the *Pigot*, the *Prince William Henry*, the *Houghton*, and the *William Pitt*, get under weigh, and sail off, on Thursday, May 23d; and, leaving their baggage at Portsmouth, they "at the same instant," returned to London.

Mr. Carey had written the bad news to Mr. Fuller on the 21st, and had suggested that the warning to the captain came from one of Mr. Thomas's creditors, which does not appear to have been the case. Mr. Fuller wrote, on the 24th, sending on the disastrous tidings to Mr. Ryland,—

We are all undone. I am grieved. Yet perhaps it is best. Thomas's debts and embranglements damped my pleasure before. Perhaps it is best he should not go. I am afraid leave will never be obtained now for Carey or any other. And the adventure seems to be lost! He says nothing of the £250 for voyage. It is well if that be not lost!

Before these words were written, however, a way of escape from the difficulties of their position was beginning to appear. The two disappointed missionaries, with little Felix, had made their mournful journey to London. Small charm for them had the flowery hedge-rows, and green fields, and blooming gardens, beside which they travelled, full of beauty as they were. What were they to do? and how could they possibly get out to Bengal? Was there any way of going by land? or of taking a passage from some other country? Mr. Carey talked wildly of demanding the consent of the Board of Directors; but their very recent outcry against Mr. Wilberforce's Resolutions, left no hope of any concession, generous or timid, from them. Baffled and dispirited, the two good men got to London at last. Mr. Thomas has left a lively description of their anxieties. He says,—

While Carey wrote to his wife, I would go to the coffee-house, with eager desire to know whether any Swedish or Danish ship was expected to sail from Europe to Bengal, or any part of the East Indies that season; when, to the great joy of a bruised heart, the waiter put a card into my hand, whereon were written these life-giving words:—

‘ A DANISH EAST INDIAMAN.
No. 10, Cannon Street.’

No more tears that night! Our courage revived. We fled to No. 10, Cannon Street, and found it was the office of Smith and

Co., agents; that Mr. Smith was a brother of the captain's, and lived in Gower Street; that this ship had sailed, (as he supposed,) from Copenhagen; was hourly expected in Dover Roads; would make no stay there; and the terms were £100 for a passenger, £50 for a child, £25 for an attendant. We went away, wishing for money! Carey had £150 returned from the *Oxford*.* This was not half sufficient for all; and we were not willing to part. Besides, our baggage was still at Portsmouth; and Mr. Carey had written to his wife that he was coming to see her; and also he entertained some faint hopes that she might now join us, if she could be so persuaded, for she had lain in only three weeks; but the shortest way of accomplishing all this would take up so much time, that we feared we should be too late for the ship.

It was, indeed, to all appearance, an impossibility that so much could be done in so short a time as probably would be available. Not a moment was lost, however. At 9 o'clock on Friday night, May 24th, Messrs. Thomas and Carey left London, and reached Northampton the next morning. They breakfasted with Mrs. Carey at Piddington, and said all they could to induce her to accompany them to India. Mr. Thomas says,—

She refused to go with us; which gave Mr. Carey much grief. I reasoned with her a long time, to no purpose. I had entreated the Lord in prayer to make known His will, and not to suffer either of us to fight against Him, by persuading her to go, on the one hand, or to stay, on the other. This expression moved her; but her determination not to go was apparently fixed. We now set off to Mr. Ryland of Northampton, to ask for money [for the passage]: and on our way thither I found Mr. Carey's hope of his wife all gone. I proposed to go back once more; but he overruled it, saying it was of no use. At last, I said, 'I *will* go back.'—'Well, do as you think proper,' said he, 'but I think we are losing time.' I went back; and told Mrs. Carey her going out with us was a matter of such importance that I could not leave her so. Her family would be dispersed and divided for ever. *She would repent of it as long as she lived!* As she tells me since, that last saying, frequently repeated, had such an effect upon her, that she was afraid to stay at home; and afterwards, in a few minutes, determined to go with us, trusting in the Lord: but this should be on

* We presume the captain of the *Earl of Oxford* retained £100 for the passage of Mrs. Thomas and her little girl.

condition of her sister going with her. This was agreed to. We now set off for Northampton like two different men: our steps so much quicker, our hearts so much lighter. The counting of the cost, however, was still enough to damp all our hopes. No less than eight persons' passage to be paid for, besides the necessaries to be bought for fitting all out for so long a voyage, would require £700 at least.

When they reached Mr. Ryland, he was just sitting down to answer his brother Fuller's despairing note; and he told them he knew not whether to be glad or sorry to see them. They told him of their success with Mrs. Carey, and made known their wishes and needs as to money for the new arrangements. He replied, "I have about £9 in my hands, belonging to the mission; and between £4 and £5 of my own. That is all with which I can furnish you." "We *must* have £200," they said. "Well," said he, "I recollect that there is at Kettering a bill for £200, sent from Yorkshire. It is, I suppose, not yet due; for it had a pretty long time to run; but that would exactly answer your exigencies." "We have no time to go to Kettering," said they: "we must be off directly."

But this Yorkshire bill, sent up by Mr. Fawcett, and representing the affectionate zeal and devotedness with which he and his aged brother Mr. Crabtree had striven to aid the missionary cause, was the effectual help provided for this time of need. Remembering this bill, Mr. Ryland begged them to sit down for a few minutes, while he "wrote letters to Mr. Newton, Mr. Booth, and Dr. Rippon, stating the case, and requesting them to advance the money," which he assured them could be immediately repaid; and then he once more parted from his two missionary brethren, never again to see them on earth.

They now hasted back to Piddington; and that Saturday was a busy packing day for the Carey family. They had, however, a most energetic helper, whose experience in such matters stood them in good stead; and, somehow or other, the needful arrangements were made, with many misgivings in the mind of the bewildered mother and aunt. On Sunday morning, Mr. Thomas put all the astonished family into two post chaises, and they arrived in London that night. Next morning, the notes from Mr. Ryland, and the emergency of the case, called forth active help. Mr. Booth, Mr. Timothy Thomas, and Dr. Rippon gave their ready aid; while Mr. Thomas went eagerly to bargain with the captain's brother. He told him, to his no small surprise, what had been accomplished since Friday; and how large a family he had brought up from Northamptonshire. His narrative proceeds,—

I continued to say that their finances were slender, and expenses very great: that the terms I had to offer him were these: That two people only—Mr. and Mrs. Carey—should be at the captain's table; that two cabins only would be required; and two persons—Mrs. Carey's sister and myself—would go as attendants, and receive their dinner from or with the servants, or any way whatever that would be convenient to the captain;—that, for these accommodations, I had three hundred guineas to offer him. I was moved with wonder to see the hand of God on this occasion, in his accepting these terms: the lowest, I suppose, that ever were heard of. He said what wrought the most with him was, such a large family being actually advanced to go.

The terms were happily settled and the passage money paid, and that same day, Monday, May 27th, the Careys embarked for Dover, to be ready to catch the ship; while Mr. Thomas hurried off to Portsmouth, to bring away the baggage which had been left there. There was not time to get it to Dover by land; and it seemed impossible to hire a boat for the purpose, the men declaring that the Channel swarmed with French privateers, and that the risk of capture was so great, they would not go for any money. Then, a boatman offered to take twenty guineas for the trip, in an open boat! Mr. Thomas was in constant terror lest he should, after all, lose the ship; yet he could not accept terms so exorbitant; and two whole days were spent by him in an agony of impotent impatience. At last, on Wednesday evening, a fisherman was found willing to go for nine guineas. The bargain was immediately concluded, the packages were put into his boat, and, the next evening, baggage and passenger were landed at Dover, "having run through all the privateers in the dark, if there were any." "With great gladness of heart," Mr. Thomas met his brother Carey there.

And now the *Kron Princessa Maria*, could not come too soon. But their patience was yet to be tried. Day after day, for a whole fortnight, passed and she did not appear. On the 6th of June, they had to write to Mr. Fuller, and ask for a further supply of money, as their funds were fast running out, at their lodgings " at Mr. Reynolds' in Crane Street, Dover." As summer advanced, holiday-keepers became more numerous there, day by day, and the cost of living grew more and more oppressive to the missionaries. The boatmen here also were found to be an extortionate set of men. Not one would agree to put the party on board for less than three guineas! The missionaries were living " in earnest hope and expectation; but no ship yet." "The winds were unfavorable for her coming down."

At last, before 3 o'clock in the morning of June 13th, they were all roused up from their slumbers by the joyful tidings that the ship was in the Roads. While the Careys got their children ready, Mr. Thomas hastily wrote to a friend in London,—

The ship is here!—the signal made,—the guns are fired,—and we are going, with a fine fair wind. Farewell, my dear brethren and sisters. Farewell! May the God of Jacob be ours and yours; by sea and land; for time and eternity. Most affectionately, adieu!

Adults and children were soon all ready to embark, and took their places in the boat. How cool and clear the waters looked, that early midsummer morning, as they made their way to the Danish Indiaman standing out before them, and only waiting their coming to start forward again upon her way. By 5 o'clock, they were on board, and had been cordially received by captain Smith, or, as he was now called, having been naturalized in Denmark, captain Christmas; and now they were speedily borne onward, out of sight of the chalky cliffs, and verdant slopes, and happy English homes, which these two devoted messengers to the heathen were never to look upon again.

Captain Christmas would not hear of the humiliating arrangements which had been so magnanimously suggested, with a view to economy. Mr. Thomas wrote,—

On our coming on board, we felt ourselves a little awkward, thinking that some there seemed very sensible that they were passengers of a better rank than we were, and considering that they had paid £100 each, whilst we, who were eight persons, paid only £315; wherefore, we expected to be treated accordingly, and determined to endure it. For my part, I looked for a very uncomfortable and lonely passage, having agreed to mess with the servants; but He who gave Joseph favor with Pharaoh had graciously provided for us and our little ones, far beyond our expectations. The captain would suffer neither me nor Mrs. Carey's sister to absent ourselves from his table: and received and entertained us all along as though we had been people of consequence; so that he has often shown kindnesses that we could no otherwise account for than by the good hand of God being upon us. On our coming on board, he immediately ordered the very best accommodation in the ship, and the largest, to be prepared for Mrs. Carey and her children, and a cabin was granted for me, and another for her sister. On their being sea sick, he ordered them soup, sent wine and other comfortable things, and would come himself and visit them, to see they wanted nothing he could supply them with.

Two days after embarking, Mr. Thomas wrote thus to his father:—

On the Atlantic Ocean, Lat. 49 N. Long. 6 W. We are most comfortably situated, and treated like gentlemen. We have been highly favored every way. We have now both our families, and our work is in view. I have lost much of my savour, in hurry and confusion. I retract,—as thinking I had not much to lose! My heart is tuned to praises, for He has been to my soul at Dover as the dew and as the rain.

The *Triton* frigate convoyed them out of the track of privateers, and they hoped to send word by her of their comfort and prospects. When she left them, however, the breeze was so strong that they could not hoist out a boat to convey their letters. No news of them consequently reached their anxious friends until the return of the ship in which they sailed.

The embarkation of the missionaries in a foreign vessel,

without the permission of the Directors of the East India Company, was regarded by some persons with displeasure and censure. Mr. Fuller's reply to their animadversions may be quoted here.—

The apostles and primitive ministers were commanded to go into all the world, and preach the gospel to every creature; nor were they to stop for the permission of any power upon earth; but to go,—and take the consequences. If a man of God, conscious of having nothing in his heart unfriendly to any civil government whatever, but determined in all civil matters to obey, and teach obedience to, 'the powers that be,' puts his life in his hand, saying, 'I will go; and, if I am persecuted in one city, I will flee to another,'—whatever the wisdom of the world may decide upon his conduct, he will assuredly be acquitted, and more than acquitted, at a higher tribunal.

The voyage was prosperous. The missionaries laboured hard in attempts to do good, and gave much of their time to Bengali. Mr. Thomas taught his beloved companion, and endeavoured to translate the book of Genesis; in difficult passages of which Mr. Carey helped him with his critical suggestions. "So," said the former, " let the goldsmith help the carpenter, and the carpenter the goldsmith, that the work of God be done." Mrs. Carey had many fears and troubles; "so that," Mr. Thomas wrote, "she was like Lot's wife, until we passed the Cape; but, ever since, it seems so far to look back to Piddington, that she turns her hopes and wishes to our safe arrival in Bengal." Many apprehensions and anxieties arose sometimes as to the course they should take when they reached Calcutta; but the prevailing idea was that they should settle on some grant of Government land, where they might procure subsistence by agriculture and could preach to the people around them. All such schemes appeared very uncertain, however, and fears often invaded their minds. Mr. Thomas wrote :—

The captain has promised to recommend us to the Danish Governor of Serampore, sixteen miles from Calcutta; which will be no small favor or convenience, if the Company should consider us as trespassers on their ground. But what is more, he has offered to recommend us to the Secretary of the Supreme Council, that we may procure land; and if this should be of God, we shall rejoice; if not—we will be contented. But in one sense, we are sure these kind favors from men are of God; and we have good hope that God will make room for us and our little ones, especially when we look back and see ourselves on the brink of sailing, but suddenly stopped and sent back: no prospect of another ship: I and my family become two bands: all darkness and threatening, fear and dismay: but in three days, another ship appears, takes us and the whole family; which we just before thought on many accounts impossible to be done! When we think of these things that are past,

"We trust Him for all that's to come."

So let the happy voyagers go on upon their way to Bengal. We will for a moment look back upon the brethren they left behind them. How did they feel, as they thought over the wonderful enterprise which had so suddenly matured itself amongst them, and the accomplishment of which had so actively engaged their sympathies and efforts? They were men of quiet regular procedure before this missionary project invaded their hearts and altars; but how completely all their thoughts and habits had been revolutionized by it! And now the strain of eager expectation and effort was over. Their messengers to the heathen were gone; and they must wait for the results of their embassy. Let Mr. Fuller tell us how himself and his brethren thought and felt. He says:—

After their departure, we had time for reflection. In reviewing the events of a few preceding months we were much impressed: we could scarcely believe that such a number of impediments had, in so short a time, been removed. The fear and trembling which had possessed us at the outset had insensibly given way to hope and joy. Upborne by the magnitude of the object, and by the encouraging promises of God, we had found difficulties subside as we approached them, and ways opened beyond all our expectations. The thought of having done something towards enlarging the boundaries of our Saviour's kingdom, and of rescuing poor heathens and Muhammadans from under Satan's yoke rejoiced our hearts. We were glad also to see the people of God offering so willingly: some leaving their country; others pouring in their property; and all uniting in prayers to heaven for a blessing. A new bond of union was furnished between distant ministers and churches. Some who had blacksliden from God, were restored; and others who had long been poring over their unfruitfulness, and questioning the reality of their personal religion, having their attention directed to Christ and His kingdom, lost their fears, and found that peace which, in other pursuits, they had sought in vain. Christians of different denominations discovered a common bond of affection; and instead of always dwelling on things wherein they differed, found their account in uniting in those wherein they were agreed. In short, our hearts were enlarged; and if no other good had arisen from the undertaking, than the effect produced upon our own minds, and the minds of Christians in our country, it were more than equal to the expense.

CHAPTER X.

How the Lord made Room for His Servants, that they might dwell in the Land.—1793-4.

THE *Kron Princessa Maria* encountered some severe weather, but, upon the whole, made a favorable voyage; yet the close of it was very tedious to her impatient passengers. The winds were fickle and often contrary in the Bay of Bengal, where, for nearly a month, the ship made little progress: the strong currents sweeping her back, as often as any advance had been gained. At last, they entered the mouth of the Calcutta river. Fishing boats came alongside the ship on the 9th of November, and with deep interest Mr. Thomas's companions looked for the first time upon the natives of Bengal. Next day, Sunday, the missionary party left the ship at Kedgeree, to come up to Calcutta in a small native boat, called a *pánsi*. When the tide failed them, they put to at a market place on the river side. Mr. Thomas preached, and a large number of the market people listened with much attention, one of whom afterwards prepared them a dinner, which was served out upon plaintain leaves, and which they ate, in primitive style, without knife or fork.

Calcutta was safely reached on Monday, the 11th of November. Mrs. Thomas with her child was there, awaiting her husband's arrival. The *Earl of Oxford*, in which she came, had arrived on the 4th of October. She had met with much kindness from many persons who knew Mr. Thomas, and especially from Mrs. Udny, who appears to have been in Calcutta on a visit to her younger son, who married in May, 1792, and was now a member in the mercantile firm of Udny, Frushard and Laprimaudaye. Mr. James Mackay of the Orphan House also was most kind to Mrs. Thomas and her little daughter.

Rám Rám Basu heard of their arrival, and came to welcome the missionaries. Their gladness in meeting him was damped by hearing that he had acted unworthily, after Mr. Thomas left. Having no Christian friend or helper, he had fallen into difficulties; and had attempted to please his kindred and connexions by compliance with idolatrous ceremonies. Now, however, he was full of penitence; and the missionaries were ready to accept all his assurances of contrition. Of Párbati, they heard good accounts; but he was at a distance. Mohan Chand also wrote to Mr. Thomas. Mr. Carey at once engaged Rám Rám Basu to be his múnshi, and was greatly impressed in his favor by all he saw of him and by his pious conversation. Notwithstanding his grievous fall, he did not hesitate to regard him as a "converted person." Mr. Thomas likewise re-engaged Padma Lochan as a pandit, to enable him to carry forward his Sanscrit studies.

Death had made some changes in Calcutta society, as Mr. Thomas knew it, during his absence in England. On the 22nd of August, Mr. William Chambers had died, and this news must have awakened many sad memories.* He had once been one of Mr. Thomas's warmest friends.

* The *Calcutta Chronicle* of August 27th, 1793, says,—

"On Thursday last, after a short illness, died William Chambers, Esq., Prothonotary of the Supreme Court, deeply regretted by those who enjoyed the honour of his acquaintance. He possessed abilities useful rather than splendid, a vigorous and cultivated mind, dexterity and application in business, a judicious mixture of liberality and economy, of mildness and vigour, and animated, yet well-regulated, warmth in support of the religion he professed, which enlarged his heart, without weakening his understanding. In the various turns of his prosperous and adverse fortune,—and he had many,—he never lost the confidence of those who were his friends nor the esteem of those who were not so. Originally engaged in the Company's Civil Service, he became embarrassed by speculations in trade; he then altered his destination and obtained the office of Master in Chancery in the Supreme Court, and discharged the duties of his situation with equal honour to himself, and advantage to the public. In March, 1792, on the death of James Stark, Esq., he obtained the place of Prothonotary and executed

DELIBERATIONS FOR THE FUTURE.

And now Thomas and Carey, with their families, were in the country which the Directors of the East India Company had resolved should not be invaded by missionaries of the gospel. But what were they to do to secure their footing, and how were they to sustain themselves whilst they preached the word of life to the Bengali people? Their plans were very indefinite. Mr. Thomas had no clear purpose as to the place they should occupy, or the methods they should adopt to obtain subsistence. He had told the members of the Society at home that, at any rate at the beginning, they must support the missionaries they sent out; but he had spoken so enthusiastically of the cheapness of provisions in India, and his statements as to the possibility of living very much as the natives of Bengal themselves do, were so unguarded, that it is not strange that the supporters of the mission concluded that a very small allowance would suffice for their brethren, wherever they might be. Mr. Carey, it will be remembered, had written a book, and therein had elaborated a theory as to the way in which missionaries to a heathen country should subsist. The following extracts will suffice to set forth the views he entertained upon this subject. He says:—

As to the difficulty of procuring the necessaries of life, this would not be so great as may appear at first sight; for though we could not procure European food, yet we might procure such as the natives of those countries which we visit, subsist upon themselves.

It might be necessary, however, for two, at least, to go together; and in general I should think it best that they should be married men, and, to prevent their time from being employed in procuring necessaries, two, or more, other persons, with their wives and families, might also accompany them, who should be wholly employed in providing for them. In most countries it would be necessary for them to cultivate a little spot of ground, just for their support, which would be a resource to them, whenever their supplies failed. Not to mention the advantages they would reap

the business of that office till his death with unimpeached integrity and general approbation.

"Such was WILLIAM CHAMBERS: let those who may object to his peculiarities—for he had some—imitate his virtues, while they avail themselves of his example."

from each other's company, it would take off the enormous expense which has always attended undertakings of this kind, the first expense being the whole; for though a large colony needs support for a considerable time; yet so small a number would, upon receiving the first crop, maintain themselves. They would have the advantage of choosing their situation, their wants would be few; the women, and even the children, would be necessary for domestic purposes: and a few articles of stock, as a cow or two, and a bull, and a few other cattle of both sexes, a very few utensils of husbandry, and some corn to sow their land, would be sufficient. Those who attend the missionaries should understand husbandry, fishing, fowling, &c. and be provided with the necessary implements for these purposes. Indeed a variety of methods may be thought of, and, when once the work is undertaken, many things will suggest themselves to us, of which we at present can form no idea.

The missionaries must be men of great piety, prudence, courage, and forbearance; of undoubted orthodoxy in their sentiments, and must enter with all their hearts into the spirit of their mission; they must be willing to leave all the comforts of life behind them, and to encounter all the hardships of a torrid, or a frigid climate, an uncomfortable manner of living, and every other inconvenience that can attend this undertaking. Clothing, a few knives, powder and shot, fishing-tackle, and the articles of husbandry above-mentioned, must be provided for them; and when arrived at the place of their destination, their first business must be to gain some acquaintance with the language of the natives, (for which purpose two would be better than one,) and by all lawful means to endeavour to cultivate a friendship with them, and as soon as possible let them know the errand for which they were sent. They must endeavour to convince them that it was their good alone, which induced them to forsake their friends, and all the comforts of their native country. They must be very careful not to resent injuries which may be offered to them, nor to think highly of themselves, so as to despise the poor heathens, and by those means lay a foundation for their resentment, or rejection of the gospel. They must take every opportunity of doing them good, and labouring and travailing, night and day, they must instruct, exhort, and rebuke, with all long suffering, and anxious desire for them, and above all, must be instant in prayer for the effusion of the Holy Spirit upon the people of their charge. Let but missionaries of the above description engage in the work, and we shall see that it is not impracticable.

Such were Mr. Carey's ideas, when projecting mission work, at home; and, when he had been more than a month in India, he wrote :—

The plan laid down in my little piece I still approve; and think it the best that can be followed. A missionary must be one of the companions and equals of the people to whom he is sent.

For this system of missionary colonization more persons were required than those who composed the present missionary party; but it appears to have been Mr Carey's wish that, as far as possible, Mr. Thomas and himself should carry out the project, by procuring a piece of land in some rural district, upon which they might set up huts, and support their families by cultivating the soil, and by the occasional use of their guns.

But now they were in Calcutta, and something must be done to settle themselves and to begin the great work they had undertaken. What were they to do? The first thing obviously was to convert the goods they had for sale into money. They had no Bills of Exchange, or Letters of Credit, upon any merchant or banker in Calcutta. What the Society had granted for their support for twelve months to come, was the sum of £150, to be divided equally between the two families; and this money had been invested in articles of merchandise, which had now to be sold to the best advantage.

For some days then, it was clear, they must stay in Calcutta, where Mr. Thomas undertook to keep house for the two families; and they all lived together. Mr. Carey looked with many secret misgivings upon the liberality of "his guide and fellow-labourer's" domestic ménage, but did not like to interfere in matters which one who had been in India before must understand so much better than himself.

Some friends, who sympathised in their missionary purpose, wished them to settle permanently in Calcutta. There, it was urged, Mr. Thomas might obtain a profitable practice as a surgeon; and, in the native population, and particularly amongst the Portuguese Roman Catholics, then wholly neglected, there was a broad and extensive field, upon the cultivation of which they might enter with good hope of success.

But Calcutta was a most expensive place, and they wished to live near to the people of the land in their quiet villages. At the end of November therefore they removed to Bandel; intending to buy or rent a house there. To buy one proved to be impossible, without far more money than they had; but they rented one of Mr. Joachim Spiegel, who kept a sort of hotel at Chinsura, in the neighbourhood, and continued there all through the month of December.

What inclined the missionaries to think of settling at Bandel, it is hard to say. It is a village immediately adjoining Hooghly, and, as early as 1599, a convent, cathedral, and other ecclesiastical buildings were founded there by Augustinian monks, whose present representatives still enjoy a grant of land made to the establishment by one of the Moghul emperors. Ten or twenty years before Messrs. Thomas and Carey went there, Bandel was a favorite and fashionable place of resort for those who desired rest and change after the fatigues of Calcutta life. It was less frequented now; and probably recommended itself as being a cheap and quiet place, where the mission families would enjoy the advantages of proximity to Europeans, whilst the missionaries themselves would find numerous villages around to which they might convey the glad tidings of the cross. "Here," wrote Mr. Carey, on the 4th of December, "we intend to reside. All the people are Catholics or Muhammadans; but many Hindus live at a distance of a mile or two; so that there is work enough for us here; and ten thousand ministers would find full employment to publish the gospel." On the 16th, he wrote again:—

We have frequent opportunities of addressing the Hindus; and their attention is astonishing. Last Lord's day we visited them at a neighbouring village called Saatgunge, and Mr. Thomas preached to near two hundred of them. They listened with great seriousness, and several followed to make further enquiries about which is the way to heaven, and what they should do to walk therein? Every place presents us with a pleasing prospect, and we are of one mind, and one soul. Pray for us: we daily remember you, and the prosperity of the Society lies very near our hearts.

Mr. Carey, however, found that he could not carry out his plans at Bandel; and they anxiously discussed the advantages of Gour, Malda, Cutwa, and Nuddea, as suitable localities for their mission. To be able to visit towns and villages on the river-side, they bought a small boat; and on Sunday, December the 22nd, they were, with Rám Basu, at Nuddea, where some of the pandits begged them to settle, and where they made earnest prayer to God for his guidance in their increasing perplexities. They appear indeed to have resolved to accept this proposal that they should make Nuddea their place of abode, for, on Christmas day, Mr. Carey wrote, "Next week, we go to live entirely amongst the natives."

But Mr. Thomas's debts had meanwhile found him out. As yet, he had nothing owing to any one in India; but whilst he listened to Mr. Carey's views, and discussed with him plans upon which no European of any sort has ever yet subsisted in Bengal, he knew that, one of his creditors having sent out his bond to Calcutta, he might any day be arrested and put into prison. It soon appeared that his only chance of escape, and of doing any good in the mission, was to try and earn money in some way which would afford his creditors a reasonable hope that payment would at length be made to them. Nothing deterred him from setting up as a surgeon in Calcutta, as some opulent natives urged him to do, with most generous promises of their patronage, but his reluctance to be detached from the brother who had come out with him from England, and who was so bent upon a rural settlement in some interior district. At length, there was hope that Mr. Carey might get employment in the Botanical Gardens just below Calcutta. This issued in disappointment; but the two families removed to Calcutta at the end of December, Mr. Thomas to open business as a surgeon, Mr. Carey to carry out his cherished plan as soon as he could hear of a piece of land procurable on favorable terms. They now separated their house-keeping. Mr. Thomas took a house in Zig Zag Lane; and Mr. Carey, who was consulting about waste lands with Nelu Datt, a native banker, from whom Mr. Thomas had taken some advances, accepted his offer of leave to occupy his garden house in Manicktolla, a north eastern suburb of Calcutta, until he was ready to go to his new home. It was a time of heavy calamity to the inexperienced missionary. At Bandel, his family had suffering severely from dysentery; and they were still sorely afflicted in the squalid place where they had found a temporary refuge.

Rám Basu was with him and was a comfort to him. He was, however, also a burden, for he wanted to be helped out of debt. Mr. Carey found on enquiry that he could obtain land to any extent at Dehatta, to the eastward, about forty miles from Calcutta. Rám Basu's uncle was the zemindar of the place, and would no doubt be kind and helpful. There he resolved to go, and to build "a bungalow, or straw-house," and cultivate about fifty or one hundred bigahs of land. His difficulty was the unwillingness of his wife and her sister to commit themselves to such a mode of life, with four helpless sickly children. They thought it very hard that, while Mr. Thomas was going to stay in Calcutta, they should be "forced to go into a wilderness and live without many of what they called the necessaries of life, bread in particular." Mr. Carey, however, was resolved, and would have proceeded to Dehatta about the middle of January, but for a most painful difficulty, which shall be stated in his own words.

January 15th and 16th, 1794.—On the first of these days, I received an account that I may have as much land as I please, for three years, for nothing, and, after that, to pay a small rent per annum. I therefore went to Mr. Thomas to consult him, and to obtain money; when I found that my all was expended, and that Mr. Thomas was already in debt. I was much dejected at this. I am in a strange land, alone, no Christian friend, a large family; and nothing to supply their wants. I blame Mr. Thomas for leading me into such expense at first, and I blame myself for being led; though I acceded to what I much disapproved of, because I thought he knew the country better, and was in earnest to go and live up the country; and that, for a week or two, while we sold our venture, it would be a greater expense to have a separate house and servants than for us to live together. I am dejected, not for my own sake, but my family's, and his, for whom I tremble. He is now at the certain expense of £400 per annum ; and, unless he has speedy practice, he must be irrecoverably involved. I must borrow five hundred Rupees, if I can ; with which I intend to build a hut or two, and retire to the wilderness. There are many serpents and tigers ; but Christ has said His followers shall take up serpents, &c. unhurt.

January 17th.—Went to Calcutta to Mr. Thomas for money ; but to no purpose. Was very much dejected all day.

January 20th.—This has been a day of seeking money. I had an offer of a bungalow, belonging to the Company, at Dehatta, till I can get a place made for myself and family ; so that it has been a day of mercy ; though, to my shame, of spiritual barrenness.

January 23d.—My temporal troubles remain just as they were. I have a place ; but cannot remove my family to it for want of money. Mr. Thomas has now begun to set his face another way. At his motion, I went to Calcutta ; then to Bandel ; at which place all our money was expended. He ordered all the expenses, and lived in his own way : to which I acceded, though sore against my will. He was inclined first, then determined, to practice surgery at Calcutta. I agreed to come and settle as near him as possible ; though I had previously intended to go to Gour near Malda ; and all this that I might not be the first in a breach of our mutual undertaking. Now he is buying and selling, and living at a rate of I know not how much,—I suppose, 250 or 300 rupees per mensem,—has twelve servants, and is this day talking of keeping his coach ! I have remonstrated with him in vain ; and I am almost afraid that he intends to throw up the mission. How all these things can be agreeable to a spiritual mind I know not. But now all my friends are but One. I rejoice, however, that He is all-sufficient, and can supply all my wants, spiritual and temporal. My heart bleeds for him, for my family, for the Society, whose stedfastness must be shaken by this report, and for the success of the mission, which must receive a sad blow from this. But why is my soul disquieted within me ? Things may turn out better than I expect. Every thing is known to God, and God cares for the mission.

January 24th.—I wish to feel myself always in the excuse of a spirit of a meekness ; but it is hard work. Yesterday my mind was much hurt to see what I thought a degree of selfishness in my friend, which amounted to an almost total neglect of me, my family, and the mission; though I do not think he seriously intends to neglect either, but inadvertently runs into such things as make it impossible to attend to either.

January 25th.—Was employed in buying some necessaries for our removal into the wilderness.

January 27th.—This morning, went to Baliaghat, to procure a boat to carry us over the lakes to the place where we hope to go. Through the delays of my companion, I have spent another month, and done scarcely anything, except that I have added to my knowledge of the language, and had opportunity of seeing much more of the genius and disposition of the natives than I otherwise could have known.

January 28th.—This morning I was at Calcutta. Again disappointed about money. Was much dejected and grieved. Advised with múnshi, who is my trusty friend; but could find no settled plan.

These paragraphs have been quoted, because they contain statements which have most seriously damaged the reputation of Mr. Thomas, ever since they were first published. Similar assertions are to be found in other parts of Mr. Carey's journal, and in letters written at the same time of trouble. So prone are even good men to remember the failings rather than the excellencies of others, that the things here stated of Mr. Thomas are just those which almost every student of Baptist Missionary history knows about him, whilst he knows no more. Our first missionary is remembered as the man who, on getting out to Calcutta with Mr. Carey, spent both his own share of their joint property and his colleague's, in reckless extravagance, and who, when all was gone, left his brother to be well nigh starved, without making any generous earnest effort to relieve the necessities he had himself created.

Mr. Carey afterwards desired to have what he had written to Mr. Thomas's disadvantage "for ever suppressed and buried in oblivion;" and there was at least as much of justice as of generosity in the request. The effect of it was, however, disastrous. Mr. Thomas never knew what had been said of his conduct; and therefore never defended himself against the charges his companion made. Mr.

Carey did, indeed, in the middle of 1797, complain of these early transactions, but the reply made by Mr. Thomas was, "I know you approved of my management at the time;" and his explanations certainly left no good room for dispute, either as to his kindness or his integrity. Mr. Carey's early difficulties, however, were too full of interest to his biographer, to be relieved of any of their original poignancy in his Memoirs; and the expressions which were so damaging to his brother missionary were reproduced there; and the selfish extravagance of Mr. Thomas, supposed to be thus demonstrated, has, in several later-written narratives, served to set off Mr. Carey's self-denial, Christian endurance, and patient excellence, under the deepest injury and provocation.

Let all the facts, however, be briefly recounted. It will be remembered that the missionary party was originally expected to include only Mr. and Mrs. Thomas and their child, with Mr. Carey and his little boy. For the support of these five persons £150 had been invested in goods, to be taken with them, and sold in Calcutta. This it was hoped, would produce upwards of £75 for each missionary, for a year's support; and the equal division of the money gave Mr. Carey an advantage, in prospect of which Mr. Thomas never complained. The inadequacy of the allowance was, however, most seriously aggravated by the unexpected addition to the party of Mrs. Carey, with four children and her sister. This doubled the number to be provided for. Whilst that difficulty naturally most affected Mr. Carey's finances, Mr. Thomas had one of almost equal weight in his separation from his wife on the voyage. She had already borrowed more than Rs. 500 from persons who knew him, to enable her to meet expenses in Calcutta, before the arrival of the *Kron Princessa Maria*.

But, quitting these considerations of the difficulties which the missionaries had to encounter with very narrow means, let us examine the truth and justice of the charges laid against Mr. Thomas by his dispirited colleague. We are happily able to do this; for an account of their pecuniary relations at this time, drawn up by Mr. Thomas, and corrected by Mr. Carey's own hand, has been preserved. An account current is not easily introduced into a narrative, but perhaps the substance of this may be rendered readable and intelligible.

Mr. Carey blamed Mr. Thomas for leading him into ruinous expense in their joint house-keeping. The two families lived together "and kept but one table," from the time they left the ship, on the 10th of November, till the end of December; and the account debits Mr. Carey for "expenses of house-keeping," including rent, servants' wages, &c., Sicca Rupees 150 only. He had to pay nothing more for the board of his family, except the half of "Spiegel's bill," for "wine, pork, gardener's wages, and rent," which belongs to the period of their residence at Bandel;—but, adding Sa. Rs. 34 for this, how could three adults and four children have been more economically provided for, during seven weeks?

We find too that the "cash" received by Mr. Carey from his colleague in several, mostly small, sums before the 31st of January, amounted to Sa. Rs. 382-5-0; whilst for "cloth for gowns," "gingham," "shoes," made necessary by the haste in which his family prepared to leave England, and their consequently most imperfect outfit, together with "earthenware," "a table," and other articles of furniture, with a few household stores, tools, and "two billhooks," before going to Dehatta, there had been paid on his behalf, in addition, Sa. Rs. 217-13-1.

Lastly, payments to the steward of the *Kron Princessa Maria*, &c. with the outlay and loss upon the boat they had jointly purchased, amounted to Sa. Rs. 56-8-0.

These sums are none of them very large, and it is easy to see how such expenditure was needful, but, added together, the items made up Sa. Rs. 840-10-1; which Mr. Thomas had paid to or for his colleague when the complaints we have quoted were written. The same account includes the sums received to Mr. Carey's credit, (some of which appear to have come in at a much later date) by the sale of cutlery, hosiery, and wine! The total was only Sa. Rs. 731-7-2¾. Mr. Carey had therefore, as he subsequently acknowledged, already over-drawn his share of the money at the very time his unguarded expressions accused his colleague of having deprived him of the scanty means the Society had allotted.

That the good men had not a clearer understanding of the state of their joint finances was certainly very unfortunate; but Mr. Thomas could have had no motive to reticence in the matter, except indeed his desire not to encourage the despondent apprehensions of Mr. Carey, whilst the later ought to have known how much he had received in money and by payment for his purchases; and, in fact, did thus possess all the data requisite for a perfect knowledge of the condition of his own affairs.

No remarks are offered upon the reflections made upon Mr. Thomas's personal extravagance, after the families separated. Mr. Carey's words were written in moments of agitation, and should not be taken as his deliberate utterances. And, without any doubt, Mr. Thomas was to blame. He was constitutionally profuse, and always reckless of future difficulties. Mr. Carey very justly estimated him, when he said that, good man as he was, he was "only fit to live at sea, where his daily business would be before him, and daily provision made for him." But it must be remembered that at the time when he was so unconsciously exposing himself to the animadversions of Mr. Carey, whose own previous life had necessarily been one of rigorous economy, he was seeking to establish himself as a surgeon in Calcutta. A conveyance was a necessity, if he was to visit patients in so large a city, and some respectability of appearance was requisite to ensure the chance of success. No further apology for expenses which he had to suffer sorely for, somewhat later, need be offered. His dealings with Mr. Carey are now under review. They have been held to exhibit self-indulgent indifference. They are certainly capable of a very much more favorable interpretation. He was in overwhelming difficulties himself, yet he not only paid Mr. Carey more than he was entitled to receive from him, but pledged his already overstrained credit to borrow money for his brother's relief.

Mr. Carey's history may be pursued for a while, before that of his colleague is resumed. He had a most dreary sojourn at Manicktola, with sick children and a dissatisfied wife, ever ready to reproach him with the discomforts of their daily lot. Yet, on Sundays especially, and on other days, he attempted, with Rám Basu's aid, to talk of the Saviour to those he met with in the bazar and shops in his neighbourhood. His journal records that on the 24th of January, he tried to find solace in the acquaintance of religious friends. He writes :—

> I went to visit a professor of religion, to whom I was recommended at the Isle of Wight ; but to my sorrow found him at dice ! Thence went to see the Rev. David Brown. He is an evangelical preacher of the Church of England, and received me with cool politeness. I staid near an hour with him : found him a very sensible man ; but a marked disgust prevails, on both sides, between him and Mr. Thomas. He carried himself as greatly my superior, and I left him without his having so much as asked me to take any refreshment, though he knew I had walked five miles in the heat of the sun.

Mr. Brown's displeasure against Mr. Thomas did not soon abate. In a letter of much later date,—March 23d 1797,—Mr. Carey says of him, " He is a virulent enemy to our undertaking."

The account current proceeds to show that, on the 31st of January, Mr. Thomas gave his colleague Sa. Rs. 150, which he had borrowed with other money from Durgácharan Datt, a native banker, at 12 per cent. interest. The next day, Saturday, Mr. Carey and Rám Basu made arrangements for departure to Dehatta. On the Monday, a boat was procured at Baliaghát, the few articles of furniture and other baggage in their possession were put on board, and on Tuesday, the 4th of February, the Carey family proceeded on their way to Dehatta. On the 6th, they arrived there, weary of their journey in the crowded boat, and with their supplies exhausted. Mr. Carey had been told that there was a bungalow at the place, in which he might for a time put up, whilst his own house was building. On his arrival he found it was occupied by Mr. Charles Short, who resided there as superintendent of the salt works in the neighbourhood. Mr. Short met them with most generous hospitality, brought them all into his house, insisted on their continuing there until they could provide themselves with another dwelling, and bountifully supplied all their wants.

As to land, there was plenty to be had here. Mr. Carey wrote :—

Hashnábád, Kollatola, and several other adjacent parishes were at that time very nearly uninhabited. I went to Hashnábád, and thence to Kollatola, where I pitched on a place ; but in a day or two, relinquished that and chose another at Hashnábád, where I began to build.

He thus describes his progress :—

February 15th.—I have taken a few acres of land at Hashnábád, near Dehatta, which is about forty miles east of Calcutta, upon the river Jabuna. An English gentleman, to whom we were entirely unknown, has generously invited us all to stay in his house, till we have erected one of our own. This I am now engaged upon. The walls will be made of mats fastened to wooden posts, and the roof formed of bamboos, and thatched. The neighbouring inhabitants yield me a little assistance in the work, and four or five hundred families intend to come and reside in our neighbourhood. This is occasioned by múnshi's representing me to them in a favorable light. Although the country is an excellent soil, it has been lately almost deserted, on account of the tigers, and other beasts of prey, which infest the place ; but these are all afraid of a gun, and will soon be expelled. The people, therefore, are not afraid, when a European is nigh. We shall have all the necessaries of life here, except bread, for which rice must be a substitute. Wild hogs, deer, and fowls, are to be procured by the gun, and will supply us with a considerable part of our food. I find an inconvenience, in having so much of my time necessarily taken up in procuring provisions, and cultivating my little farm ; but, when my house is built, I shall have more leisure than at present, with daily opportunities of conversing with the natives, and pursuing the work of the mission. Here is certainly a large field for usefulness :—much larger than you can conceive, both among the Hindus and Mussulmans. They are very numerous, very inquisitive, and very attentive to the gospel. When I know the language well enough to preach in it, I have no doubt of having a stated congregation, and I much hope to send you pleasing accounts. I can so far converse in the language as to be understood in most things belonging to eating and drinking, buying and selling, &c. My ear is somewhat familiarized to the Bengali sounds. It is a language of a very singular construction, having no plural except for pronouns, and not a single preposition in it: but the cases of nouns and pronouns are almost endless, all the words answering to our prepositions being put after the word, and forming a new case. Except these singularities, I find it an easy language. I feel myself happy in my present undertaking, for though I never felt the loss of social religion so much as now; yet a consciousness of having given up all for God is a support; and the work, with all its attendant inconveniences, is to me a rich reward. I think the Society would do well to keep their eye towards Africa or Asia, countries which are not like the wilds of America, where long labour will scarcely collect sixty people to hear the word: for here it is almost impossible to get out of the way of hundreds, and preachers are wanted a thousand times more than people to preach to. Within India, are the Mahratta country and the northern parts to Cashmire, in which, as far as I can learn, there is not one soul that thinks of God aright.

February 23d.—Though I am surrounded by mercies, yet for this fortnight past my life has been rendered useless as to spiritual things, being for the present wholly occupied in temporal concerns, and the Sabbaths now are quite disconsolate. In one of these Sabbaths I am seeking communion with you, and I feel that a distance of ten or fifteen thousand miles, cannot prevent the communion of saints. Though deprived of a personal intercourse with my European friends, I have at least onè religious friend, and that is Rám Rám Basu, He has indeed much timidity, but is a man of very good understanding, and well-informed; he is also a person of strict probity. The part where I am building my house is within a quarter of a mile of the impenetrable forests called Sunderbunds: and though quite deserted before, through fear of the tigers, the people are now returning, encouraged by my example, and we shall soon have three or four thousand in our vicinity. These people and all others in the neighbourhood are much pleased with my coming, and two or three days ago a deputation of five or six Brahmans, with a present in their hands, came to thank me; or rather to say that they were *glad* I was coming to live among them, for they have no such word as *thank you*, nor any expression of *thankfulness*, in all their language. With respect to personal safety, I am just the same here as in England. My health was never better. The climate, though hot, is tolerable; but, attended as I am with difficulties, I would not renounce my undertaking for all the world.

These extracts breathe a noble spirit of devotedness to the great work the writer had undertaken,—devotedness undisturbed by the most adverse circumstances conceivable. Mr. Carey had to sustain the burden of domestic misery, in the displeasure of his wife and family with all his present arrangements. He was separated from his colleague, who also had no ability to send him help. He was almost penniless, for the little money he had on leaving Calcutta was now all gone, notwithstanding the relief to his finances afforded by Mr. Short's kind help. He had no supplies in prospect for many months to come. He was now about to dwell in a hut altogether unfit for the occupation of Europeans new to the country, and erected in a malarious uncultivated district, with a family already predisposed to dangerous sicknesses. Strong in faith, Mr. Carey felt himself safe in the hands of God; and he was so; but surely all must feel that his deliverance from disease and death depended, under God, upon his speedy removal from his present position. Hitherto the miseries of his situation had been mitigated by the circumstance that he and his family lived in Mr. Short's house and were fed at his table. He was now about to occupy his own dwelling, and to become dependent upon his own exhausted resources; whilst the hitherto moderate heat of the climate was daily becoming more and more oppressive to those who had never before experienced its intensity.

But unexpected relief was near at hand. He who had so wonderfully "furnished a table in the wilderness" for His servant, was now providing for him an escape from the dangers which beset him at Dehatta; and if Mr. Thomas be held responsible for some of his brother's calamities, it is pleasant to mark how the providence of God made him the joyful instrument of obtaining for him a most happy release from them. To do this, we must revert to the progress of affairs in Calcutta.

Very little can be said of Mr. Thomas's prospects of success as a surgeon. He kept no journal at this time, and information as to his doings is very scanty and imperfect. But there can be little doubt that the issue of his attempt to establish himself in Calcutta must have been an utter failure, had it been continued. As it was, he contracted debts which very seriously added to his former embarassments; and, as he himself felt and acknowledged, the effects of his anxious struggles to succeed, and of his endeavours to discover some method of overcoming his difficulties, were most unfavorable to his spiritual life and missionary usefulness. Thus the feeble infant mission appeared, under all these adverse circumstances, to be about to expire, in the death or ruin of its first agents. No human eye could have foreseen its recovery from disaster so complete and overwhelming.

We left Mr. Thomas attempting to establish himself in practice as a surgeon in Calcutta. A few days after he had made his arrangements for this, an event occurred which was related by the *Calcutta Mirror*, of January 7th, in the following words.

A most unfortunate and melancholy accident happened on Friday evening, January 3d. As Mr. R. Udny, his lady, Mr. Laprimaudaye, and Mr. Robinson were crossing over to Calcutta from the opposite side of the river, their boat, getting athwart the hawser of a ship lying at anchor, was suddenly overset, and carried down under the ship's bottom by the rapidity of the tide; by which accident Mr. and Mrs. Udny unhappily perished. Mr. Laprimaudaye was taken up in the course of a few minutes, but was insensible. Some doubt was at first entertained of his recovery; but we are happy to understand that he is free from danger. Mr. Robinson was carried along between the boat and the ship's bottom, from which he was much torn and bruised.*

* In the Old Burial Ground at Calcutta is the following inscription :—" Here lie interred the bodies of Robert Udny and of Ann his wife, who, on the 3d of January, 1794, were overset in a boat, as they were crossing the river opposite to Calcutta, and perished,—he aged 31, she aged 26 years. They were lovely and pleasant in their lives, and in their death they were not divided.—2 Samuel i. 23. Prisoners of hope.—Zachariah ix. 12."

This deplorable catastrophe overwhelmed the Malda family with distress, and especially the tender mother of the deceased young man. Mrs. Udny was so sorely afflicted that it was feared she would sink under the terrible stroke. As the reader will suppose, Mr. Thomas was greatly affected by this sad event. Robert Udny had been one of his earliest acquaintances amongst those who feared God in Bengal ; and his death under circumstances so painful occasioned very deep feeling. We have seen that Mr. George Udny had most kindly aided Mr. Thomas down to the time when he left India. He, however, had " declined the support of the mission," and no appeal was made to him for assistance in the difficulties in which the missionaries found themselves placed. Now, however, on hearing of the illness of his kind friend Mrs. Udny, Mr. Thomas wrote at once to her surviving son, expressing his warm sympathy and saying that, but for the impossibility of leaving Calcutta at the time, he would have set off for Malda as soon as the news reached him. His affectionate overtures were gratefully welcomed. Mr. Udny wrote at once, begging that he would come to them. Early in February, therefore he set off to Malda, leaving his family in Calcutta. Some particulars of this visit are related in the following extracts from a letter written on the 10th of March, at Baddaul, sixty miles to the eastward of Malda, whither he had accompanied the Udny family on a trip for change of air. Speaking of his interview with Mr. George Udny, he says :—

We met, with two hearts overflowing with affectionate remembrances of each other, and recollections of the sad occasion of our meeting now. Many tears fell, and many steps were taken, before one word was uttered on either side. We went and mingled our tears with those of his dear mother, who lay smarting under the afflicting hand of God, in body and mind : carrying about with her deep marks of heart-breaking grief. The same morning, I directed her to get a word from Christ, by preaching from Canticles viii. 13. I fatigued her body with long walks, hoping thereby to render her mind less capable of grief : and the Lord gave His blessing.

This led to most important results. Re-established in the affections of his Malda friends, Mr. Thomas did much to restore their tranquillity, and they were wishful to retain near them a friend so useful, both as a physician and as a Christian minister. While these wishes were as yet unknown to him, he was one day in the chariot with Mrs. Udny, when she said, "You have no mind, Doctor, for indigo works, have you?" "Yes, madam," was the reply; "I should like it very much, if any one would so employ me." She spoke to her son, and he at once acquiesced in the proposal that Mr. Thomas should take charge of the factory he was erecting at Moypáldiggy. He had another set of works also building at Mudnábatty, and Mr. Thomas's entreaty that his brother Carey also might be employed in the same way met with a ready acceptance. Before the end of February therefore, he was able to write to his sorely tried brother and to make him the offer of employment as an indigo planter. In the letter already quoted he goes on to say,—

I intended no other than to return to Calcutta; but during my visit at Malda, Mr. Udny proposed that I should superintend one of his indigo manufactories; and I have acceded to his proposal. It appears to me a great opening for usefulness; as it affords large opportunity of communicating knowledge by schools and stated instruction. Here I shall at length have perhaps five hundred of the natives in employ; and, from November till June, be entirely at leisure to pursue my usual labours. Mr. Carey is offered another of the manufactories; but I have received no answer from him yet. If he accepts it; as I think he will, we shall be within twenty miles of each other. I consider this employment for us and our people as every way becoming and suitable; and I hope it will afford the Society pleasure and satisfaction.

When our salary will commence, or what it will be, I know not as yet. We wish to know: for our money is all gone: and I have borrowed for both, and that is gone also. Poor brother Carey was sadly grieved in behalf of Rám Rám Basu, who had a debt to discharge, and his wages were due. He was beset for the debt, and we were two months before we could spare him relief. Having never maintained a family, nor lived at my own expense, in Calcutta, I little thought how much money it would require to keep house in the same line and proportion as Mr. Carey had lived in at home. We should have written soon, and entreated the Society to spare us more: but now, I hope, we shall soon be able to do with less, perhaps with nothing, from them; but may add something to the strength of their hands.

I have not seen Párbati yet, nor Mohan Chand. The former is four hundred miles away, up the country. He is expected down; and when he and Mohan Chand, and Rám Basu are all together, your letter is to be solemnly read and explained, and delivered to them. Let it not grieve you that it has been so long delayed. We have been much favored and helped of God, and are happy and comfortable with each other. O that I could tell you how useful, and how successful we had been in bringing the Hindus to Christ! I mourn to find my time and thoughts so dissipated with cares, and so unhinged for this great work: but, notwithstanding this, I hope for precious times to come.

Mr. Carey received the welcome invitation to remove to Malda on the 1st of March, but he was detained at Dehatta some time after he knew that a home was provided for him elsewhere. On the 23d of May, he started with his family, on the journey to Malda; and reached it on the 15th of June. Mr. Udny and his mother gave them a most kind reception. Next day was Sunday, and Mr. Thomas came in to the services, and there was a joyful reunion between him and his colleague. Mr. Carey delighted in the opportunity to preach again, and had an attentive and intelligent congregation of sixteen, in the scene of Mr. Thomas's early labours. Mr. Charles Short who had so generously entertained Mr. Carey's family at Dehatta became shortly afterwards a member of it. On the 15th of November, 1794, he was married at Chinsura to Miss Catharine Placket, Mrs. Carey's sister.

Mr. Udny made generous arrangements with his missionary planters. The monthly salary of each was to be Rs. 200; but very large returns were looked for from the factories, and, over and above their salaries, they were to obtain a commission upon all the indigo made; and, if things answered expectation, a proprietary share in the works was also to reward their efforts. For the present, their business was one of preparation. Houses had to be erected, factory buildings and vats constructed; and a busy time was before them, in which they could not hope to do much to their higher work of making known the truth. But they looked forward to the quiet times which would follow, and rejoiced that God had so graciously provided homes and profitable employment for them, in which they could hope to be so useful in His cause.

However the indigo manufacture might answer in time to come, one thing was already clear to the two missionaries : further support from the Society was now needless. Let the funds collected for them go to evangelize some other country. They in Bengal could now sustain themselves, if indeed they could not do much more. They wrote therefore, in the spirit of true Christian generosity, declining further remittances, yet holding themselves as closely as ever bound to the Society at home, whose sympathy and help had done so much to promote their hearts' desire.

Our narrative has shown how necessary the support this employment gave to the missionaries really was ; and, all things considered, it appears to be impossible to conceive of any situation which would have better suited them and the work they had come to India to accomplish. Events subsequently showed that, without secular employment of the kind, they would not have been permitted to stay in India ; and an arrangement which, while it gave them support, left so much time at their disposal, whilst it also placed them under the protection of a man of Mr. Udny's character and commanding influence, was so singularly felicitous, that we must see in it the finger of God. How important an instrument in bringing about this arrangement Mr. Thomas was, must appear to every one who has read the foregoing pages. Imprudent and erratic, as we freely admit that he was, the Lord employed him in a remarkable manner to facilitate the entrance of His word into the long benighted province of Bengal.

CHAPTER XI.

Moypaldiggy.—1794-7.

MOYPALDIGGY, the place of Mr. Thomas's residence was not destitute of antiquarian and other interest. In his *Description of the District of Dinajpur*, Dr. Francis Buchanan Hamilton thus speaks of it :—

In the North East part of the Bangshihári division, is a very large tank, supposed to have been dug by Mohipál rájá, and called after his name, Moypáldiggy. This sheet of water extends 3800 feet from North to South, and 1100 from East to West. Its depth must be very considerable, as the banks are very large. On the banks are several places of worship, both Hindu and Moslem, but none of any consequence. Nothing remains to show that Mohipál ever resided at the tank or near it; but there is a vast number of bricks, and some stones, that probably belonged to religious buildings, erected by the person who constructed the tank. The people in the neighbourhood have an idea, that there has been a building in the centre of the tank, but this is probably devoid of truth, as there is no end to the idle stories which they relate concerning the tank and Mohipál. Both are considered as venerable, or rather, awful, and the rájá is frequently invoked in times of danger. A canal and road, formed from the earth thrown out, lead south from the tank about four miles, where they join others, leading east and west.

From "bricks of an uncommon size," dug out of the pavements around this tank, the house Mr. Udny erected for his factory was in great part built. The outlay was very considerable, not less than £12,000 being expended upon the buildings at Moypaldiggy and Mudnabatty. A letter written by Mr. Thomas to his father, in August,

1795, supplies a rude sketch and description of his dwelling house. He says,—

This is a little like the part of the house we have begun to build, and this a plan of the whole when finished. It will have two piazzas, a hall, and four store rooms below; two piazzas, a hall, and four bed rooms above stairs; and a study at the top of the house. On the other side is the head of the staircase.

The situation was, upon the whole, very healthy and pleasant. Numerous villages of people to whom the gospel might be preached lay within an easy distance all around. The noble sheet of water close to the house was pleasant to the eye and, when the wind blew over it, greatly conducive to coolness. And, away to the north, was to be seen, when the atmosphere was clear, the magnificent peak of Kunchinjinga, 28,177 feet above the level of the sea, with adjacent mountains, covered with everlasting snows, and speaking ever to the missionary of the people dwelling in ignorance in the valleys at its feet.

Mr. Thomas regarded it as a great mistake that "in the first setting out of Moypal," lands of a very low level were secured for the indigo cultivation, and that they were so widely scattered. In one of his notes to Mr. Udny he says, "It is not much less than thirty *krosh*,* to go quite round the borders of our lands." This was a very "expensive inconvenience," rendering inspection of the growing plant very laborious, and occasioning much outlay at the time of manufacture to bring the indigo to the vats.

The district of Dinájpur is very populous, yet large tracts were uncultivated, and wild animals abounded in many parts of it. Tigers were considered rare. In August 1796, however, Rs. 800 was paid in rewards for killing them, by the collector of Dinájpur, at the rate of Rs. 12 per head. The most injurious beasts there were leopards, wild boars, and buffaloes, especially the last named, which were so numerous that more than sixty were killed in the neighbourhood of Moypaldiggy, in little more than three years. It was no uncommon thing for Mr.

---

* The *krosh* is about nine furlongs.

Thomas to be summoned to assist some poor neighbour who had received frightful hurt in an encounter with one of these animals in his rice fields.

The inhabitants of the district were a very simple inoffensive people. Mr. Thomas illustrates this, in one of his letters to Mr. Samuel Pearce, as follows :—

When I call the Hindus harmless, what do I mean ? I do not contradict the bad name given them by Europeans for deceit, treachery, &c., but I have done business with some thousands of them, and I say again they are the most harmless and inoffensive people I know of in the world, or have ever heard of. I speak, of course, not absolutely, but comparatively. If I look at the American continent, the African, the European,—if I think of the lower class of men in England, Ireland, Scotland, or Wales,—if I visit the Malays, the Tartars, or the Chinese,—I still come back to the Hindus, notwithstanding all their frauds, as a man would come home from people of fierce brutal lusts and passions to his own quiet neighbours. Not far from my place of residence, there was a European of high rank riding one day through the rice fields, which are very extensive in this district. The road from here to Mudnabatty is eighteen miles or more, all the way through rice fields, with here and there a village whose little straw huts are surrounded by bamboo and mango trees. This gentleman had lost his way, but came upon people ploughing their fields, by whom he wished to be directed. They, however, seeing him approaching, left ploughs, bullocks, and all, and fled, as if death was behind them, having had experience of the way such gentleman treat them. He rode after them, and unhappily overtook a poor man, whom he ordered to be severely flogged, and then made him and his son go on before to show him his road. You may be sure that, at parting, the poor fellow gave this gentleman as many saláms as if he had made him a liberal present. This was told me by the person himself. Now had he ventured to do so in the countries I have named above, he would soon have found himself overtaken by stones, bludgeons, pitchforks, kreeses, daggers, or the like, before he had gone far upon his journey.

Any person might enter my house at midnight ; for I have neither bar nor bolt, hasp nor lock, nor any thing of the kind ; and yet I am as safe here, as you are in Paul's Square, Birmingham, at noonday. Could I venture to sleep so any where in Europe, America, or Africa ? Much has been said of the murderous Fakírs and of dacoits ; but the acts of violence of these lawless depredators do not affect the character of the people at large.

Such Europeans as the one mentioned above were not the hardest oppressors the poor ryots of Dinájpur had to complain of. In March, 1796, Mr. Thomas writes,—

A few days ago the rája of the district came into this neighbourhood hawking. One of his hawks seized a bird, and fell with it close to a poor man's hut. The man supposed that it was a wild hawk and, in trying to catch it, broke its wing. Another hawk was lost. For these two misadventures the rája fined two Chowdrees, or head men, who were with him, Rs. 600. They, in turn, extorted the money from the poor cultivators; and the messengers employed to make the collection aggravated the evil by taking still more than they were ordered to do. It is truly fearful to see how the poor are fleeced and plundered. One of our own factory people had his bullock seized and sold, and Rs. 8 taken from him, on account of these wretched hawks; but I got it back for him. It was all he had in the world.

So, in 1797, he says,—

The rája, who did me the honour of calling to see me, has been very extravagant this year, so he has levied upon his ryots, not a forced loan, but a forced gift or 'benevolence'! of about 6*d*. per acre; and I am told that the amount of the contribution made up some two months ago, was more than £12,000 sterling. It was then not completed!

How unhappy was the condition of a people who were defenceless against such cruel extortion! No marvel that the indignation of the compassionate missionary was often roused by the spectacle of their miseries.

The history of Mr. Thomas's residence at Moypaldiggy has many points of great interest. In some respects, it was the happiest period of his missionary life. He began it with a good knowledge of the language of the people around him. He had business relations with many hundreds of them, which naturally secured him influence over their minds, and this seemed likely to contribute to the success of his missionary efforts. He had at a least a sufficient maintenance, in the allowance made for his services in the indigo manufacture, by Mr. Udny. His family were with him; and he enjoyed the advantage of affectionate intercourse with a devoted and judicious colleague, deeply interested with him in every detail of missionary effort or success. He had also the encouragement and stimulus afforded by his connexion with the Baptist Missionary Society, some of whose members corresponded with him, and were always delighted to receive notices of his encouragements or progress.

The indigo cultivation had been commenced at Moypaldiggy, towards the end of 1793 ; but when Mr. Thomas took charge, little was done towards completing the requisite buildings. Both he and Mr. Carey at Mudnábatty had much to do in superintending bricklayers and carpenters. In July, 1794, a small beginning in the manufacture was made ; and both missionaries spent much time in visits to neighbouring factories, that they might acquaint themselves with all the details of the business. On one of these occasions, as they were riding together, near Bhulaháth, they found " a basket hung in a tree, in which an infant had been exposed. Its skull alone remained: the rest had been devoured by ants."

The circumstance reminded Mr. Thomas of a somewhat similar occurrence, which took place when he was living close by, at Harla Gáchi. A mother had hung up her puny infant in that same tree. The poor wailing child struggled, and at last fell out of its basket; and a jackal was making off with it, when it was rescued and carried back to its home by the indignant missionary. Such exposure of sick infants, supposed to be bewitched, was a common practice in those cruel days. Sometimes a child survived, and was reclaimed. Far more frequently, it fell a victim to the superstition of its parents.*

* In the Rev. Dr. Claudius Buchanan's "record of the superstitious practices of the Hindus, which inflict immediate death, or tend to death, deducted from the evidence of the pandits and learned Brahmans in the College of Fort William," and printed in the Appendix to his *Memoir of the Expediency of an Ecclesiastical Establishment for British India*, 1805, he says of the "exposure of children,"—

" If a child refuse the mother's milk, whether from sickness or from any other cause, it is supposed to be under the influence of an evil spirit. In this case, the babe is put into a basket and hung up in a tree for three days. It generally happens that before the expiration of that time the infant is dead ; being destroyed by ants, or by birds of prey. If it be alive at the end of the three days, it is taken home, and means are used to preserve its life."

On the removal of Mr. Carey's family to Mudnabatty, they suffered very severely from the fevers which were prevailing at that time in the neighbourhood. The situation appears to have been a very unhealthy one. All September, Mr. Carey was terribly ill with a malarious fever; and, at the end of the month, his third son, Peter, a fine engaging boy of five years old, fell a victim to the same disease. In this affliction, the sympathy and help of his medical brother were of course freely given; and they were a source of very great comfort to the distressed family. In one of their conferences held during this season of trial at Mudnabatty, Mr. Carey records that Mr. Thomas and himself " agreed to spend the Tuesday morning of every week in joint though separate prayer to God for a blessing on the mission."

As Mr. Carey did not speedily regain his health, Mr. Udny was anxious to settle him elsewhere; and, hoping that a change of air might prove beneficial, he asked Mr. Thomas to accompany the invalid on a journey of exploration to the northward, lending them his own pinnace that they might travel in comfort up the Tangan river.

On the 22nd of October therefore Mr. Carey arrived at Moypaldiggy, where he and Mr. Thomas enjoyed happy union in prayer, and profitable discourse, and, next day at noon, they proceeded on their excursion. On Saturday, they arrived at Sádamahal, where they spent their Sunday, thus making their first acquaintance with a place with which Mr. Thomas afterwards was closely connected.

Having advanced as far as the shallowness of the river permitted in the pinnace, they went yet farther in a small boat, hoping to be able to reach the foot of the Boutan hills; which, however, they soon found was impossible. They enjoyed some fine opportunities for preaching the gospel, and arrived again at Moypaldiggy by the end of October.

As the result of their report to Mr. Udny, he wished to remove Mr. Carey from Mudnabatty to Sádamahal; and sent him back thither to make arrangements accordingly; but the project was given up; and, after some improvements had been carried out at Mudnabatty, that place seems to have been found very healthy.

When the ships from Europe began to arrive, the missionaries looked eagerly for letters from their friends at home. Mr. Thomas's correspondents, at least, had had sufficient experience of the Indian mails to avail themselves of the ordinary opportunities of sending to him. Neither they, however, nor the members of the Society, appear to have done so; and the missionaries who quitted England on the 13th of June, 1793, received their first letters from the friends they had left behind them, in the middle of May, 1795! To be so long without any communications from those to whom they looked for sympathy and encouragement in their arduous undertaking, must have been a severe trial of patience. A yet more serious disappointment would have befallen them had not the good providence of God relieved them from dependence upon their brethren at home, inexperienced as they were in the art of remitting funds to India. The first remittance from the Society was made in stationery and drugs, to the value of £50, sent in May, 1794. This was despatched "at a venture" by Mr. Fuller, during a visit which he paid to London. A more important consignment, amounting in value to £145, was to be sent in the autumn of the same year; but, through a mistake made by Mr. Savage, of the East India House, who undertook to ship the goods, they were stored in a London warehouse, until April, 1796, when, having been accidentally discovered, they were despatched the following month. Mr. Fuller very truly remarked on the occasion,— "If our brethren had not been provided for another way, such an oversight might have been very serious in its consequences!"

Meanwhile the utmost harmony and affection prevailed between the two missionary brethren. They met together as often as possible, prayed together, discussed plans of usefulness together, and were helpers of each other's faith and joy. Preaching in the villages around them was carried on, and schools were set up for the children, which, however, the ignorance of the parents led them to neglect.

To remedy this evil, the missionaries formed the following project, described by Mr. Carey, in January, 1795,—

We formed a plan for setting up two colleges, for the education of twelve youths in each. We intend to clothe and feed them, and educate them for some years in Sanscrit, Persian, &c., and particularly to introduce the study of the Holy Scriptures and useful sciences therein. We intend also to order types from England at our own expense, and to print the Bible and other useful things in the Bengali and Hindustani languages. We have reason indeed to be very grateful to God for His kind providence, which enables us to lay out anything for Him. May our hearts be always ready.

Much of all this they found themselves unable to carry into execution; but hearty practical efforts were steadily made by both brethren to sustain their high calling as missionaries in a heathen land.

Mohan Chand visited them both; but Párbati was still at a distance, and seemed to be little disposed to come to them, owing to a quarrel he had had with Ram Basu. The accounts they received of his character were, however, very encouraging.

Rám Ram Basu was still Mr. Carey's teacher of Bengali, and was helpful to him in his efforts to preach to the villagers, but the hope that he would become a professed Christian grew less and less confident as his character more fully developed itself. Mr. Thomas had Padma Lochan as his pandit, and began to entertain hopes of his conversion. He was silent, his master said, when asked, "What think you of Christ?" but he put into Bengali verse the hymn,—

> Jesus, and shall it ever be,
> A mortal man ashamed of Thee!

which for several years was used by the Bengali Christian congregations.*

The work of translation was not neglected. Mr. Carey had already begun to display that extraordinary perseverance and facility in this labour, for which he afterwards became so eminently distinguished; and had translated the

---

* This Bengali hymn commences,—হে স্বর্গের ছয়া প্রভু শ্রীষ্ট ।

book of Exodus into Bengali, besides bestowing much toil upon the revision of the portions previously executed. Luke was also begun by Mr. Thomas, and they both hoped, when the expected profits of the indigo manufacture for 1795 were realized, that they should be able to print and send abroad some portions of the work at their own proper cost.

They hoped also to form a Christian church, without delay. Mr. William Long, whom Mr. Thomas baptized in June, 1788, was living within a few miles of them, at Bámangola, where he superintended an indigo factory, and Mr. Samuel Powell, who was at Moypaldiggy as Mr. Thomas's assistant, and who had derived much spiritual benefit from his cousin's close and affectionate conversation, was anxious to be baptized. His severe illness, however, in July, 1795, made it necessary to postpone these arrangements for a few months.

Mohan Chand's conduct and conversation excited much hope in Mr. Carey's mind that, although very timid and irresolute, he was really sincere. He read with great interest the portions of the Old Testament which had been put into Bengali, and found much in the Mosaic ritual which pleased him greatly, since he was disposed to think that the Hindu ceremonies far more nearly resembled the Jewish, than any practices he had witnessed amongst Christians! Mr. Carey had also a young pandit in his employ, named Kasináth Mukerjea, of whom he saw some reason to hope well.

Meanwhile a dreadful calamity was befalling Mr. Carey, in his wife's insanity, which took the form of the most odious suspicions regarding her husband, and sometimes assumed a very violent character. In this terrible trial, Mr. Carey had the tenderest sympathy and help from Mr. Thomas, who wrote him on one occasion as follows,—

I have many things to say, and this is a very imperfect way of conveying thoughts in comparison with talk. You know Mrs. Carey sent a letter express to me yesterday, and gave a man a rupee to bring it. I was seriously frightened.—Her false surmises may bring on true troubles, that are rising to such a height that I know not what will be the issue of it. You must endeavour to consider it a disease. The eyes and ears of many are upon you, to whom your conduct is unimpeachable, with respect to all her charges; but if you show resentment, they have ears, and others have tongues set on fire. Were I in your case, I should be violent; but blessed be God, who suits our burdens to our backs. Sometimes I pray earnestly for you, and I always feel for you. Think of Job. Think of Jesus. Think of those who were 'destitute, afflicted, tormented.' It is but a little while, and all will be over. Times of trial are special times to serve and glorify God, by patience, by meekness, by gentleness; all which I am striving for, and following after; for they are comforts as well as duties, and duties as well as comforts. 'Physician, heal thyself!' Ah, my dear brother, I am sensible you may always use with propriety such a word whenever I endeavour to provoke you to love and to any good work. God be praised, His word is still extant, His throne of grace still accessible. I still have space. Still I am on this side of that door of perdition,—'past feeling.'—Still out of hell. Glory be unto God: and you will say, Amen.

And so each of our first missionaries had his own peculiar and most heavy trials. The foundations of the mission work were laid in tears of anguish, and with the deepest consciousness of humiliation and insufficiency; and its success was finally given by Him "that comforteth those that are cast down."

After the first letters came from England, Mr. Thomas went over to Mudnabatty, to discuss their contents with his fellow-missionary, and to preach to the people Mr. Carey had collected to hear the gospel. Such a day of prayer, conference, and preaching, brought back the memory of the happy Ministers' Meetings in Northamptonshire! A few days after, they invaded an old temple of Shib, which stood near the house, for the purpose of a solemn prayer meeting. Poor Rám Basu was with them, and all of them engaged in supplication for the revival of godliness in their own souls, and for the prosperity of their work amongst the people of the land. "That day of prayer," wrote Mr. Carey, "was a good day to our souls."

Not a little discussion was occasioned in England when the news arrived that the missionaries had obtained employment as indigo planters. It had been intended by the Society from the first that their brethren should endeavour to support themselves in India; but now that the providence of God had placed them in circumstances so much beyond expectation, great disquietude was felt on their account, and "though, upon the whole, the Committee could not disapprove of their conduct in accepting the engagement; yet, considering the frailty of human nature in the best of men, they thought it needful to send them a letter of serious and affectionate caution." They further very kindly intimated their readiness to resume their payments to them, if help was at any time needful.

Mr. Thomas wrote in reply to this letter of admonition,—

You are very dear to us, and your counsels of love are exceedingly welcome to our hearts; and I hope efficacious in strengthening our hands.

We entertained the same thoughts and fears on our entering into trade, which you have so kindly expressed to us; and we think, more than ever, that missionaries had need to be dead indeed to this present world. Getting of money we are quite strangers to; not having gained one shilling yet above necessaries; and the thought of ever enriching ourselves, or our families, is far from us. On our arrival in this country, we both suffered many straits, fears, and reproaches, on the score of temporal things; but the Lord quickly, wonderfully, and unexpectedly opened a door to us, for providing for our families, and perhaps for many others. We thought, upon the whole, that it was quite right in itself to enter upon our present undertaking, and that the Society would be pleased to hear of it.

We are both very thankful for the resolution of the Society on our behalf, in case we should request them to supply us again with money. We resigned our salary whilst yet poor, not with the least idea of becoming independent of the Society, but to enable it to extend its benevolent exertions to other parts of the world.

And oh that God may yet cause His face to shine upon us, and bless us; that His way may be known upon the earth, and His saving health among all nations! May we still more than ever be remembered in your prayers, that we be kept from the evil, and may do good.

On the 7th of October, 1795, Mr. Thomas wrote to Dr. Ryland of Bristol :—

We cannot say that the mission has been blessed with that visible success we could wish. Never was a people more willing to hear. Never was a people more slow to understand. Yet I dare not say that no success has attended us, and we may now be casting that bread on the waters which shall be found after many days. Since tasting the social pleasures of religion in England, I have felt more than ever the gloom of my lonely situation here. The letters of religious friends in Europe have proved very quickening and refreshing to me. Do write. I shall read it with avidity. I shall eat and drink your words; and you may do as much good to the mission, as some have done to the commercial interests of this country, by sending a bit of the prickly-pear plant, with the cochineal insect living upon it. In the hands of the original owner it was not worth six-pence; but here it may prove eventually to be worth millions.*

Should any more brethren come to us, I think I should receive them with rapture; and to have a few more would greatly strengthen our hands, and tend to establish the work in which we have engaged. I must conclude. Notwithstanding our discouragements, I indulge a hope, that through this very mission, the Gospel will certainly spread over all Hindustan into Tartary itself, and cover all the mountains above, and all the valleys below us—spread in Bengali, Boutani, Persian, Sanscrit, and other languages to us as yet unknown and unheard of, and then the devil himself may say, 'Behold! how great a matter a little fire kindleth!'

The letters from the Society brought communications to Mr. Thomas which it must have given him much pain to receive. Mr. Fuller had now become acquainted with Mr. Charles Grant, whose advice on matters connected with India was much esteemed, and he heard from him some things

---

* This allusion may be best explained by an extract from the obituary of the *Calcutta Gazette* for March 9th, 1797. It says,—

"Died, on his passage from Madras to England, Captain Neilson, of H. M.'s 74th Regiment of Foot, a meritorious officer and a worthy man.

"It was to the enterprising spirit of Captain Neilson that India was indebted for the introduction of the cochineal insect, about eighteen months or two years ago."

Some varieties of this valuable insect are indigenous in India; but the finest species was a desideratum there for many years after the death of Captain Neilson. In the year 1807, the Court of Directors offered a premium of £2000 to any one who would introduce "the fine grained cochineal" into their territories, in a state fit for propagation there, provided the insect was brought in a British vessel. They did not wish other nations to profit by their enterprise.

which tended to lower Mr. Thomas in his opinion. He had listened to his own statements as to his connexion with Mr. Grant, when they first met, in January, 1793. He now had heard Mr. Grant's side of the same story, and he could not but be deeply mortified to find that one of the missionaries he had helped to send out to India had parted from his former friends after disputes so unpleasant, and that he was so hopelessly involved in debt. Mr. Fuller was a man of severe integrity; and debt, however honestly contracted, was to him a most odious thing, so that Mr. Thomas's difficulties now appeared to him to be a very serious disqualification for usefulness. It is greatly to be regretted that any such cause for Mr. Fuller's displeasure existed, and that it wrought the unpleasantness it did in Mr. Thomas's later missionary life. He evidently felt that he was misjudged, and the severity of Mr. Fuller's remarks ultimately led him to refrain from that freedom of correspondence which was desired at home. In reply to one of the earliest letters from the Secretary, he wrote on the 11th of January, 1796,—

Considering the information which you acknowledge I gave you, and the knowledge you had of my affairs by reading my letters to Mr. Booth, I am quite at a loss to imagine in what manner I 'ought to have been more explicit.' However, I reckon all these things into that inevitable 'sweat of the brow' which falls to my lot as a son of Adam; and I shall be glad to have my hopes realized of rendering to my creditors all their due. You give me pleasure after pain by saying after this, 'you all love me.' Every token and every expression of your love is always very precious to me, and although in my daily life you may find occasion enough to think ill of me, I am satisfied that, upon the whole, your opinion of me is quite as good as I deserve, nay, better. You say, 'Our Episcopalian friends have set their faces against you.' Well, they serve me very right; for I remember how I set my face against them; but now I am bound to bless and pray for them.—Matthew v. 44. I admire the next passage of your letter.—' Mr. Newton says, in a letter to me of last week, 'Now they are both connected with Mr. Udny, I shall cheerfully pray for the success of both.' You see what influence connexions have, even upon our prayers! True. 'This corruptible must put on incorruption, and this mortal must put on immortality.' Till then, we shall see no end of this. Little differences make great difficulties among people who have to act together; and I rejoice always to have to do with persons of one mind in the work of the mission. To maintain the conflict between truth and error with proper spirit, and to preserve peace and love, however, is not impossible with some men. I am grieved to hear you mention 'mean and mercenary conduct' in one so near your own sentiments as I. '*This* mortal must put on immortality' too; so love him still, with all forbearance.

When the letter to which this was a reply was written, Mr. Fuller had received Mr. Carey's representations of the events of January, 1794, and those statements also had produced their natural impression upon the mind of the worthy Secretary to the mission. He did not indeed say any thing about those things; for Mr. Carey had entreated that the matter might not be referred to. Mr. Thomas therefore could not vindicate himself from the effects of the misrepresentation by an explanation of the facts. He could only reply to matters of which his correspondent explicitly wrote.

The letter goes on to deal with some remarks which had been made upon Mr. Carey's request that a few ordinary English garden seeds and roots might be sent out to him. This seemed to the excellent Mr. Sutcliff even, to be something like the "looking back" of one who had "laid his hand upon the plough." Mr. Thomas stood up stoutly in his brother's defence. He says to Mr. Fuller,—

What you say about brother Carey's seeds, and what brother Sutcliff says about *letting the dead bury their dead*, is a little awry. Brother Carey keeps a garden, and a man to look after it: but if he saw the least occasion so to do, he would give up, not only his garden, but all he has. I confess, my own occupations *do* most certainly prove such an interruption to my great work, that I sometimes think of taking such a step as perhaps would turn the consciences of men into quite another channel. If I thought it was the will of God, I had rather be a fugitive and a vagabond to-morrow, and go and translate all the rest of my days in Calcutta jail, than be an indigo maker. But when I consider my debts; my wife, so delicately brought up; the remarkable appearance of providence in working out, unasked of men, such a provision for us all, and so preventing us from *begging* by giving us an opportunity of *working* with our own hands, 'I am in a strait.' I proposed to brother Carey to give it up; but his wiser solid reason was a check to my folly.

You see in Mr. Carey and myself some differences in taste, manners, &c., and there are many differences between us which you do not see. Do not be alarmed, for our very noses are not alike; but our hearts are one. We may differ in faces, but not in hearts. One heart, one soul, one Lord, one faith, one baptism. There may be one Lord, one faith, and two baptisms; but this is like a house on fire at one corner. I admire the grace of God, in knitting together diverse people, like brother Carey and myself; for we never differ, but we agree to differ; and in things respecting which it is no matter whether we differ or not. We often fall into each other's opinions, are always delighted to see each other, and we love each other fervently. This information, though you have had it before, I consider far from uninteresting.

We often lay our heads together, and form large plans, for all we produce such little executions; but we have difficulties you know nothing of. Sore troubles; implacable enemies; jealous eyes over us; and a variety of opinions formed on our conduct and designs. Some think we intend at bottom to turn this part of the world upside down, as missionaries; others think we have quite forsaken the mission, and gone after filthy lucre, in the way of Balaam: some think us wise, others think us foolish; some sober, others mad: and all these contrary opinions have their use, perhaps. On this paragraph, I could fill a ream of paper.

One of our difficulties is that the people hereabouts speak a mixed language, part Persian, part Bengali, and part Hindustani or the Moor language; so that we do not understand them nor they us, half so well as though we were nearer Calcutta; but whenever we meet with Brahmans, the case is different. The majority of the people here are not Hindus, but Muhammadans.

Under date of January 13th, he says that the Indian Government had required of every individual Englishman, not in the Company's service, to give in his name, place of abode, occupation, and date of arrival in India, in order, if permitted to remain, to enter into covenant, and find two securities for the due performance of it, in £2000 each, or, in other cases, £500 each.

Had the two missionaries not been engaged as indigo

planters when these requisitions were addressed to them, they must inevitably have been forbidden to remain in the country. This action of the Government was considered very oppressive at the time, and some persons ventured to refuse the Company's demand. In particular, Mr. Fairlie, a prosperous merchant in Calcutta, defied the Government to deport him, if it dared. "But," said Mr. Thomas, " such great words cannot be uttered by little mouths!" The part of the missionaries evidently was compliance; and the covenants were entered upon : Messrs. Udny and Carey becoming securities for Mr. Thomas ; Messrs. Udny and Creighton for Mr. Carey; and Messrs. Thomas and Carey for Mr. Powell. These covenants, however, were not immediately executed, but, after many delays, in the middle of 1797; after which the missionaries enjoyed greater security than ever before. They were now, for five years, recognised residents in India ; and no man could call their right to dwell there into question.

In the letter from which so much has been already quoted, Mr. Thomas mentions the deep dissatisfaction generally felt and expressed against the government of the East India Company in India at this time. He says,—

The whole army of India is full of loud murmurs on account, as they say, of the little regard which has been paid to their remonstrances and petitions. All the officers are of one mind, and have formed regular councils, in Fort William, Cawnpore, Fort St. George at Madras, Bombay, and every settlement in India. I have conversed with some, and have heard of the language of other officers, who have never seen each other, and their minds are one ; and the oppressions which many Europeans here have suffered, who are not in the Company's service, but form a large majority, will induce them also to take part against the Company. They all say it can be no treason ; for they will not be found acting against the king, but only against a parcel of merchants. Upon the whole, we seem to be upon the very eve of————a change!

Both missionaries had begun to feel great anxiety to arrange for the extension of the Society's labours to some other countries, contiguous to India, where perhaps the same difficulties in the way of the progress of the gospel might not exist. Towards Boutan, in particular, they both looked with strong desire. In the same letter, Mr. Thomas says :—

The Boutan people have no caste, neither have the Rajmahal Hill people, which hills are inhabited by men of very different appearance, habits, language and religion from the Hindus. These hills are situated about thirty miles from Malda, to the N. E. of us ; and Boutan is about eighty or a hundred miles to the northward of us. I heartily wish that three or four young men and their families were settled among the Boutan people, and four on the Rajmahal Hills. Dr. Coke talked of sending missionaries there ; and, if he did, we should be bound to help them all in our power.

At present indeed we have but maintenance for ourselves, for the indigo was almost all drowned by the floods of last year, otherwise we had agreed together to lay out about £300 of our profits in printing the gospels, or such parts as are ready ; and other large sums we both had appropriated to similar purposes. Indeed it is possible that one good season would enable me to pay off all my debts, and furnish me with overplus, several hundreds besides. If ever this is the case, when I am out of debt, I mean to have less to do with indigo than I now have, for the sake of the work of the mission.

This letter also contained some distressing particulars as to Mr. Thomas's circumstances. At the close of 1794 his debts were reckoned as about £1300 ! This he hoped almost to clear by the profits of the indigo season for 1795, and the lawyers who represented his creditors, had been content to wait the results of the year, before pressing their claims. Now that all hopes of profit had failed, they had, of course, become more urgent, and he was glad to make terms with them by the payment of £100, which he contrived to borrow for the purpose, thus in fact adding to his difficulties. He had confidently hoped for more than release from the pressure of debt, and had planned many schemes of usefulness to be supported by the gain which not he only, but also his employer and his colleague looked upon as sure to be realized. His disappointment was not the less severe because the unattained advantage was to be devoted to the payment of his debts and to benevolent purposes. " If God puts money into my hand," he wrote, " it shall not stay there ; but I will study to do good and to communicate.

My past wants make me feel for others, and I cannot endure to see any in need and distress without relieving them; and this is a sweet and pleasant duty, and I see how much more blessed it is to give than to receive, even to me, a frail worm, how much more so to Him, who is abundant in goodness, and 'giveth liberally and upbraideth not.'"

Who can wonder that, in such circumstances, he sometimes gave way to "a spirit of dejection?" Mr. Fuller, in some letters of his which have been preserved, expostulates with his missionary brother, tenderly, yet closely, in reference to this; and to other correspondents he admitted that he sometimes "thought hardly" of Mr. Thomas because of it; but how little did he then understand all the anguish of his unhappy brother's despondency, rendered doubly poignant by its reaction from the sanguine confidence which was so natural to him in his happier healthier moods.

The manufacture of indigo at Moypaldiggy and Mudnabatty was not expected to yield any very considerable returns in 1794; since it was then conducted under the disadvantage of imperfectly completed apparatus and a very limited extent of cultivation. Great anticipations were, however, cherished as to the results of the year 1795. The crops promised excellently; but at the setting in of the rainy season the low lands, which were chiefly under cultivation, were at once inundated, and very much of Mr. Thomas's "plant" was immediately destroyed. At the beginning of August, however, he wrote to his father that he still confidently expected to make, "at the worst," a profit of between £600 and £700. The bulk of this was to go towards paying off his debts; but a portion was to be expended upon the long desired work of printing Bengali translations of Matthew, &c. Grievously was he disappointed. Flood after flood swept away his growing indigo; and when at last the poor residue of the crop came to be manufactured, the amount made in 1795 actually fell short of that secured in the previous year, by more than one fourth! At Mudnabatty, the out-turn was even worse. To complete the misery arising out of this great calamity, the unfortunate missionary-planters learned that Mr. Udny was disposed to trace his ill-success in the two factories to their bad management. "His countenance was not toward them as before." Their letters to him remained unanswered for weeks; and both felt that it was necessary to come to a clear understanding with him. On the 2nd of November, therefore, they sent him a joint letter, stating that they had hitherto "laboured under several manifest disadvantages, inconsistent with responsibility;" that they had been allowed "neither to appoint nor discharge the principal agents by whom they had to conduct the business of their factories;" and that they regarded the men Mr. Udny employed as "either unfit, incapable, or dishonest," that they had suffered much insult, and Mr. Udny much loss, by these arrangements, and that they thought, if they really were managers of their respective factories, that orders and enquiries from Malda should not be sent directly to the servants who ought to work under them. Much of the avoidable disaster had arisen, they said, from these irregularities in conducting the business.

On the day before this letter was written and despatched, much more pleasant occupation engaged both missionaries at Mudnabatty. On the 1st of November, 1795, Mr. Samuel Powell was baptized there by Mr. Carey. Mr. Long was present; and the two mission families, with a Mr. Rebellio, Mr. Carey's Portuguese assistant, and Mr. Thomas's black boy Andrew, made up the afternoon congregation, when Mr. Carey preached from Matthew xi. 19, "Wisdom is justified of her children." About forty natives were gathered as spectators at the water side, and Mr. Thomas addressed them in explanation of the rite they were to witness. The baptism then took place. Afterwards, Mr. Thomas, Mr. Carey, Mr. Long, and Mr. Powell solemnly united as a Christian church, and having given each other the right hand of fellowship, proceeded to partake of the bread and the wine which the Lord has ordained to be received by his disciples in remembrance of Him, till He come.

This was the first Baptist church formed in India. A little band, indeed; and soon to be discouraged by defection and separation; but it was the beginning of a fellowship which has since embraced thousands, both of European and of many Indian tribes, and which has now many happy representatives, not only upon earth, but "before the throne of God."

Just at this time, an incident occurred which interested and encouraged the missionaries not a little. The following letter was sent them from Dinájpur, by persons they had never seen. The English date of the document is October 29th, 1795:—

Three years ago, Mohan Chandra, Brahman, came to Dinájpur, and we then heard a little about the gospel of God. At that time he also promised to send us seven or eight chapters of the Bengali translation thereof. After this, we sent to his house for the same; but did not obtain it. Now the brahman is here again. Many people have heard the unparalleled words; but the promised translation we have not yet obtained, and he does not wish to stay here longer. On this account we write to you, that you would shew favor to us sinners, and send us a few chapters of the translation, and also that you would order the brahman to stay with us a few days longer, that he may make the path of the gospel plainer to our apprehensions, and that we may cast off our old idolatrous and evil customs.

We are servants, and if we should leave our services to visit you, we should have nothing to eat. Should the brahman stay with you a little time, we will after that send to fetch him for a few days, if you will give us leave; and then we will hear again from his mouth, and will come with him to hear the word from you—the word of faith—the manner of prayer—the joyful news from heaven; and, having heard it, be blessed. This is our desire—this grant.

(Signed) BALARAM DAS.
RADHA MOHAN BASU.
KRISHNA MANGAL GUPTA.
BRAJA MOHAN BASU.
PRASAD DAS.

Kartik 15th, 1202.

Nothing appears to have arisen out of this letter. The missionaries were full of hope that the writers would continue their correspondence, and in the end prove to be sincere seekers after salvation. But they wrote no more; and, afterwards, when enquiries were made after them in Dinájpur itself, no trace of them was to be found. It seems but too likely that the letter was concocted by Mohan Chand himself, with the intention of magnifying his own services in speaking of the gospel, and so inducing his missionary friends to supply him more liberally with money.

The remonstrance written to Mr. Udny brought about a reconstruction of arrangements, and a much happier understanding with him. At the close of 1795, Mr. Thomas spent a fortnight with him at Malda; and, when he left, Mr. Carey also went for a similar period. Whilst there, they learned much which awakened their sympathies on Mr. Udny's behalf. He had suffered greatly from other disasters besides his disappointments in their indigo manufacture. By the failure of the mercantile house in Calcutta, in which his late brother had been the principal partner, he had sustained heavy losses, estimated at upwards of £35,000; and his large outlay upon his indigo manufactories had hitherto yielded him no returns.

Thus the year 1796 opened with the promise of increasing usefulness. The houses and factory buildings, the erection of which had occupied so much care and time, were now completed; and both missionaries were able to give fuller and more vigorous attention to the delivery of their divine message to the people around them. They rejoiced greatly in this. "We are now entering," wrote Mr. Thomas, towards the end of 1795, "upon a very agreeable change in our circumstances. No more building! Nothing more to learn of the art necessary to conduct our manufacture; except such things as naturally and continually occur to observation and experience. The noise of axes and hammers will now give place to the sweet silence of solitude and retirement, broken only by the echo of a song of Zion."

On returning from his visit to Malda, where he preached on Christmas-day, New Year's-day, and two

Sundays, he resumed his work with great zeal and many encouragements. He preached frequently in neighbouring villages, and, every Sunday, the *tomtom* was beaten slowly at Moypaldiggy, "for the purpose of assembling the servants of the family and factory, and neighbours, to hear the word of God." In fine weather the usual place for preaching was "under the great tree," about one hundred yards from his door, but on rainy days the assembly came within the house. The enquiries made by some of his hearers proved that a very intelligent interest was taken in his sermons by many. More than a hundred usually came on a Lord's-day. He also had a regular preaching service every week at a populous village called Basattipára, where sometimes two hundred hearers assembled.

His medical skill was greatly in request, and Moypaldiggy became the place of resort for all the sick and poor in the district around. Several sheds were put up for the shelter of such poor applicants, and the generous assistance of the compassionate missionary was never refused in any case of distress. His time passed rapidly in the discharge of a variety of duties. He wrote to his father, "I act part of the day as a servant, part as a master, doctor, missionary, merchant, justice of the peace, and can even make bread occasionally! I like the part of a strolling missionary best of all; and, next to that, it is a pleasure to heal the poor and relieve them from any of their pains and diseases. I have patients from all parts, all poor and costly, but some of my sweetest moments are spent in giving them relief." As to itineracy, he and Mr. Carey were projecting "a journey of one thousand miles, preaching Christ all the way."

Much of his time was spent in the translation of Luke into Bengali, and occasionally in examining translations prepared by Mr. Carey, whose progress was far more steady and rapid than his own. He was also endeavouring to prepare a set of Bengali letters, simple and compound, to send to England, that punches might be cut from them there, and type for printing the scriptures cast. Mr. Carey was often disappointed by his delays in this matter, which, indeed, was never accomplished; but probably it was very

DESIRE FOR A BENGALI BIBLE.

advantageous that the plan proved a failure. The delay in printing, however discouraging at the time, certainly conduced to accuracy in the translation, by permitting more careful revision; and, afterwards, unexpected facilities both for type-founding and printing became available at Serampore.

In the meantime Mr. Thomas was as fervently anxious as ever for the publication of the scriptures in Bengali. At the end of January, he wrote to Mr. Fuller,—

I would give a million pounds sterling, if I had it, to see a Bengal Bible. O most merciful God, what an inestimable blessing will it be to these millions! The angels of heaven will look down upon it, to fill their mouths with new praises and adoration. Methinks all heaven and hell will be moved at the Bible's entering such a country as this. O Lord, send forth thy light and thy truth!

Some other extracts from letters written about this time may be given here. To Mr. Pearce, Mr. Thomas wrote as follows :—

February 6th.—We have reason to praise God for some appearance of the power and effects of His word on a few of our hearers; but it seems more as the moving of the Spirit on the face of the waters, than like the particular acts of creation.

My pundit, Padma Lochan, asks questions, sheds tears, and requires parts of the scriptures of us. Brother Carey has another enquirer or two, and some people have sent us a hopeful letter from Dinájpur; so that they are not totally indifferent about the gospel, although they have only heard the conversation of Mohan Chand. And the Lord has appeared to answer the prayers of brethren in England, and has remembered His former mercies in gracious revivals; so that, for my part, I, who, but a little while ago, feared to stand up and speak to the natives, now long to be thus employed; and say, I will speak that I may be refreshed; and instead of preaching as out of a pump, I speak of the overflowings of my heart. Our congregation here increases; and, on the Lord's-day, we see the natives coming across the fields from all parts to hear the word of God. Yesterday, at the market, which is held twice a week under the great tree near my house, many strangers asked if I should preach next Lord's-day, professing their desire to come and hear me.——Two translating assistants are just come in, and I must take leave; but let me just say, this great, but not noisy part of our labours, I have set my whole heart upon. Much of the holy scriptures is already intelligible to the inhabitants of this country. O that this light may not go out, and that we may by no means quench or grieve Him who comforts our hearts, and strengthens and enlivens our hopes and expectations. I can no more doubt that the Lord will bless our mission now, that I can doubt of the rising of the sun again.

To Dr. Ryland he wrote, on the 7th of March,—

I have just been talking to sixty or seventy of the natives of this country, about the power and glory of our Lord Jesus Christ, in cleansing a leper and healing the centurion's servant. I came among them very spiritless; but when I left them I felt like one that had been anointed with fresh oil. It was a sweet season, in which the strength of Christ seemed exerted and shewn in a time of much weakness. Padma Lochan, who is very inquisitive, first of all read the eighth chapter of Matthew; after this I said a few words, intending it as a general preface; but was led away into the heart of my subject ere I was aware.

I paused, and we sang a hymn; then I prayed, and resumed my discourse; then prayed, sang again, and again continued my discourse. This will perhaps appear very singular, unless I farther explain myself. The preface is always delivered in consideration of some among the number who never heard before, and who are sure to reply to what you say, and ask questions in the midst of your discourse, unless they are expressly desired not to do so; and besides this, there are truths already stated and known to those who hear the gospel regularly, with which the new comers, being totally unacquainted, are so much the more in danger of misapprehending the meaning.

The people at both our factories sing, as they work, Ram Basu's '*Ke áro?*' 'Who besides can recover us?' and some few appear to be under very serious impressions. A number of creditable Mahomedans paid brother Carey a visit lately, on purpose to hear the gospel. Another messenger came to him from a village in the neighbourhood of which there are several thousands desirous of hearing the gospel; and I had some few come to day from a considerable distance, though the weather was very rough and threatening. Both of us have been encouraged and animated by these things, though we have still fears and distresses if we enquire, To whom, in particular, is the arm of the Lord revealed? I trust God will appear at last. The devices of the heathen are as nothing before Him, and every difficulty under which we now labour, shall fly anon, like chaff before the hurricane.

Repeated mention has been made of the interest felt by the missionaries in the neighbouring country of Boutan. They were disposed to think that the gospel would encounter fewer hindrances there than on the plains of India. This country lying beyond the territories of the East India Company, their restrictive jealous policy would be escaped there; and as the people of Boutan have no caste, they would not be deterred by that from professing Christianity, as Hindu enquirers had been. Both Thomas and Carey greatly desired therefore to obtain such a knowledge of Boutan as might enable them to secure an entrance to the people; and hoped, if the Society would send out some missionaries for the purpose, that they might be able to promote their settlement there.

The following extract from a letter sent to the Society describes one of Mr. Thomas's attempts to obtain fuller knowledge about this country.—

In order to examine into the practicability of a mission to Boutan, and to obtain necessary information, I have endeavoured many months to procure a múnshi from that country, but in vain. Lately, I have taken a different course, which may succeed better. Early in April, I went to a great fair, called the *Nekmurd Mela*, about forty miles from Moypaldiggy, towards Boutan, where the natives come down yearly. I found there only two real Boutanese, and enquired the reason. I find that they have suffered losses, by thieves; which has discouraged them from coming to the fair. These two persons were a merchant and his servant, with woollen blankets, elephants' teeth, &c., for sale. I was truly surprised to behold a people situated so near to us, and yet so totally different from the inhabitants of Bengal, in all their customs and manners, dress, persons, and features. The worthy merchant's name is Shreecha, and, on my first approach, he was a little disconcerted; but I spoke familiarly, sat down on his blanket, bought some of this commodities, and asked him some five hundred questions; for I was so much pleased with my visit that I frequently came again; but the crowds of people wishing to hear me were so great, that nothing could be bought or sold while I remained with him. I made him amends for this afterwards. Shreecha was dressed in many folds of loose garments, and complained of the heat of Bengal. His cap was of neat basketing, in shape of a bell, ornamented at the top with peacocks' feathers. He spoke a little

Hindustani, and was attended by a Bengali writer; so that, with his help, I was able to converse very largely. With great difficulty I prevailed with Shreecha to come and sup with me in my straw hut. We sat down on the ground and ate and drank together, and conversed much. He came readily the next evening; and, after many refusals, he at last consented to go with me to Moypál, on condition of my promising not to detain him by force, but suffer him to return to Boutan after two days. Next morning, we all set off; Shreecha and six of his servants; but the other Boutan native could not be prevailed on to go with us. After two days' abode in my house, he took leave, and I sent two guides, according to his desire, to conduct them to Rániganj, about twenty-four miles on their way. Shreecha promises to return in about two months with a múnshi from the Penlow-Rajah; to whom I have sent some few rare and acceptable things as a present; with a letter, requesting permission to visit his dominions, in the month of March, 1797. The Penlow-Rajah is subordinate to the monarch called the Deb Rajah; and he is said to be a very humane man, protecting and providing very carefully for the subsistence of orphans and other destitute people among his subjects, and continually requiring his officers to use gentleness among his people, especially to the poor and distressed. His place of residence is at Paragong, a little distance from the capital. His palace is said to be very lofty and large; built of huge timber and stones, and the materials overlaid with silver and gold. There are commonly about two thousand persons within its walls, and these are his household. The city of Paragong is said to be very large; but no European has been known to visit it. They use bread; and wheat, with every other sort of corn, is very cheap there; and the land in the plains and valleys is very rich and fruitful. Hogs and sheep are dear; for they eat these, and all other sorts of cattle which are commonly eaten in Europe. They worship they know not what. I must obtain much more information before I touch on this point; however, it seems clear to me that their chief object of worship is the Grand Láma. They use the inner peeling of the bark of a tree for paper, and it looks like thin parchment, and is very pleasant and strong to write upon. The inhabitants of this country seem very frank and open, manly and generous, and have refined ideas of friendship, and great vigour of body and mind. Their la nguage is soft and easy to be pronounced.

About this time, a very painful disappointment befell the missionaries. A report that Rám Rám Basu had been guilty of adultery with a young widow, and that the offspring of his guilt had been murdered, was brought to Mr. Thomas by some of the people at Moypaldiggy. He wrote immediately to Mr. Carey, urging him to investigate the matter thoroughly. This was done; and the unhappy man's guilt was established. He at once departed from Mudnabatty, leaving both missionaries to mourn over this bitter disappointment of their long cherished hopes of his sincerity and change of heart.

Mr. Carey wrote to Mr. Pearce of this sad calamity and of his hopes at Mudnabatty,—

I have written to some of my correspondents an account of poor Rám Basu's awful fall. He is gone, I know not whither; and it appeared as if all was sunk and gone. After the múnshi's fall, my school fell also, as I found my income could not possibly support it, and, the school-master going with the múnshi, his relation, it was broken up; nor is it yet resumed, though I much desire it.

In this situation, I was for some time much dejected; but one Lord's-day, although I preached in a very low, distressed frame of heart, I was very earnest with poor souls. The text I have forgotten; but I now remember that I used the words of the Psalmist with much affection:—' Whither shall I flee from thy presence?'— Psalm cxxxix. 7. I had almost lost the recollection of this circumstance the next morning; but, walking out on the Monday, three Mussulmans came, and, with apparent agitation, asked me,' Sir, what must we do to be saved? কেমন পারি হইব? How shall we get over?' I talked much with them, and hoped God was beginning a work. In a short time, however, two of them ceased their enquiries: but the other, Sookman, is still in a hopeful state. He has been conversing with me this morning with increasing earnestness, and I have reason to believe ' he prayeth.'

On the 2nd of September, Mr. Thomas gave Mr. Fuller the following account of some enquirers at Moypaldiggy:—

Brother Carey has some hearers under great concern, on one of whom, a poor labourer, he thinks the word of God has taken effect. I also have two or three, of whom I should think more hopefully, perhaps, if past experience did not check me. One is a blind brahman, who came, about six months ago, for medicines for his eyes: which, however, were then quite lost. He lives in a Moypal hut. He hears me constantly, and says that he prays to Jesus Christ night and day. When I have been absent on a Lord's day, and preached elsewhere, he comes on my return, and professes regret at not hearing the word of God that day. One week day, having some close conversation with him, he said, among other things, 'I am the servant of Jesus Christ in my heart!' 'But,' said I, 'if Jesus Christ were to come and touch your dinner, you would throw it all away directly, and refuse to eat a morsel more! What,' I added, 'would you think now, if I were going from home, and bade a servant let off such a vat of indigo within half an hour, telling him that if he should forget it, or by any means let it steep longer, it would be all spoiled? I warn him, repeat it, intreat him to take care, and take leave. After a long time, I return, and find this vat still steeping; and of course utterly lost. I call this servant, and say, 'How is it that you have not done as I said?' He answers, 'O sir, it was in my heart to do it. I am a faithful servant to you in my heart: therefore you will excuse the outward act!'—Brahman, Jesus Christ declares plainly that many will say to Him in the great day, 'Lord! Lord!' But not these, but only such as do the will of God, shall enter into the kingdom of heaven. He says, 'Except a man hate all, forsake all, and follow me, he cannot be my disciple.' He went away dejected; and still makes enquiries; but the great deep, I fear, is not broken up.

The other two appear more deeply concerned at present, and are both Mahomedans. One of them, whose name is Yárdí, often asks Mr. Powell, myself, and my little daughter, how such an one as he is can be saved; acknowledges that he is 'a poor ignorant sinner,' and says he is greatly disturbed. He and the other Mahomedan are easily to be known in our stated times of worship from all the rest, by their uncommon seriousness. These enquirers comfort our spirits and animate our depressed hopes.

In another letter of about the same date, Mr. Thomas says of the same two men,—

They make frequent and lively enquiries for the way to Zion; but many have done so, and gone further, and left us lamenting after all, saying, 'I have laboured in vain.' 'Who hath believed our report?'

In the middle of September, a third missionary arrived to join the brethren, in the person of Mr. John Fountain, and he immediately proceeded to Mr. Carey's house. He reached Mudnabatty on the 10th of October, and, just afterwards, the following letter came in from Mr. Thomas.—

I wish you could step up here; for I am at a loss how to proceed.

The Lord has certainly appeared to this poor people: and my heart is full of joy and thanksgiving. There are five here under great concern. One of them, Dúrgatia, has suffered threats and persecutions from his family, unknown to me; and it has made a noise in the neighbourhood. Yárdí, who is more enlightened, says that Dúrgatia's father came to him to ask if his son was gone out of his senses or not? for Dúrgatia and the others declare they will no longer be Mussulmans. Yárdí says he cannot sleep at night. Many tears are shed. The sins of their youth are brought to their remembrance, so far beyond what anything of my preaching has extended to, that I have no doubt at all that the Spirit of God has wrought in them. They seem willing to do anything Christ would have them; and, by their expressions, they would part with all for Him. Now, I say, I am at a loss; for when I hear them speak so sweetly and experimentally of the things of God, mourning over their sins, and glad at heart to hear of Christ, I am struck with that word: What doth hinder them to be baptized? I should like you to hear them, and talk with them; and, if your opinion is like mine, I shall say, 'Be baptized.' They are all going to learn to read and write. I preached at daylight last Lord's-day, and had a very uncommon day throughout. God appeared in Christ in all that was said and done.

Such of your people as would be willing to join any of these who may be found sincere and ready to give themselves up to the Lord, might be asked, and they might all join together and become free at once;—or would it be better to wait longer, and see?

In compliance with this invitation, Mr. Carey rode over to Moypaldiggy, on the 15th of October, taking Mr. Fountain with him. The younger missionary says,—

On the Saturday we went, with eager expectation. I was kindly received by brother Thomas, as I had been before by brother Carey. On the Sabbath, at sun-rise, worship began. Nearly a hundred people were assembled. After prayer, brother Thomas preached from Ezekiel xxxvi. 27 :—'And I will put my Spirit within you.' After which, brother Carey preached from Acts iv. 12 :—'Neither is there salvation in any other.' Very great attention was paid by all. After breakfast, three persons concerned about the salvation of their souls, came again, with whom brethren Carey and Thomas spent a considerable time. They appear hopeful characters. They daily pray together. One of them, Yárdí, is a man of good natural abilities, and seems to possess much Christian simplicity. They appeared much affected when I informed them, through brother Thomas, how the people of England were praying for the salvation of their souls. 'What!' said they, 'do they pray for us?' At twelve o'clock, brother Carey preached in English, from James i. 6 :—' But let him ask in faith, nothing wavering.' At half past three o'clock, the natives assembled more numerously than in the morning. Brother Thomas preached from Acts xvii. 30 :—' But now commandeth all men everywhere to repent;' and brother Carey from Psalm lxxxix. 15 :— ' Blessed is the people that know the joyful sound: they shall walk, O Lord, in the light of thy countenance.' In the evening, brother Thomas preached in English from Isaiah lviii. 11 :—' And thou shalt be like a watered garden.' They both declared I had seen more attention and seriousness, my first Sabbath, than they had seen all the three years they had spent in India. Brother Carey returned home the following evening; but I staid near three weeks. The congregation increased the two following Sabbaths that I was there.

Mr. Carey also was most favorably impressed by what he saw and heard during this visit. He wrote,—

Three at Moypal appear to be in earnest about eternal things, and I am not without hope that some good may be found in others there. There is a great stir in all the neighbourhood, and many come to hear the word of God. This is, in some degree, owing to Yárdí, who is a man of a sweet natural temper, with good abilities, a readiness to discourse with others, and a zeal for Christ.

Mention should be made here of one of Mr. Thomas's European neighbours, Mr. Gready, an indigo planter. He had once been a member of the Moravian church at Bristol; but his life in Bengal had led him to forget the fear of the Lord, and he had ceased to walk in the narrow way. His unhappy condition was made known to Mr. Thomas, and he felt the most tender interest in the backslider. He invited him often to his house, and amongst his correspondence there is a letter, dated October 6th, 1796, in which, with most affectionate importunity, he seeks to win him back to the service and love of Christ. In this letter he says,—

As to myself, I have experienced all that you express. I have made a profession of religion these fifteen years; and, the farther I go, the more I am convinced that all that is in the world, though enjoyed for a thousand years, is not to be compared with one hour's holy enjoyment of Christ. Formerly I thought I should be a great Christian; but now I sink into nothing, and Christ, my precious Saviour, is all in all to me. All my hopes of salvation now are in the free unmerited favor and mere sovereign mercy of God, through Jesus Christ. My former hopes were more lively, but my present hopes are more solid, lasting, and satisfactory. The punctuality of God in His word, both in threats and promises, makes me 'rejoice with trembling' sometimes. I believe I have obtained the good part which shall never, no never, be taken away from me, and oh that God may grant me the pleasure of being, in any way, the instrument by which He may convey to you any help and encouragement in His good ways, where you will be sure to find peace and pleasantness now, and everlasting blessedness in the end. Let us pray often for ourselves, for our children, and for one another, remembering the words of our Lord Jesus Christ, 'Labour,' 'Strive,' 'Watch,' 'Pray,' 'Ask,' 'Seek,' 'Knock,' &c.

Another most encouraging circumstance occurred at this time. Mr. Ignatius Fernandez, of Dinájpur, but a native of Macao in China, a gentleman of European parentage, who had been intended by his friends for the Roman Catholic priesthood, but had declined to take the vows, owing to a growing dislike to the principles and practices of the Romish church, having heard of Mr. Thomas, applied to him through a friend for some books which would afford him instruction in the doctrines received by Protestant Christians. Mr. Thomas sent him Bishop Newton's *Dissertations on the Prophecies*, and some other works; and while Mr. Fountain was paying his first visit to Moypaldiggy, he and Mr. Powell rode over to Dinájpur to see Mr. Fernandez. They spent two very pleasant days in his society, and met many enquiries which he made in his anxiety to be informed upon religious subjects. He then came back with them to Moypaldiggy, and spent Sunday, the 23d of October, there, when Mr. Fountain preached, from Psalm xiv. 7, "the first gospel sermon he ever heard in all his life." From this time, Mr. Fernandez attached himself to the missionaries with much affection, was always glad to receive them at his house, and laid himself out to make their ministry available for the benefit both of Europeans and natives at Dinajpur, striving by every means in his power to promote the spread of the gospel. To this end, he immediately undertook the erection of a brick house for worship, at his own cost, where people might be gathered to hear the word of God, whenever one of the missionaries was able to visit Dinajpur.*

But the history of the indigo manufacture must be resumed. The year 1796 opened with fairest promise. Mr. Thomas had striven to remove his cultivation to higher lands than those before chosen ; and as the young indigo sprang up, he was able to regard his as " one of the finest crops in India." His neighbours who saw it congratulated him on his bright prospects for the season ; and all went well until within a month of commencing the manufacture. Then the annual " rains descended, and the floods came," and the waters rose to a height almost unprecedented, " several feet higher than those of the former year," thus following up the plant which he thought he had placed quite beyond the reach of such disaster. As the result, only about one third of the expected quantity of indigo was made. Although this was considerably more than double the amount made in 1795, and was beyond the average secured by neighbouring factories, Mr. Udny was greatly disappointed. Poor Mr. Carey, at Mudnabatty, did yet worse. He " had a woeful season," and he wrote to Mr. Fuller in November that the abandonment of his factory was inevitable. " My place," he said, " cannot be tenable much longer ; Moypal may. Large floods have destroyed the whole crop almost every successive year." He ascribed the disaster to the unfortunate position of the factories, which had been determined, before the missionaries entered Mr. Udny's service, by native servants, utterly ignorant of the principles of agriculture, who had chosen " the most improper places that could be thought of."

* Dinájpur is not a very favorite place in the present day, and is reported to be very unhealthy. It seems to have enjoyed a different reputation formerly. When Mr. Thomas had paid his first visit there, he wrote, "Dinajpur has greatly exceeded all expectation, and is, I think, the most beautiful situation I have seen in India, not excepting even Pondicherry."

In August, Mr. Thomas obtained Mr. Udny's consent to the establishment of a small out-factory at Sádamahal. Here were lands not likely to be inundated, and he thought that a profitable crop of indigo might be cultivated upon them at a very small annual cost. The works were to be superintended by himself from Moypaldiggy.

He was also eager in his attempts to persuade Mr. Udny to make vigorous preparations for the year 1797 at Moypaldiggy. He wished to secure the higher lands, and to increase the extent of the cultivation; but, to accomplish this, the prompt outlay of a very large sum of money was required. Many of the ryots, having lost their crops in the floods of former years, were unwilling to undertake the precarious work again; and all who consented to cultivate indigo needed to be bound down by advances made to them now, in anticipation of the coming season. Other capitalists also were in the same neighbourhood, engaging people to rear silk worms, or to grow opium; and the competition for labour enabled the cultivators to increase their demands, and to refuse the old terms of engagement. On the other hand, repeated disappointments had made Mr. Udny more timid, and the heavy losses he had suffered in Calcutta made it difficult for him to do all that Mr. Thomas saw to be necessary for future success. He was indeed labouring under a double disadvantage: the quantity of indigo produced at his factories was small; and, owing to the large supplies sent into the market from other places, its average value was very low.* All this diffidence as to enlarged projects for the future, however, Mr. Thomas found comparatively easy to bear; but when, after a visit to Calcutta,

---

* A notice in the *Calcutta Gazette* gives the prices of indigo sold by the East India Company, in November, 1794, as ranging from 2s. to 10s. 6d. per lb. and a note written by Mr. Udny early in October, 1796, says: "Moypal and Mudnabatty indigo of 1794 sold at an average at 4s. 0¾d. per lb. 1795 is expected to be as low, if not lower, as 50,000 went home. The Company gives 12 per cent. for money; which has made it very scarce, and almost impossible to be had. I pray you to effect this point: the reduction of charges and all expenses immediately, without loss of time. If I had only a small sum embarked in indigo, I should be for giving up altogether, and putting up with the first loss. News bad from England. War! War! It is feared that Tippoo is preparing! In packing the indigo, care must be taken that it be thoroughly dried first. Mr. Carey's, last year, was, some of it, damp."

Mr. Udny wrote, at the beginning of November, imperatively enjoining him to put a stop to all he was doing at Sadamahal, and to send back to Malda all the money in hand for advances at Moypaldiggy, he felt that he was humiliated in the eyes of the people, and that the necessary conditions of success for the coming indigo season were being most disastrously interfered with.

Other afflictions befell Mr. Thomas at the same time. In July, his wife, always very delicate, was suddenly attacked by a severe spasmodic affection, which happily was soon relieved, but it left her "trembling, weak, and low." Mr. Carey also suffered severely, towards the end of October, from "an imposthume, near his throat;" which was the more alarming, because his mother had died an almost sudden death from the same disease, the carotid artery having been, in her case, corroded by it. Mr. Thomas skilfully lanced the abcess, and immediate relief and speedy recovery followed.

It is sad to say that the close of 1796 found him as deeply involved in debt as he was at the beginning of it. Mr. Fuller solicited from Mr. Carey a confidential statement concerning his colleague's character and affairs, and a few sentences may be taken from the reply written in November of this year. Mr. Carey says,—

There are some such traits of genuine and hearty religion in Mr. Thomas as are perhaps equalled by few; but on the other hand he has such eccentricities and foibles as can scarcely be found in any one else. He is either very warm, or exceedingly cold in religion. He is a hearty friend; but so very delicate in his sense of honour, that though others must bear everything from him, he will unhappily misconstrue the most affectionate admonition into a reflection upon his conduct. Besides his debts in England, when he was about to set up as a surgeon in Calcutta, he borrowed Rs. 1200 from a native. This is still unpaid, I believe. Mr. Udny has advanced about Rs. 1500 for his relief, which was paid to his creditors; and I expect Mr. Thomas owes him much more, and is in debt besides to almost every one who would give him credit, either little or much; and I dread the consequences. Mr. Udny cannot help us now, as formerly, on account of his recent heavy losses, and he refuses to advance Mr. Thomas more, and retains his commission on the indigo he has made this year, to liquidate the amount already owing to him. The consequence is, that Mr. Thomas is constantly in danger of an arrest. Depending upon Mr. Udny's helping him as before, he had promised to go to Calcutta, and to pay off a large proportion of some of his debts this month, his works having been more productive than some others; but Mr. Udny refuses, and the attorney threatens.

You will ask, 'What does he do with his money? Does he live high and luxuriously?' I reply, 'Though he lives more expensively than I, who have neither tea nor wine, yet not luxuriously; but his compassion to the poor leads him to give far beyond his ability, and his mind is so unsteady that whatever he sees which excites his desire to possess it, he must have at any rate.

He is a man of great closet piety, and has lately preached much amongst the natives. I have great hope of some people there. He is very compassionate to the poor; and in instructing those who are enquiring after the truth, he is indefatigable. He has excellent aptness for that work. In translations, the gospel by Luke is all he has done since we came to the country.

These sad statements as to Mr. Thomas's circumstances and infirmities of character could not in fairness be withheld from the reader. Who does not pity the unhappy man, so entangled in the meshes of debt and difficulty, and so little able by natural disposition and steady resolution to make the best of the advantages his present situation afforded, uncertain and often disappointing as they were?

In December, Mr. Carey paid a short visit to Calcutta, borrowing Mr. Thomas's boat for the purpose. On his return, both he and Mr. Thomas hoped to enter the Boutan country and to endeavour to secure a footing there.

At the close of January, 1797, a party of five men from Boutan came to Moypaldiggy, with ponies, musk, and blankets for sale. They were welcomed with great delight by Mr. Thomas; but we may quote a short account of them from one of his letters.—

Glad was I to get rid of them without bloodshed; for they quarrelled amongst themselves like tigers, and threatened our people that if any man came near them in the night time, they would cut him down. This threat fell the heavier because of the sense we had of the heavy broad-sword which every man carried at his side, and the muscular strength of each man, which appeared to be twice that of a Bengali. But the hearts of all men are so entirely in the hand of God, and 'all power in heaven and earth' so minutely dispensed, that we have no reason to fear going to 'preach the gospel to every creature.' If I could only speak their language but a little, I would go up among them. They drank tea and dined with us, eating—or rather, devouring—every thing that was given them. I was sorry to see them so excessively fond of strong liquors, and ready to drink an immoderate quantity. I detected one of them in a theft; but did not appear to notice it at the time. However, next morning, I gave him an admonition, if it was only for his neck's sake. After all, there is something about these men so open and manly, so sociable and free, that I take great pleasure in seeing them. 'The Desire of all nations,' shall come! What a lovely people they will be then! It seems, to sense and reason, that these people, having no caste, would be more easily converted than the Bengalis. No such thing! The depravity of the heart is the great difficulty in all countries; which, if once overcome from above, all the rest will vanish. Mr. Carey was saying the other day, however, that if we had no more obstacles than the missionaries in the wilds of America, we should have baptized several this last year. I gave these men a letter to one of their great men to enquire after the letter and present I sent last April to the Penlow-Raja, and to ask again for a múnshi.

The hopes entertained of the enquirers at Moypaldiggy are spoken of in the same letter. Mr. Thomas says,—

You have been told of Yárdí and Dúrgatia. My bowels of love yearn over them. Yárdí's wife told him the other day that she would kill herself and her child if he was baptized. His eyes are full of anxiety and his poor troubled heart may be seen through his face, as Nehemiah's was. Dúrgatia's father and brothers set upon him, and dissuade him with all their might; but he is resolute and unmoved. Yárdí suffers far more from his wife than from all others. She mocks him cruelly. They agreed very well before, he says. He is a man, in whom natural patience, mildness, and meekness are remarkably apparent; but our blessed Lord's words are herein partially fulfilled,—'Suppose ye that I am come to give peace in earth? I tell you, Nay, but rather division.'—Luke xii. 51. How it will all end, I cannot say. He has at times determined, if she will depart, to 'let her depart;' but her threats as to destroying herself and the little one terrify him greatly.

How many difficulties stand in the way of the gospel here! If any of the natives are baptized, they cannot marry or be married to any others than to their fellow Christians; nor will it be proper to marry Christians according to the customs of the Mahommedans or Hindus; neither will it be expedient to go to the other end of the world for a clergyman of the Established Church to marry them. What is to be done? I suppose, any particular appointed method, agreeable to the word of God, would be religiously lawful? But the legality and propriety of such marriages, amongst men, are topics I should like to see well discussed.

In company with Mr. Carey, he made the long anticipated journey to the borders of Boutan, in March, 1797. They travelled northward from Moypaldiggy, to Bote-Háth, beyond which they were not able to proceed, though the snowy range of mountains appeared to be nearly as far from them there as it was at Moypaldiggy. On their return, they went through part of Cooch Behar and Rungpur, visiting all the indigo works met with upon the way, and trying to learn something from the experience of those who conducted them. The following account of the excursion was sent by Mr. Carey to Mr. Fuller, dated March 23d:—

Mr. Thomas and myself are just arrived at home from an excursion to Boutan, in which we preached Christ in many places where His name was never heard before, and were attended to with great ardour. The name of our Redeemer has been declared in that unknown country; and we have the greatest encouragement to hope that a mission may be begun to great advantage in those parts.

I will relate a little of our expedition. We set out from Moypaldiggy on the 6th instant, and arrived on the 10th in the Boutan country, viz. that part of it which is below the hills; for we did not ascend the mountains: our time not being sufficient to permit us to go through all the formalities requisite thereto. We went to a place called Gopálganj, and waited on a Bootea officer called the Zinkaff. He received us very kindly, and we presented him with a few articles, with which he was much pleased. Here we found that it would be necessary to see some more officers, and to get a regular permission to ascend the hills. During the greatest part of the day, we were in his house, which is large, and made of bamboos and mats; with saul-tree pillars; and has an upper floor, on which he lives, made of split bamboos. He made us a present of some pieces of bacon, about a foot long, but which were so stale as to be smelt at a great distance. After that, he treated us with tea. The tea-pot is a large bamboo, with a hole perforated through one of its knots on the inside, which is the spout. Their tea is made into cakes with some composition, and, when used, is mixed with boiling water, *ghí*, and salt! We tried in vain to swallow it, though the Booteas drank very copiously of it. His kindness, however, was very conspicuous, and he drank of our rum more than we wished him. The Booteas are much addicted to drinking spirits, and pride themselves upon drinking much; though drunkenness is reckoned a shame among them. However, all will intoxicate themselves, if they can get English spirits. They are taught to drink spirits as soon as they can talk, and in all their houses you see large pitchers, called *kalasís*, about the size of a small bucket, full of Bengal arrack, which they drink as we should water.

The natives call themselves Botes, but the Hindus call them Booteas. They are very stout, robust, people; and, with respect to dress, colour, and appearance, are like an amazing stout athletic English waggoner, very much weather-beaten. They have no stockings, but their dress is like a waggoner's smock-frock, except the higher ranks, who have a dress very much like an English gentleman's morning gown, made of blue, red, or green stuff, with large figures wrought in it like diaper. The women are tolerably white; their dress consists of a petticoat, and a cloth which is so fastened from the shoulders to the waist as to appear like a monstrous pouch over the breasts, in which they keep every article, as in a pocket. Their hair is parted on the top of the head, and we saw no covering for the head of the females, though the men in office had different coverings for the head.

From Gopálganj we went to Bote-Háth, to see the Súbá, who is the greatest officer: that is, a kind of viceroy, below the hills. A letter having been sent to him from the Zinkaff, he sent two horses to attend us, and the Zinkaff himself went with us. The procession was the most comical and singular that could well be imagined, yet it strongly proved their great attention to us. We were preceded by a band of Bengal music, if such it can be called. We were six horsemen, and servants, and a number of spectators, besides people to carry our baggage, tents, &c., which in travelling by land in this country must be carried on men's shoulders. On one horse was the Zinkaff, led by two men: notwithstanding which, he was sometimes first, sometimes last, and sometimes turning round, his horse being ungovernable. Every mile or two, he was stopping to drink spirits. A Hindu on another horse was much like him, except in drinking; and we had enough to do to keep our horses out of their way; to effect which we were always wheeling to the right or left.

At our approaching the town, a number of women met us, and made their sálam; after which they ran before the horses, and all the inhabitants of the place, I should suppose, to the number of two or three thousand, all Hindus, joined the procession.

We went in this manner to the Súbá's house, who received us with great politeness, and made us presents of silk; viz. a white scarf in the name of the Grand Lama, a red one in his own name, and another red one in a friend's name. After receiving the presents, we ascended the ladder to his house, which was like the Zinkaff's, but much larger and more elegant. It had four rooms on the upper floor, which were entirely covered with mats. At the farther end of the principal room was the seat of the Súbá, raised about two feet from the floor, covered with red cloth, and hung round with thin gauze curtains. Here we were seated by the Súbá. On two sides of the same room were seats for the servants, raised about six inches from the floor; and, like the Súba's, made with planks of saul-timber, but covered with sack-cloth. A window of about a foot deep, made of lattice-work, ran throughout the two sides on which the servants' seats were placed, these only being the outward walls; and a curtain of white cotton cloth was placed just above the window. On this curtain were hung shields and helmets, and under it matchlocks, bows and arrows. The under part of the house serves for a stable, &c.

The genuine politeness and gentleman-like behaviour of the Súbá exceeded every thing that we could have imagined, and his generosity was astonishing. He insisted on supplying all our people with every thing they wanted: and if we did but cast our eyes on any object in the room, he immediately presented us with one of the same sort. Indeed he seemed to interpret our looks before we were aware; and in this manner he presented each of us that night with a sword, shield, and helmet; also a cup made of a light beautiful wood, used by all the Booteas for drinking. Perceiving that we admired the wood, he gave us a large log of it, which appears like fir, with a very dark beautiful grain. It is full of resin, or turpentine, and burns like a candle, if cut into thin slices, and serves for that use.

In eating, the Súba imitated our manners so quickly and exactly, that he appeared as free as if he had spent his life with Europeans; though he had never seen any of them before. We ate his food; though I confess the idea of the Zinkaff's bacon made me eat rather sparingly.

We then talked about Boutan, and about the gospel; and the appellation of Lama was given to us, which appears to mean teacher, and which title is by them emphatically given to the Grand Lama.

We found that he had determined to give all the country a testimony of his friendship for us in a public manner, and the next day was fixed on to perform the ceremony in our tent, on the market-place. Accordingly we got instructed in the necessary etiquette, and informed him that as we were only come a short journey to see the country, we were not provided with English cloth, &c. for presents.

The time being come, however, we were waited on by the Súbá, followed by all his servants, both Booteas and Hindus. Being seated, we exchanged each five rupees, and five pieces of beetle, in sight of the whole town. And, having chewed beetle, for the first time in our lives, we embraced three times in the eastern manner, and then shook hands in the English manner. After which he made each of us a present of a piece of rich Debang, wrought with gold, a Boutan blanket, and the tail of an animal; but we could not ascertain what animal it is. The Súbá says they are kept tame, are as large as a buffalo, and live only on the tops of the highest mountains, which are covered with snow. The tail is as bushy as a horse's, and is used in the Hindu worship.

When the ceremony was over, we were conducted to the Súba's house, where we found another officer, I believe, the Vakeel, or attorney of the court below the hills. This man was just the reverse of all we had seen. He had been to Calcutta, and was a man of great consequence in his own eyes. He sat on the Súba's seat like a statue, not rising when we entered, which the Súba, a much greater man, always did. When we sat down, he began a long discourse with the others in the Boutan language, and, as we did not understand it, we also talked to each other in English. All this time a servant, by his orders, held a lighted torch just in our faces, that he might stare at us. Mr. Thomas ordered it away. He then asked how many servants we kept. Mr. Thomas told him that, if he would go to our houses, he might satisfy himself about that. All this was to see whether we were great men or not. He then enquired if we had a tent. We answered in the affirmative. We treated him with as little ceremony as he did us, and, after exchanging a few words with the Súba, he took his leave abruptly. The Súba was then transported with rage, and threatened him dreadfully. He tore off his upper garment, seized a *kreese*, a kind of dagger, stuck it into the table, beat his breast, threatened to go after him and kill him! We tried to appease him, and were successful.

We declined going up the hills, as we found it was necessary to wait for an order from Paragong, the seat of the Penlow-Rajah, who is a kind of minister of state to the Deb-Rajah himself, whose palace, if we were not misinformed, is at Tassisudon.

Our people were much afraid: for though the Hindus had till now expressed the greatest confidence in the gentleness of the Booteas, yet they now began to propagate a great number of bloody tales; and nothing was talked of but the insincerity of the Booteas. As for ourselves, we were not quite so timid, though we were not without our cogitations. We, however, laughed at the people, and told them to run away for their lives, if any danger appeared. For fear of wild elephants, &c., we had taken a gun or two; but we ordered that no gun should be loaded, nor any additional care whatever manifested, though we were certain the people would not sleep much that night. We then commended ourselves to God in prayer, and slept till morning. In the morning the Súbá came, with his usual friendship, and brought more presents, which we received, and then took our leave. He sent us away with every honour that he could heap upon us, such as a band of music, guides to show us the way, &c. In short, the whole of his conduct towards us was invariably as generous, polite, and friendly as I ever witnessed. I suppose the disagreeable conduct of the Vakeel arose from his thinking himself to be a great man, and somewhat slighted in not having any present from us; but in truth we had nothing to present. The Súbá proposed paying us a visit in a little time. Should he do this, I hope to improve the interview for the great end of settling a mission in that country.

I have never before seen so great a contrast between two neighbouring nations as in the case of the Booteas and Hindus. The latter are small, puny, fearful people; the former athletic and fearless. They have a great deal of curiosity. We gave them several articles, as a looking glass, a pocket compass, &c., which were examined in every point of view.

They have a written language, and, I am informed, many books written in it. The names of the letters are the same as the Bengali, with a few exceptions, and are written in the same order, with only this difference, that the Bengalese have five letters in a series or line of the alphabet, but the Booteas only four. I think the accent of the Bootea language not much unlike that of the French; but more acquaintance with it may alter my mind in that particular. I am to be furnished with a Bootea múnshi, and Mr. Thomas with another.

Boutan is a very large country, subject to the Deb-Rajah. The Lama Guru, as they call him, is, I think, only considered as a representative of God; and they have his image in their houses, about the size of a large man's thumb. The Suba said there was a greater object of worship, which could only be seen by the mind.

To say any thing of my own personal exertions, would be only filling up paper with a long tedious tale about myself; I therefore decline it, and only say that I have daily cause to complain, yet complain in reality but little. I need all the advantages of godly society to set the springs in motion; yet this is a blessing of which I am nearly destitute. Brother Fountain is a great advantage; but we can scarcely vary conversation so much as to keep up its zest. I labour in the word; public exercises are pleasant to my soul; though I want that aptness to converse closely about the things of God which is so conspicuous in brother Thomas.

The accounts of Yárdí, Durgatia, Sukman, and others will, I trust, give some pleasure to the Society and the numerous friends of Christ in England; and will shew that their prayers have not been in vain, while it affords encouragement to us. One of these persons has, however, entirely deserted us. I have great reason to hope that the others are really converted to Christ. They speak in an interesting manner about the things of God, and grow in knowledge, and I trust also in grace. So great an opposition to their baptism has been stirred up, that I am not sure when we shall have the happiness to receive them as members of our communion; but hope that will be the case before a long time shall have elapsed. Brother Thomas labours with greater and greater vigour in preaching the word, and appears alive.

As the result of this visit to Bote-Háth, a friendly correspondence with the Súbá was maintained for some time. At the beginning of April, he sent some of his men to Moypaldiggy; from whom Mr. Thomas obtained much information as to routes of travel in Boutan, with particulars as to some of the tribes occupying the border country between Boutan and Bengal. Amongst these, it is curious to find the Gáros mentioned,—"a people who eat dogs!" and who have a savage propensity to attack their neighbours and carry off their heads as trophies of valour; but who in these later years appear to be well prepared to receive the gospel. In October, the Súbá sent a múnshi to Moypaldiggy; but his extravagant demands for brandy could not be complied with, and he would not stay. This was Mr. Thomas's last opportunity of learning or teaching any thing by personal intercourse with this people. His interest in them was, however, unchanging; and Mr. Carey also never ceased to long for the establishment of a mission to Boutan.*

* The notices of the Booteas given in the foregoing pages, may be compared with the estimate of the same people written by the Hon'ble Ashley Eden, after his Mission to Boutan, in 1864.

"The lower classes are very superior to the higher classes; though amongst the surrounding tribes the name 'Dhurma Bootea' is supposed to signify every thing that is low, treacherous, and fraudulent. I must say that I did not form an unfavorable opinion of the peasantry. They seemed intelligent, tolerably honest, and, all things considered, not very untruthful. Looking at the Government under which they live, the only wonder is that they are not worse. They are immoral and indecent in their habits to an extent which almost surpasses belief. They have no sort of sense of shame or honour. The outward form of Polyandry, which once existed in North Boutan, is not even adhered to in the present day. The conversation of the highest officers of State would put the lowest Bengali to shame. Of the upper classes generally, it is impossible to speak in sufficiently unfavorable terms. Physically, the Booteas are a very fine people. There are some really tall men amongst them; but, though very robust as compared with the people of the plains, they are not nearly such a stalwart race as the Sikhimese and Thibetans; which is possibly to be attributed to their immorality and drunken habits. Their dress is a loose woollen coat reaching to the knees, bound round the waist by a thick fold of cotton cloth. The full front of the coat is used as a pocket, and is well stored with beetle-nut, prepared chunam, &c. The higher classes have their mouths perpetually filled with this disgusting stimulant. They almost live upon it. The woman's dress is, like that of the Sikhimese, a long cloak, with loose sleeves. Their chief ornaments are amber beads, corals, with those who can afford them, and large pins. The women would not be bad-looking, if they were not disfigured by having their hair cut short, like the men. The Booteas are an idle race, indifferent to every thing except fighting and killing one another, in which they seem to take a real pleasure. They are dirty in their persons and habits, to a degree. The insecurity of property makes exertion quite useless, and a Bootea's energies never take him further than the provision of the day's meal, which, if he cannot obtain by fair means, he will by foul. They live on meat,—chiefly pork,—turnips, rice, barley-meal, and tea made from the 'brick-tea' of China, which is the main article of sustenance throughout the Himálayas and Central Asia. The 'brick' is cut up with a knife, and the leaves

The pecuniary difficulties which beset Mr. Thomas at the close of 1796, he found means to escape. A wealthy native patient, whom he had "cured of a total deafness," lent him Rs. 1000; and, in February, Mr. Udny also enabled him to make such remittances to Calcutta as quieted the impatience of his creditors there; so that for a little while he was able to feel relief and comfort. The evil day was, however, only postponed. As to the indigo cultivation, the year 1797 brought about an abundance of new anxieties and troubles. Some of the readers of this book may remember the agitation which prevailed in Bengal more than sixty years after the period now written of. They can call to mind the conflict of statement which then arose between planters and ryots, wherein the alleged oppressions of the one and the frauds of the other party, were discussed; whilst several expedients for placing the manufacture of indigo upon a more satisfactory basis were advocated. The history of the Moypaldiggy factory during 1797, might furnish an epitome of this later and wider dispute. First, the zemindars made a claim upon their ryots for *bhikhyá*, or a forced benevolence, and took away the bullocks of many of them, thus rendering them

are placed in a large hollow bamboo. Hot water is first poured on, and then boiling butter, with salt and a little crude soda. A cover is put on the bamboo, and through a hole in the cover the tea is churned for about ten minutes, with a stick, at the end of which is a notched round piece of wood. The tea is then put into large tea-pots, many of which are really very handsome and highly ornamented silver vessels. It is poured out into little handleless china or wooden cups, and as many as twenty of these are consumed by one person in a sitting. A little parched barley-meal, rice, or Indian corn is thrown into the cup, and this is often the only food that a Bootea cares for for days together. It is unquestionably a very nourishing diet. A cup or two of such tea is most invigorating after great exhaustion or cold. Their favorite drink is *chong*, distilled from rice or barley and millet. It is really not a bad substitute for whiskey. The Murwa beer, made from fermented millet is largely consumed. As a race, their failings were very correctly described by Captain Pemberton, in 1837, in the following words:—'I sometimes saw some few persons in whom the demoralizing influences of such a state of society had yet left a trace of the image in which they were originally created, and where the feelings of nature still exercised their accustomed influence; but the exceptions were indeed rare to universal demorality, and much as I have travelled and resided amongst various savage tribes on our frontiers, I have never yet known one so wholly degraded in morals as the Booteas.'"

unable to plough their fields. Then some poor ryots, cultivating indigo for the neighbouring factory at Berole, were harshly treated by the superintendent, and thereupon brought a complaint against him in the judge's court at Dinajpur, where Mr. Parr fined the oppressor Rs. 60, with costs, &c. This victory of ryot over planter excited the cultivators in all the neighbouring district to hope for release from their engagements with the factories. Agitators went round, and endeavoured to stir up the villagers to a general repudiation of their agreements to cultivate indigo; and many people flocked in to Dinajpur, with all sorts of complaints against the planters. Then, in the disputes thus created, it came to light that the cultivation of indigo was rendered odious to the people not only by the risk of loss it involved, but by the peculation and exactions carried on by the native servants of the factories. Mr. Thomas had the distress to find that Padma Lochan, of whom he hoped so well, was deeply involved in this way; and he discharged him on account of it. In the midst of all these great difficulties, he appears to have acted with commendable judgment and prudence. His letters to Mr. Udny show that, with a careful regard for his employer's interests, he was most anxious that every just complaint brought forward by the ryots should have candid and generous hearing and redress, and his suggestions as to the measures which should be adopted, to conduct the cultivation upon principles just and advantageous, at once to labourer and capitalist, appear to be those which subsequent experience has approved. But he found difficulties which thwarted his best intended efforts, on both sides. As to the ryots, he had to say, "I would sooner undertake to persuade their bullocks to walk on their hind legs only, than to induce this people to act like the rest of the inhabitants of the earth in any point of advantage in agriculture!" On the other hand, he wrote to Mr. Udny, in June, in the following very plain terms,—

As to its being better for you to put up with the first loss, and to leave off making indigo, I really think it would be altogether so. You never had, and it is most probable you never will have, sufficient confidence in those you have employed, to let them proceed on any plan which the circumstances of their case really require, unless such and such persons, who are situated in totally different circumstances, happen to do the same; while you readily adopt the most ruinous measures, if proposed by strangers. I have never had the happiness, after the most elaborate attempts, to persuade you to do any one thing in consequence of its being, in my opinion, the best. I do not say these things in ill humour, as you may suppose; but to acquit myself, by mentioning them to you; as they appear to me to affect your interest, and to contain some reasons why you should abandon indigo making; for I do not think that you will ever gain by it. It has often struck me with surprise, how you can be so easily led about, this and that way, by strangers who are not at all concerned, while you are so difficult to be persuaded by those in your immediate employ, whose interests are blended with your own.

Mr. Carey laboured under similar disadvantages at Mudnabatty, although he did not allow himself to be so much disquieted thereby. On the 12th of August, Mr. Thomas wrote to him,—

I heartily sympathise with you in all your afflictions. Mr. Udny's letter must distress you. How cautious we ought to be in writing letters, while the evil passions are in motion. A word spoken amiss by the tongue may be afterwards immediately softened, changed, recalled, or turned right about by the tone of the voice; but half as much written in a letter enters the bones like a sharp arrow, and there sticks, burns, and galls. I pray God, for Christ's sake, to forgive me all this iniquity of afflicting others with my pen, and I intend evermore to take care.

This great letter, with the improved or rather altered plan, I cannot answer now; but I am most decidedly and calmly of opinion that Mr. Udny, all things considered, had better go no further at Moypal.

I am so sadly afflicted with boils, that I cannot move from my bed to a chair without crutches, otherwise, I believe, I should have come down to Mudnabatty. This is a time of Jacob's trouble, but he shall be saved out of it.

My new enquirer is a Hindu, and appears very anxious. Yárdí has got him in the drying house. He can read, and Yárdí says he always has the hymns in his hands.

Together with these difficulties, both with employer and

with cultivators, there were others in 1797 which made success almost impossible. Rain indeed fell early, which admitted of favorable sowings, and notwithstanding all the unwillingness of the ryots, and their want of bullocks, Mr. Thomas induced his people to cultivate indigo nearly as extensively as before. But now the district had to suffer for want of rain. So little fell throughout the wet season, that it was only by much labour the crops were kept alive. The rice fields were burned up. The rivers became almost dry; and people from considerable distances were constantly employed in conveying water to their fields from the great tank near Mr. Thomas's house. Famine threatened, and a malignant fever was frightfully prevalent. At Mudnabatty, "seven out of twelve" died. "At Moypal," he wrote, on the 14th October, "we have people falling down with it every day; but I am happy to say none have died of it yet; for if any die of any disorder near me, and under my care or within my reach, I feel more or less as if I had killed him by negligence or unskilfulness! I have seen thousands almost fall on my right hand and on my left, by this fever; but, in all these years, God has not suffered it to touch me yet."

When the time of manufacturing indigo came, another difficulty arose from the general drought. The plant, when cut, could not be brought in by boat, as in other years, and it seemed impossible to convey it to the vats.

Notwithstanding all these great hindrances, however, the quantity of indigo made at Moypaldiggy in 1797 was considerably in excess of that obtained in any former year, though it still fell very much short of Mr. Thomas's early expectations, and of the success needed to repay Mr. Udny's outlay upon his works.* Something was done

---

* The following particulars are taken from Mr. Thomas's accounts. The manufacture of indigo was,—

	At Moypaldiggy,—		At Mudnabatty,—	
In 1794,	maunds	69-19¼	maunds	15-3½
In 1795,	,,	46-29	,,	39
In 1796,	,,	109-31¼	,,	no record.
In 1797,	,,	139-23¾	,,	,,

In 1796, a yield of 400 maunds appears to have been regarded as a very moderate expectation for Moypaldiggy.

also to complete the arrangements at Sadamahal; and Mr. Thomas hoped to establish a *nopalerie* there, for the production of cochineal.

In other respects, the year was one of trial. For some months, he was confined to his bed by an abscess in the thigh, and afterwards by very painful boils. His missionary work was thus greatly hindered, but not wholly suspended; for his congregation assembled within the house, and he preached to them as he lay upon his couch. Mrs. Thomas also was in very delicate health. In September and October, Mr. Fountain was most seriously ill of the fever. He removed to Moypaldiggy, in order to obtain the benefit of his missionary brother's medical care, and, by God's blessing upon it, he regained his health.

On the 10th of October, Mr. Thomas received intelligence of the death of a sister, Mrs. Pearce of Tewkesbury. The news deeply distressed him. "Death," wrote he, "has now come into my very blood; and what an effect it has upon me!"

In the mission, little progress was made. As the year advanced, Yárdí and Dúrgatia appeared to grow colder in their enquiries and there was reason to fear that, like others before them, they were turning aside from the gospel of Christ. Párbati came about the middle of the year, and remained some time at Moypaldiggy. He still exhibited much interest in the way of life, and after hearing a sermon, could give a full and exact account of the truths set forth in it. But his conduct and conversation too clearly proved that his whole heart was not engaged in the word of Christ. The present world held the first place in his affections; and he could not be induced to declare himself upon the Lord's side.

Another sad discouragement to the missionaries occurred in August, when Mr. Long, a member of their little church, had to be excluded from it for dishonesty. This was a terrible disappointment to Mr. Thomas. From the time of his baptism, in 1788, he had taken the most affectionate interest in Mr. Long, and, for several years, thought very highly of his piety and consistency of deportment. He was now compelled to think badly of him; but his letters and journals show that he never ceased to care for him tenderly, and to pray earnestly for his restoration to the right and good way.

How full of disappointment were the first years of this mission! Who does not admire the stedfastness with which those who laboured in it retained their confidence in the ultimate triumph of the gospel, and their enthusiasm in preaching it, notwithstanding all discouragements. This confidence is expressed in an interesting manner by Mr. Thomas in a letter written in the year of which we now write. He says,—

We often enjoy very sweet liberty, zeal, and abundant utterance in preaching to this people. The language of our hearts has been, 'I will speak that I may be refreshed;' but yet, 'Who hath believed our report, and to whom hath the arm of the Lord been revealed?' is our sorrowful complaint that remains after all. When I have been abundantly refreshed in private, I have gone out with an overflowing sense of a realized eternity, and have laid hold of natives to whom the gospel was no longer a novelty, and have uttered my thoughts so plainly, that I have wondered that they have not seen with my eyes and heard with my ears; and at last I have quite tired out the poor mortals' patience; and found, as good Mr. Flavel says, that 'you may tie a carnal man to a whipping post, and soon preach and pray him to death!' Sometimes, I am not humble, nor lowly, nor meek enough to go on without such thoughts as these: —'Why should I preach any more, or wait any longer? Why not go to England, and sell holy ballads for my bread, rather than live in these suburbs of hell, where religion itself is as cold as death, and where Satan's seat is, visibly? Why not go and feed with the flock of Christ in my native country, and give this work up, as one which the Lord will not prosper?' I suppose there is a good deal of flesh and blood at the bottom of all this. But again, I think of my adorable Master, and of some of His servants, like Jeremiah, and, at a very humble distance, I follow on, determined at all events to pray and preach among them here, till I die myself. That cannot now be very long hence, for I am forty-one years of age, and I feel myself begin to change, and to lose my health, natural spirits, and strength. I would therefore have you look out in time, for another man to take my place;—but do not let him be such an one as I am!—But now I am forgetting the Lord of the vineyard.

He will send by whom He will send:—sometimes by an angel, and sometimes by an ass!

One very cheering incident has yet to be recorded amongst the events of 1797. On the 1st of November, the place of worship Mr. Fernandez had erected was opened. All three missionaries were there, and the proceedings of the day were thus recorded by Mr. Fountain :—

At 8 o'clock in the morning, I began the services. After singing, I read Isaiah xlix. and prayed. After this, brother Carey preached from Luke ii. 10,—'Behold, I bring you good tidings of great joy which shall be to all people.' A great number of the natives having afterwards assembled, amongst whom were the heads of the place, the rajá's servants, &c., brother Thomas preached to them from 1 Timothy i. 15,—'This is a faithful saying and worthy of all acceptation, that Jesus Christ came into the world to save sinners.' At this service we sang three hymns in Bengali. In the afternoon they assembled again, and brother Carey discoursed from 1 John iii. 8,—'For this purpose the Son of God was manifested, that He might destroy the works of the devil.' The hearers paid great attention. In the evening, brother Thomas preached to us in English. We then agreed that one or the other of us should go over to preach on the first Lord's-day in every calendar month.

Early in December, Mr. Thomas obtained Mr. Udny's permission to visit Calcutta, as he had so long proposed to do. He intended, when he left Moypaldiggy, to be absent only two months; but, alas, he was leaving it to return there, as to his home, no more!

Of his journey down the river, he gave the following account to Mr. Carey :—

Nothing can be said to describe how well I was received at the college below Rangamatty and also at Cutwa, where I remained on the Sabbath day and preached. I also attended to some hundreds of sick folks, and ate and drank blessings from all hands, and hearts too, I suppose. I was surprised to see what a truly magnificent temple they have built at Nuddea. It is an edifice that would adorn any European neighbourhood: built by one man at his own cost, of the best materials, and by a European architect. It cost a lac of rupees and more. I did not stop anywhere else with equal pleasure, reserving myself for the return. But alas, when that will be, I cannot tell!

All sorts of preaching in Calcutta. Mr. Ringeltaube, a young man, the most evangelical of all. You will be surprised; but I stay in Calcutta, and have hired a pretty little place to preach in!

The reasons which led to so momentous a change in his plans and circumstances shall be stated in the next chapter, as far as they can be ascertained. Here it may suffice to glance back upon the hopes and expectations entertained during the period included in this chapter. When he first went to Moypaldiggy, he cherished bright and not wholly unreasonable expectations of release from debt and shame, and he had many encouragements to look for most happy results from his missionary labours. But now he was going away, and nothing but disappointment was left behind him. His converts were all "as grass upon the house tops, which withereth afore it groweth up; wherewith the mower filleth not his hands, nor he that bindeth sheaves his bosom." The cheering hopes entertained of Ram Ram Basu, Mohan Chand, Párbati, Padma Lochan, Yardí, Dúrgatia, and others, had all proved deceptive, and, in leaving Moypaldiggy, he had to feel that the hopes with which he had gone there, both as to missionary usefulness and as to deliverance from his many difficulties and long contracted debts, were all disappointed. It seemed all a blank failure; and he had the world to begin anew, with burdens and disadvantages which might well have broken a more stedfast spirit than he possessed.

Yet surely he had been a blessing to many. The afflicted and the poor had lived under his shelter, and had good cause to bemoan his departure. Nearly a year after he left, Mr. Fountain wrote of him:—

Brother Thomas's removal is a great loss to this part of the country. I understand he has been thronged with patients from place to place, wherever he has gone. Perhaps there never was a person in this country who has done so much in this way for the poor and needy as he has. The blessings of hundreds ready to perish have fallen upon him. His regard for them is so great that I have known him to get no sleep for a whole night when he has had a surgical operation to perform the next day. He has many qualifications which render him the fittest person for a missionary that could anywhere be found.

To a similar effect Mr. Carey had previously written,—

Brother Thomas has been the instrument of saving numbers of lives. His house is constantly surrounded by the afflicted; and the cures wrought by him would have gained any physician or surgeon in Europe the most extensive reputation.

The stranger who visits Moypaldiggy now finds it a scene of desolation. The foundations of the house occupied by Mr. Thomas may yet be discovered, at the side of the great tank, and the indigo vats are still there. Mango and other trees which he planted, a few of them otherwise unknown in the district, retain their vigour; but the neighbourhood is most of it covered with jungle. The visitor who lingers to trace out the remains of the English home once planted there, will probably be accosted by some villager who can tell him the traditions of the place, amongst which he may hear of the *Doctor Sáhib* who once lived there and generously ministered to all the sick who sought his aid. Nearly three quarters of a century have elapsed since Mr. Thomas quitted Moypaldiggy, but the recollection of his humanity still survives in the place where all his efforts to communicate the knowledge and love of Jesus Christ proved to be abortive.

CHAPTER XII.

Having no certain dwelling place.—1797-9.

AS Mr. George Udny is going to England very shortly, and has agreed with Mr. Carey and me to dispose of his works, and as we have not gained to ourselves any money above our expenses and those of our families, and as the Society has resolved to supply us when necessary, I have this day given Bills of Exchange for £100, payable on account to Christopher Dexter or order, which you will please pay on behalf of the Particular Baptist Society for spreading the Gospel. As I have written largely, and am writing, by these ships, I need not say more here.

Such was the letter, bearing date of December 28th, 1797, which reached Mr. Fuller in explanation of the change in Mr. Thomas's circumstances. The Bill for £100 also came duly to his hands, and was paid; but the other letters spoken of came not, and it was clear enough from the communications of Messrs. Carey and Fountain that Mr. Udny's works were not given up, and that Mudnabatty, at least, was still carried on as before under Mr. Carey's superintendence.

What did it mean?—was a question hard to answer at the time; and necessarily yet more difficult to satisfy now. Little information concerning the matter survives in any documents which have been preserved. Mr. Thomas abandoned the use of his journal from the end of October, 1797, to the 8th of July, 1798, and a few letters alone remain to tell what his intermediate history was.

His object in visiting Calcutta had been the adjustment of his affairs there, and this required the payment of a considerable sum of money. His commission upon the indigo made in the season just past might have enabled him to arrange matters; but Mr. Udny detained it to cover the advances he had himself made. This, however right and just, was fatal to Mr. Thomas's hopes of effecting a settlement with his creditors in Calcutta; and, upon his journey down, he wrote to Mr. Udny proposing some plan which he thought would enable him soon to repay his Malda debts, but which required the immediate use of the money in dispute between them. But his employer still refused to let him have it; and, receiving this news on his arrival in Calcutta, he was driven almost to despair of any accommodation with his impatient creditors. Just then, he met with Dr. Barron, a medical man, who proposed to him to become his partner in a Calcutta practice, and hoping and believing that he might thus escape from his difficulties, as he now despaired of doing by means of the uncertain cultivation of indigo, he wrote to Mr. Udny resigning his service, and withdrawing from further connexion with Moypaldiggy!

But what can be said concerning Mr. Udny's alleged purpose of retirement from his works? If no very satisfactory explanation is possible, in the absence of complete and exact testimony, it is any how clear that, three years later, Mr. Thomas met the charge that he had not represented things fairly, with a most unfaltering assurance that he said only what he believed in this matter, when he put his name to the unfortunate letter above quoted. And perhaps the reader has himself seen, in facts already related, reason enough to think that in Mr. Udny's letter of refusal to pay him the money he asked for, there may have been an intimation that these works would very probably be at once given up?—If indeed he was fully determined to carry them on, he was interested in pacifying the claimants who had it in their power to arrest a superintendent whose services he had no wish to lose. In that case, his own claims might be satisfied in the future. But if he meant at once to give up the works, he was wise to take payment of his advances while he could. Evidently Mr. Udny's mind had long wavered upon this subject, as appears from his words quoted at the bottom of an earlier page. And Mr. Thomas, for his own part, had been confident that his employer *must*, sooner or later, abandon these factories, and so, after many unpleasant uncertainties, he was in too much haste to believe that this decision had actually been arrived at.* The further history of both places proved but too well that such a decision would have been wise.

No better solution of this mysterious and unhappy business presents itself. But if Mr. Thomas resigned his post under such an impression as to Mr. Udny's purposes, he was soon conscious of the mistake he had committed, and of the hopelessness of his success as a surgeon in Calcutta, and, in the middle of January, 1798, he hastened back to Malda, to regain, if possible, his engagement at Moypaldiggy. But he was too late. Mr. Udny had given the situation to Mr. Powell; and was so seriously displeased as to be not at all disposed to listen to Mr. Thomas's entreaties for restoration to his patronage. By his precipitancy therefore the unhappy man was at once reduced to a condition of almost helpless poverty. For property left at Moypaldiggy, he was to receive a monthly remittance from Mr. Powell of Rs. 100, for several months to come. The Society's aid he had availed himself of already, and had paid away the money. How he should live and support his family for the future was a question impossible to answer.

One most disastrous consequence of this change in his arrangements was the permanent loss of Mr. Udny's favor. He had been an unfailing friend, whose kindness, notwithstanding any occasional disputes and misconceptions, had been shown in many ways, and with a very extraordinary degree of generosity. He evidently had desired to retain Mr. Thomas's services, and was greatly offended by the withdrawal of them. It appears

* That the above explanation is correct seems to be corroborated by a passage in a letter to Mr. Carey, dated July 8th, 1799. In this Mr. Thomas says, "I wrote a letter to Mr. Fountain, explaining my sentence, with many quotations from Mr. Udny's letters, which will enable you to write of it." Mr. Fuller had asked Mr. Carey to explain the matter. He, however, declined using the information furnished to Mr. Fountain, because it would have been "highly improper to transcribe" passages from Mr. Udny's confidential correspondence.

also that his resentment against his poor unhappy friend was heightened by some who told him that, in quitting his service, Mr. Thomas had but carried out a long premeditated design. This assertion had no other justification than could be found in the hasty expressions which had been sometimes provoked by vexatious disappointments, such as were but too frequent at Moypaldiggy, but which had never been uttered outside the privacy and confidence of his own family circle.

His attempts to regain Mr. Udny's patronage having all failed, he left Mudnabatty, where he had gone to take counsel with Mr. Carey, and, at the end of February, went to Serasing, at the foot of the Rajmahal Hills. His cousin Miss Powell had married an indigo planter there, and he was invited to visit them, and to inoculate their children for the small pox. Mrs. Thomas and the little girl were still in Calcutta with a friend, waiting until he could find a new home to which they might be brought. He reached Mr. Hasted's house on the 7th of March. In a letter written just afterwards to Mr. Carey, he says,—

> I have been variously affected under these dispensations, since I saw you: but am more composed now. The word of God affords me grounds and reasons enough to be content for the present, and to hope for the future.
>
> I have had some conversation with the Hill people, and learn from them that they have no history, nor books of any kind, nor method of writing, except the very few who may chance to write the Bengali or Nagri. They have *gosains*, who, I suppose, rule them. They have also four regular festivals; of what kind I know not. I shall ascend the hills, I suppose, before I leave.

On the 14th, he wrote to Mr. Carey again :—

With respect to spiritual welfare, it seems to me as though I had ruined myself by doing and suffering little things in my own strength. I come back once more to this point, ' Power belongeth unto God.' ' He giveth strength and power unto His people.' ' Without me ye can do nothing,' &c. When such texts of Scripture are abused, they are 'a savour of death unto death,' sloth unto sloth, deadness unto deadness. But where they enter, they give light, life, and encouragement to activity. It seems to be your opinion now again that I had better follow the mission alone, but you have not annexed any reasons. I am a poor judge of my own mind, I confess; however, it seems to me as if I should like this; but that my embarrassments, my family, and the Company's proceedings are objections apparently at present totally insuperable. I have much and frequently entreated of the Lord that He will also plainly guide me at this crisis, that I may surely do that which will be best on the whole for the glory of the gospel, for my own soul, and for others, and I have some hope that He who hath been my help by wondrous events of past providence, will not leave nor forsake me now. Join me in this request at a throne of grace; and let me attend to the leadings of providence and do valiantly for the best: and the Lord do as seemeth Him good.

Psalm cxix. and the whole word of God seems to have doubled and trebled its produce to me by this fermentation; and I have been cordially thankful for it as a mercy that I was in need of, and as an instance of divine faithfulness and everlasting mercy to an undeserving wretch. How quiet it is after a brisk storm! So it is with me. I sit still. I hope I shall have to write to you of the furtherance of the gospel yet.

On the 24th, he wrote again. His medical charge was not yet fulfilled. He had sent off his boat to bring up Mrs. Thomas and his little girl; but the failure of the *hundi*, or draft, expected from Mr. Powell had detained her in Calcutta, and put them to sore inconvenience. The main object of his letter was to beg Mr. Carey to use his influence to secure the remittance without further delay; and, since April was at hand, to obtain also the payment of the amount due for March. "I am sorry," he says, "to make these complaints and give you all this trouble; but, remember, I have no one else to help me now. I suppose Mrs. Thomas and Betsy will stay at Mr. Hasted's till I have prepared a shelter for them."

Poor man, the shelter he projected was but ill fitted for the protection of himself, to say nothing of any risk of evil to a delicate wife and child. But the hot season was at hand, and his boat was so small that "only Betsy could stand upright in it." To live in it under the sun of a Bengali May was not to be thought of. He proposed therefore to find some suitable place near Nuddea, where, as he had done before, in 1791, he might put up a hut to dwell in. Mrs. Thomas preferred to accompany him; and after her arrival they all left Serasing. Towards the end of April, they were at Berhampore, again disappointed of the money which, if it had come, would have been all too little for their needs. But they had to go on without it to Kishnagur, a few miles to the north of which, at a place called Harin Danga, he proposed to make himself a home. Indeed he seems to have intended to cultivate indigo there for his support. Mr. Hasted had offered him as much seed for the purpose, as he needed. The people there "heard the gospel with avidity." But his purpose to establish himself at this place could not be carried out. On the 7th of May, he wrote to Mr. Carey. "No *hundi* for the month of March or April: and this is May! As you were so good as to say you would see to this for me, and I know it is of no use to expect help from any other man in your neighbourhood, I must beg you to consider and recollect my case, with all the obvious concomitants; for I have but Rs. 3 left!" More than a week later, he was still unrelieved, and wrote with excusable bitterness that "his inconveniences, though patiently borne by others, were severe to his family." Amidst these distresses, however, the interests of his great work held place in his heart. He wrote,—

I am quite weary of hearing and seeing hopeful beginnings end in a hopeless manner, or near it. Yárdí, like all the rest, is going; and if I ever meet with any that distinguish themselves by enquiry, attention, and seriousness, they only give me pain, where once I only felt pleasure.—I heard a voice saying, 'All that the Father hath given me shall come unto me.' The Holy Spirit never designed this truth to encourage wicked and slothful servants in their evil habits; but He designed it for various uses to His church and people; one of which may be to encourage faint hearts still to go on in their use of the appointed means. The people hear and attend here with that spirit which would charm and delight me, if these appearances had not so often vanished and deceived.

He speaks of kindness received in his need.—

The Magistrate of the district received me with very pleasing attention and politeness; offered to send us, and does send, bread, butter, biscuit, &c., in quantities; and when I eat a tiffin with him, I think I have a feast fit for a prince. The rájá also is very friendly, and I attend him as my patient: a very shrewd, sensible man, and a man of eastern learning. I have met with very great friends amongst the natives, who have laboured night and day for me, without any apparent prospect of reward. I am crowded with patients from morning till night.

The season was insufferably hot, but "we still," he wrote, "live in a boat, and have had many a storm to weather, night and day. Not a bamboo bought yet: and good reason why! He that is a refuge to those in trouble meets my expectations, as He does those of the worthless, when no one else will accept of them. He raises up one and another, to pity me and help me. Oh for a more thankful heart!"

On the 17th of June, the straitened family were "still in the boat, learning how to endure." A *hundi* for March, bringing, like that for February, Rs. 80 only, instead of 100, had come. He was now at Nuddea, and wrote to Mr. Carey:—

"I find the pandits clever fellows; but none behave with asperity. I have hundreds of patients; and I go on in my old way. I maintain here and there a most deplorable object, while I am in want myself; but it looks to me like murder to neglect those who are actually ready to perish, on any pretence whatever."

His letter closes with an entreaty to Mr. Carey to pay some small sums due to servants at Moypaldiggy, which had been overlooked. "To fail in this drought, would be shocking," he says, feeling tenderly for others, whilst suffering so sorely himself.

On the 21st of June, they were in the same state, but "through wonderful mercy, all well," except the boils from which himself and his daughter suffered. That, however, was "not to be compared with the heaviness and perplexity they had undergone through the neglect and vain excuses, from time to time, which they were supplied with instead of money." The rains had begun; and it was needful that they should seek some better shelter than their boat. They were intending to remove to Chinsura. He adds,—

We have long been without the common necessaries of life, and, for about ten days, we have been obliged to do without bread, butter, &c., and, as to wine and tea, they are never thought of. I have such a number of poor people come every morning for medicine as would astonish you. I am frequently six or seven hours before I give over my morning attendance, and then generally leave many begging in vain for relief. I disposed of nearly five hundred pills yesterday, besides other medicines; and several persons have obtained great relief.

The distressed family, after moving down the river, found a little upper-roomed house at Chandernagore, "with four rooms and an enclosed verandah above, and fourteen or fifteen little places below, at Rs. 16 per mensem," and proceeded at once to remove into it, and so "got into shelter from the rains." The preserving goodness of which they were, in all their troubles, the objects, appeared to them very singularly at this juncture of their affairs. Mr. Thomas wrote to a niece,—

We had taken all our trunks, baskets and stuff of every kind out of the boat: and then, and not till then, a plank which the water-worm had eaten gave way,—and down she went to the bottom, though several men attempted to prevent it by baling her. Had this happened in deep water, and far from shore, you would have heard of us no more till you had ended your pilgrimage.

Two brahmans had followed him from Nuddea, "with the avowed intention of reading and hearing the word of life;" but he feared they were really seeking "the word of *this* life." He says, in a letter to Mr. Carey,—

Instead of having my hopes enlivened by my late excursions among these people, I feel greatly disheartened. The gospel, however, the glorious gospel, is quite sufficient for all the great ends and purposes we have in view, for ourselves and others. The Lord's hand is not shortened; but His face does not shine upon me. I sometimes am swallowed up in a dark thick cloud of dejection; so that it is distressing to speak. I have several times gone out to preach in this frame, and found it all pass off; but lately, especially on Sabbath days, I have gone, found people, attempted to speak; but a ton weight was on my soul; and oftentimes I have gone moping through the villages, followed by a crowd, without saying one word about the gospel; and, if I replied to any other question, it was with distress and difficulty. Of all the missionaries on the earth, I am one of the most hopeless. Mrs. Thomas has had much more of the spirit of a missionary in her than I have, and though she cannot keep it long out her head,—' What shall we eat, and wherewithal shall we be clothed?' yet, to her praise I speak it, she has advised me to give up all things for the mission, and sometimes has reproved me for my inactivity, in which I heartily joined her; but then it is, as I have said elsewhere: I have the heart of a dead dog in it. I use David's argument when entreating deliverance: 'for I am brought very low.' The heavens over my head are become brass, and the earth is iron to me.

He still complained of the delay with which he received instalments from Moypaldiggy. Out of Rs. 700 which was due, he had received Rs. 260 only; and he entreated Mr. Carey's interposition. On the 27th of July, he wrote of the long delay in answering his letters. Driven to the last extremity, he was thinking of going to Calcutta to "write for his bread," and he knew not how he could await the return of the post from Mudnabatty. He adds, "I thought you never more would have heard from me; being a few days ago laid up with liver disorder and fever. Let me entreat you to reflect on what you suffered in my case, and how I acted; but I am determined to say no more. If I perish, I perish!———Not I! No: I shall never perish; but what effect all these troubles may work upon this mortal body, I know not."

Help was now at hand. On the 11th of August, he writes to acknowledge the receipt of letters which had been lying at the Post Office at Kishnaghur for weeks; and, better still, relief from England was soon to be available. The kind providence of God, which had so often interposed for him before, was manifested now in the action—unsolicited by the missionaries—of the Committee of the Society. A resolution of theirs, dated August 29, 1797, of which the news now reached India, was as follows:—

Our brethen having, in a disinterested manner, declined their ordinary income from us, at a time when they thought they could do without it; and various unforeseen circumstances having since occurred, which render it necessary that we should afford them substantial assistance, resolved, that at this time we will pay them those arrears, which they voluntarily declined, that is, that we will make up what has been sent out in goods at different times to £100 per annum to each family, for four years, viz. from November 7, 1793, to November 7, 1797.

Mr. Thomas's share of the money thus voted was to be about £220. He says to Mr. Carey,—

How seasonably has the Lord sent us help! We have had great discouragements to flesh and blood ; but the hand of Lord is not shortened. Let not the axe murmur against the hand that lifts it. It is peculiarly good for missionaries to both hope and quietly wait for the salvation of God. I have read much of the word of God this last month, both in my family and in private. I am ashamed of all my afflictions and sufferings, as not worthy to be mentioned, when I see what is written there. I repent of my grievous complaints to you in my last letter; but you know what they are; the scum and spawn of ingratitude and infidelity to God. By the word of God, I see a needs be for myself in every pang, and it is good for me that I have been, am, and shall be, afflicted.

In this letter he adverts to a very painful subject, which Mr. Carey had brought to his knowledge. Párbati was now at Mudnabatty, and there was reason, from his own admissions, to believe that he had from the first been a deceiver, and that his marvellous dream and subsequent conversion were matters fabricated between himself and Mohan Chand at Bhulaháth. Mr. Thomas wrote,—

I feel myself sorely hurt to this day at hearing of the device of Mohan Chand and Párbati. I had no suspicion of them. My budgerow is just fit to float, and I intend to go and sow the good seed, from town to town, and village to village, next week, making Chandernagore my place of residence.

On the 22nd of August, leaving his family behind, he took his little boat and went forth preaching the gospel, which in some places was listened to with apparently genuine interest; whilst elsewhere the utmost indifference was manifested to whatever he said. He wrote on the 24th,—

I see by experience how necessary it is to make a longer stay among the people, and I am also taught that this is necessary by the Acts of the Apostles; though as I am going from place to place, I will not refuse to speak of the gospel, because I cannot tarry. Our blessed Lord sometimes preached at several towns in one day, where he made no particular stay. But who is sufficient for these things? To go from place to place, in the darkness of Egypt, a man had need have God at hand, to keep his heart up. Without you stay and reason with them, once preaching amounts to this: '*You* are all in the wrong, and *I* am all in the right.' If you stay to reason with them, the people you begin with to-day disappear to-morrow. If you sum up all you have to say in a few words, it is like the index of a book, or a syllabus of lectures, and is received by them as a dry uninteresting subject, or, at best, as the plan of a chain of reasoning by those who have never yet begun thinking. I find these and other discouraging barriers and impassable gulfs between this people and the gospel, so that except the Lord be merciful to them for Christ's sake, and come forth with irresistible power, it is impossible that any of them should ever be converted. But who can tell but the Lord may do this? It is all the hope I have left. The difficulties are very great, but the work is still very sweet and desirable. It is a little heaven to me to go and speak to these sheep without a shepherd, of the great things which concern their everlasting peace.

This preaching excursion appears to have afforded him much interest at many places, and especially at Malanpara, where, having one evening promised to preach next morning, he was accordingly called out of his boat a little after day-light by a pandit, who said the people were all ready. All day long, he was engaged with them in eager debate. He wrote in his journal,—

No indifference here! I think this is the first congregation that ever tired me out, and stayed longer than I asked them. I have been speaking loudly to them for the space of eight hours in all, and have suffered in spirit very sorely because of the many blasphemous opinions which have been uttered, and on account of those notions they firmly hold, which strike at the root of all religion and virtue, and make sin to be a sort of play-thing which God ordained, as well as righteousness.

The discussion was renewed the next day, and he left them with a very solemn exhortation and remonstrance concerning the pernicious doctrines they had advanced against the truth.

During this journey a great sensation was produced amongst some of Mr. Thomas's hearers by the discovery that he was in possession of the mysterious Sanscrit verse called the *Gáyatrí*. He wrote,—

I found it, about seven years ago, in Roman letters, in a book written a hundred years ago by a Portuguese priest,* and I immediately put it into the Bengali character. Then, one day, I met a pandit in the open field, who proved to be a man of uncommon candour, and, after a long talk, I told him I had the *Gáyatrí*. He read over my copy of it; and by his remarks I discovered some blunders, which I corrected with a straw dipped in the mud. Thus I obtained a copy which all admit to be correct. It is difficult to express, by any words, the reverence in which they hold this text. When questioned as to the *Gáyatrí*, they thrust the tongue out as far as they are able, and clap their hands over their ears; as though they were deaf and dumb. They have disputed my knowledge of it, but no sooner have I silently written the first letter of it on the palm of my left hand with my finger, then they have covered their eyes and run away, in a crouching posture, as though they had seen something forbidden to mortal eyes.

A Brahman from Orissa, "very illiterate, wonderfully simple, but a very intelligent man," attached himself to the missionary as an enquirer during this journey; and, for a time, there seemed to be reason to hope that he and one of the boatmen were disposed to become followers of Christ. Indeed he wrote of all his boatmen,—" They are all moved, more or less, and sit and ask questions, and acquiesce, and wonder." But the end of it was only disappointment.

Other interesting details must be omitted. On the 11th of September, he rejoined his family at Chandernagore. During his absence he saw reason to think that he might sustain his family, and do something to defray his debts, by purchasing cotton cloth from the weavers in country places and selling it in Calcutta. This he accordingly attempted, and was for a little while encouraged by the results. Unhappy as he had been in his earlier engagements and involved as his circumstances were, he found people in Calcutta who were ready to offer him encourage-

* Sir William Jones refers to the same book in the following words,—
"The original *Gáyatrí*, or holiest verse of the Veda, has already been published, though very incorrectly, by Fra Manuel da Assomcaon, a successful missionary from Portugal, who may have received it, as his countrymen assert, from a converted Brahman."

ment in new speculations. In the middle of September, he had proposals made to him to undertake the charge of two indigo factories, with the promise of substantial help to carry forward the undertaking. He, however, declined these offers. "The very sound of indigo," he wrote to Mr. Carey, "is shocking to me; and I have become quite averse to running into any more nooses. I think Providence smiles upon me in the small way, and seems willing to give me my daily bread, and what lack I more?" It had been happy for him had this resolution been maintained.

He would have been glad to make a home in some spot in the wilderness, as he had thought of doing at Harin Danga; but he heard the most dreadful reports, every where as he travelled, of the atrocities committed by dacoits. Harmless villagers were attacked and cut to pieces by them, and their heads hung up upon the trees, and the most revolting cruelties were perpetrated upon any who were supposed to have hidden away their property.

In carrying forward this traffic in native cloth, he seems to have travelled mostly in the district around Nuddea, and he was a very frequent visitor at that place. There he had some hearers of whom he hoped well; especially a man named Rám Mohan, a *poddár*, or money-changer, whose simplicity and interest in the gospel won the heart of the missionary. He had also a wealthy patient, "the famous Ganga Gobind Singh, Mr. Hastings's Dewan," who built the *nabaratna*, at Nuddea, of which he had written with so much admiration to Mr. Carey. His attempts to win men to Christ here seemed as though crowned by the blessing of God, towards the end of the year. Rás Chandra, a Brahman, and two or three others professed to be Christians; and he wrote a letter to Mr. Carey, begging him to bring Mr. Fountain with him to Nuddea on the 28th of January, 1799, that they might be present at the public baptism of these converts. The request ran in the following confident terms,—

I hope you will not fail me, but consider how greatly the cause of Christ calls you on this occasion. Let nothing prevent your coming. Let not our past disappointments, which have discouraged me from writing much to you about the work of the Lord lately at Nuddea, discourage your hope. Doubt not, but be assured, the Lord has appeared, and does appear, making bare His arm. You will find the simplicity of the gospel, and that divine mark in their foreheads, love to the brethren, with repentance towards God and faith toward our Lord Jesus Christ. It would take up too much time to tell you how the Lord has been with me lately in daily prayer, and in expounding and reading the word of God to them in Bengali; but come and see. Come over and help us. I want your advice; and long, day and night, for your speedy coming.

Mr. Carey went to Calcutta in January, and was able to comply with the request made to him that he should visit Nuddea; but, before the date fixed for the baptism came, the Brahman's conduct showed that he was a deceiver; and yet another disappointment was added to the retrospect of missionary failures.

At the end of 1798, the Rev. Nathaniel Forsyth, arrived in Calcutta as a missionary of the London Missionary Society. He had been one of the number intending to come to India with Mr. Robert Haldane; and, on the failure of that enterprise, he still persisted in his purpose to labour in Bengal. It does not appear that he ever acquired either of the vernacular languages of India, but he was indefatigable in his attempts to do good, as he had opportunity, and he supported himself by his own property. On his arrival, Mr. Thomas met him, and found great pleasure in his society. He describes him as "a very grave, sensible and pious man, about thirty years of age;" and in sentiment "an unbigoted Presbyterian." Mr. Forsyth began to preach in Calcutta in the lecture hall of Dr. Dinwiddie; where he had very small encouragement; for his congregation was "sometimes only two, seldom ten."

Towards the end of April, a startling change in Mr. Thomas's arrangements suddenly meets us. Notwithstanding his aversion to indigo planting, he was induced to rent on his own account a factory at "Cooleadean, half a *krosh* inland from Lál Ganj, which is opposite Santipore, and near Culna, and about six *krosh* to the southward of Nuddea." He says to Mr. Carey,—

I have been in great trouble and conflict, but at present there is such a probability of retrieving my temporal circumstances as leaves room to hope; but that hope is founded, I confess, on the uncertain turn of an indigo season. Thus far my temporal circumstances. My soul, I cannot say, is prosperous. I do not see how it should be so. As I have opportunity, I speak, with apparent concern of heart, the great truths of the precious gospel; but with no more efficacy than before. Poor and wretched art thou, my soul, in these respects; but I cannot add, 'and knowest it not;' or, 'thou sayest, I am rich.' And now in return, my dear brother, tell me how it is with you. Do your souls prosper better than mine? Then be thankful for what you have received. Does the Sun of righteousness shine on your labours?—though this is a hard question; because He shines sometimes as brightly when the darkness of the clouds prevents our observation, as when the light of His countenance fills our unbeclouded hearts with joy and peace through believing. I see with some satisfaction and quietness that, in all these tossings, God is at the bottom.

This rash undertaking at Cooleadean, proved an utter failure. The unhappy adventurer felt himself to be singled out by providence for disappointment and ruin! The neighbouring factories, both above and below him, had seasonable rain upon their fields; but he had none, and could not put in his seed till late in June, when such a deluge descended as speedily drowned all his hopes. "His indigo concern thus sunk to nothing, and almost sunk him with it." His circumstances were more hopeless than ever. He wrote to his father that he had now "done with all indigo works. But some thing must be done, to render to every one his due."

While at Cooleadean, Mr. Thomas had, as one of his nearest neighbours, Mr. Cardin, " the Company's distiller," whose house was at the Dhoba Distillery, near Mirzapore. Mr. Cardin had been a planter in the West Indies, and had proved by experiment that a very great improvement in the cultivation of the sugar cane and the manufacture of sugar and rum might easily be attained, if the West Indian methods were followed. Communications with this very kind neighbour gave a new bent to Mr. Thomas's efforts to support himself and to pay his debts. There was now a great demand for sugar. People said that the Russians had found out the use of it, and that the demand for it was likely to become more and more active. He therefore entered into partnership with a Calcutta merchant who was to advance the money needed for very extensive purchases, and he began this new business with the liveliest confidence in the success it was to yield. On the 8th of July, he wrote to Mr. Carey of his undertaking. He was then " in a 500 maund boat, on his way to Cutwa, to buy sugar for shipping," wherever he could procure it in that neighbourhood. He was full of hope that " with the blessing of God on the labour of his hands," his new occupation would " yield back all his losses." This employment also gave him good opportunities to visit different parts of the country, and he was active in preaching wherever he went. He said to Mr. Carey,—

The Lord will have His will and His way, and His means, and He will work, and who shall let it THEN ?—Till *then*, we *must wait*, and *wait long*, perhaps, as the husbandman does for the fruit. But if we have any expectation in our hearts, and if that expectation is in God only, we shall not be finally disappointed. I do truly and deeply mourn and lament with you our want of success in the gospel. For my part, I have shame, and fear hangs about me when I attempt to speak again of people who hear at all hopefully:—I have been so exceedingly deceived and disappointed. This part of the country is favorable. A Bible is much desired and asked for at Cutwa. 'It seems more unlikely than ever that we shall do any good.' This is the language of sense; but the language of faith is, ' We are as likely now as ever we were.' To attempt is ours: to succeed is not ours; nor is it expected of us, but of God only. O for more of Christ dwelling in our hearts, and more of His sweet name in all our common undertakings, and more of His interest, honour, and glory in all our designs (Ezekiel xxxvi. 23); but I have walked contrary to Him, and He has walked contrary to me, according to His word, and blessed be His name; but I feel His sovereign mercy and enjoy it. I have all along thought myself something, while I was nothing. I had need of all my trials, and envy no man his prosperity. O bleeding Lamb of God for me, may my pride bleed to death through thee, and my loftiness be thoroughly brought down; and be thou, thou alone exalted. Then will I teach transgressors thy ways, and sinners shall be converted unto thee.

I earnestly entreat you to pray much and often for me, that Christ may come and dwell in my heart by faith more than He has done. Pray that I may be upheld and, 'after suffering awhile, stablished, strengthened, settled.' And, oh, may the God and Father of our Lord Jesus Christ be in us all of a truth, that we may glorify Him here on earth, while we stay, by doing or suffering, and enjoy Him for ever in heaven, where neither the evil root of sin, nor the bitter fruit of sorrow shall ever again interrupt our joy in the Lord.

In all this time since leaving Moypaldiggy, Mr. Thomas had wholly neglected to write to Mr. Fuller. He "left it all" to Mr. Carey. On the 17th of January, 1799, indeed, he did post a letter to the Secretary, but it was written two years before, and had been lying by him all that time. It was, nevertheless, published in the *Periodical Accounts*, and was read with great interest by many. Mr. Fuller also printed two letters which Mr. Thomas wrote to his nieces on hearing from them of the death of his sister Mrs. Pearce. He said of these letters,—

Truly the spirit which they breathed, the sentiments they enforced, and the complicated trials which they implied on the part of the writer, dissolved my heart in tender affection towards him. I read the letters to our congregation as a part of the afternoon worship. Many of our friends felt with me; but they must wonder that all we know of Mr. Thomas is by copies of letters sent to his relations.

The new undertaking seemed likely to succeed. Towards the end of August, he informed Mr. Carey that he had carried his cargo of sugar to Calcutta, where he had been offered a good profit upon it. "For once, he had gained." In a letter to his father, a few days later, he gratefully acknowledges the same success:—" I ought not have said, I had been smitten in *all* my labours; but we are prone to overweigh afflictions, and to overlook sins and mercies. This is no uncommon mistake."

The district of Bírbhúm offered the most inviting field for the business Mr. Thomas was now carrying on, and he found it needful to secure a depôt at Etinda, where his sugar might be refined and prepared for transmission to Calcutta, and where he also set up a small distillery.

So greatly was he encouraged by his present prospects, that he was eager to induce Mr. Carey to profit by his experience, and "to turn his eye to sugar, instead of that precarious indigo, which would exist neither a dry month nor a wet one, without loss or damage; while the sugar-cane would do both, without either, and would afford a missionary more regular and more numerous advantages." Nor did his representations fail to take considerable effect upon his less excitable colleague. On the 18th of October, Mr. Thomas wrote him a long letter in reply to questions he had propounded upon the manufacture of sugar and rum. Let not the reader be shocked by the fact that these good men could hold the labours of the distiller innocent and compatible with the missionary calling. The moderate use of spirits was not then accounted an evil thing. As to this matter, the Christian conscience had not been educated in accordance with our present standards.* Country rum was the commonly used beverage of such Europeans as could not afford claret, madeira, or porter, and the production of it was not held to be an iniquity, on the part either of the manufacturer or of the Government. So far was Mr. Thomas from any thought of wrong-doing in this business, that after answering all Mr. Carey's queries, he wrote,—"I beg and beseech you to consider the matter well, and, for your own sake, for your family's sake, and for the gospel's sake, have no more to do with the precarious deceiving indigo!"

* A yet more curious illustration of the fact that even an enlightened conscience takes much of its tone from the society around it is supplied by the excellent John Newton, in whose Olney hymns every Christian finds the record of his own experience. This good man says, in his autobiographical narrative:—

"During the time I was engaged in the slave trade, I never had the least scruple as to its lawfulness. I was, upon the whole, satisfied with it, as the appointment Providence had marked out for me; yet it was, in many respects, far from eligible. It is, indeed, accounted a genteel employment, and is usually very profitable, though to me it did not prove so, the Lord seeing that a large increase of wealth could not be good for me. However, I considered myself as a sort of gaoler or turnkey; and I was sometimes shocked with an employment that was perpetually conversant with chains, bolts, and shackles. In this view, I had often petitioned, in my prayers, that the Lord, in his own time, would be pleased to fix me in a more humane calling, and, if it might be, place me where I might have more frequent converse with His people and ordinances, and be freed from those long separations from home, which very often were hard to bear."

CHAPTER XIII.

Serampore.—1799-1800.

AN extract from Mr. Carey's essay on Christian missions, given upon an earlier page, has informed the reader as to the method in which he thought they ought to be conducted, when he formed his plans in England. He was anxious to put those plans into operation, as far as possible, at Dehatta; but the providential opening for him at Mudnabatty induced him to abandon his half finished house and farm there; and the project he had elaborated at Moulton and Leicester was laid aside to be reconsidered whenever circumstances should render a reconstruction of affairs desirable or necessary. Such a time seemed to be at hand at the close of 1796, when, as has been seen, the failure of the indigo manufacture at Mudnabatty made the immediate relinquishment of his works there appear inevitable. Thinking that it was so, he addressed to Mr. Fuller the following project for the establishment of the Bengal mission, as soon as his support from Mr. Udny should cease.

I will now propose to you, what I would recommend to the Society. You will find it similar to what the Moravians do. Seven or eight families can be maintained for nearly the same expense as one, if this method be pursued. I then earnestly entreat the Society to set their faces this way, and send out more missionaries. We ought to be seven or eight families together; and it is absolutely necessary for the wives of missionaries to be as hearty in the work as their husbands. Our families should be considered nurseries for the mission; and among us should be a person capable of teaching school, so as to educate our children. I recommend all living together, in a number of little straw houses, forming a line or square, and that we have nothing of our own; but all the general stock. One or two should be selected stewards to preside over all the management, which should, with respect to eating, drinking, working, worship, learning, preaching, excursions, &c., be reduced to fixed rules. Should converts from amongst the natives join us, all should be considered equal, and all come under the same regulations.

The utility of this community of goods in the beginning of the gospel church here, will be obvious, by considering the following things:—

1. Our finances being small, it will be necessary to live economically; but one set of servants will do all the work for the whole, if thus organized, when, if otherwise, every separate family must have the same number as would be necessary for the whole, if united: and, if God converts the natives, they would in time supersede all want of servants, being partakers of the public stock, and therefore bound to labour for the public benefit.

2. Education of our own and converted heathens' children is a very important object, and is what might, if followed by a divine blessing, train up some of them to be useful preachers or other members of the mission themselves.

3. The example of such a number would be a standing witness of the excellence of the gospel, and would contribute very much to the furtherance of the cause of Christ.

4. Industry being absolutely necessary, every one would have his proper work allotted him, and would be employed at his post; some cultivating land, some instructing, some learning, some preaching, and the women superintending the domestic concerns.

In order to this, I recommend about one or two hundred bigahs to be cultivated for the mission, which would produce most of the articles necessary for them and their cattle; that all these people should not come at one time, but one or two families in a year, or in two years or so. But as brother Thomas, for obvious reasons, could not join this family, and as there is a far greater probability of his being torn from the work than not, we are in immediate want of more, say one family more, of missionaries; and I entreat the Society to send them, as the only way of keeping the mission together: but pray be very careful what stamp missionaries' wives are of.

Should this place be continued to me, I recommend the seat of the mission to be here; and my income and utensils will be immediately thrown into the common stock. Or any part of Bengal would do; though the north is most agreeable, and will produce wheat, a very necessary article: the heat also is more moderate. Should we go south, the neighbourhood of Nuddea is most eligible; but, I fear, too near Calcutta. All provisions also are much cheaper in the north; and by keeping a small boat, which can be bought for thirty rupees, two persons may travel any where at a time. Cultivation, and all except superintendence, must be performed by natives.

EXPENSE. The number of servants kept would fall under two hundred rupees per month; I think, about a hundred and thirty: and the expenses of clothing and articles of furniture would be near one hundred for the number mentioned. The table might be well supplied, for all above mentioned, for one hundred rupees at furthest: I think, for sixty; but I say the utmost. Now, if eight families were distinct, their monthly expenses could not, with the utmost frugality, come under one thousand rupees per month: the whole of this would only be four hundred, and the produce of the land would go to lessen even that; so that we should receive from the Society for such a number £30 per month, or £360 per annum, till we were able to say we could do with less. It would be a great saving of even this, if the Society were to send £50 a year of this in woollen cloths, light shoes, strong stockings, hats, and garden seeds. This £50 would save the mission about £100 or £150 a year. Having said this much, I recommend it to your serious consideration. The calculations may all be depended upon.

The communistic scheme thus propounded would probably recommend itself to very few directors of missionary societies in the present day; and many objections to it will, no doubt, occur to every reader. Mr. Fuller's sagacity and strong common sense, however, found nothing in it to object to. His reply was a model of laconic, but most complacent, acquiescence. "Do whatever your own judgment dictates, all circumstances considered. We have great confidence in your prudence."*

---

* That Mr. Fuller's ready acceptance of Mr. Carey's plan did not imply an unqualified admiration of all his performances, a quotation from this same letter will prove, in a somewhat amusing manner. Mr. Carey had asked that his mode of spelling Indian words might be always adhered to, when any of his letters were printed. Mr. Fuller wrote in rejoinder,—

"But you do not always spell alike. Sometimes you write *moonshee*, and sometimes *munshi*. 'If the trumpet give an uncertain sound, who can prepare

But Mr. Carey's fears as to the immediate abandonment of Mudnabatty were not realized. The works there were still, for a time, carried on. In 1797, the results of the manufacture were more favorable. In 1798, Mr. Carey wrote to Mr. Thomas "sad accounts of the season;" yet his ill-success did not bring about the expected crisis. But it came in 1799. Scarcely had the seed begun to spring up, when the young indigo was almost totally destroyed by an inundation. The matter was now decided; and, in September, Mr. Carey received notice that the works were to be closed. He most frankly acknowledged that his employer did wisely in determining to abandon his unfortunate speculation at Mudnabatty forthwith. With the year 1799, his allowances as superintendent of the factory ceased.

Now therefore it was necessary to make new arrangements. In view of such an event he had already agreed with Mr. Udny to purchase from him a small out-factory at Kidderpur, twelve miles from Mudnabatty. It had not answered Mr. Udny's expectations, and he consented to transfer it to Mr. Carey, upon his paying for it about Rs. 3000, the sum already laid out. Here therefore, Carey and Fountain proposed to erect houses, a printing office, and other buildings for the accommodation of themselves and the brethren about to reinforce the mission, of whose coming they had been apprised; and, in doing this, they proposed to follow the plan advocated at the close of 1796.

The missionaries were, Mr. William Ward, Mr. Joshua Marshman and his wife, Mr. Daniel Brundson and his wife, Mr. William Grant and his wife, and Miss Tidd, who was to marry Mr. Fountain. All were to settle with Mr. Carey at Mudnabatty; but the Committee were apprehensive of difficulty in obtaining a footing for their brethren there. They knew well that the permission of the Indian Govern-

---

for the battle?' You must again allow me to remind you of your *punctuation*. I never knew a person of so much knowledge as you possess of other languages write English so bad! You huddle half-a-dozen periods into one. Where your sentence ends, you very commonly make only a semicolon, instead of a period. If your Bengali New Testament should be thus pointed, I should tremble for its fate."

ment was not likely to be granted for their settlement as missionaries, and they thought it best not to ask for it, but to let them go quietly to the place of their destination, unnoticed, if that were possible, by the authorities. Mr. Fuller wrote,—" On advising with Mr. Short," who was then in England, " and also with Mr. Charles Grant, the Director, they recommended that the missionaries should not be landed in Calcutta, but at Serampore, a Danish settlement, between Calcutta and Hooghly. We have therefore," he added, "ordered matters so that, in Calcutta river, they, instead of going into the city, get out of the ship into a boat, take their chests with them, and go immediately to Serampore." There Mr. Carey was to make arrangements to meet them, and to conduct them to his place of residence.

The *Criterion*, an American vessel, commanded by Mr. Benjamin Wickes, a very excellent Presbyterian of Philadelphia, sailed from Gravesend with the missionaries, on the 26th of May, 1799, and reached Calcutta on the 12th of October. The missionary party followed the instructions given them in England. A little below the city, they all left the ship in two boats, and went on without landing to Serampore, which they reached at day-break on Sunday morning, the 13th. They hoped to be met by one of the brethren from Mudnabatty, and to travel thither under his direction.

But unexpected difficulties arose. When Captain Wickes went to enter his ship at the Custom House in Calcutta, he was ordered to produce his missionary passengers ; and permission for him to trade at the port was made conditional upon his giving them up, or engaging that they should be sent out of the country. These harsh conditions were afterwards withdrawn, and the good captain's difficulties were surmounted ; but it was found that there was little or no hope that they could be allowed by the British authorities to labour as missionaries in Bengal. So jealous was the Company's Government of all " interlopers," and so opposed to all religious agitation amongst the natives, that there was reason to fear that even the enlightened Governor-General, the Marquis Wellesley, would deport them, if they attempted to set up their press and to carry out the other purposes for which they had come to Bengal, either at Kidderpur or at any other place within the British territories.*

Whilst they were discountenanced thus by their own countrymen, God gave the missionaries a generous protector in the person of Colonel Bie, the Danish Governor of Serampore. From the time of their arrival, he was their adviser and friend. They waited upon him the day after they reached the place, and "found him very friendly and disposed to do them all the service he could," but his help could avail them little beyond the limits of his small territory. He counselled them as to the communications they should make to the authorities in Calcutta, and assured them of his protection if they chose to remain within the Danish settlement.

Mr. Thomas was deeply interested in the anxieties of the newly arrived brethren, and wrote to them frequently. It was his strong wish that one or more of them should join him, now that he had such favorable prospects of both temporal success and missionary usefulness in the Bírbhúm district. They, however, had heard much at home which made them unwilling to enter into needlessly close relations with him; and the rumours which now reached them of his debts and entanglements filled them all with most painful apprehensions of discredit to the mission on his account. Mr. Ward, indeed, did not hesitate, within a month of his arrival in India, to suggest to Mr. Fuller that Mr. Thomas's connection with the Society ought to be severed.

* The manner in which the ship was reported in the newspapers was thought to have led the Government to suppose that the missionaries were French spies. The *Calcutta Gazette* of October 17th thus announced the arrival of the vessel:—

"The American ship *Criterion*, Captain Wickes, came into the river on Thursday last. She left London on the 26th May, and saw the Land's End on the 8th June following. On this ship came passengers:—Sir John Meredith, Bart. and four missionaries deputed by the Papist Mission Society."

Of these passengers, two died before the month in which they landed in India had expired; *viz.* Sir John Meredyth on the 27th, and Mr. W. Grant, one of the missionaries, on the 31st of October, 1799.

Colonel Bie made it evident that he well appreciated the great objects for which the missionaries had come to Bengal. When they commenced a public service at their hired house, he came to it with his guests and friends; and, that he might the better introduce the missionaries to the notice of the residents at Serampore, he invited them one Sunday in November to preach in his own large hall to as many as could be induced to come. He had no wish however, so to employ his official influence as unduly to constrain others in matters of religion. Having once had the service in his house, he "intimated that he had now brought the people under the word, and could do no more. He must leave them to their own discretion." The services were therefore afterwards again held at the missionaries' house; but the Governor still set a good example by being himself a regular attendant.

In the midst of all their anxieties, the missionaries suffered the loss of one of their number in a very unexpected manner. Mr. Grant was, upon his arrival at Serampore, apparently in perfect health. On the 27th of October, he suffered from a cold; but no thought of danger arose till the morning of the 31st, when a convulsive fit alarmed the family around him, and, in the afternoon of the same day, he expired. His death was a severe shock to his brethren, by whom he was much beloved; and he left behind him a widow and two little girls.

Mr. Carey did all he could to obtain permission for the removal of the missionaries to Mudnabatty. He wrote to every influential friend he had in Calcutta, whither Mr. Udny was now removing, to take his seat in the Board of Trade. Dr. Roxburg, Mr. Carey's botanical friend and correspondent, was also asked to help; but all was to no purpose. The conclusion the missionaries arrived at was:—" The Company do not wish for the settlement of Europeans in Bengal. No European can be a proprietor of lands, nor indeed can any one properly come or stay here without their permission. That permission we shall never obtain; and without it we could never be secure. We therefore rejoice that here there is a resting place; and from here we can itinerate to any part we choose. The paper, the press, and the types are at Mudnabatty; but in other respects the mission is surrounded with gloom, and we are almost disheartened. Europeans every where laugh at us, and God seems to cover Himself with impenetrable clouds."*

This was written on the 9th of November. Mr. Fountain had come that day to meet them, and they had called on Colonel Bie, who renewed his offers of protection and assistance if they liked to remain at Serampore, and proposed to help them now by giving one of them a passport to Mudnabatty. This would enable them to confer with Mr. Carey more freely than was possible by letter, and something might then be resolved upon.

On the 14th of November, therefore, Mr. Ward, protected by the Governor's passport, set out for Mudnabatty, in company with Mr. Fountain. They stopped at Nuddea, and heard of Mr. Thomas there, as well-known by his preaching and his kindness to the sick. They reached Mudnabatty on the 1st of December, and, by the next morning, Mr. Carey's mind was fully made up to leave the place in which he had so long laboured, and to join the missionary band at Serampore. To do this involved the abandonment of many long cherished hopes of usefulness in the Dinajpur district, the loss of much money laid out at Kidderpur, and the sacrifice of the amount still owing for the premises; but there was no help for it; and, on the 25th of December, he finally quitted Mudnabatty, and set out on the journey to his new home,—the place to which his learning, ability, diligence,

---

* Mr. Brunsdon wrote to Mr. Chamberlain, then a student at the Bristol Academy,—

"This is indeed a land of darkness and the shadow of death. The primate of Bengal seems to think they are too much sunk in sin and ignorance for divine grace to work upon! What views he must entertain of his own nature and of the grace of God! He says, when he came first to this country, he used to try what could be done; but he had then more zeal than knowledge. Oh may I ever remain ignorant as I am, if an increase of knowledge is to abate my zeal and diligence in endeavouring to set before these poor heathens the unsearchable riches of Christ."

and stedfast zeal and piety were soon to give so much celebrity.

On Friday, January 10th, 1800, the travellers reached Serampore; and Mr. Carey was received by Colonel Bie with all the kindness he had already shewn to the rest. He had tried in vain to find a suitable house for them. Then he offered them a piece of land upon which they might build. This they were intending to accept, and meant " to build six mat houses, of three or four rooms each ; a school, a place of worship, and a printing office." But the ground offered them was too small for all this; and consequently they embraced an opportunity which arose, a few days later, to purchase of the Governor's nephew " a large house in the middle of the town." " It consisted of a spacious veranda and hall, with two rooms on each side. Rather more to the front, were two other rooms separate, and on one side was a store house. It stood by the river side, upon a pretty large piece of ground, walled round." For these premises they paid Rs. 6000. Here they were comfortably provided with a home, and were able to arrange to set up their press, and for the school, which for many years to come was a source of great benefit to the European community in the neighbourhood of Calcutta.*

A series of rules for the management of the mission family was immediately drawn up and adopted.† They

---

* The *Calcutta Gazette* for March 20th, 1800, contained this advertisement.

"*MISSION HOUSE*
"SERAMPORE.

" ON THURSDAY, the 1st of May, 1800, a SCHOOL will be opened at this House, which stands in a very healthy and pleasant situation by the side of the river.

"TERMS,
"INCLUDING BOARD AND WASHING,
Per month Sa. Rs.

" Reading, Writing, Arithmetic, Book-keeping, Geography &c.,.... 30
" Latin, Greek, Hebrew, Persian or Songskrit,................... 35

" Particular attention will be paid to the correct pronunciation of the English language.

" A Persian and Songskrit *munshi* will be employed.

" ☞ Letters addressed to MR. CAREY will be immediately attended to."

† As these rules are numerous, only the more important of them are reproduced in this note.

were in some respects unlike those devised at Mudnabatty; but they soon required other modifications, and the history of the Serampore mission proved how little suited to the genius of Baptist missionaries "the Moravian system" was. Those who contend for a very precise adherence to missionary methods, may with advantage compare the plans devised by Mr. Carey at the outset of his missionary life with the actual procedure of his own career, devoted and useful as it was, and with the experience developed by practical contact with his colleagues,—several of whom were remarkably pious and excellent men, and who all exceedingly admired and loved him.

Colonel Bie at once reported to his Government the arrival of the Baptist missionaries, and the encouragement he had given them. A kind response speedily came from Copenhagen. Full permission was accorded to the missionaries to establish themselves at Serampore, and the Governor and Council there were instructed to afford them protection, in the confidence that, as good citizens, they would pay all due obedience to the laws and regulations.

The brethren of the mission form a community, in which no one has the pre-eminence.

Every question relative to the affairs of the Society shall be determined by a majority; to whose determination the minority shall peaceably accede.

Any brother may call a meeting of the brethren in the evening after worship.

Whatever worldly employ the brethren, as a body, may think it expedient to pursue, no one must refuse to take the share assigned him, nor shall any part of the profits arising therefrom be accounted private property, except so appropriated by the majority.

No brother shall engage in any private trade whatever.

Each of the brethren, in rotation, shall superintend the affairs of the family for a month. In case of inability, the next in turn shall supply. This superintendence shall extend to providing for the table, presiding at meals, keeping the family accounts, watching over and paying servants, preserving order and a due observance of family rules, waiting on strangers, and whatever may properly belong to the affairs of the family. The superintendent shall deliver up his accounts the last day of the month, or as soon as possible afterwards.

A prayer-meeting shall be held on the first Monday in the month for the success of the gospel.

Saturday evening, a meeting of the brethren shall be held to consult on the affairs of the family, and promote brotherly love.

All censures shall be passed by a brother selected for the purpose.

CHAPTER XIV.

Cast down, but not destroyed.—1799-1800.

MR. THOMAS's history must now be resumed. Early in November, he removed his residence for a time to Súpúr, not, however, giving up his premises at Etinda, and the fatigue, exposure, and anxiety which he underwent in carrying out his arrangements, resulted in a very alarming illness. He gave the following account of it in a letter to Mr. Carey.

I have been very ill indeed, upon and since the 9th of November. I thought I should never more see your face in the flesh, or write you again. I received a letter from my father on the morning of the 9th, telling me of the death of my last surviving sister. My head became giddy, my heart palpitated, and I set down the palanquin and rested. After having spoken the word of God to the bearers and others who were with me, with much solemnity, I again got into the palanquin, and told them to go on to Mons. Chamboo's, who lives on a mount two *krosh* off. I now felt myself worse and worse; my hands became livid, and I found I was fast going. My pulse stopped, and then went on again, till I was quite unable to proceed further.—I was within two arrow's-shot of the house. I sent for M. Chamboo, and told him I was dying. He gave me vinegar, which revived me. I gave him my letters, and made what I supposed to be my last requests. I had little or no fear, or doubt of mercy, at that moment. I now fell into a fit, or phrensy, and convulsion, tore my palanquin to shivers, wounded my body severely, which wounds and bruises are not even yet healed, and, for three days and three nights, I ate no food, but was insane. I thought I was in heaven; and that heaven was like earth; only all was extasy. I leaped and sang, 'Arrived! Arrived! How came I here?' &c. Much of my talk, indeed almost all of it, was of the rising of the dead, eternity, and future judgment, the millenium, and the spread of the gospel. But He who is a God of order and not the Author of confusion, restored me to my senses on the 12th. About the 14th, I felt myself going off again, at noon, just in the same manner; and I sent for the Doctor who now attended me, and requested him to bleed me. He did so, freely; and I immediately fainted; but received complete relief in my head and heart, and have been very well since. Glory be to God. But I feel my soul touched with a lively solemn sense of death, judgment and eternity to this hour. I feel my soul also restored, quickened, filled. I am satisfied and refreshed, as with living water, marrow and fatness, I was so weak, I could preach to none but those who called and found me out. But now I preach to every body: and, when alone, to myself. If I should gain more than suffices to pay my debts, I continue in the same mind. *I* am not, neither is anything I have, or shall have, *my own*, but the Lord's. I intend to build a factory, about 1000 cubits round, as I am directed to do, also a dwelling house, of necessity, also a place of worship. I have no doubt but God is now working my deliverance by providence and grace, and giving the world one more instance of His patience, forbearance, kindness, and mercy to the evil and unthankful; and may I also through your prayers be, in gentleness to all men, a child of God, not only to the good, but also to the froward. Let us all cease from evil, do good, follow peace and pursue it, cease from anger, noise, and clamour, and awake to righteousness, meekness, love; and Christ shall give down light and life more abundantly than heretofore. I have all things. I want nothing, but that the will of God be done by me and every one of us. I desire to place myself below the least and lowest of all the missionaries, and to lay my mouth in the dust, and humble myself before God and all men, especially among the natives.

Expectation was bright when the foregoing letter was written. His business engagements still promised the most favorable results. In another part of the same letter, he says,—

The Lord has given me Rs. 2000 profit, towards paying my debts; but the sugar is not yet delivered, nor the money paid. It has now pleased the Lord to hear and answer my prayers old and new, offered up ten years ago and since, that He would remember His word, 'The silver and the gold is mine,' and grant me money to pay my debts, and that I may have to give to him that needeth; that I may render to every man his due, and owe no man anything.

It was his cherished desire to present to the younger missionaries an address adapted to stimulate their zeal, and to convey to them the results of his own experience, and he spent much time in writing his thoughts upon Ezekiel xxxvi. 23, in which he dwelt particularly upon these truths, —1. That it is the will of God that the heathen should be brought to the knowledge of Himself; and 2. That there is a divinely ordained connexion between a missionary's holiness and his success. It is far too long to be reproduced here, although in many respects very interesting. The serious attack of mental disease through which he had passed, no doubt indicated a very disordered condition of his system, and he subsequently had many symptoms threatening a similar malady. The hopeful condition of his affairs as indicated in the above extract very speedily underwent a disastrous change. In a later communication, he tells Mr. Carey that there had been a very extensive demand for the sugar which he was buying up, with the prospect of a considerable profit, and he had secured an extensive contract; but, before this could be executed, "news came from England that at the taking of Surinam there was sugar enough for all the markets for a whole year and more!"

About the middle of December, Mrs. Brunsdon, the wife of one of the newly arrived missionaries being very unwell, Mr. Thomas was asked to visit Serampore and to give his advice upon her case. He arrived there on the 20th, and after much pleasant intercourse with his new friends, took Mr. and Mrs. Brunsdon back with him to Súpúr. The change of place speedily restored the invalid, and there was much to interest the young missionaries in the labours Mr. Thomas conducted, and in the attention those labours excited amongst all classes around them. A congregation of sometimes nearly three hundred people attended his preaching every Sunday, and large numbers assembled to hear the gospel wherever it was preached in the neighbourhood. Many hearers seemed to be powerfully impressed. A *gosain* and several of his disciples heard the gospel and appeared to be inclined to accept it. Mr.

Thomas's East Indian assistant, Mr. Carlo, gave some evidence of a change of heart, and his neighbour, M. Chamboo, at whose doors he had suffered his late alarming attack of mania, appeared to be casting aside his deistical opinions and had anxiously procured a French bible. The *gosain* composed Christian hymns, and sang them with his people; and a movement in favor of the gospel seemed to be going on, which it was hoped would issue in most satisfactory results.

Many very interesting accounts might be quoted in illustration of these statements, but the reader may well be weary of the history of promises never fulfilled and of hopeful occurrences issuing only in bitter disappointment.

Mr. and Mrs. Brunsdon returned to Serampore towards the end of February, and, on the 8th of March, Mr. Thomas also went there. It was an unspeakable pleasure to him to see Mr. Carey again, and to join with the brethren in preaching, prayer and conference. But the object for which he visited the neighbourhood of Calcutta was to endeavour to arrange his miserably entangled affairs. He had given up the indigo factory at Cooleadean without obtaining a legal release from the responsibilities its occupation involved. In the sugar business, he had not been sustained by the necessary remittances, and had therefore obtained help from others to carry on distilling, but he now found his partner claiming the right to share in that to which he had contributed neither labour nor capital. He seems to have effected no settlement of any of his difficulties; but he was politely treated, and the evils which threatened him were at any rate postponed.

The day before he went back to Bírbhúm, Mr. Thomas visited the place where he held his interesting conference with a college of Brahmans, in January, 1792. The place was not far from Serampore, and he wished to bring the Brahmans into friendly intercourse with the missionaries. He found the students busy learning. Many of them immediately recognized him, and two accompanied him to Serampore, to see his brethren there. It appeared but too evident, however, that their motives were mercenary, and nothing came of this interesting endeavour. What a series of bright expectations, utterly disappointed by the results, did the early history of the Indian mission present!

As he travelled back to Bírbhúm, his mind was greatly troubled by all these discouragements, and he wrote in his journal,—

My most ardent addresses fail, and my heart despairs within me when I think of speaking again to men steeped in blasphemy, prejudice, and sin, and hardened in all. Some do feel emotions visibly; but they soon disappear, and leave them more insensible than ever.

If the Almighty has any people to save by me among the Hindus, He will still carry me on through and over these discouragements. Perhaps He will meet my very determination to preach no more by His word running into all my bones, like fire, and make me as weary of forbearing, as I am now of preaching in vain, and will, in some other unknown or unexpected way, bring it to pass, and they shall be converted.

If He has none to save by my ministry; yet this is no proof that I may neglect it; for *who* preached and worked miracles at Chorazin and Bethsaida? all which failed to convince and convert; yet who is bold enough to assert that any of the doctrines there preached or the miracles there wrought were preached and wrought in vain? Grant me, O Jesus, thy light, and give me patience and zeal still. Give me wisdom to follow thee, that thou mayest yet make me one of thy 'fishers of men.'

Amidst all discouragements and doubts, therefore, he continued to exhort all around him; and, but for the dread of too greatly enlarging this narrative, many interesting details, regarding both his preaching and his benevolent efforts to heal the diseases of the poor sufferers who every where resorted to him for help, might be given.

His temporal circumstances did not improve, and he was every way discouraged. Out of many interesting enquirers at Súpúr only two remained, one of whom, a sugar boiler, Fakír *mistrí*, seemed to be very hopeful still. A letter to Mr. Carey, dated June 23d, says:—

All my temporal concerns turn out as theirs did of old, to whom the Lord said, 'Ye looked for much; and, lo, it came to little.' The

Lord blows upon it, and smites all the labour of my hands, and I know not what to do, where to flee, or how to change my course. To sit down in debt, and do nothing, seems not right. To preach the gospel to the heathen is still pleasant; but, oh, how dried their bones are! Oh how far off! As to my soul, it is like a garden much neglected; but I hope the tree of liberty is planted in it—the tree of life, I mean; because I find still, though all things are so, and though I have now no prospect of any temporal comforts any more, such as I have had; yet I can find reason to be very thankful and glad in the midst of all; for the word of God is a marvellous light in this darkness.—Habakkuk iii. 17-19, and Micah vii. 8.— I murmur less and hope more. Therefore, seeing that His sweetest mercies are yet lengthened out to me, I conclude that His compassions fail me not, because,—Oh wonder of wonders,—having loved me and given Himself for me, He will never leave nor forsake me utterly, and because He helps me by faith to take for my great wants, out of the fulness of Christ, that righteousness and grace that is sufficient for me. And my hope is in Him; and this hope I find keeps my prayers from sinking after rising, like arrows shot short of the mark; for my Intercessor's incense which He offers up with the prayers of all saints, is enough to make the poorest prayers of the very least of them a sweet smelling savour unto God. One so poor and low as I in religion, who has nothing at all to trust to, is forced to go to Christ for grace, faith and promises, having nought besides. There is indeed nothing for me to hope upon in all my past life, or present endeavours, or future performances, but what has turned out in the fiery trial to be dry wood, hay, and stubble.

At the end of July, he was again in Calcutta, endeavouring to bring his perplexed affairs into order, with, as will be supposed, very little success. Still matters seemed to assume a brighter aspect; and pleasant intercourse with his brethren at Serampore greatly cheered his spirits. The gospel of Matthew,—in the main his own translation,—was now actually printed in Bengali, and copies were ready for distribution. He was able at last to send Mr. Samuel Davis some copies of the book he had so long ago encouraged him to publish, and could take a supply with him to give to enquirers wherever he met them. He was cheered too by receiving letters from his relations, with a kind message from Dr. Ryland, to whom, as he was returning to Birbhúm, he wrote in the following terms of his troubles and present prospects.—

I thought I should have been delivered before, but such is my peculiar depravity that if the Lord had granted my desire when I wished it, I should have been ruined. I required stroke upon stroke. I have been brought very low, and thought it very strange. Brute as I was, the Lord's hand held me up from utter despair; but I had almost gone! I began to look upon myself as forsaken of God and man; nay worse, if worse can be. I saw all things working together against me. *That was flesh, and sense, and sight.* Now I kiss, and bless, and hear the rod. *This is faith.* The difference between the two kinds of experience is like the difference between a taste of hell and a taste of heaven. In the one, it appears as if there was no God; or, if there is, He is against you. In the other, it appears strongly there is a God, there is none like Him, none besides Him. He is all in all. Wherever you look, you see Him; wherever you are, you enjoy Him; and in whatever is yet to come, you expect Him. In the former condition it is impossible to praise Him. In the latter it is impossible to refrain. Glory, honour, blessing, and praise will spring out of the heart,—will come out of your mouth. And this is my present condition. All things turn to His praise. I am all the day amazed at the goodness, the mercy, and the glory of God in Christ, all in all. I wish—I do not know whether I dare wish. I know He who satisfieth the desires of every living thing, will fulfil every pure wish; but I hardly know what it is yet to wish for His glory,—but more or less for the sake of my own, and this is poison. O thanks be to God for a Christ lifted up.—But I was going to say, I wish I could tell you of many souls saved here by coming to Christ; but I cannot. Yet I can tell you of tokens for good. Our heavenly Father would never reveal his Son in us in this manner among the heathen for nothing. But we know the word of God that whenever He is so revealed that sinful men behold His glory and are changed into His image, then God is glorified in them; and when God is glorified in us, I think, the result we long for cannot be far off; because of that sure word in Ezekiel,—'The heathen shall know that I am the Lord, saith the Lord God, when I shall be sanctified in you before their eyes.'

The mission sustained a severe loss in the death of Mr. Fountain, on the 20th of August. He had been induced to go to Moypaldiggy, to undertake the charge of the factory, as Mr. Powell was leaving it to join Mr. Fernandez at Dinájpur. He had been ill at Serampore, but now his disorder became worse. He was taken to Mr. Fernandez's house and there, after a few days, he expired. Mr. Thomas felt the event deeply. A letter which he wrote to Mr. Carey in reference to it, gives an interesting account of labours carried on at Etinda, where his family now resided, and of his hopes, particularly of Fakír *mistri*. Of his own spiritual state he gives the following description :—

My walk is all fits and starts, jumps and hot extasies, slips and cold fits. Yet, after all, through the unsearchable riches of the grace of God in Christ Jesus, I believe that I shall be saved.

His temporal prospects seemed for a little to revive after his return; but very soon he found himself in more serious difficulties than ever. Without money, it was impossible to carry forward his factory; and there was no market for his manufactures. At the beginning of October, he was again obliged to go to Calcutta, and he now took his wife and daughter with him. After arriving at Serampore, on Friday, the 10th, he read with intense interest a small book which gave an account of some remarkable revivals of religion, in America.* As the result, he came amongst his brethren, in Mr. Ward's words, "with a sweet savour of divine things on his mind." His soul was inflamed with desire for a revival of God's work in himself and his brethren, and he induced them to establish a weekly prayer meeting, to be held every Tuesday morning, with the especial object of imploring the gift of God, the Holy Spirit, to co-operate in all their labours. This meeting was sustained for many years and was, without doubt, a source of great spiritual blessing to the mission.

But nothing could be done to avert the disaster which had befallen Mr. Thomas's secular business. On the 17th of October, he wrote,—

I see no use of going on in this; no prospect of anything else; no hope but in God. I see no way out; but He may. I know not what to do, nor where to go. The Lord now gives me comfortable exercises in His word, but in nothing else. No answer of prayer

---

* Glorious News! A brief Account of the late Revivals of Religion in a number of Towns in the New England States, and also in Nova Scotia. Philadelphia, January, 1800.

respecting my temporal affairs. Yet will I wait *on* Him, and wait *for* Him, and look to Him. He has the hearts of all men in his hands. He is rich.

Some previous extracts have displayed the confidence and joy which, amidst many trials, Mr. Thomas was able to realize. The following will show how extreme was his dejection in this time of tribulation.

October 25th.— Oh what a wretched being am I! A burden to myself; a vile cumberer of God's earth ; a plague and weariness to many of my friends ; without any relish of life. All this week, I have been tossed, afflicted, and not comforted. The hand of God hath touched me. He bloweth again on my hopes and labours, and blasts them all, and I know not what to do, or where to go. I am weary. My life is a burden to me. Every beast of the field, and every fowl that flies in the air is happier than I am.

Is there no hope ? No relief ? No helper ? No refuge ?——What is the use of a refuge to him that does not flee to it ? Is there no God ?——What is the use of having a God that can save, that can deliver, that does deliver, and will deliver, if I regard iniquity in my heart, if I ask amiss ?

Somehow or other, God is 'a very present help in time of trouble ;' but I do not find Him so. And what is the reason of it ? His hand presseth me sore, instead of relieving me, and is there not a cause ?

'Because thou hast forgotten the God of thy salvation, and hast not been mindful of the Rock of thy strength, therefore.'——Isaiah xvii. 10.

The next morning " hope and quietness" revived ; but, in the miserable condition of his affairs, it will not be matter of surprise that he was often terribly cast down. It is pleasant to see that, amidst all his perplexities and sorrows, he never manifested any disposition to charge God foolishly. The Lord was always justified, whilst he acknowledged with shame his own evil deserts.

Whilst in the neighbourhood of Calcutta, he enjoyed much intercourse with the brethren at Serampore, and his journal contains interesting notices of their engagements in preaching to the heathen and in devotional exercises amongst themselves. One extract may be given.—

November 7th.—Attended the experience meeting. Spoke of my

consolations. Brother Carey spoke of his gifts dying away, &c., in such a manner as amazed me. Brother Marshman also spoke of the fulness he knew in Jesus Christ; but complained in rather a desultory way of not finding his way into it. I left the room with fear and humiliation. The sisters complained also. Most of their complaints ran in one line: that they found so little in themselves. I deeply sympathise, and hope they will soon be delivered. But it sounded to me like the branch of a tree saying, 'Alas, in what a wretched state am I! Were I to fall to that ground, what should I do? I fear I shall; and then I have no body; no trunk; no root; no sap; and I must wither and die!' not once recollecting the sap as its own. O Lord, make bare thine arm. Reveal thyself.

On the 21st of November Mr. Thomas met his friend Mr. Burney once more. He was now head-master of the Orphan School for officers' sons, which had been removed from Howrah to Kidderpore, a southern suburb of Calcutta. It was delightful to the poor troubled missionary to meet one to whom his early ministry had been blessed, after so long a time, and to talk with him about the progress of gospel truth in the neighbourhood of Calcutta. He says in his journal,—

I was glad to find a man, after fourteen years standing, all alive, strict and conscientious, deeply humble, swift to hear, rejoicing in Christ Jesus, having no confidence in the flesh. Rejoiced to hear that he expounds, with prayer, the word of life to all the children under his care; and that one of them, now gone to Patna, had been found in secret, praying; and he gave other consistent reasons to hope that his humble labours among the children had not been in vain in the Lord. Rejoiced to hear that one. Michael, a Portuguese, assembles a few people of this tongue, in his house, and expounds the word to them, with prayer. Also that a Mr. Da Costa, a Portuguese, discovers a similar disposition. A Portuguese Protestant also preaches at the mission church every Lord's-day morning, in Portuguese.—After about two hours fervid, soul-renewing communications with Mr. Burney, I departed.

That night, Mr. Thomas lodged at the house of Mr. Robertson, a cooper, with whom he had business transactions, and he mentions with peculiar interest the fact that he "slept, or rather lay, in the very room where the Lord called him to be a missionary, and where he had prayed all night." What a review of humiliating disappointments and failures must his sleepless meditations there have embraced, as he thought over all that had happened since January, 1787. Now, in lowly contrition, he renewed his vows; and, he asked, since the Lord had withheld from him success in all his efforts to extricate himself from debt,—since every attempt after gain had but increased his indebtedness,—was it not right that he should abstain from further endeavours to make money, even for his creditors, and simply apply himself to his missionary work? So it seemed to him now. He would try and support himself and family upon the annual £100 allowed by him by the Society, and, as to his creditors, in his own utter helplessness regarding their claims, let the Lord do as seemed good in His sight. He trusted that His providence might yet open the way to his emancipation from debt. He laid before his brethren, early the next week, the following "five reasons for giving up all trade and business."

1. God has called me to the ministry. To me is this grace given, that I should preach the unsearchable riches of Christ amongst the heathen. My heart turns away from all other pursuits with disgust, and follows this with delight. God has owned my labours, though few.

2. Missionary work requires a man to give himself to the word and to prayer wholly, and to reckon other good employments as 'serving tables.' What is the chaff to the wheat?

3. The business I have been engaged in has been a very great hindrance to my great work.

4. The Lord hath blown upon all my labours in trade, and nothing has ever prospered.

5. My time is short: I shall die soon, or become old and feeble. My days are over, and I need employ every hour, and lay out every moment to the best advantage to redeem the time I have left. Amen.

On the other hand, there are my debts, and it is my duty to pay, and to owe no man anything.

So entangled were his affairs, that it is no marvel that his missionary brethren found it almost impossible to give him any counsel, in a matter involving such difficulties.

On the whole, however, he concluded that they inclined to his present opinion.

He now therefore drew from the Society a year's allowance, which, at the very unfavorable rate of exchange then current, gave him but Rs. 800, and resolved to apply himself wholly and actively to the work of evangelization. That he might do this in the most economical and efficient way, he resolved to assume the Bengali dress, to travel like a native, and to go from village to village, preaching and distributing gospels and tracts as opportunity offered. His Bengali outfit was at once purchased, at the cost of Rs. 16-3½, and he was eager to set forth upon his expedition. His communications with his brethren at Serampore appear to have been very delightful to him. He met them frequently in fervent prayer, and was stimulated by this fellowship to ardent devotedness. His journal speaks of the blessedness he enjoyed in secret also, when he sought the Lord " in Carey's bower." "There," he wrote,—

He granted me sweet access to Himself early in the morning, and, though I am so vile, He restoreth my soul daily, and makes this my joy, that He is *that He is*, and there is none like Him, none besides Him. Amen. Compassed as I am with clouds and darkness, God is light to me; and light enough. Though in want, I am contented. Though disturbed, I am at peace and in quietness. Though in need, I have all and abound.

On Tuesday morning, the 25th, the weekly prayer meeting which he had induced his brethren to establish was held. They asked him to pray, and before doing so he delivered a short address upon the Lord's Prayer, which shall be introduced here. It embodies the meditations which occupied his mind as he lay awake the preceding night.

Whoever can say the Lord's Prayer aright, will be saved; for none can say to him, 'You are of your father, the devil, and his lusts you will do.' He is a child of God, and God is his *Father who is in heaven*. His Father's name, his Father's kingdom, and his Father's will occupy the first place in his prayers, the first place in his thoughts, and first place in his proceedings. *Hallowed be Thy name*. Seeking first the kingdom of God and His righteousness,—his own supplies for soul and body are secondary things: his own name, his own interest, his own will, come easily to be .

as nothing, so that the name of God be sanctified, the kingdom of God advanced, and the will of God be done. *Thy kingdom come.* Like persons unskilled in physic, who yield up their own will, and the management of themselves, to the superior skill of an eminent physician ; or like a person in a law-suit, giving up easily his whole case, his reputation in the law, his wishes, into the counsellor's hand, and submitting to be guided by his judgment, even so does the believer say to his heavenly Father,—*Thy will be done!* Such a man also is contented with a little ; and knowing that he wants that for to-day only, he is not anxious for the morrow ; but says,— *Give us this day our daily bread!* The necessaries of life are all he wants : he does not ask for the conveniences, and he despises the luxuries of it. He has such a heart-affecting sense of his own sins against God, beholding the magnitude and number of them, that he looks upon an insult, an injury, or an affront, from a fellow-creature, as a very little thing, and is ready to forgive it. He forgives from his very heart ; and is so clear in this matter, that he can say to the Searcher of hearts,—*Forgive us our sins, as we forgive them that trespass against us!* Withal he is so humble, and so sensible still of his own frailty and of the weakness and wickedness of his depraved human disposition, that he begs of God,—*Lead us not into temptation,* lest he fall ; *but deliver us from the evil* within us, which he is so apprised of.

But that to which I would direct your minds and my own this morning, as an encouragement in prayer, is this, The arguments which our Saviour teaches us to use with God, and the reasons why He should hear us and do for us as we ask :—*For thine is the kingdom.* This kingdom is of thine own right-hand planting, and thou hast set thy King upon thy holy hill of Zion. Thou hast commanded all the ends of the earth to look to Him, and be saved ; to hear Him ; to behold the Lamb of God, that taketh away the sins of the world ; and to come to Him for righteousness, life, and salvation.

Hear us, and do as we ask ; for *Thine is the power,* to lead us into this kingdom, and to bring in the heathen. Above all, *Thine is the glory.*—Though we deserve nothing, yet, for thine own name's sake, thou hast promised to hear us, and to grant our petition.

And further : we ask, for Jesus Christ hath bid us ask. As I told Fakír yesterday, ' Suppose you were to go to Mr. Carey, and ask him for two gold mohurs ; you would go with doubts and fears, lest you should not be able to obtain ; and even if you did obtain what you asked, would he not say, ' *Mistri,* I owe you nothing ?'

And would you not expect to be brought to an account hereafter, like the men with the talents? But if *I* bid you go for two gold mohurs, you go in my name: you have access and boldness, without fear, without doubt, because I bid you go; and you ask in my name, not your own; on my account, and not your own.*—So it is in prayer: if we go in our own name, we have fear and distrust; for He owes us nothing: but if we go in the name of Jesus, we go boldly; we have access; we expect supplies; saying and remembering, that Jesus Christ bid us go to His Father, and ask.

Brethren, we are now come to ask of God His Holy Spirit! Let us ask in His name who sent us hither. This is God's own appointment, and He is faithful who hath promised. He is punctual to his *time*:—*this* is the time; for we are in trouble about the mission. 'Call upon me in the day of trouble: I will deliver thee, and thou shalt glorify me.' God is punctual to *place*:—and *this* is the place, where two or three are gathered together in His name. And He is punctual to His *promise*:—'*Ye shall* receive.' Let us draw nigh then.

On the same day, he mentions, with evident delight the success of his attempt to adopt the Bengali dress. After putting it on, he walked through various parts of Serampore and visited several acquaintances, particularly the missionaries, who did not recognise him, but treated him as a Bengali. The natives themselves looked upon him as one of their own people, and men and women talked freely with him, supposing him, from his complexion and speech, to have come from the North-Western provinces.

Fakír *mistrí* had come with Mr. Thomas down to Serampore; and all the brethren were much pleased with what they saw of him. A few sentences may be quoted from Mr. Brunsdon's notice of him, which are interesting as pointing out what has often since been observed with deep concern in the case of Hindu converts. He says, "He certainly appears very different from the rest of the natives; but there seems to be no sense of guilt in him. He is full of love. The salvation of Christ appears to be a very delightful subject to him. I have thought that perhaps

---

* This illustration is explained by an entry in the journal of November 24th, "Paid to Mr. Carey eight gold mohurs, to be kept in his hand for me, and repaid when I return."

any who are awakened here may not be filled with that distress for sin which is common elsewhere. These people have hardly any idea of moral good or evil, and till they have learned this, they will lack enlarged views of the desperate depravity of their hearts, and the criminality of their conduct in the sight of God. The salvation of Christ may nevertheless fill them with joy." On the 25th of November, Fakír was formally accepted for baptism. He seemed to be sincere and disinterested, and all hoped,— especially he who was most deeply interested in him,— that at length the grace of God had subdued the fatal obstacles which had hitherto withstood the thorough conversion of a Hindu. Mr. Thomas had soon to return for a short time to Etinda. It was arranged that Fakír, who was a widower, should go with him, and bring away his little girl. On coming back to Serampore, he was to be baptized.

Next day, the journal contains an interesting entry.—

I was sent for to set a man's arm, a Hindu. I found it to be a dislocation of the shoulder. I tied his body to a tree, and while brethren Carey and Marshman made the usual extension, I reduced it, so that he could move the arm, though it was still painful. This man had heard the gospel. When his arm was set right, he complained still of the pain, but more of himself, as a sinner; and, with many tears, cried out, 'I am a great sinner! A great sinner am I! Save me, Sahib! save me!' Then with unusual light and enlargement of soul, I renounced all power to save him myself, and referred him to Jesus, *my* Saviour, of whose mission and power to save all those who come unto God by Him I spoke many things, but chiefly on the knowledge, confession, and forsaking of sin, of obtaining righteousness and liberty, by and through Him, as a free gift. I explained His command to all men everywhere to repent and believe; but still more pointedly dwelt on the command to confess, the tendency this had to forsaking sin, and the promise of God belonging to it, that such a sinner should find mercy.— Proverbs xxviii. 13. I made him repeat that text; but he failed about ten times, which I pointed out to brother Ward as an instance of their being a people slow of understanding, dull of hearing, not having their senses exercised to discern good and evil, and whose minds are like iron, impenetrable till red-hot, and requiring repetitions, 'line upon line.' In order to impress this man's memory the more, I called it 'THE TRUE GAYATRI,' which if any man could pronounce rightly, acting upon it, he would be saved, and he only. It was reduced at last to this form :—

পাপ সিকার করিলে	He that confesseth his sins,
পাপ ত্যাগ করিলে	And forsakes them,
যেশুর ধর্ম্ম পাইলে	Obtaining the righteousness of Jesus,
মুক্ত হয়।	Is free.

This is easy to be understood, and, having been explained well in an itinerating sermon, it may be left behind as a good key to the law and gospel; for no man can confess or forsake his sins till he know them: no man can know them without the law, for 'the strength of sin is the law:' no man can be delivered from the law and sin, but by the gospel: and he who believes the gospel, is a righteous person, made free from sin by the Son of God, and therefore free indeed.

In the evening, accompanied by Ward, Brundson, and Felix, he went out in his native dress, and "preached the Gáyatri." After another visit to the house of the man whose arm he had set, the night found him in " the bower," and he " enjoyed access to the Lord, where He had often met him."

Next day, at noon, he left Serampore, with the cordial prayers and good wishes of all his brethren, and began his missionary tour. He had intended to go on foot, but he found that he could travel as cheaply and much more conveniently, as far as Cutwa, in a small boat; and one was engaged for twelve annas a day. What heavy cares he carried with him, however he travelled! "As I am indebted in great sums of money, to several persons," he wrote, "and have no prospect of paying them, without some special help of God; and as I have prayed for, and do expect this, I am still in doubt about the way I ought to take : whether I ought to give up all and devote myself to the mission only, or not; and as I cannot give up the mission with any comfort of conscience, nor give myself wholly to it without giving up every thing else, therefore I intend to read through the whole Bible, seeking for that direction I have asked. O Lord, cause me to find out my duty in that word which thou hast given as a lamp to my feet, and a light to my path."

We cannot follow the several stages of this journey. He proceeded up the river, with Fakír and Kingkar, a Brahman from the neighbourhood of Cutwa, of whose conversion he had strong hopes. He stopped at every place where a good audience could be hoped for, preaching abundantly, with great ardour, and with most encouraging results in the interest he everywhere excited. He had, for distribution, copies of the gospel of Matthew, of the new *Gáyatri*, of the Bengali translation of Pearce's *Letter to the Musalmans*, and of Ram Basu's *Harkará*, a poetical tract, intended as an introduction to the gospel, which this singular man had written and presented to the missionaries.* Never had he been so well equipped before. Printed books were strange to the Bengalis then, and he soon found reason to think that those he gave away would have been received with more favor had they been more thoroughly native in shape and appearance. At Gúptipára, a pandit told him that he would have read the gospel to his pupils, if only it had been in a shastra-like form, *i. e.* with each page consisting of six or eight very long lines.

From Cutwa he went on foot to Etinda, preaching all the way, and with such enlargement of heart, melancholy as was the prospect before him there, that "all the road," he said, "was like the way to heaven." He reached his house on the 6th of December, and remained there about a week. Fakír left him to go to his home and make arrangements with his family, after which he said he would accompany his teacher back to Serampore.

During his travellings, Mr. Thomas had thought of a scheme for his future support, which he trusted would combine great usefulness with some considerable pecuniary profit. This was the publication of a monthly magazine in English. He calculated on getting at least one hun-

---

* It is worthy of remark that this tract has ever since been useful both in its Bengali form and in translation into other Indian languages. In Orissa, the *Jewel Mine of Salvation*, as it is now called, has been instrumental in the conversion of many readers.

dred subscribers, and with not a little zeal he set about the preparation of papers for the original department of the periodical. His plan is thus stated to a friend in Bírbhúm, whose patronage he solicited:—

On the last of January, I begin to publish an *Evangelical Magazine*, monthly, consisting of forty pages at least, on good paper and in fair type; chiefly compiled from a work of that title published in England, in which some of the first divines of every denomination join; so that it contains all the principal events that happen in the religious world, with anecdotes and an obituary, chiefly relating to the remarkable deaths of such persons as die triumphantly or otherwise. To this will be annexed monthly interesting anecdotes and dialogues with the natives, discovering more of the principles of their religion and the bad influence of these on their practices than has been yet made known to the world. This work to be delivered in Calcutta the last day of every month, at Rs. 2 per month. It has proved a very useful publication in England, and I am in hopes it may, through the blessing of God, be much more so here, where advantages for the Christian religion are fewer.

He left Etinda on the 13th of December, having made such arrangements with his servants and the money lender there as a moneyless man could. He travelled back to Cutwa on foot, and thence took boat to Serampore, preaching all the way, and meeting with very much encouragement to believe that many of his hearers were deeply impressed by the truths he brought to their ears. His journey was laborious; but he rejoiced in the belief that, since he began it, many thousands had been taught something of the grace of our Lord Jesus Christ by his endeavours.

On the 17th of December, he again reached Serampore; but without Fakír. Alas, like so many unfaithful ones before him, he had disappointed the hope that he would come out from heathendom and, leaving all things for the truth's sake, become the Lord's servant. The mission families at Serampore were in very great distress and alarm, owing to the dangerous state of Mr. Brundson. With a malignant fever preying upon him, he had been longing for Mr. Thomas's return, feeling quite sure that he could relieve him. And now he had come, two or three days earlier than was expected; and it was believed that this was in answer to prayer, When he saw the sick man, he felt that there was no time to lose. "He had that twitching of the tendons, with glaring eyes and delirium, which few recover from." Mr. Thomas, with the consent of the doctor who had been in attendance, at once put the sufferer into a hot bath; and the result was his immediate relief. He was, however, in a most critical state, and although Mr. Thomas was greatly wearied with his toilsome journeyings, and with incessant preaching and prolonged exposure to the sun, for so many days previously, he now sat up the whole night with his beloved patient, and wrote in his journal: "This, I feel, is my joy, that I should be permitted to be a comfort and service to the body of His saints."

The next morning, a letter from Mr. Fuller was given him, dated August 25th, 1799. It was late in coming, and it reproached him with his long continued silence, which he had already broken; but there was no delay in replying now. He sat down at once to write, although he had had no sleep since his arrival. He thanked Mr. Fuller for his letter, "stripes and all." The worthy Secretary had said that Mr. Thomas's procedure in leaving Moypaldiggy "conveyed an idea of the mission being only a secondary object with him." His humble rejoinder was, "It may appear so; but, still, if the Society were to leave me, and every mortal upon the earth, I, nevertheless, had rather die in the mission work than live upon the wealth of all India out of it." In reply to some expressions of sympathy with him in his disappointments and in the great difficulty of the missionary work, he related the recent case of Fakír, adding, "I think there is a work of grace in Kingkar, a Brahman, in Mohan *poddár*, and perhaps in Gholám *mistrí*. Brother Carey also has hopes of several; *and if all these should fail, and as many more,* WE SHALL THEN BEGIN AGAIN, 'KNOWING,' *what we cannot prove, perhaps,* 'THAT OUR LABOUR IS NOT IN VAIN IN THE LORD.' We are not sufficiently humbled, perhaps, yet; but, blessed be God, we shall be; and we know it." Surely such words revealed a very noble spirit of faith and undying devotedness to the work of the Lord.

In the afternoon of the same day, he went with some of his brethren across the river, and preached to groups of hearers near Barrackpore. He was delighted on this occasion to hear Mr. Marshman speak Bengali "so very feelingly, so fluently, so well to be understood, and so far beyond all expectation, considering the time he had been learning it." At night, there was a conference of the missionaries, at which he introduced his new project of a monthly magazine. All his brethren seemed to approve ; but some doubts were expressed as to his stedfastness in carrying on the periodical. These he strove to remove by assurances of his unchanging purpose to be punctual ; and he wrote in his diary, " O Lord, think of me for good, and bring this promise to my mind, and give me a faithful, stedfast, humble heart to perform it."

He was engaged the next morning in looking for a small house where his family might live at Serampore, and he succeeded in finding one. To his great joy, Mr. Brunsdon, although exceedingly reduced in strength, was still improving. A visit from an English gentleman to the mission house filled him with affectionate and prayerful interest, since it appeared that, though the visitor made no pretensions to piety himself, he had been a pupil of "that great man of God, his former correspondent, Mr. Ryland of Northampton." Was it not to be hoped that the seed sown by that excellent teacher might yet be fruitful, even in a heathen land !

But visitors of yet greater interest came afterwards. These were Krishna Pál, the man whose dislocated arm he had set on the 26th of November, and his friend Gokul. Both professed a firm conviction of the truth of the gospel. Mr. Thomas was delighted with each of them, but especially with Krishna, who spoke with deep emotion of the day his arm was set, and of the words then addressed to him. "I shall never forget them," he said ; "Oh, how they have softened my heart. I am a very great sinner, Sahib ; but I have confessed my sins ; I have obtained righteousness of Jesus Christ; and I am free." "This," wrote Mr. Thomas, "was saying the *Gáyatri*, with a witness!" Both men declared themselves quite ready to relinquish caste and be baptized. Here was an unexpected blessing! In the contemplation of it, his heart was filled with rapturous gratitude and joy.

That afternoon, he, Mr. Ward, and Felix Carey went to Krishna's house. Felix, of whose piety they were all well assured, had never yet been able to overcome his youthful timidity, so as to preach the gospel. Now, at Mr. Thomas's urgent request, he did so, and spoke, "leaning his hand on Mr. Ward." Gokul, Krishna, and the women of the family were eager listeners, and when Mr. Thomas afterwards addressed them, taking up the stripling's words and enlarging upon them, many tears were shed. The missionaries then found a congregation of attentive hearers "under the great cotton tree," and having distributed papers, they came away weary, but "abundantly cheered in soul!"

"What a day has this been!" wrote Mr. Thomas in his diary. "It is now midnight, but it is still noon-tide with me."

We must not multiply particulars. His days passed thus,—in anxious watching over Mr. Brunsdon,—in exciting interviews with Krishna and Gokul,—in laborious preaching to the heathen,—in eager conferences with his missionary brethren,—and in fervent wrestling supplications at the throne of divine grace. Quiet and refreshment for his wearied body appeared to be of no importance amidst the spiritual interests which claimed his whole heart and filled his thoughts. On Sunday morning, he preached from 1 Thessalonians v. 17,—"Pray without ceasing." His emotions were almost incontrollable; but he asked for God's help, and believed that he received it. Afterwards, Krishna and Gokul came to the mission house, and since some of the missionaries appeared still to mistrust their sincerity, Mr. Thomas put it to the test by inviting them to come the next day and deliberately relinquish caste by eating with the brethren there.

From a letter written this day to his friend the Rev. W. Staughton of Philadelphia, a few characteristic sentences must be extracted. They describe the men who were engaged in the mission; and the reader will not fail to observe the generous commendation which now, as always, the writer bestowed upon his colleagues.

Brother FOUNTAIN was called away from us a few months since, and brother GRANT about a year ago. But there remain now, the indefatigable CAREY, a man made on purpose for the work;—Mr. MARSHMAN, a good scholar, a circumspect Christian, a diligent, persevering man, with a soul easily put into motion by every fresh view of the abominations and perishing condition of the heathen, on the one hand, and by every ray of hope of their salvation by any means, on the other;—Mr. WARD, a printer, a regular, warm Christian; zealous without enthusiasm; a man of a circumspect walk, with a care of souls upon him; a man acquainted with the fulness and freeness of sovereign grace, and the efficacy of appointed ordinances; one that ploughs, sows, and harrows, without forgetting the rain and the sun,—and one that remembers the rain and the sun, without forgetting to plough;— Mr. BRUNSDON, a man of a warm heart, lively feelings, good natural abilities, laborious and very promising;—and, lastly, one JOHN THOMAS. This man has one ground of hope at the very opening of that text,—1 Corinthians i. 28.—'And base things of the world, and things which are despised, hath God chosen, yea, and things which are not, to bring to nought things that are.'

On Monday, according to the invitation given to Gokul and Krishna, they came; and the decisive act was performed. At length then the barrier of caste was broken! Mr. Thomas's delight was unspeakable. In an ecstasy, he wrote in his journal,—

This blessed day, thrice blessed blessed day, I praise the most high God, Possessor of heaven and earth; for Gokul and Krishna have thrown away their caste! Yesterday, I was so confident that the time was come, that all my brethren imputed it to my too sanguine disposition,—which also Mr. Grant complained of. But, O my God, what had my disposition to do in this matter? or what my polluted hand? or what any arm of flesh? No hand was here but Thine. Thou alone hast done it, when some of us least expected it; and I was not too sanguine in Thee, neither can any ever be. I'll tell you how it was; for the sweepings of the house must be kept (Psalm cii. 14), because the time is come when the servants of the Lord take pleasure therein. Yea, the set time is come, the time to favor Zion, the time when the heathen shall fear the name of the Lord, and all kings of the earth His glory.— Who would not wait for this? Oh how unutterable is my joy! But, lest I be exalted above measure, some terrible messenger is at hand!—Welcome, good messenger, terror along! for my soul is not afraid. He who sent thee knows I want thee; why should I refuse thee? Sing, soul, sing. O sing quite aloud, that all the heavens may sing along. All the heavens, sing! All the earth shall sing.—Not all, but some;—and why not all? for 'tis the Lord.——*

The incoherence of the above is followed by even more unmistakeable evidences of insanity. This long-craved blessing, of seeing Hindus led by the love of the truth as it is in Christ Jesus really to abandon their accursed caste—that evil which had hitherto thwarted all his endeavours and blighted so many fond hopes,—coming, as it now did, in connexion with so much bodily exhaustion,

---

* The whole of this day's entry might be quoted as a psychological curiosity. It exhibits nothing but the extravagancies of a disordered mind, conversant with the Bible, and with the hopes and disappointments of missionary life. But as he wrote on in delirious joy, his words arranged themselves in a wild cadence, and an unstudied rhyme, as though his very heart was dancing within him. The history of Nehemiah had often been pondered by him, in his "great affliction and reproach," owing to the failure of his best efforts. See how he turns the elements of the same story to account now in his disordered triumph. He wrote, "Let all the people sing for joy! and yet not all, but some. And why not all? for 'tis indeed the Lord. Why thy head so much cast down? Why cast down to-day? Why cast down the more for this? Pray, what's thy name and nature, man? 'Tis poor Tobiah's look! And who are you, so sad, so low? Ah, poor Sanballat! Fie! Pray where's your foxes? Where's the wall,—that one poor fox will now throw down,—if down it comes at all? Sing a song of fifteen years, —if, my soul, thou canst, for tears.—Sing of hope, and sing of doubt.—Sing how all is well made out.—All but poor Tobiah sing.—All but poor Sanballat sing......Oh, the joy! The fifteen years seem fifteen moments now; and, Oh, the joy, it seems to me as if 'twould never go.—Alas, Fakír,—if thou wast here,—sure all thy fear—would flee away;—for see, 'tis day,—and night's for ever chased away. But not for all!—Yes, yes, to all;—and not alone to you, Bengal.—I said, To-day,—and they said, Aye.—Away, away,—they throw away, —they throw away the devil's caste. They throw it off to-day.—Angels, see.— Who are we?—You can see.—But we are blind.—If you've a mind,—we'll come and learn;—we'll come and burn,—along with you above.—What is this?—So great a bliss!—This is heavenly love!"

painful anxiety, and nightly watchings over his sick brother, with all the sleepless worry arising out of his miserable embarrassments, was more than his too excitable brain could bear. His mania was a religious transport, however, and his brethren thought no particular attention to the case was called for. At night, he was with them at their church meeting, when Felix Carey, Krishna, and Gokul came to relate their experience and to ask that they might be baptized. "All were well pleased with the good confession they made;" but he was so excited by what was taking place that he was fast losing self-control.

On Tuesday morning, the weekly prayer meeting which he had induced his brethren to establish, took place. He was there, and took part with the rest in the offering of prayer. He even gave them an address upon Psalm lxvii. But his condition became rapidly more alarming, and after speaking and writing throughout the day with the utmost wildness, he was at length put under restraint by his distressed brethren.

On a much earlier page we have mentioned a dream which was regarded by Mr. Thomas as a revelation of God's purposes regarding him. This was not forgotten now, after some eighteen years. Indeed, in his exultant triumph and wild fantasy, he believed he now understood the dream and the interpretation thereof.

His journal records with considerable fullness these and other disordered fancies. All the entries testify to the intensity of his concern for the glory of God and for the salvation of the heathen of Bengal.

For some days, the restraints of the mission house sufficed for the sufferer. It was hoped that the balance of of his mind would speedily be restored. But he became worse, and the mission family had another maniac there,—Mrs. Carey,—whose unhappy condition was a source of perpetual distress to them all. Mr. Thomas's thoughts and expressions, though wild, were all of the character indicated by the extracts from his journal given above. Mr. Powell indeed wrote of his disorder, "Afflictive as such a situation appears to be, yet the joy and rapture he experienced while in that state stripped it of all that was distressing [?] and he seemed to enjoy as much of God, even then, as he did in the full use of his reasoning faculties."

On Sunday, December 28th, Gokul drew back; but Krishna Pál and Felix Carey were baptized in the river by Mr. Carey, in the presence of the Governor of the settlement and many Europeans, East Indians, and natives. Mr. Brunsdon was now so far recovered that he could be taken to the river's bank in a palanquin, and he lay there a delighted witness of the happy event. Alas, the beloved physician, who had so evidently been made the means of his restoration, and who had anticipated this day with such intensely ardent desire, was incapable of any partipation in its pleasures. Perhaps, however, he was not wholly so. His place of confinement was the school room of the mission house, which was so near the bank of the river that he could distinctly hear the congregation as they sang Padma Lochan's hymn, হে স্বর্গের স্বয় প্রভু খ্রীষ্ট ।

The next day, Mr. Marshman went down to Calcutta to endeavour to procure admission for him to the Hospital for Lunatics. He did not immediately succeed; but returned on Wednesday with an order, obtained through the kindness of the chaplains, Messrs. Brown and Buchanan, that the patient should be admitted " at the Government expense." This seems to have been the last point of contact between Mr. Thomas and Mr. Brown. Had the poor sufferer been aware of it, the fact would doubtless have given additional pain to his deep humiliation. The next morning, January 1st, 1801, Messrs. Carey and Marshman took him down with them, and placed him under the care of Dr. William Dick at the Asylum. It surely was not a reliable recollection of the history of his confinement, but only one of those hallucinations which sometimes so long survive an attack of positive mania, which led him to write, five months later, that he " lay in that dreadful place of Dr. Dick's, fast bound, wounded and distracted, many days and nights, without one soul to visit him in his affliction !" Alas, what measures of time and space can compute the wild troubled wanderings of a mind which has lost its balance? He was in confinement from the 1st to the 24th of January. The day he went to the Asylum, Mr. Fernandez arrived from Dinájpur, with Mr. Powell. Hearing of Mr. Thomas's situation, Mr. Fernandez went to see him on the 11th. He was then quite deranged, but was preaching to his fellow patients, and talking of the millenium as already begun. On a later visit, he was asked by his kind friend if he would not come, with his wife and child, to Dinájpur, and stay with him there, until the Lord opened up some new abode for his occupation. He revived at the proposal. Dr. Dick warmly recommended its adoption, and, with the consent of the missionaries, it was resolved that it should be acted upon.

The second day after his release from the Hospital, however, he received from England letters conveying very severe strictures from the Society there, on account of his neglect of their wishes as to correspondence, and regarding his discreditable pecuniary entanglements. Unquestionably, there were but too sufficient reasons for the rebuke; yet, had Mr. Fuller known upon what a poor bruised reed his weighty censures were to fall, he would on no account have written them. Coming at this unhappy time, they all but occasioned his relapse into the disorder he had just escaped from. "He tore them up, for his health's sake, the day he received them;" but his repeated feeble attempts to answer them show how deep was the agitation into which he had been thrown by them. Before they came, he had sent full accounts of his labours to Mr. Fuller, and he had now by him a very voluminous series of extracts from his recent journals, which was ready to be despatched by the next opportunity.

CHAPTER XV.

Dinajpur and Sadamahal.—1801.

MR. FERNANDEZ had come down to Serampore to be baptized. On the 18th of January, his wish was fulfilled, and Krishna's sister-in-law, Jaymani, was baptized at the same time. On the 28th, Mr. Thomas and his family, with Messrs. Fernandez and Powell, started for Dinájpur. It was a relief to the convalescent to be away from the scene of his recent disorder. He felt himself humiliated in " having been publicly pronounced to be in a state of insanity." Crushed and dispirited as he was, even the solemn condolence of his brethren upon his " awful visitation" was a source of painful irritation to him.—His affairs too were more than ever entangled since his disorder, and friends seemed to " stand aloof from his sore." They were ashamed of his circumstances : and not without good reason. They valued their own respectability and reputation,—as what good man does not ? and his was now an ill-repute, which might affect the credit of the entire brotherhood. They " had no room for him" at Serampore. But, yet a little patience, and their unhappy afflicted brother shall vex and trouble them no more.

Seldom has a more melancholy journey been made than this was. The river between Calcutta and Malda had been traversed by him so often that it was familiar to him in all its parts. Perhaps no missionary ever since has preached in the towns and villages skirting it more frequently than he who was the first to announce the glad tidings to Bengali ears. In how many of the places upon which he now gazed in passing, had his hopes of success been bright and strong. Now, a broken, ruined, helpless man, he was leaving them all, one by one, behind him, and in none of them had the arm of the Lord been revealed. Chandernagore, Bandel, Nuddea, Cutwa, Bhulaháth,— how many recollections of supposed success and actual failure were associated with them all! Yet, though feeble in health, and often oppressed by the miserable dread that his mind would again give away, he continued to preach almost daily, and found many attentive hearers. Years after, as Mr. Fernandez travelled past the same places, he called to mind this journey and the spots where Mr. Thomas had stood, earnestly declaring to the people " all the words of this life." At Bamangola, the poor invalid wrote, "I went up in the evening, and viewed the place which Bill Long resided at, with emotions of pity and sadness;" and, next day, "At Nulla, in the evening, I was greatly dejected again, especially as I looked towards deserted Mudnabatty. Mr. Fernandez, seeing me alone, came and fetched me out of the field, and I was a little relieved."

The party was visited very early in the morning of February 11th, by river dacoits, who were discovered only when they had made off with their booty. It was afterwards found that they had robbed Mr. Fernandez of about Rs. 5000. On the 18th the boats were left, and the remaining part of the journey was accomplished across country, with horses and an elephant.

Dinajpur was reached in the evening of the next day, and he found most generous entertainment with Mr. Fernandez. There were a few other residents at the station whose society was a pleasant solace to him. Chief amongst these was Mr. W. Cuninghame, a young civilian who had previously profited much by the visits and labours of the missionaries from Moypaldiggy and Mudnabatty, and who now gladly united in the meetings for prayer and for preaching, held by the missionary and his friends. On Sunday morning, the 21st, Mr. Thomas preached in English from Matthew i. 21,—" He shall save his people from their sins." It is to be feared that his discourses were seldom short. He remarks of this one that it was "rather too long, having taken up fully two hours;" but he "spoke with great liberty and solemnity of spirit, of the two great events since the creation :—the coming in of sin, and the coming of the Saviour." He esteemed it a token for good that "God evidently touched the hearts of His people as they heard him," so that "they received the word with gladness, with tears, and with acknowledgments of an encouraging nature." In such engagements, in preaching to the heathen, and in visiting a native school which Mr. Fernandez had established, he found quiet and happy employment, while he gradually regained a little strength, and lost those distressing apprehensions of relapse which had haunted him ever since his confinement in Calcutta. Alas, if he could but have been freed from those other corroding thoughts of debt and shame which were the sad issues of his struggles with the difficulties of his situation for so many years! Things now were worse than ever. The tangled threads of his affairs had wholly dropped out of his hands when he became insane, and he could do nothing yet to recover or adjust them. At the beginning of March, he sent off the extracts he had made from his journal, to Mr. Fuller, and a few sentences from a letter forwarded at the same time to the Rev. Dr. W. Rogers, of Philadelphia, may be quoted. This had been written at the end of November, but was laid aside then; and now the recent baptisms enabled him to re-write it, so as to tell of actual additions to the church at Serampore from the heathen. He writes :—

You ask, 'WHAT SUCCESS?' I know of no question so difficult to answer with precision, just now. Some say, 'None at all;' others say, 'The time is not come :' some say we never shall have any : others laugh at our labours altogether, and pity the Society at home. We know of ourselves, that 'except the Lord build the house, they labour in vain that build it :' except the Lord remove all the impediments, lay down all the plan, and find all the materials, we labour in vain. Is a foundation to be laid? Alas, in this work, here is a Mount Vesuvius in every heart to be taken away. We have laboured on the rubbish, and the materials being now in sight, we begin to think little of what our neighbours say; even though Sanballat the Horonite, and Tobiah the Ammonite themselves were here: for our Master-builder is too wise to send all these materials, at the cost of so much blood and treasure, without any design to build.—'WHAT SUCCESS?' Some of the rubbish is taken away,—the foundation is prepared,—the word of life is translated,—part of it is printed and daily distributing,—many of the natives are eager to read it, the holy unction appears on all the missionaries, more especially of late; times of refreshing from the presence of the Lord are solemn, frequent, and lasting.—'WHAT SUCCESS?' I cannot tell; for some say all this is nothing, and we have been too ready to join them. But the Builder sends, and encourages us to go on, and now we have a 'mind to work.' Six persons have been baptized, four of whom are natives.—'WHAT SUCCESS?' Who can tell, when only one little grain, like a mustard-seed, is sprung up? Here is a door of faith opened, which no man shutteth. Who can tell of what divinely penetrating degree this leaven is, and how far it reaches, even now? Multitudes are moving, bone to bone! Glory be unto the most high God, Possessor of heaven and earth! Amen. Let all the people say, Amen. Let all the angels in heaven say, Amen. And let Christ, the All in all, say, Amen!

Earnestly did he desire that by God's help he might be extricated from his debts, and that all his sorrowful experiences might work out in him a truer conformity to the will of Christ. Reading in Scott's *Commentary* of some who were "not cured of their self-importance and self-indulgence," he wrote.—

This has been, for many years, exactly my case, in a large degree; and if my dear Saviour has done something lately with His rod and His staff towards my cure, 'tis well; but I am not cured yet. I desire, not to be *diffident* of myself, but *despondent;* and to be not only *sanguine*, but *confident* in the Lord whom I serve.

His project of a magazine had, of course, been interrupted by his illness; but, towards the end of February, he had written to his brethren at Serampore to say that he had resumed his preparations, and would be ready to send materials for the first number to be issued some time in March. They, however, wrote back altogether refusing to print the periodical, and employed terms so distant and forbidding, that he was sorely hurt and distressed. The poor deserted man wrote in his journal :—

I have this sad and mournful day been very low. I now feel my conflict very sore,—my burden very heavy,—my sense of mercy gone. My faith still remains like a small, glimmering lamp, trimmed this evening, and kept from expiring by these three words of life, which I record to His praise,—' The Lord will provide ;' ' I change not ;' ' Cast down, but not destroyed.'

What was he to do? His creditors were angry and impatient; his way was shut up; his situation as Mr. Fernandez's guest was becoming burdensome to his spirit. His thoughts turned again to the indigo cultivation! He was advised by some of his Dinájpur acquaintances to resume it. Twenty-four miles off, at Sadamahal, lay the little out-factory which he had commenced while at Moypaldiggy. It was now lying vacant, and Mr. Udny wished to sell the property for Rs. 4000. After taking counsel with his friends, Mr. Thomas resolved to write to his former patron, offering to purchase it, on such terms as were alone possible for one who had no money wherewith to buy. He would pay interest at 12 per cent. upon the price, until this could be paid off out of his profits of manufacture; and if, before he could pay for it, any better opportunity of selling the property were found, he would at once make way for the other purchaser.

These proposals were sent to Mr. Udny on the 9th of March, " without any arguments to induce him to comply." Mr. Thomas wrote,—

I leave it to the Lord to determine for me as seemeth good in His sight, seeing it is my duty to provide for my household, and yet, finding I can provide nothing : leaving it, and hoping in the Lord that He will provide.

Next day he writes,—

The consolations I recorded yesterday, lasted and supported me under dismal distracting sensations in the first part of the night, and enabled me to lay hold of the unchangeableness of God in bestowing grace and shewing mercy, while my dejection of natural spirits and momentary horrors continued. Having slept upon it, I awoke this morning, and the whole creation seemed lighter and pleasanter. In prayer, I had little liveliness; but considerable humiliation before God. In private prayer, I enjoyed real liberty. I was strengthened to draw near, with all my guilt and folly, in hope, expressing unfeigned sorrow, with confession of sins of my past life, which now find me out every hour, and lay me low in darkness and distress. I was strangely, yet soberly and seriously, affected with the righteousness of God, for I am 'cast down;' and with His enduring mercy, for I am 'not destroyed.' I felt as a culprit child, speaking, between the strokes, to his Father with the rod in his hand. I receive correction this time, I think, and 'hear the rod,' more than usual, 'and Him that hath appointed it,' turning to Him that smiteth me. Yesterday, I was lamenting my state in this world,—friendless, forsaken, poor, indebted to many, censured, despised, and treated coolly by those of whom better might have been expected, and, when my wife was vexed at some trifle, I was ready to say I had not one friend left in the world. Today, I perceive more friendship, and comfort, and relief, in these three words, 'I CHANGE NOT,' than all my friends could give me, if they were ever so kind,—more than all the world is worth, if it was laid at my feet this moment. Oh then, why do I, by dissipating desultory thoughts, follow after vanity and reap vexation: and, by sowing to the flesh, prepare for myself corruption? The love of Jesus Christ is to be extolled in this one view of it, that it should maintain all its energy in the times of my coolness and shameful indifference to Him and His concerns in this world, wherewith I am entrusted, over all which His grace abounds, His love extends itself to my view, brings me back with stripes, in cords, as I am able to bear, and stays His hand, when I am not able. I was almost gone, I was distracted with divine terrors yesterday; but I am renewed in strength to-day, by the same hand. He rebukes me, but does not destroy me.

In reading 1 Corinthians iv. 9—13, the Lord shewed me His apostle Paul's condition in this world;—despised, counted weak, suffering hunger, thirst, and nakedness, having no certain dwelling place, buffeted, reviled, defamed, persecuted, and made as the filth of the earth and off-scouring of all things, and laboured, working as a common labourer, with his own hands, and how he behaved under all this; and I felt compassion for my rich brethren in this country, to whose shame and dishonour I have suffered many things which I can mention to no man.

We might give many such extracts from his diary, which was very regularly kept throughout this period, but these may for the present suffice to show the deep abasement of his spirit, and the intense sadness of his reflections upon the condition of his affairs. Though now in somewhat improved health, he suffered not a little from bodily ailments, and had but too much reason to forbode a speedy termination of his career. Alas, how little had he accomplished of all the grand expectations with which he commenced his mission to the people of Bengal. A broken hearted, dishonoured man, he looked back with distressful gloom over his disastrous mistakes and unhappy failures; and, if he thought of the future, what could he anticipate as now to be achieved, when the chill and gloom of the even-tide of life were gathering over him?

He could speak for Christ, however, even now, and he did so constantly, finding a special pleasure in visiting Mr. Fernandez's Bengali school and catechising the pupils, one of whom afforded him great encouragement by the readiness with which he acquired gospel truth, and by the interest he displayed in all that related to the way of salvation.

On the 16th of March, Mr. Thomas and his family accompanied Mr. Fernandez to Jharbárí, where he found a congregation, sometimes amounting to about three hundred people, to listen to the word of life from his lips. Upon some of them the gospel appeared to produce a deep impression. He remained there three weeks, and was in almost daily intercourse with a few of these persons, and when he left had strong reasons to think that they were very hopefully affected by what they had heard.

After his return to Dinájpur, he felt so much concern for these enquirers that, on the 21st of April, he again went to Jharbárí, without his family, to renew his instructions. He stayed this time about a fortnight, and then came back, with some encouragement as to their state.

It was a matter of sorrow now to learn that his friend Mr. Cuninghame was about to quit Dinájpur. He could ill afford to lose a friend, and he had special reason to thank God for this friendship, which had resulted not only in much pleasure to himself, but in great and acknowledged profit to Mr. Cuninghame, whom he had been privileged to assist in his early Christian progress, and who carried away with him very tender feelings of gratitude to the much afflicted missionary.*

On the 12th of May, some hope and comfort came, with a letter from Mr. Udny, consenting to his proposal to take Sadamahal. He trusted that this was a token for good, that it was the Lord's doing, and that, by His favor, he might at length be wholly released from his terrible embarrassments and debts, and might even be privileged to provide "a nursery for the mission." But he had no capital wherewith to work his little factory. Mr. Cuninghame had, however, kindly given him a horse, "which was another favor of Providence," and he still held a place in the generous affections of some of his friends. Mr. Cardin, Mr. Burney, Mr. Fernandez, and others were asked to advance him a few hundred rupees to proceed with, and to some of them the application was not made in vain.

On the 18th of May, he "arrived at Sadamahal, at noon, and dined in Bengal fashion, using a plaintain leaf." The place offered no accommodations for his family, and he had left them behind him, under the generous care of Mr.

---

* This will appear from a letter written by Mr. Cuninghame for publication, in January, 1808. An unscrupulous opponent of missions had asserted that Mr. Thomas "died raving mad in Bengal." Mr. Cuninghame says,—

"From the summer of 1796 till May 1801, I held an official situation in the Company's civil service at Dinájpur; and during the last six months of this period, I had very frequent intercourse with Mr. Thomas, and heard him preach almost every Sunday. I considered him as a man of good understanding, uncommon benevolence, and solid piety.

"In May, 1801, I quitted Dinájpur, and never again saw Mr. Thomas; but I had more than one letter from him between that time and his death, which happened, I think, in October the same year. In the last of them he wrote (with the calmness and hope of a Christian) of his own dissolution; an event which he thought was near at hand.

"After Mr. Thomas's decease, I had an opportunity of learning the circumstances of it from the late Mr. Samuel Powell, a person whose veracity none who knew him could question; and I never had the smallest reason to believe or suspect that Mr. Thomas was in any degree whatever deranged in mind at the time of his death. On the contrary, I always understood that he died in possession of his faculties, and of that hope which nothing but an unshaken faith in the gospel of Christ can give."

Fernandez. He was therefore all alone in the place where he trusted the Lord would appear for his help and would enable him to work out his deliverance.

The next day he was thrown into much perplexity, by the refusal of the ryots to sow indigo for him. "Troubles," he wrote, "soon make me faint and grow weary now: my courage flies away. My situation is unpleasant; but I'll pray." That evening, whilst walking out, a very little inconsiderate exertion brought on an attack of violent palpitation of the heart, which sorely distressed him. He had become physically unfit for any toil and excitement; but he must encounter both in the prosecution of his undertaking.

On the Lord's-day, he had a considerable company of hearers, to whom he preached the gospel. Monday was devoted to fasting and prayer; and he gratefully records that his difficulties with the ryots were surmounted. They appeared now to be well-disposed; they had taken seed for four hundred bigahs, and his enterprise was fairly commenced. The weather too was propitious, and his fervent petitions ascended for the blessing of the Lord to succeed his efforts.

Under these encouragements, hope revived; and its cheering influence appears in the daily entries in his journal. If, however, there was any risk of his losing sight of his misery, that was soon prevented. On the 30th of May, a letter reached him from Mr. Brunsdon, giving honest utterance to the displeasure he and his brethren felt in regard to Mr. Thomas's past doings, and, as it would appear, to his present undertaking also. They seem to have thought that nothing but increased debt and shame could be the issue of his attempts at Sadamahal, and some things they had heard about his former business affairs had given them a very unfavorable impression of his conduct. A few sentences from the reply which this afflictive rebuke called forth, must be quoted.

You say my former transactions have opened the mouths of God's enemies to blaspheme. This expression, with others in your letter, gave me so much grief, that I had no rest or sleep till

3 o' clock in the morning; but I turn your letter into prayer, and pour out my griefs unto God. With respect to my resolutions to give up all worldly business, I stated them to you as five reasons why I would not wish to go on, while one great reason on the other side was my debts; but my brethren said not a word to me. Their lips were all sealed up. The difficulty of the case did not allow a sudden positive determination perhaps. Many months have passed since, and I have received not one word of counsel, reproof, advice, or remonstrance from any of them, till your letter, for the Christian frankness, openness and good design of which, I both love and thank you.

He then recapitulates to him the circumstances of his first great disaster in the speculation he entered upon before he left the *Earl of Oxford*, and adds,—

All I have done ever since has been unsuccessful almost. As soon as the news of my loss came, I saw men's countenances and conduct change toward me, as they do now, and as it undeniably ever will be, for it is written, 'Men will praise thee when thou doest well for thyself,' and *vice versa*. I do not presume to say or think I have at all times been as sparing, economical, and discreet as I ought to have been, and think I would be if I was to go over my time again; no, my own mouth would condemn me. Foolishly flattered with a prospect of great gain, as we all were perhaps, and otherwise blamable in things peculiar to my natural dispositions, I relent, I repent, and earnestly implore that forgiveness that is with God, that He may be feared. I have been very guilty of trusting in an arm of flesh. You know the consequences are awful. —Jeremiah xvii. 5.—I have trusted in my own wit and parts, and in the friendship, love and help of man!

He then details the steps which led him to Sadamahal, "where," he adds,—

I have little expenses, use strict economy, have a promising season, a stated congregation, and now, who can tell but that He whose mercies are very great, and who keepeth not His anger for ever, may by this very means accomplish deliverance for me?

He concludes this affecting letter with the desire,—

May my chastisements turn to your advantage. How so? If you are truly thankful for that wisdom, prudence, or whatsoever it may be, that you have, which I have not, and that would prevent you from the same miscarriages in the same circumstances,—' What hast thou that thou hast not received?' If you pray for me earnestly, and frequently, that, for the honour of that dear Name, I may be enabled to render to every one his due.—If you are more cautious, more jealous of yourself, more single in your eye to God, more blameless in your life and conduct, <u>more useful to others, than I have been</u>,—which God of his infinite mercy grant, for Christ's sake. I believe,—whatever they may say,—that my worst evil speakers think in their hearts, I would pay every mite if I could. For your comfort, I would add that I have had hitherto a favorable season, and, with the utmost frugality, watchfulness, diligence, and prayer, I use means of relieving myself; and, though heretofore I have been denied success, I have no warrant to conclude I always shall be. 'Man's extremity is God's opportunity.' The more hopeless my case is in itself, the more occasion is there for me to hope in God.

Mr. Brunsdon's letter occasioned him "the sharpest pain and grief in his heart," as the entries in his journal but too plainly show. A few days after replying to it, he went back to Dinájpur, and remained there till June the 23d. Here he "preached five times in English," and had his hopes of the school boy and of one of the enquirers from Jharbárí much encouraged by what he saw and heard of them during the visit.

On returning to his solitude at Sadamahal, he wrote,—

At Dinájpur, I received a threatening letter, which occasioned great trouble and tossings of mind. The hand of the Lord still smites me. I came up hither, and began, this morning, a new life once more, by devoting myself to the Lord, reading His word, submitting to His rod, and instructing the people here. Let me seek His mercy, and wait till He be gracious to me, knowing that I have sinned against Him. I have done evil. It is of the Lord's mercies that I am not consumed. May I be able to accept of His punishment thankfully, always, come what will.

Next day he wrote,—

Glory be unto Him. I went to bed comfortable after all; for He comforted me by His word, 'Labour not for the meat that perisheth,' &c. 'Come unto me.' 'I will in no wise cast out.' 'Let the wicked forsake his way.' Reproach hath broken my heart; but the world, and caring for to-morrow *is worst of all;* and trusting to the Lord by the day, obediently submitting to His will, *is best of all.*

Extracts must not be multiplied, or a curious Biblical study, in a collection of the "scripture terms for affliction,"—a mournful assemblage of the most sorrowful expressions of the word of God, might be quoted from his journal. Such a study was congenial to his depressed mind, and not wholly unfruitful of comfort. "My troubles," he wrote in a *Nota Bene*, "look like mice, before these thunderbolts, already."

He also gave himself up to the more abundant reading of God's word, and found that, by making this the business of all his leisure moments, he could in a very short time read through the entire Bible. In twenty-eight days, he now completed it ; and wrote,—

It has been like going over the garden of God. It has been the happiest month of the present year to me. The word has been sweet to my taste, especially the four evangelists, and, amongst these, the Gospel by John. I find myself very ignorant of the scriptures ; but am abundantly encouraged to future diligence in reading, searching and meditating upon them, and to hope for that divine power which will enable me, by and bye, to understand those things which now I do not. The prophets and apostles reflect light upon each other, and give light on all the affairs of this life, great and small ; and the precepts teach us how to act in every difficulty, and how to behave ourselves at all times ; and, as our times change, those precepts which once signified little to us become more important ; so that I do not perceive how it is possible for any man to be a doer of the word, without he makes a point of constantly reading it.

About the same time, Mr. Thomas perused, with deep interest, but not with perfect approval, Hervey's *Theron and Aspasio*. The principal subject of these dialogues was one of supreme importance to his mind, and his daily memoranda show how closely he was intent upon the investigation of it.

A few further extracts from his journal will show how varied and exciting were the exercises of his spirit, under the influence of his many perplexities and in his experience of divine consolations.

What a conflict in my poor soul, in this solitary abode. Sometimes, in great fear and distress ; and, at other times in the same day, in a transport of joy. Was David so? This evening, while reading on quite another subject, I laid down my spectacles, to rejoice with exceeding joy on these words, 'Thy people shall be willing, in the day of thy power.' How came I willing? Who made me willing?

At another time :—

To-day, after much reading of the scriptures and prayer, towards evening, I have been greatly cast down, and, suddenly, my spirit was overwhelmed, and I felt myself truly a miserably wretched man. I walked out, and cried for mercy; and the horror and darkness is a little over since I began to consider that text, 'Why should a living man complain, a man for the punishment of his sins?' and I began to count up my mercies.

So, a little later in the same day,—

While reading and expounding to some Brahmans, on Saul and David, I was struck with such horror at the Spirit of the Lord leaving Saul, and an evil spirit from the Lord troubling him, that my blood ran up in my face, and there was no more strength in me; but my body and spirit were so moved and affected that I soon gave over, and continued in great distress for some time, lest I should be as Saul: but I could not find my David in all the world, against whom my heart is inveterate and implacable. After prayer, I continued low.

Who can fail to discover in all this tumultuous agitation the action of disease, which demanded the soothing influences of loving tenderness, with the guardianship of most watchful care, to shield the sufferer against every occasion of excitement or perturbation? Was a man like this, so dejected and oppressed in spirit, and so infirm and broken in bodily health, fitted to live all alone, burdened with anxious uncertain business engagements, harassed by impatient claims for money he was utterly unable to pay; lover and friend far from him; without sympathy or encouragement, save that alone which his broken heart could find in lowliest supplication at the throne of grace? Yet there were times when that sufficed "to turn the gloom of his solitude into cheerfulness and joy."

Upon the 23d of July, he received tidings of the death of Mr. Brunsdon, after a most painful illness; and other letters, upon business, greatly added to his distress. On the 28th he went again to Dinájpur. For some days, he had been suffering severely from the palpitation at his heart. He feared that the disorder which occasioned it was gaining ground. The country around Sadamahal was flooded by the heavy rains. His indigo crop was threatened with complete destruction. He could do nothing to avert the disaster, and he needed the solace of friendship, and longed for the affectionate care his family alone could give him. His heart revived as he journeyed to Dinájpur, partly by boat and partly on horseback. He wrote,—

Pleasant and refreshing exercises in the boat. Much instructed and quickened by reading Erskine's *Gospel Sonnets*. I found the words of Christ, and did eat them, and was strengthened. Sweet refreshing from the same book on horse-back; so that I came to Dinájpur, rejoicing in the Lord, like a strong man to run a race; all my burdens become 'light afflictions,' hoping in God, trusting in the Lord. But how soon was all this changed! I received on my arrival here a letter from the Church at Serampore, in which they allege my having borrowed money, with little or no prospect of paying it, to the dishonour of the gospel, &c., and they have suspended me! This letter filled me with astonishment and grief, although the mercies received just before it supported my spirit from falling suddenly. I perceive in it that my brethren profess to glorify God themselves, to condemn my conduct, and to justify my accusers. I believe I am under the chastisement of God, for sin; but on other accounts; so that, whilst I justify God and condemn myself, I cannot allow any truth or propriety in some of my brethren's proceedings. They first suspend, and then accuse: they have stated matters very erroneously; yet this also, through the divine blessing, shall turn to my account, and to the glory of God.

After a restless night, "having only two or three hours' sleep," and with "a violent soreness and palpitation of heart," he began to write a reply to this distressing letter. After this, he wrote, "I revived a little in prayer. In the family, still more, and, while the way was open, I retired to my closet, and was able to cast all my burdens of sin and sorrow on the Lord. Went to bed rejoicing in the Lord;" not, however, to sleep until "about 2 o'clock."

His letter to Serampore was finished on the 31st. In it, he evidently used a very severe self-control, carefully avoiding any expressions which pride or indignation suggested. His brethren had referred, first, to a pecuniary transaction which took place shortly after he became acquainted with Mr. Fernandez, in 1796, whereby, it was said, that gentleman had been made to doubt the reality of religion; and they further very severely reflected upon his recent entanglements at Etinda. As to the earlier matter, Mr. Fernandez was now at hand to assure him that no such impression as that ascribed to him was ever produced upon his mind, and that though, "some years back, he had been asked some sifting questions" about the matter, he was confident he had never said anything so opposed to his honest convictions as was now alleged. As to the rest, Mr. Thomas's affairs in their worst aspects had been laid before his brethren, months ago, and their counsel in his perplexities solicited, and none of them had censured him in regard to what he had done. They had never before called in question his integrity of purpose before God and men. How could they do it now? This indeed was the stress of his letter:—The affairs to which you refer are not new; and, so far as they are true, I myself told you all about them. Did you blame me then? Who among you has admonished me at all? I was with you for weeks together, going out and coming in, and taking part with you in your holiest things; and nothing was said of your unfavorable judgment upon my conduct, which I had fully set before you. Why condemn and suspend me now? He added,—

If I have now said any thing amiss, unreasonable, or unscriptural, I beg you will show me no mercy. Do not talk of *my* being offended, who am as a hunted flea, a broken vessel, like a dead man out of mind, a sunken worm. You need not care whether *I* am angry or pleased. Times are altered. Since all these calamities have happened to me,—especially the disorder I had in my faculties,—I find all things very different with me. My high spirit is brought down. I have not the same sense of provocation by injuries from men, since I have been so touched by the hand of God, as I had before. Men do not appear to be the same men, nor things the same things as they did. These unhappy circumstances, the subjects of your letter, these and their train, have given me much perplexity and sorrow. But this is not all. I am afar off from all relations and friends. My brethren are more than cool. Driven from among men, I sit alone, friendless, almost comfortless, as to this world, for weeks together. My secret sins are brought to remembrance. These chastisements, so heavy on my heart, so sore, so many, so long continued, plainly relate to my faults; or, if it will please you better, to my crimes! But to whom shall I mention them? Where shall I begin? Where shall I leave off? 'My spirit made diligent search.' But I believe no such things as you imagine; and any mere cant of my self-sufficiency, self-complacency &c., would add to my guilt. To mention my sins to those whose hearts are healthy and stout would add to my difficulties; and to detail them to you would answer no purpose. I pour out my grief unto God. I have been in doubt and perplexity of soul, such as I never knew before; in darkness, without any light: my bodily strength decayed; my heart literally sore; my spirits drunk up. But I know the light as well as the darkness,— the voice of the Shepherd, as well as the voice of the wolf. I have heard Him say, 'Come unto me.' I know His voice, and feel His glorious power also, strengthening vile me unto patience and long-suffering, with some joyfulness, giving thanks unto the Father.

The disorder at his heart grew worse daily. He suffered continual pain there, which any effort, even in speaking, greatly aggravated. The palpitations became more frequent and insupportable, and his nights were usually sleepless. He could not understand his symptoms, but suspected the formation of "a polypus, or some evil" of an organic nature, at his heart, which he thought would soon put an end to his mortal life. The prospect had no terrors. On the 11th of August, he wrote,—

I seem quite willing at present, if the will of God be so, that this disorder may be unto death; and I feel as if I could die this hour triumphant in the Redeemer, satisfied with the mercy of God, which is above the heavens, and nothing like human mercy, yea, wholly unlike human thoughts of divine mercy, being far higher, surer, freer, richer, and more abundant. I have no confidence in the flesh: all my hope is in God. I earnestly prayed the Lord to fit and strengthen me to suffer all His will, if further affliction and stripes should be necessary for me. I also asked the Lord to guide me, and grant me discretion and prudence in every step of my future proceedings; and asked in hope. Enjoyed sweet quietness and peace, acquiescing in all the divine dispensations toward me, hoping in His mercy. My mind is no longer tossed with surges of trouble as before; though the circumstances of my case all remain as they were.

On the 19th, he suffered from a severe spasm at his heart, with aggravated symptoms of disease in the liver also, and, as was common when he slept, "dreamed of his distress and safe refuge, all night."

But his affairs needed him at Sadamahal. Unfit as he was to bear the burden of them, he must somehow do it. On the 27th, he went there, and the irritation of his poor enfeebled body, so unequal to the toil of the journey, "grieved his soul exceedingly." He got to Sadamahal "very weary, waspish, sun-burnt, and stupid." He was really sinking fast. "Every little extra motion" or mental excitement " brought on fluttering palpitation and distress, which was a death-like sensation not to be described."

Dreams often indicate the ordinary current of thought. On the 29th, he wrote: " Dreamed of the dead; and thought brother Brunsdon said, the oldest missionary would be the next; and I said, 'The will of the Lord be done.'" Next day, he was engaged in a review of his life, and left in his journal a list of its several stages, or more remarkable incidents. It is curious to see, "Answer to prayer, Isaiah xlix." and "Dream of the crab, lilies, and wheat," enumerated amongst these. What could he think now of the vast expectations to which these things had once been the index? It was a gloomy retrospect, made upon a miserably cold day. " Poring over his manifold troubles all day, and being chilled in body, though wrapped up in flannel, he took cold, and lost the sweet savour of truth he had in the morning; and at night woke up after his first sleep in a very alarming state of mind." But on casting himself upon the Lord, he regained comfort. "When I look back," he said, "I conclude, if the Almighty had no more concern for my salvation than I have had, I should have perished long ago."

On the 1st of September, he " began making indigo, with a heavy heart." The results could not be sufficient to answer his expectations, and he suffered much in anguish of spirit, as he "thought of the door of providence shut against him every way, and the hand of God still upon him, chastising him, and shutting him up. Yet," he added, " the door of faith seems open, and I will knock at that door and wait; and who can tell, but I, even I, may yet obtain relief from above? Wait, O my soul, on the Lord. Keep His way. Wash thine hands in innocency, and so compass His altar."

On the 3d, he writes again,—

Such an amazing dejection as no words can describe. My food I could not touch. My soul in extreme distress. I left business, and tried to pour out my heart in prayer. I seemed to be lost, soul and body. Though I cannot rejoice yet, I seem to have some refreshment from the precious word of life. It is not what is in me, but what is in my Christ, that I am to look to: 'His fulness,' His 'unsearchable riches,' out of which all the Apostles received and all believers. I am truly 'heavy laden;' and I must first be so, must needs be so, to be within the invitation. Heaviness, mourning, sighing and groans, I spend my life in; and it seems to me as though my heart was literally broken, having pain in that part for some months daily. I feel myself a weak, empty, helpless, trustless, useless creature; but, desperate as my case is, I see here One able to relieve me. He also invites me, and that not at an uncertainty, but assuring me He will give me rest. O Jesus, who didst once manifest thyself so satisfactorily, shine forth again. Return, O Sun of righteousness. Restore my soul. Thou only hast power over sin. Glorify that power in me. I ought to look upon every one of my afflictions as the cross on which I willingly am to crucify my *self*, my flesh, my evil nature; and thus I may rejoice in them, though grievous. Let me humble myself under the mighty hand of God.

Thus his days passed by. One might be "all agony, anguish, fear and dismay," whilst he felt himself "visited of God, abhorred by men, guilty and totally helpless." Another would be as "a glorious morning," when "the Sun of righteousness arose, and he saw His beams, and felt their effects, warming his garments, and gladdening his soul." Now "afflicted and ready to die;" and again so full of joy that no words could express it. Upon the whole, however, the happier experience began now to predominate. His toilsome journey was well nigh finished. Its gloom and dangers were, for the most part, overpassed. Something of the warmth and brightness of his eternal home began to reach his weary longing spirit. He wrote on the 6th of September,—

This day, let it be recorded, and remembered, O my soul, that the High and Lofty One that inhabiteth eternity, hath looked upon me, and revived the spirit of the contrite. I was brought low, very low. I sought Him, and found Him not; yet it was but a little, and I found Him whom my soul loveth.—I was afraid He had forsaken me. I called upon Him day and night; but this afternoon I set myself to meditate on the power, willingness, truth, and love of Christ as a Saviour; and drew out from memory and Scripture several testimonies that God has given of His Son in these particulars. As I meditated on His power, His word was sweeter to me than my necessary food. I began to lift up my sunken soul in praise; and especially when I came to that text, 'Verily, verily, I say unto you, he that heareth my word, and believeth on Him that sent me, *hath* everlasting life, and *shall not* come into condemnation, but is passed from death unto life.' These words were a sweet charm to my spirit. The impressive manner in which they are ushered in,—*Verily, verily, I say unto you;*—the pointed address and application of them, singling out him *that hath His word &c.;*—and the three-fold utterance of the happy comforting conclusion, *hath everlasting life,—shall not come into condemnation,—but is passed from death unto life.* Although my faith is lacking, little, weak, and unfinished, yet it exists, and is revived by this word in a solid satisfying manner: not rapturous, but inexpressible. Blessed be God for hope! Blessed be the Son of God, who hath not left me comfortless! Blessed be the Spirit of God, who hath not utterly forsaken me, but takes of the things of Christ still, and shews them to me! O Thou, who art able to keep me from falling, keep my soul near; do not depart, let me be filled, and revive, and bring forth fruit, instead of being cut down! Thou hast begun to compass me about with songs of deliverance. This is the first day I could sing for many days past. Trust in the Lord!—Wait!

So two days later,—

How precious is Christ to me at this moment. How truly I enjoy Him as the fountain of living waters. How different from all stagnated cisterns. I drink out of His fulness and find a plenteous redemption, and see clearly it is from Him we receive grace for grace; and He is all in all:—repentance to repent,—faith to believe,—patience to endure,—hope to expect,—quickening to desire,—light, life, and joy to rejoice in Him, and to deliver from confidence in the flesh. I find this hymn exactly expressive of my experience, in every verse and every line, especially these lines:—

> Thou art my Pilot wise;
> My compass is thy word;
> My soul each storm defies,
> While I have such a Lord.
> I trust thy faithfulness and power,
> To save me in the trying hour.

> Though rocks and quicksands deep
> Through all my passage lie,
> Yet Christ will safely keep,
> And guide me with His eye.
> My anchor, hope, shall firm abide,
> And I each boisterous storm outride.

> By faith, I see the land,
> The port of endless rest.
> My soul, thy sails expand,
> And fly to Jesu's breast.
> Soon shall I reach that heavenly shore,
> Where winds and waves distress no more!

More than a month had now elapsed since he wrote his remonstrance to his fellow missionaries at Serampore. He marvelled much to find so many weeks pass by without one line from them in answer to that or to any of his letters; and he addressed them again, on the 8th of September, remonstrating with them forcibly upon the manner in which he had been dealt with.

Little has been said of late concerning his missionary efforts; but they were never intermitted. He was continually talking either to the people at Sadamahal, or to strangers who came to hear him from neighbouring villages; and in his solitude he thought over subjects he would preach upon when next he visited Dinájpur. His mind just now was busy upon Jeremiah ii. 13,—the broken cisterns of earth, and God as "the free overflowing fountain of goodness, mercy, and benefits."

We have very little more to relate. In the latter half of September, he was compelled to leave his solitude at

Sadamahal for the last time, and to seek such help as medical advice, with the attention of his family and friends at Dinájpur, could give him. Perhaps he could not delay whilst arrangements were made to secure a boat for the journey; for he appears to have made it throughout on horse-back. Nearly all the country lay under water. The roads in several parts had been broken up by the floods. Heavy showers alternated with scorching sunshine throughout the twenty-four miles he had to ride. He reached his journey's end at last; but in a condition of utter exhaustion. Cold and a violent fever were the natural results; yet no alarm seems to have been felt by his friends. So shattered in health as he had previously been, one might suppose that his condition now would have been seen to be one of extreme danger. This, however, was not the case. Dr. Gardiner, the Company's surgeon at Dinájpur, kindly gave him all the assistance in his power. At first, the fever appeared to yield to the treatment employed, and, on the 26th of September, the poor patient wrote that it had left him for two days, but that his " head was giddy, heavy, and weak."

Next day was Sunday, and he was well enough to sit up. He wrote,—

In much weakness, spoke a few words in the family on the woman of Canaan. In the evening, we all read in the Psalms, and I occasionally commented, and prayed. Went to bed in much pain.

On Monday, he wrote,—

O Lord, I mourn over my unfruitfulness to God and man. What shall I do? From Thee is my fruit found. To Thee will I look, and as I receive, devote my life to Thee—devote a weak, an empty, a wretched, worthless thing. But, O Lord, Thou art a strength to the needy, and a fulness of grace and truth to Thy people in all their straits; therefore to Thee will I look. Since I grow better in health, and to-day especially, I have been very anxious and sorrowful to see the condition of my soul. So little zeal,—nay none; so little love,—nay none perceived. Only, if I love not, why are these mournings? Retired this afternoon, to pour out my complaint to God, who revived me afterwards in family prayer.

On the 29th, he made the last entry in his journal,—

Still refreshed with a sense of the mercy received yesterday. Still more, by reading *Gospel Sonnets*, those sweet, enlightening, and blessed truths to my soul. O Lord, accept my early thanks through the Redeemer, in whom Thou art well pleased, and may they never cease to flow from this heart.

'And the truth shall make you free.'—John viii. 32. As the truth maketh a man free, so error brings him again into bondage. We are as prone to error as we are to sin. We slide into it, and know it not; till darkness, fear, doubt, and confusion surround us; and it is well if we know it then. How necessary is our Lord's good counsel,—'Take heed of the leaven.'

I conversed with a Brahman on death, on the shastras, on idols, and the worship of them, till he made a sudden bow, and disappeared!

Thus to the very last he was eager to do the work of his high calling as a messenger to the heathen.

But a relapse now took place. His fever regained its violence, with new and dangerous symptoms; and it soon became evident that his case lay beyond the reach of human succour. He could write no more; but continued powerless and resigned to all the will of God in "the dying strife," which, for a whole fortnight, preceded dissolution. Mr. Powell, to whom we are indebted for most of these particulars, wrote:

During the nine months he was in this neighbourhood, notwithstanding the weight and burden of many afflictions of a very trying nature, he possessed his soul in patience: and seemed to enjoy a heavenly frame of mind, which nothing could long disturb. Frequent and fervent in prayer, he experienced its efficacy, and found it a comfortable solace under all his woes. Though crucified to the world, he felt her hardships and endured her frowns; but he drew near to God, dwelt under the shadow of His wings and lived with the prospect of eternity continually before him. He talked in a most familiar, but solemn manner of death, and more than wished for a final release from the troubles which were pressing upon him.

Towards the close of his sickness, his bodily pains were exceeding great. For several days, he had periodical cold fits, then a raging fever, and then a violent vomiting, and afterwards a dreadful oppression upon the stomach, which threatened suffocation, so that it occasioned the most painful sensations to all who beheld these alternate sufferings. On his recovering a little from one of these severe daily attacks, Mrs. Thomas asked him how he felt himself? 'I feel,' said he, 'like a man who wants to die, but cannot.' Dr. Gardiner gave him small doses of opium to alleviate his pain. This affected his brain; and therefore Mr. Thomas was not satisfied in his conscience that he did right to take it. 'O God,' he cried, 'take away the effects of this drug from my mind and imagination, and forgive me this sin.'

A day or two before his death, with great difficulty, he repeated the first verse of the hymn,

> Jesus, lover of my soul,
> Let me to Thy bosom fly,

in a most impressive manner, so that I thought I perceived more beauty in it than I ever did before. When he came to the first line of the second verse,

> Other refuge have I none,

he stopped, and enlarged upon the ability of Christ to save. 'Yes,' said he; 'we want no other refuge.' All his hopes centred in Christ. He knew no rock but the Rock of ages. Upon that foundation he built for time and eternity, and found that no open assault or secret machination, though aided by all the powers of darkness, could undermine it. His sickness was a dreary melancholy season. Nothing but the happy prospects he had in the future sustained him in those gloomy hours while tossed to and fro, and wearied with the pains of dissolving nature. Unable to read, his mind was so stored with Scripture that he would often cite passages appropriate to his situation and circumstances, from which he derived much comfort. His soul was continually breathing after God. Once, while he was in great pain, he cried out in triumph, 'O death, where is thy sting!' His last agonies were exceeding great. Several hours before his death, he became speechless, and continued so, till his soul burst from her prison and winged her way to a brighter and better world, where pains and sorrows are unknown. He expired on the 13th of October, and was buried by the side of Mr. Fountain.

Far more interesting particulars of Mr. Thomas's last days, might, no doubt, have been preserved, but what has been quoted is conclusive as to the dying peace and hope of the much-tried man whose history has been set before the reader.

A few notices of this event written by his fellow missionaries at Serampore may also be gathered up. Mr. Ward wrote as follows :—

Brother Thomas is dead! He departed with a hope full of immortality. He had a great many faults : but never shall I forget the time when, after setting Krishna's arm, he talked to him with such earnestness about his soul's salvation, that Krishna wept like a child. I hope that this preaching led to his saving conversion. Thus brother Thomas led the way to India, and was the means of the planting of the church, by the conversion of *the first native*. Brother Carey preached a sermon on the occasion of his death, on November 8th, from John xxi. 19,—' This spake he, signifying by what death he should glorify God.'

Mr. Marshman wrote of him,—

When every thing is considered, he was a most useful instrument in the mission. To him it is owing, under God, that the Hindus now hear the word of life. His unquenchable desires after their conversion induced him to relinquish his secular employment on board the *Earl of Oxford* East Indiaman, to devote himself to that object alone, which ultimately led our beloved Society to their engagement in the present mission. Though he was not without his failings, yet his peculiar talents, his intense, though irregular, spirituality, and his constant attachment to that beloved object, the conversion of the heathen, will render his memory dear as long as the mission endures.

Thus did his brethren bestrew his tomb with their floral offerings. Would that the fragrance of their loving acknowledgments of his fidelity had but reached him whilst his fainting broken spirit might have been cheered and sustained by it; but now he had fled away and was at rest. He no longer needed their sympathy or forbearance: he no longer dreaded their censures. His hard conflict was over. He had passed from the scene of his failures and humiliations, to the society of the spirits of just men made perfect, whence none could exclude him; for the people that dwell therein are forgiven their iniquity. " Blessed are the dead that die in the Lord. Yea, saith the Spirit, that they may rest from their labours, and their works do follow them."

On the 22nd of October, the *Calcutta Gazette* announced

his death, speaking of him as "formerly surgeon on board the *Earl of Oxford,* Indiaman, and latterly a zealous promoter of the knowledge of Christianity among the Hindus."

A letter addressed to his widow on the 25th of the month may be introduced here. The writer, Mr. Udny's mother, had known Mr. Thomas most intimately from August, 1788, and her words of condolence reveal an affectionate esteem for him, which is a strong testimony to his many excellencies. It is as follows,—

I scarcely know what to say on an event which has distressed and afflicted me beyond measure. I do not presume to offer you consolation, being well persuaded that only He who caused this affliction can be our Comforter under it. Be assured that I most tenderly sympathise with you under this severe loss. I had a very sincere regard for the dear departed, and recollect with gratitude the many obligations I have received from him. But why should we lament, where there is so much cause for rejoicing? Mr. Powell spent the morning with me yesterday; which was passed in mourning and tears. He gave me much cause for comfort, and repeated many things which I wished to hear. Alas, why should we grieve for him who has so much the advantage over us? That he is happy, I am firmly persuaded. Throughout all the changing scenes of a troublesome world, Jesus was his sure Rock and Refuge, and never left him till he died. Be comforted, my dear friend. A gracious and kind providence, I trust and doubt not, will support and be with you in this time of severe trial. I can write no more at present, but to assure you of my warmest and best services. My son does not know of my writing, or I am sure he would unite his most cordial regards and best wishes.

Mrs. Thomas and her daughter were invited by the missionaries at Serampore to remove thither, and to reside in the mission family. They had, however, very attached and generous friends in Mr. and Mrs. Cardin, who offered them a home at Mirzapore, near Nuddea; and they accepted it. The widow did not long survive her husband. She rapidly declined in health, and died at Calcutta, on the 6th of April, 1803. A monument was erected to her memory "by her disconsolate daughter," in the Old Burial Ground. In 1805, Miss Thomas accompanied her kind friends to England, and rejoined her father's family there.

The little factory at Sadamahal was bought by Messrs. Fernandez and Powell. Mr. Fernandez afterwards occupied it as a missionary station; and some converts were made, whose descendants are still living on the spot where our first missionary, in solitary sadness, passed so many of the last weeks of his life.

Near the present jail at Dinájpur is a little spot of ground, once a garden belonging to Mr. Fernandez, but now the property of a Musulman. There are to be seen five long neglected old tombs. Three stand near together. Beneath that to the west, Mr. Samuel Powell lies buried. The two next bear inscriptions which mark them as the graves of infant children of Mr. Fernandez. The remaining two are at a little distance to the east. These bear no names, and the masonry has crumbled down to an unsightly heap of bricks, overgrown with rank vegetation, and especially with the fern called "the maiden-hair." There it is that Thomas and Fountain, side by side, await "the voice of the archangel and the trump of God." Very few lovers of the mission cause have ever visited the spot. In 1804 the noble evangelist John Chamberlain stood there with a heart thrilling with loving tenderness for the "dear brethren," who "would speak no more for God on earth."*
But since the death of Mr. Fernandez, no one has been able to say with certainty which of the two graves is the resting place of the first messenger of the gospel to the people of Bengal.

* In Mr. Chamberlain's journal for March 10th, 1804, written at Dinájpur, he says,—"This evening I have been reading some of dear Thomas's letters, which I hope have humbled and affected my heart. Oh what a saint was he! Great as were his failings, his excellencies were very great. His letters are full of a godly savour, and well worth preserving. How well versed was he in the Scriptures, and how evidently did they affect his heart! His last days evidently showed that he was ripening for glory; and now, dear man! he is doubtless in bliss, secure from sin, and full of holiness, in possession of all his hopes."

CHAPTER XVI.
Concluding Observations.

"I AM more and more convinced of the real piety of Mr. Thomas, though he is a man of like passions with others." So Mr. Carey wrote upon the arrival of the *Kron Princessa Maria* in Bengal, in 1793, and so the reader of this history may probably be disposed to say in review of the facts which have been laid before him. Of many faults, many weaknesses, many failures, and much inconsistency, irrefutable evidence has appeared; but many uncommon excellencies, and remarkable piety and devotedness are also disclosed in the life here portrayed. Seldom perhaps has a character been more unsparingly revealed to public view than this, in the materials before the reader. It may be thought that the biography might very advantageously have used far greater reserve, and that many of the more unlovely features of it should have been wholly omitted, or left more in the shade. But, in biographies, who does not like to know all the truth, if any genuine interest in the subject be awakened? and the whole truth must be far more instructive than the too common one-sided representations, by which men and women are untruly depicted as faultless beings. It was believed too that Mr. Thomas might be fearlessly set forth as he was. Faulty he was indeed; but his admirable qualities redeem him from contempt. It may be lamented that capabilities for usefulness so large, and consecration so sincere, were marred by defects so grave and injurious; but the facts will awaken sorrow and not scorn.

There is another point of view in which this history is valuable. It records the feeble beginnings of missionary effort in Bengal : the first of a series of occurrences which have set wide-open a door once closely barred against the approach of Christian truth to the millions of this province of India. In the face of determined opposition to missionary effort here, Mr. Thomas began to preach and to translate the Scriptures. He subsequently drew the attention of the newly-formed Baptist Missionary Society to this immense country, which otherwise they certainly would not have selected; and his experience and enterprise remarkably assisted the entrance of his earliest colleague into the field, so carefully guarded against intruders, wherein that eminent man's prudence and success were followed by such vast and happy results. A life upon which so many consequences depended, certainly deserved to be written; and it must have special interest to the Christian reader. God's methods of operation are not like ours. Have we not occasion to admire them here, in the train of events which have given the gospel to India?

Now that the story of Mr. Thomas's life has been completed, it may be well to add a few remarks upon some of its more prominent features. Let us begin with those which are the most displeasing.

We have, in Mr. Thomas, the deplorable spectacle of an *insolvent* missionary : a man who, whilst it was his great duty and his actual endeavour to set before the world an example of Christian integrity, was in fact so involved in his circumstances that the just demands of his creditors were not met, whilst he was sometimes reduced to pitiful shifts and contrivances to escape the consequences of failing to meet his engagements. Perhaps no fact in his history was so productive of reproach and dishonour to him as this. His best and most constant friends were put to the blush by it; and even now, after the lapse of so many years, the fact outrages the very spirit of respectability, as we read of it.

But, with all deference to this commendable spirit, we may ask, Does not a case like that before us show that sometimes its censures and frowns may be given to the unhappy, rather than the guilty? Mr. Thomas became a debtor, to an amount utterly beyond his power to defray, at the outset of his missionary career, and through unforeseen and disastrous circumstances. *That* calamity gave its color to all his after-life. It has been matter for heavy blame that in subsequent years he "embarked in speculations." But in all that he thus did, he was prompted only by the laudable desire of obtaining the means to pay his debts. The result, indeed, was the increase of debt; but his purpose was unquestionably its honest discharge. As to "speculations," all Europeans in India speculated in those early days. Mr. Grant and Mr. Udny were both very extensively "embarked in speculations," although they occupied situations of great prominence in the Company's civil service. What Mr. Thomas's speculations were we have seen. He might have been more prudent in entering upon them, he was unhappily unsuccessful in conducting them, he may have been fickle in abandoning them,—but that his purpose throughout was honourable and good, no one who has studied the undisguised expressions of his daily memoranda can for a moment doubt. So far indeed was he from suspecting that he was doing wrong in these unhappy business transactions, it is clear that, in them all, he believed he was following the most explicit providential guidance. His difficulties and desires having been laid before God, with earnest entreaties for deliverance, he was ready to conclude that any apparent outlet from his troubles which subsequently offered itself was the method of divine succour. He refused to accept the large relief which his friends were ready to afford him in 1789, because the obligations it would have imposed upon him were inconsistent with his convictions of duty to God; and, to the very end of life, he firmly trusted that the Lord would enable him to pay every man his due. We cruelly wrong his memory if we think he was ever indifferent to the just claims his creditors had upon him; and his deep humiliation and sorrow for his unhappy failures have been made sufficiently evident in the preceding pages.

Whilst all this is said in extenuation of Mr. Thomas's conduct as a debtor, his example can give no encouragement to extravagance or other imprudence in worldly affairs. The details of his life will be misread if they do not supply a most forcible and stern admonition against recklessness in expenditure and the other unhappy peculiarities which wrought for this good man so much shame and sorrow. How have these things blotted the records of a noble Christian life! Had he guided his affairs with more discretion, how bright a history might his have been. Heavy was the penalty he paid for his imprudence. Humiliated and disgraced in life, the memory of his goodness and services in the cause of Christ has been beclouded ever since his death; and it demands some courage even now to bring the facts of his history to the knowledge of the Christian world. Surely one of the plainest lessons to be read in this volume is a warning to all against the failings which slurred the character, destroyed the happiness, and impaired the usefulness of him whose story it narrates.

Another very unhappy fact set forth by our narrative is Mr. Thomas's *irascibility of temper*. This belonged to his natural disposition, and was evidently the object of most anxious self-restraint. That he did not succeed in more habitually controlling it, was an occasion of painful humiliation to himself, and may well be regretted by those who love his memory. Such a disposition is often associated with many noble and generous qualities, and it was so in his case. It is also, we believe, attendant upon mental disorder such as he appears to have been constitutionally liable to suffer, and perhaps, if his case be rightly weighed, there is really more reason to admire the extent to which he held this morbid irritability in check, than to deplore its manifestations, except as they were the occasion of alienating his friends and of beclouding his own spirit with doubt and remorse.

Other features of eccentricity will not have escaped the eye of the attentive reader of these memoirs. The almost *arrogance* of his claims as a minister of Christ, his forward-ness to censure sharply any presumed errors or misconduct of others, and to obtrude his views on the attention of those who were not dependent upon his counsels will, no doubt, be remembered. May not these things be largely accounted for, in connection with his peculiar natural temperament, by the unfavorable circumstances of his religious education ? From the time when as a wayward refractory lad he quitted his father's house, to the day of his conversion, he could have seen little of godly society ; and, subsequently, until he became a missionary, he enjoyed few of the advantages which the ministry of the gospel and the influences of Christian fellowship supply. At sea, in the *Earl of Oxford*, he was without any pious associates, save those reclaimed from the irreligion of the ship's company by his own endeavours. His study of the Bible and of a few approved Christian books was constant and close, and his habits fervently devotional ; but he had little opportunity to compare his conclusions as to scriptural truth with those of intelligent fellow-Christians, or to have his views expanded by free intercourse with men who were better instructed than himself. With such a preparatory experience, it is little surprising that, on coming amongst the few persons who were seeking after truth in Calcutta, and on being greatly flattered by their admiration of his gifts, and their deference to his judgment and knowledge, he should be led into the mistakes and extravagancies which disfigured his subsequent relations with them.

If we now turn to the more pleasing elements in Mr. Thomas's character, surely there is very much that was exemplary. How remarkable was his *benevolence*. Wherever he went, he was followed by the indigent, whom he fed out of his penury, or healed with a patient care which has rarely been equalled. His sympathy with the suffering was intense and constant, and his hand was ever open for their relief. He was indeed surrounded by wretchedness in India. He once wrote to Mr. Fuller,—

Do not send men of any compassion here, for you will break their hearts. *Do* send men full of compassion here, where many perish with cold, many for lack of bread, and millions for ' lack of knowledge.' In England, the poor receive the benefits of the gospel, in being fed and clothed by those who know it not, and know not by what they are moved; for the gospel puts some men in fear, and others to shame; so that, to relieve their own smart, they provide for the poor;—but, here!—Oh miserable sight! I have found the pathways stopped up by sick and wounded people, perishing with hunger and distress, and that in a populous neighbourhood, where plenty of people pass by, some singing, others talking, but none showing any more compassion than as though they were dying weeds, and not dying men. There is such a blessedness and sweetness in giving, especially to those who have been accustomed to feel distresses of their own, that I wonder that all men, who are able, do not indulge themselves in this pleasure. What a luxury it is, and my eyes are full of sweet tears while I write it, to see poor helpless creatures come to your door. Half despair, half fear fills their countenances, and their bodies seem half dead! Relieve them, and, lo, these dead bodies spring into motion! Down to the earth they fall in a moment, overjoyed with your small donation. Again they look up at you with tears of joy; then look in their hand again, for fear it should be all a dream. I say, this is luxury; and the most luxurious pleasure I have tasted here; except only, 'the exceeding riches of God's mercy towards us in Christ Jesus,' who, though He was rich, for our sakes became poor.

All this was no mere sentimental effusion. We have followed the writer day by day in his journals, and can testify that in his direst straits, and they were sometimes very sore, the needy never looked for his help in vain; and that nothing afforded him keener, more gleeful delight than to surprise a poor destitute beggar with a gift, which however small in itself, vastly exceeded expectation.

His medical aid was never withheld from the suffering, and his tender sympathy for those who came to him for such relief, was often even morbidly acute.[*]

[*] Mr. Thomas's skill as a medical man was very highly esteemed by those who had experience of it, and his journals contain some interesting notices of his practice.

The absence of any mention of the disease now so frequent in India, and so well known, as the Cholera, is the fact which appears most strange. He does refer to the Cholera Morbus, and to native remedies for it; but no case is spoken of in his journals at all resembling the present Asiatic Cholera.

His *fidelity* to the missionary work is also especially worthy of notice. He had to do many things in his struggles to obtain a livelihood for his family, and to provide money for his creditors; but, whether engaged as indigo-factor, sugar merchant, distiller, or surgeon, the duty of preaching Christ to the heathen was never overlooked, discouraging as the labour was in the delay of its long expected results. The following words were written in a period of great perplexity and sorrow, and they may be taken as expressive of his ordinary feelings in reference to this work.

I have preached many a time among the Hindus unsuccessfully; whilst at the same time I have enjoyed such enlarged views of the solemn truths I delivered, however undervalued by them, such liberty in expressing them, and such a clear, sweet, soul-satisfying taste of the goodness of God, and of the baseness of every other independent enjoyment, if there be an independent enjoyment, as did put it out of all doubt that Jesus Christ had fulfilled His word

Cases of hydrophobia and of the bite of serpents appear to have attracted very close attention. Several instances of death from the former occurred under his notice. The latter, if brought to him speedily, he very successfully treated by a ligature, with mustard oil, "as hot as he could make it," applied to the bitten part, and with a few ounces of the oil administered inwardly.

"We have a fly here," he wrote to his father, in 1791, "which kills more people than all the tigers in the country. It is exactly the same kind as that which blows on the meat, as the term goes; and here it watches its opportunity to light on a running sore and there deposit its maggots, which eat up a man's flesh voraciously, and in ten days will strip the bones. A woman with a sore arm was brought down to this holy river, as they call it, at Nuddea, to die I went to see her, and her bones were bare, with these vile insects hard at work, devouring her alive. She died about an hour afterwards. A poor wretched man came to me, a few days ago, with a mortification in his leg. I found the same insects making rapid progress; and, as they devoured, the evil proceeded. I made a mixture of aloes, mercury, and lead, with a bottle of rum, and two gallons of water. This bitter punch soon stopped their work, and, after two days, they were all destroyed, and the man is recovering. Another man had got them in his nose, but spirits of turpentine, which is best of all, soon ridded him."

Some curious memoranda of native remedies are to be found here and there in the journals: *e. g.* "*Rosho Cheenta Monee*," "a medicine which has cured hundreds in locked jaw, lunacy, and palsies;" the poison of the "*Allad*" snake, "in very small pills, used by the Hindus as a great specific in cholera morbus;" and "two common scorpions boiled in two ounces of oil, as an excellent liniment for the cure of an inveterate itch!" In hydrophobia, Mr. Thomas recommended that boiling *ghi* should be poured into the wound, as soon as possible, and stated that, in forty cases, this remedy had proved invariably effectual.

to me: 'Lo, I am with you alway, even unto the end of the world.' If there were no world to come, happiness is happiness; and I am sure, amongst mankind, I have had my full share, and have had as much joy as any worldly success has afforded the worldly,—as much as any of them have when their corn and their wine increase,—in preaching the unsearchable riches of Christ amongst the Hindus. The presence of Christ is all. It is enough. I know of no persons to whom the presence of Christ is so necessary as it is to missionaries, neither do I know of any persons to whom it is so pointedly and plainly promised, or pronounced and verified, as it is to them. I know that the worldly always smile at these reports. Father, forgive them; for they know not what they do!

If any man be truly converted to God himself, and has a scriptural zeal for the conversion of the heathen, and at such a juncture as this is, while Christ is saying so loudly and repeatedly, 'Who will go for us?'—if such a man were to say, 'Here am I, send me,' I cannot help thinking that,—though he might be at present,—nay must be,—unfit for the work, yet Christ would fit him and qualify him for it by degrees. 'Jesus Christ is the same, yesterday, and to-day, and for ever.' Read the life of Berridge, the narrative of Scott, and a hundred more that might be named, who set out in the ministry, trembling in the dark, and preaching they did not know what; yet there was that sincerity and divine simplicity in their intentions, which is always begun by the Author of the faith; and it was followed by clear manifestations and great success at last, from the Finisher of the faith. I have been thirteen years a missionary, the lowest of all missionaries in every thing, and the least successful. But I hope that He who has employed me in removing the rubbish, will let me have something to do in the building. At any rate, I do not affect unworthiness:—'I speak the truth before God, and lie not.' It follows, if God, through Jesus Christ, has been so faithful and gracious to the least of His missionaries, He will be so to all that follow.

I know what the delicacies of life are, for I have tasted them. I know what it is to live in 'the glory of all lands,' and under the best of all governments, as I think. I know what social enjoyments are: and I know what it is to enjoy myself, as the world calls it. And now, could I multiply all that I know a thousand times, it would be dung to me in comparison of that joy, that new life, that tenfold satisfaction, that inexpressible everything, which the presence of Christ affords. In a hot and wearisome climate; surrounded by various things unpleasant to flesh and blood;

absent from all the Churches; from all my friends and relations, banished for ever——No, no! All are here. This barren climate is a paradise,—this fiery atmosphere is cool and refreshing,—all the Churches, and all my friends are here, when Jesus Christ is with me. But it is said, 'God went up from Abraham.' As it was in the beginning, it is now; and this befits our present state of infirmity, and shews His 'wisdom and prudence.' Still, if human visits often leave lasting impressions behind them, as if they still continued, how much more do these!

When I think of all things, instead of murmuring because I have not been more successful, I am amazed that I am what I am, and still have my name and place among them that love the Lord Jesus Christ in sincerity. I am neither fit for, nor worthy of, success; yet I dare not say I have had none at all; nor would I part with the hope of success that I yet have for a globe of gold as large as Jupiter. Therefore, if this is really and truly the case, though I am poor in experience, I am rich in hope. Glory, honour, blessing, and thanksgiving in the highest to 'the God of hope!' My hope indeed is not pure; but, in our motives, God knoweth those things that are His, as we distinguish diamonds from pebbles.

If an angel were to come and ask me where I wish to be, I would say, 'Where I am.' If he asked me what I wish to be, I would say, 'A faithful witness of Christ amongst the Hindus, till death.' If he were to ask me what corruption I wished to have vanquished, or what grace I wished enlarged, I would say, 'I wish to know more of Christ: for that will slay all my corruptions at once, and invigorate and replenish the new man at all points.' And my situation amongst the heathen sometimes seems to make Christ appear more precious, as the want of a Christ amongst them renders their condition more and more inexpressibly deplorable.

Another characteristic of Mr. Thomas was his great *intrepidity* in the service of Christ. His history abounds with instances of his dauntless avowal of allegiance to his divine Master, amongst those who despised all the restraints of godly fear. Such an instance we find in a letter of most affectionate and faithful rebuke addressed to his captain on board the *Earl of Oxford*, in reference to the choleric blasphemy which marked his daily life. At Malda, amongst the visitors at the Factory, were many, high in social position, whose infidel principles and immoral lives received from the young missionary most courageous reproofs, whenever these could with any propriety be administered.

Most persons find it difficult to speak out faithfully, when there is a risk of offending wealthy men upon whom they are largely dependent; and riches are supposed to secure to their possessors freedom from close and unwelcome admonition. Mr. Thomas knew nothing of such weakness as this. Soon after getting to Malda, he recorded his discovery that £200 out of £10,000 per annum, was about as much as one half-penny a day from a labouring man's wages; and could be spared with far less inconvenience by the wealthy donor. In that light he regarded his pecuniary obligations to Mr. Grant and others, and if he saw occasion to admonish them, he was embarrassed by no dread of their displeasure or its consequences. No consideration of self-interest ever sealed his lips. Nor did he refrain from a telling rebuke, in the apprehension that it might provoke reprisals. Let them come: he held it his duty to speak out for God and truth, in complete fearlessness of man.

It seems to have been his rule never to allow profanity or other open sin, committed in his presence, to pass unreproved; and, if the reader calls to mind the character of Indian society when Mr. Thomas lived, he will see that to bear witness for God thus required a most noble courage. But this might have been so displayed as to create disgust and resentment. It was not so in his case. The tact with which he succeeded in administering most forcible rebukes without giving offence was very admirable. The effect was often marked and beneficial, and in several cases, lasting.

This boldness for the truth was not of himself. In a letter, written only two months before his death, in reply to Mr. Cuninghame, who complained of his own timidity, he says,—

I am very sensible of the same frailty you speak of, the fear of man which bringeth a snare; and I remember with remorse how basely it affected me when you asked me to crave a blessing at your table, before the face of two or three fellow-worms, who, I feared, would despise me. I suppose at other times, when I have despised myself, I have been willing that others should do so too, and have solicited the opportunity before many strangers. How could we ever account for such different principles, so opposite to one another, existing in our own minds, if we had not the decision of Scripture, which marks out the old Adam and the new man in every one who believes? It is a good thing to count the cost of taking a decided part with the gospel when we have an opportunity, lest, being overcome by the shame and fear within us, we neglect it, and lose our reward. In the first case, we may suffer the sinner's jests and the ridicule of men who are enemies to their own Redeemer, and we may lose several advantages of life; but we are not sure that these enemies will continue so; nor do we know but what an open frank profession of Christ among them may be the very means of their conversion, as the faithfulness of others was of ours. And, whatever we lose, we are sure of gaining; for, first of all, there is a blessing in it.—Matthew v. 10, 11.—We are more blessed of Christ then, than when we are at our ease, and all men speak well of us; and those who leave or give up father, mother, life, or the things of it, their own reputation, honour, and ease, for Christ's sake and the gospel's, shall receive a hundred fold in the life that now is, and, in the world to come, the peculiar gracious rewards that belong to an everlasting life. And how often have we seen His hand, who hath all power in heaven and earth, fulfilling His word. The arrows of conviction have turned men's slanders into praises, and grace has changed the hearts of His people's enemies, and they have become fellow-citizens and heirs of immortality. How often has a brand been plucked out of the fire by a bold and open confession of Christ before men. How often has He caused His people to wax bold in the faith, and greater faith has yielded in this life more than a hundred fold of 'joy unspeakable and full of glory,' and made the possessors of it look back with contempt on all they had lost for Christ's sake, because of the recompense of the reward; for godliness hath the promise of the life that now is, and of that which is to come.

I would not cast my pearls before swine; but this I would fain have, a heart so filled with a sense of obligation to my Saviour, my heart of stone so changed by divine power, that, instead of fearing man, and being ashamed of Christ, I may have a greater fear, to overcome it,—the fear of God; and rather burn with a shame of my own shame, than let the shame of Christ appear. O for more of His likeness and Spirit, 'who made Himself of no reputation,' and 'endured the cross, despising the shame.' A close observation of what passes in our own breasts will show us our need of His hand, and make us cry for it; and He will hear us, and increase our faith, and strengthen us to fight the good fight, and to finish our course with joy.

I cannot look back on my past life without recollecting how, at one time, I have forced a religious conversation in a company; and, at other times, I have quite neglected much fairer opportunities. 'Who can understand his errors?' But there is a free independent energy of spirit I have known at other times, which opens the mouth with a sovereign ease, to give vent to a free flowing stream from the abundance of a heart overflowing from heaven, and the conversation at such a season carries all before it; neither the witty profligate nor the bold infidel is able to gainsay or resist it; but every mouth seems stopped up and every conscience touched.

We must advert finally to Mr. Thomas's remarkable *efficiency as a missionary*. None will dispute his possession of that most essential qualification,—a fervent and immutable belief in Him who sent him, and in the supreme value of the message He had entrusted to him. But, in other respects, his qualifications for the work were very high. It would be unfair to expect in him a large and critical knowledge of the vernacular language, which he had acquired under such very great disadvantages. But he evidently had an exceedingly useful knowledge of it. He was well understood wherever he went, and he so spoke in Bengali, that crowds everywhere delighted to listen to his addresses, and were often deeply moved by his pungent and affectionate appeals. In dealing with those subtle and difficult metaphysical questions which the learned or unlearned Hindu is ever ready to propound and discuss, and which are so well adapted to blunt the edge and turn the point of ordinary exhortation, he showed great ability and power. Those questions, in their Bengali aspects, he was perhaps the first to encounter as a Christian evangelist; and the ingenuity, practical good sense, and profound reverence for the divine honour which his arguments displayed, are worthy of all admiration by his successors. To exemplify these particulars would demand too great space, and they are to some extent illustrated in the foregoing pages. He seems to have been singularly fitted to announce the gospel to the Hindus, "speaking to them by many similitudes, such as they themselves use," "who never argue long without a quotation or a comparison."

The very disasters of Mr. Thomas's life contributed not a little to the wide diffusion of the gospel message. Instead of having one certain dwelling-place, where he could have reached comparatively few people, his changes of employment and abode led him so to traverse Bengal that he was brought into contact with many thousands in several of its most important divisions. We have seen how laboriously and faithfully he used these opportunities to preach the word, and how, to an extent seldom equalled perhaps ever since, he did " the work of an evangelist."

His labours of a more private nature, in conversing with, and instructing, enquirers after the way of life, were also wonderfully constant and faithful. These persons were always welcome to him, and he was never weary of talking to them about Christ. In such conversations, his attractive address and earnest endeavours to win souls appeared to the utmost advantage. He was, as Mr. Carey declared, "one of the most affectionate and close exhorters to genuine godliness, and to a close walk with God, that could be thought of."

Can any thing be said here of those large expectations with which the missionary life of Mr. Thomas was begun? Were those hopes all delusive? and was the end of them a disappointment? Certainly his personal experience failed to realize them. Where were the numbers wherewith he thought to be surprised, and all the other bright panoramic scenes suggested by Isaiah xlix.? Ah, what a contrast was there between these early anticipations and the small uncertain results of his labours for Christ in Bengal. Yet from the outset he well knew "that no prophecy of the Scripture is of any private interpretation." He knew that Isaiah spoke of Christ, and that "all the promises of God in Him are yea, and in Him, Amen, unto the glory of God by us." As to his own share in them, he did indeed greatly miscalculate its importance and immediate results; but when the Redeemer's triumph shall be complete, will His servant survey it with disappointment? or when He shall acknowledge the doings of "the called, and chosen, and faithful" who "are with Him," will He despise the toils and long-suffering patience of him who began the conflict with the powers of darkness in Bengal? It is pleasant to know that, even at the beginning of his missionary life, Mr. Thomas had so true an appreciation of the value of success as to feel that a very small amount of it would largely repay any labour or sacrifice his own life might exhibit. Writing to his brother, in August, 1788, he said,—

Oh, what blessedness to gather in, if it were but one single stalk of the first fruits of that great harvest, the seed of which has been so long and so surely sown in promises, in prophecies, in tokens, and in stirrings of hope in the church. Our children, I trust, will live to see many churches of Christ among the heathen.

These hopes at least were verified, and it was his joy to gather the first fruits of Bengal to Christ, though "but one single stalk." But how stupendous is the bliss which still lies before this faithful labourer for Christ, when "he that soweth and he that reapeth" shall "rejoice together!"

Many may be inclined perhaps to estimate the results of his missionary work as he did himself; and will think that he "spent his strength for naught and in vain;" but they will do more wisely if they judge nothing of this nature before the time. *That day* will reverse many premature human judgments, and bring to light many unexpected results of apparently fruitless toil; and then very much that in man's eyes seemed to be weak and contemptible "shall be found unto praise, and honour, and glory."

Here then we will take leave of our readers. We have endeavoured to set before them the faithful history of a confessedly imperfect Christian and missionary life. May its faults serve for our admonition, its troubles awaken our tender sympathies, and its excellencies stimulate our loving emulation.

APPENDIX.

The foundation stone of any valuable building is laid with much observance, and with hearty interest, and in the foregoing account of the efforts which led to the establishment of the Baptist Missionary Society, several minute particulars have been preserved in the belief that they will not be deemed redundant. In the same confidence, an abstract of the income and expenditure of the Society's first year, from October 1st, 1792, to October 1st, 1793, may be here introduced.

It would take up too much space to record the name of every individual donor, but some of the names are worthy of special remembrance. The grandest donation in the entire list was that which Mr. Thomas received at Bristol, and the "worthy name" of Mr. William Newcomen, of Barnstaple, deserves mention. Mrs. Atwell, near London, Mr. John Collins, of Devizes, and Mr. Fishwick, of Newcastle, the early patron of Mr. Ward, came next, each with a donation of £20. The next largest donations were seven of £5-5 each. Guineas and half guineas made up the bulk of the amount. Some of the names are interesting. Not again to mention the Northamptonshire and Birmingham men, who projected the Society, we find Booth, Dore, Swain, Rippon, Timothy Thomas, Francis, Birt, Fawcett, Hughes, Steadman, and Tommas of Bristol, amongst the Baptists; and Robinson of Leicester, Toller of Kettering, and Hey of Bristol, amongst those of other Christian bodies.

One other name possesses a special interest, as constituting the link between the earliest Baptist Missionary enterprise and the American Baptist Churches. The Rev. William Staughton was a donor, and was present at the farewell service at Leicester, when also his name was added to the Committee of the Society. He shortly after emigrated to the United States of America, where, especially in Pennsylvania, he attained great eminence in the ministry and as an instructor of young men, and he did much to awaken the missionary spirit in the country of his adoption. His love for Thomas and Carey was never extinguished, and his correspondence with them was a source of mutual delight to himself and to them.

APPENDIX.

INCOME.

	£	s	d
All the personal donations made up,	335	18	6
Anonymous contributions and sundries,	11	3	6½
Sale of a translation and version of the Hymn by Ram Ram Basu,	1	2	9

LOCAL COLLECTIONS:—

	£	s	d
Bristol, collection at the doors of Broadmead meeting house,	15	8	6
Contributions received at the vestry of Castle Green ditto,	4	6	6
Ditto at Pithay meeting,	1	1	0
From persons unknown,	7	7	6
Students at the Baptist Academy,	1	1	0
Bath, collection at the doors of the Baptist Meeting-house,	22	8	6¼
Downend Chapel, collection, with other small benefactions,	2	16	0
Birmingham Assistant Society, by the Rev. S. Pearce,	70	0	0
Monies collected by the said Society, besides the above,	126	3	6¼
Yorkshire Assistant Society, by the Rev. J. Fawcett,	201	16	0
Hampshire and *Wiltshire*, Assistant Society,	42	0	0
Arnsby, Baptist congregation,	9	8	6
Colchester, ditto ditto,	9	1	0
Cambridge, ditto ditto,	18	1	0
Folkstone, Assistant Society,	5	0	0
Foxton, Leicestershire, Baptist congregation,	1	9	10½
Frome, ditto ditto,	9	10	0
Ipswich, ditto ditto,	2	12	6
Isleham, Cambridgeshire, ditto ditto,	5	19	6
Kettering, ditto ditto,	15	17	8½
Ditto club,	1	1	0
Long Buckby, Baptist congregation,	3	14	7
Longham, ditto ditto,	8	8	0
Leicester, ditto ditto,	19	15	9½
Leighton Buzzard, ditto ditto,	2	2	0
Newcastle, ditto ditto,	3	1	2
Norwich, ditto ditto,	3	13	6
Nottingham, ditto ditto,	13	13	0
Northampton, ditto ditto,	23	1	6
Olney, Bucks, ditto ditto,	10	15	6¾
Plymouth Dock, ditto ditto,	20	2	9
Road, Northamptonshire, ditto ditto,	1	12	0½
Salisbury and *Devizes*, ditto ditto,	16	16	0
Sheepshead, Leicestershire, ditto ditto,	9	9	6
Spalding, Lincolnshire, ditto ditto,	5	5	0
Tewkesbury, ditto ditto,	8	1	0
Thorn, Bedfordshire, ditto ditto,	11	5	5
Worcester, ditto ditto,	9	9	0
Weston by Weedon, ditto ditto,	0	9	0
	£ 1091	9	3¼

APPENDIX.

DISBURSEMENTS.

To Mr. CAREY, for time and travelling expenses on the concerns of the mission, for three months, with the removal of his family to *Piddington*,..................£	26	16	6
To Mr. THOMAS, for time and travelling expenses, for three months,	28	9	6
Expenses of Messrs. CAREY and THOMAS, during the months of April and May, in endeavouring to obtain a passage, ...	19	19	0
Travelling expenses of Messrs. CAREY and THOMAS, from *Portsmouth* to *Northampton*, and removing the whole of Mr. CAREY's family thence to *London*,................................	13	7	5
To Mr. CAREY, for expenses attending the removal of himself and family to *Dover*, and incurred during his and their residence there, whilst waiting for the ship,.........................	25	5	0
Mr. THOMAS's journey to *Portsmouth*, and removal of goods by sea to *Dover*, ...	15	5	6
To Mrs. CAREY during her residence at *Piddington*, according to agreement, in case she had not gone with Mr. CAREY, one quarter in advance, and five guineas for expenses attending her lying-in, ...	17	15	0
Journeys of Messrs. FULLER, SUTCLIFF, TIM. THOMAS, and PEARCE, on collecting and other business, with supplies for their congregations during their absence,...........................	16	2	0
To printing, carriage of goods and parcels, with postage of letters,..	8	15	4
To books and globes taken to India for the use of the mission, ...	13	13	0
To passage money for ten persons, *viz.* five adults and five children, together with supplies of linen, &c. for the voyage, and for their use when arrived in *India*,............................	719	16	11
To allowance to the missionaries in advance for the first year after their arrival, ...	150	0	0
To balance in the hands of the Treasurer, October 1, 1793, ...£	36	4	1¼

www.ingramcontent.com/pod-product-compliance
Lightning Source LLC
Chambersburg PA
CBHW030543300426
44111CB00009B/841